SOCIAL STRATIFICATION AND POWER IN AMERICA

The View from Below

THE REYNOLDS SERIES IN SOCIOLOGY

Larry T. Reynolds, *Editor*

by **General Hall, Inc.**

SOCIAL STRATIFICATION AND POWER IN AMERICA

A View from Below

Lynda Ann Ewen
Marshall University

GENERAL HALL, INC.
Publishers
5 Talon Way
Dix Hills, New York 11746

Social Stratification and Power in America
A View from Below

GENERAL HALL, INC.
5 Talon Way
Dix Hills, New York 11746

Publisher: Ravi Mehra
Composition: Perfect Setting, Bridgehampton, NY

LIBRARY OF CONGRESS CATALOG CARD NUMBER: **98-71776**

ISBN: 1-882289-52-8 [cloth]
1-882289-51-X [paper]

Manufactured in the United States of America

DEDICATION

This book is dedicated to my students:

those rebellious students
from the University of Wisconsin
who helped break me in as a college teacher;

those ethnically diverse students
at Wayne State University and the Detroit Labor School
who taught me about urban realities;

the receptive students
at the University of Dar es Salaam
who taught me that the love of critical thinking is worldwide;

and especially to
the Appalachian students
at West Virginia Institute of Technology
and Marshall University
whose ability to learn and "leap"
in their understanding
never failed to amaze me.

Contents

PREFACE

It is easier to give birth to a baby than to give birth to a book. This one has taken me five years, and during this time I was surrounded by family, friends, and colleagues who held my hand, encouraged me, and argued with me.

There were those who took the time and effort to respond to the manuscript itself. Cheryl Joseph gave a careful reading to two drafts, complete with corrections and suggestions for resources. Carol Axel Ray provided valuable feedback and help. Judy Aulette was a gold mine of suggested references. Colleagues who provided help in their areas of expertise were David Curry, Diane Binson, John David, and Jan Young. Reviewers who provided invaluable feedback were Marta Gimenez, Nancy Buffenbarger, and James Geschwender. And community activists Barb Steinke and Bruce Copeland took time from their busy lives to give their responses.

I must also acknowledge those friends whose ongoing conversations continued to stimulate and prod me as I worked on the book. These include Bob Newby, Rita Wicks-Nelson, David and Janet Greene, Sally Roberts and Bettijane Burger. My partner, John Taylor, was my daily springboard and I am grateful for his long-suffering patience.

Larry Reynolds is responsible for encouraging this book in the first place. His vision of a series of texts that escapes the mediocrity of the publish-only-for-profit syndrome provided the space for me to write this kind of text. Ravi Mehra's commitment to provide an independent publishing house is an important part of that vision. And Irene Glynn's careful, and supportive, editing greatly improved the overall quality of this book.

This is only a very partial list. For while I was writing this book I attended numerous conferences, meetings, rallies and other events that fueled my understanding of social stratification and power. I was intimately involved in Charlotte Pritt's first gubanatorial campaign that was organized from the grassroots and once again demonstrated the awesome power of social movements in America. Persons I know, persons who are only names, and persons whose names I do not even know at all contributed to my understanding of power and resistance. I thank you all, and I thank all those fighters and dreamers who came before me and helped make the history that undergirds this analysis.

In the end, my students were those who provided the inspiration and rationale for the form taken by this book. Drafts have been used by three classes, two at West Virginia Institute of Technology and one at Marshall University. I must give special attention to those students who endured through the first primitive draft and who throughout the semester wrote lengthy criticisms and analyses of each chapter. I promised that for their unflagging efforts they would be named. They are Virgie Arthur, Nancy Beard, Donna Cale, Tom Freeman, Anita Greathouse, Meredith Hall, James Harbison, Ron Haynes, Jennifer Highlander, Jeff Johnson, Martin Kigudde, Matt Lilly, Tiffany Maynard, Sherri McNeely, Charlie Morris, Michael Patterson, Jeremy Richmond, Yowan Selvaraj, Kathryn South, Andrea Taylor, Bryan Toney, Roger Toney, and Kevin Young.

Of course, in the end I put it all together in my own way. I did not accept all the criticisms and suggestions offered, although I always found them helpful. If a book is like a birth, one can assume this is only a beginning. Whatever is useful here is only one step in the understanding of ourselves and our society. I know that I continue to grow and learn each day, and so what is written here is not some definitive "answer" but only a tentative suggestion as to how we might view our world. Please read it in that spirit.

INTRODUCTION

This is a different kind of textbook. I have tried to make this book "reader friendly." Most textbooks are boring and many are unnecessarily difficult. Often the author uses fancy language and tries to prove that he or she knows all about the debates in the field to protect against any possible criticism. I did not try to do this. This book is not written just for sociologists or even sociology majors. It is written for everyday ordinary people who really want to know about power and social stratification as it has an impact on their lives.

The book is subtitled *The View from Below* because the perspective is not that of those who run the system. I don't blindly assume that this country is good for everybody. I know too many working people who have lost their jobs; too many children who go hungry at the end of every month; too many women who have been beaten by a husband or partner; too many minority youths scarred by the daily insults of racism in their lives; too many streams that have been polluted. Many of you know these things too. You want to know what has caused such problems and what can be done about it.

On the other hand, a few people will read this book and be offended by it. For them, this is a great country. They have good educations, good jobs, and good futures. They may not even really understand what I am talking about. Well, I couldn't write a book for everybody, and so I made a decision for whom I would write.

There are a couple of things you should know about this book. The first is that I try to give everybody an equal shake. That means that I have tried to make my language and my examples reflect everybody's reality. At first, the use of "she or he" may seem strange, but when you think about the number of times it is used in this book, you realize that had I stuck with the traditional use of "he," women would have been left out of all those references. Likewise, I often use the term "Euro-American" because it seems fair that if we talk about Asian Americans, African Americans, and Latino or Hispanic Americans, we should also stick a label in front of those of us whose ancestors came from Europe!

In my twenty-five years of teaching in higher education I have never taught at an elite school. I have always taught students who were mainly working or middle class. My students did not find mainstream theories of social stratification very useful to their reality. They could memorize a summary of Weber's theories or recite the arguments of Pareto, but what they really wanted to *know* was how they got to be in the position they were in and how one acted to end inequalities in American society. I wanted to write a textbook that answered *those* questions.

This textbook will not prepare you very well for the Graduate Record Exams' sociology section on social stratification. If you are going to graduate school in sociology you should probably also read some mainstream text. But if you want to leave college with a better understanding of who's messing with whom, and how it got to be that way, you will do well to pay close attention to this book.

I have also tried to avoid a lot of complicated statistics. Almost any argument can manipulate numbers to prove whatever they want to prove. ("Figures don't lie, but liars can figure.") I have used some numbers, and of course I have used them because they help prove *my* argument. But what is really important is the framework of my analysis. In other words, the *way* I approach a question dictates which figures will be most useful to my argument. So when someone runs a bunch of statistics by you, it's more important to understand the underlying logic of the person's argument than to quarrel about the figures!

I have *not* tried to avoid referring to history. I know that many of you hated your history classes because all you learned were a lot of names and dates that you promptly forgot after the final. That's because history is often taught in the wrong way. There's a saying that I think really applies: "Those who do not learn from the mistakes of the past are bound to repeat them." If we are ignorant of those lessons, we cannot use them to change things. So I use a lot of history to show how power and social stratification *came* from somewhere. And to help explain how we can have an impact on the future.

Throughout the book I use a lot of references. The notes are there because you have a right to know what sources I used and where I'm getting information. When I use facts or statistics without giving the reference, that means the fact is generally known and accepted or that I got it from a "standard" reference like the U.S. Government's *Statistical Abstract of the United States*. Please don't get bogged down by references—use them only if you want to or need to.

I have been working on this book for five years and have tried to update statistics as I went. But numbers change, and by the time this is printed, some of my figures will be obsolete. The important question, however, is whether my arguments and the trends I identify are still applicable.

This book is critical of the *system* of social stratification and power in this country. But I want to make it very clear that I firmly believe the vast majority of *people* in America really do want a more equal and just society for all. Throughout history Americans have fought to expand the rights and liberties laid out in the beginning: "We hold these truths to be self evident." The problem today is that so many ordinary people are confused by the changes that are rapidly taking place in our society. Without a clear understanding of the problems, finding equitable solutions is difficult. This is one of the main reasons that I am writing this book—to help people figure out how to bring about greater justice and equality.

There's one last thing I want to say to you, the reader. If you disagree with me or if I make you mad—that's OK. During my own college education, the courses from which I learned the most were the courses in which I disagreed. Those courses made me rethink things I had previously learned and forced me to develop a defense. Sometimes my defenses held, and sometimes they didn't. But if what I had learned earlier was wrong, I wanted to know what was right. I know that there are probably things I have written in this book that are wrong because I am still learning. And I am sure that readers who disagree will let me know about it!

I believe education is an interactive process: professors can always learn from students. This is my third book, but the first textbook I have written. It's dedicated to my students because I have learned so much from them. Over the years, the thousands of lively minds that have argued with me, agreed with me, and laughed at me have kept me intellectually alive. It sounds silly, but I truly love my students. I hope that some of that love is evident in this book. And I hope that you, the reader, will not hesitate to let me know what you think—just as my students do to my face.

Lynda Ann Ewen
Department of Sociology and Anthropology
Marshall University
Huntington, WV 25755

Spring, 1996

E-mail: EWEN@MARSHALL.EDU

PART 1

THE LADDER OF STRATIFICATION

The first five chapters of this book sketch out the idea of a "ladder" in our society. Everyone in America gets assigned to a place on this ladder. As you read, try to picture yourself on the ladder. Look at the people around you—are they on the same rung? Think about the people you see on the evening news on television. Where is the president of the United States on the ladder? Where would you put homeless people? the teenage school dropout? What about the people you can't see? Are there powerful and rich people you never hear about? Where would they go on the ladder?

- **Chapter 1** begins by discussing the glue that holds the ladder of stratification together—social power. We can guess that people on the bottom of the ladder aren't happy about being there. What kind of social pain do people at the bottom feel? Did somebody put them on the bottom on purpose? This chapter tries to answer those questions.

- **Chapter 2** takes an in-depth look at two groups of people that our society has historically put on the bottom rungs of the ladder—the very poor and Native Americans. By using these examples we try to show how social forces acting through history have denied certain groups full access to the opportunities and resources of American society. We often ignore these groups because it makes us feel bad to know that some people have suffered. And it makes us ask questions about the way our society is run.

- **Chapter 3** looks at the current distribution of resources. This chapter has more statistics in it than any other chapter. That is because many resources can be measured in terms of money. Money is easily counted, and it can show some social relationships in numbers. Don't be put off by all the statistics. What is important is to use those figures to see the relationships between groups of people. One doesn't need to memorize the percentage of wealth held by the richest people in America. But one should ask if this percentage is increasing or decreasing, and why?

- The people on the ladder who we often don't see are the subject of **Chapter 4**. They are what we call the "invisible" groups. The fact that we may not be aware of their presence, however, doesn't mean they are not important for social stratification in America. As you read this chapter you might ask yourself whether these groups have been invisible to you. Or maybe your grandparents or even parents were members of these groups!

- **Chapter 5** begins by showing that all through our history, people at the bottom of the ladder have not accepted the reasons they are given for being on the bottom. Thus the ladder is often "shaken" by the groups at the bottom. We look at the major social move ments in American history that have done this shaking. This chapter is important because it reminds us that the ladder is not a permanent thing. All through history people have acted together to change their position on it.

Each chapter puts important concepts into boldface type—**like this**. At the end of the chapter these concepts are defined. But unlike many other textbooks, this book doesn't stress learning vocabulary. Words are important only if they help us identify things in our world. It is more important that you learn to see what the word is talking about. For example, can you identify any ways in which the group to which you belong is oppressed or degraded? How do you experience power in your own life? Do you think you are middle class? How do you know?

The summaries at the end of the chapters are what I think were the most important points. These are "dry" because they are only conclusions. And maybe there are things in the chapter that *you* thought were important that I don't mention. So, remember, the summaries are only to help you organize your learning—they can't take the place of the chapters themselves.

There are also discussion questions to help you think about what you have just read. It is important to remember that there are no "right" or "wrong" answers to these questions. How you, as a person, answer those questions will have a lot to do with your own experiences in life—and where *you* are on the ladder!

Finally, there are videos and books recommended that illustrate ideas in the chapter in greater depth. Of course, the notes and bibliography give a much greater documentation, but you probably don't have time to look all of that up. So the resources listed at the end of the chapter are picked out because they are interesting and easily available to college students.

1

THIS THING CALLED POWER

"May the Force be with you."

—Luke Skywalker in *Star Wars.*

This book looks at the way social stratification in America affects both the individual and the entire society. **Social stratification** is the ranking of individuals and groups in a society in ways that make some superior and others inferior. If we think about it in a physical sense, we can see it as layers or rungs, as in a ladder. Some are on "top," and others are at the "bottom."

SOCIAL POWER

The "glue" that holds this ladder together is social power. Before we look at all the ways people in American society are ranked we must first understand the glue for social stratification. What is this thing we call social power? We can't see it or feel it in any physical sense, but we all know when it is there. A teacher has power over you—the power to give you an *A* or an *F*. A police officer has the power to stop you for speeding and give you a ticket. Wealthy individuals have power to influence politicians by making large campaign contributions.

We also know when power *isn't* there. If your instructor gives you an *F* when you feel you deserve an *A* you may feel powerless to object. If you get a speeding ticket when you really were n't speeding, you may feel powerless to protest. When you don't like certain government policies, you may feel powerless to do anything about them.

Power is like electricity. When we turn on a light, we see the *result* of electricity. No one has ever actually seen electricity itself. We know that when this "thing" called electricity is around, certain events happen—lights turn on, motors run, shocks are felt. We measure electricity through its *effects* on us or our environment. Electricity, itself, remains a mystery. It is a force, or an energy, that has no actual physical substance but by its impact can *cause* things to happen that we can observe and measure.

Physics and applied fields such as electrical engineering are the sciences that observe and measure the effects of electricity. Social scientists, like physicists, study some things that cannot be directly seen, felt, or measured. Social power is one of the most important "forces" in the social sciences. We measure the *effects* of it just as the effects of electricity are measured.

It is easy to study something when a cause leads directly and immediately to an effect. When we switch on a light, the electricity flows and "causes" the bulb to turn on. We see one thing—the electricity—as being directly responsible for the second thing—the light.

What happens if the cause is *not* immediate or direct? There are scientists today who are studying the possible effects that high-voltage power lines may have on the people and environ ment surrounding those lines. They discovered that children in a school very near such power lines had more health problems than other children. But how does one show that the high voltage line is responsible? Maybe the water in the school is polluted with some sort of chemical? Maybe the air is polluted with a chemical that would not hurt the children *unless* that chemical was exposed to high voltage? Maybe the electricity affects the nervous system of the parents, who yell at the children more, which causes stress for the children, which affects their immune systems, which causes more health problems?

In other words, we often have to study a relationship between two things embedded in a whole complicated set of relationships—all acting on one another. The same problem holds for the study of social power. Many social scientists have tried to investigate the power that television has over the minds of young children. Does television undermine the power and authority of parents? Does television affect children more than school? Will children watching violent television shows behave in more violent ways? Again, it is hard to answer these questions because television is only one factor, or "force," in a child's environment.

The application of social power is often obvious, such as the coach who throws you off the team if you don't obey the rules or the police officer who stops you when you speed. It is much more difficult to judge the indirect and interrelated results of social power. For example, the advantage that men have over women is a form of social power. Rarely does a man walk into an office and say "I demand to be paid 40 percent more than a woman." As a matter of fact, most men would assume they will be paid the same as a woman doing the same job. Yet our society sets up expectations that men's work is worth more than than women's. This assumption is taught and accepted without persons thinking much about it. These assumptions lead to expectations of behavior that we discuss in detail in later chapters. But the end result is a social pressure to make us behave in ways that are expected.

We might see the power exerted by society as similar to the generalized electricity that floats around the high-voltage line. It "seeps" into our interpersonal interactions without our being consciously aware of it. Indeed, we might even deny it is there.

As we discuss power throughout this book it is easy to think of individuals or groups as "having power" as though it is a thing that can be owned. Yet power is never a possession of an individual or group in itself; power always comes because that person or group is in a certain relationship over or above some other person or group. If that relationship changes, then power relationships can change. For example, people need electricity and gas to provide the energy to live and travel. Those who control the coal mines, oilfields and refineries, and power stations have power over those of us who need energy. But if tomorrow we found a way to get our energy directly and cheaply from the sun, those who owned the other energy resources would lose their power over us.

WHO USES IT ON WHOM?

Electricity existed before humans gave it a name or studied it scientifically. Early humans saw lightning outside their caves; the Romans who scuffed their feet on rugs gave each other electric shocks. Likewise, there has been social power as long as there has been human society. The earliest written records show that humans knew social power existed even though they did not study it scientifically. And from those earliest records we also know that humans raised the ques tion of how power was exercised.

Social power *never* occurs by itself. Power is *always* embedded within historical and cultural relationships. Humans not only observe the effects of social power but evaluate the use of power. The examples given above—the unfair grade, the undeserved speeding ticket, the corrupt politician—would all be perceived as negative uses of power. Power can also be perceived as good and beneficial. Parents can use their power to punish a small child who runs out into the road without looking both ways. Police officers can stop drunk drivers and prevent them from hitting us. A coach can use his or her power to ensure the team has a winning season. Again, we would almost all agree that these are positive uses of power.

It is more complicated when the effects of power are observed but we *don't* agree on whether it is good or bad. A politician might vote to provide a government subsidy to a big defense corporation and vote against government aid for college grants. Most of you reading this would probably feel the politician had misused his power because you favor government subsidies to students and not to defense corporations. But the chief executive officer or major stockholder of the defense corporation might feel that the politician had exercised power wisely. In other words, how the effects of power are evaluated depends on *who* is doing the evaluating!

Social power can even affect how individuals measure and evaluate the "natural world." For example, it should make no difference whether a politician, student, or police officer looks at a breathalyzer that measures alcohol levels. The reading should be the same. But if the police officer is anxious to make an arrest, that might influence the way he reads the results of the test. The student stopped for drunk driving doesn't want to be arrested. If he looks at the results, he may see something different. And a politician who is anxious to prove he is "tough on crime" may see the results according to his interests.[1]

We who study social power are members of a society that has already taught us morality. We automatically evaluate what we are studying. For example, few people today who study slavery in the American South would argue it was a good system. We are taught today that slavery was degrading and exploitative of other humans and only benefited a few. Yet two hundred years ago, there were many educated scholars who studied slavery as a positive system that benefited the Africans by bringing them "civilization."

Whether we agree or not about the pain that negative power can cause, we can usually agree on its *consequences*. If money is one important basis for power (and very few would argue against that) then the *distribution* of power in America is changing. According to the U.S. Census Bureau, in the two decades between 1969 and 1989 the proportion of Americans who were rich grew, and the proportion of Americans who were poor grew. At the same time, the proportion in the middle class shrank.[2]

It is easy to measure power in terms of money, but social power is more than just money. It is more accurate to think of power as control over resources—the things that people need. The vast majority of resources are material things like food, clothing, housing, and health care. But the power to give us a job or lay us off is also a very real power. And the power to meet or deny our emotional needs can be a source of power.

If we see "good" and "bad" in what we study scientifically, can we say we are objective? neutral? truly scientific? In other words, if I think you've used power in a negative way, and you think you've used power in a positive way, we can ask a double question: (1) what kind of power was it and how did that power get used? and (2) *why* is it that I see it as bad and you see it as good?

Many social scientists answer those questions in two ways. First, they admit that their own cultural background—the way they were raised, their education, and their life experiences—will in fluence their study of social power. They argue that even though our culture affects our view of the social world, it is possible to understand how those with a different background will see social power. There are, however, still social scientists who claim that their view of social power, and other social phenomena, is the "objective" view, and therefore the only right view.

THE PERSPECTIVE OF THIS TEXT

This book treats power as a force that affects human beings in their relationships. **Negative power** creates what we will call "social pain." In other words, someone in that relationship is being hurt by the exercise of that power. The person, or group, causing the hurt may or may not realize or understand the social pain being caused. But the fact that they don't know, don't understand, or deny the pain does not make the pain go away for the person who is suffering.

In individual social interactions, the use of power and its painful consequences are a lot easier to observe, as in the case of the police person or the coach. When we examine how structures of social stratification create power, and are institutionalized for groups of people, the consequences of power, like the electricity of the high-voltage line, are much more difficult to trace. How do we identify those responsible for the growing number of homeless people in America? Do they know and understand what they did? We certainly cannot argue about the pain of homelessness, but who benefited from homelessness? Who has the power to end homeless ness?

You, the reader, might not always agree with how I evaluate the use of power in this book. That is all right. The purpose of this text is *not* to get you to agree with all the evaluations; the purpose of this text is to get you to recognize and understand what social power is and how it can be used. What you do with that knowledge and how you use it in your own life is your decision.

There have been many important social scientists who see social stratification very differently. They would argue that stratification is necessary; it is for the good of a society to rank individuals. They would disagree with my argument that such ranking causes social pain and would say that those with lower rank suffer the pain through some fault of their own. We examine these arguments more closely in Chapter 12.

The point of social science is to explain why and how it is that something exists. You would not want to go to a doctor with a painful lump on your neck and have him or her tell you that "your lump is .5 cm big and it is red." You want the doctor to tell you what is *causing* the lump. And you want the doctor to tell you how to make it go away. Thus, we expect social science to do more than describe or even explain. We want it to provide insights that allow us to make things better.

CONCEPTS OF POWER

The idea of negative power means that some sort of idea of positive power is possible. This book agrees that positive power exists. **Positive power** occurs when individuals in social relationships enable each other to realize their individual potentials fully. In more everyday language, positive power is the relationship between equals. We do not mean equal in the sense of "same." Under conditions of equality, individuals and groups have access to the resources to develop their different potentials, whether it be as an athlete, an artist, an administrator, or a teacher. Although much of our focus is on the use of power that creates social pain, individuals and groups have had alternative visions of positive power throughout much of our history. In the American tradition, these visions have been captured in our ideals about equality and democracy

Do people always understand the power exercised on them as positive or negative? No! Indeed, this is perhaps the most complicated aspect of the question of power. An example is the relationships that occur between men and women. We are raised to believe that those ways of thinking and acting are good and necessary. Indeed, we are uncomfortable if we are not acting appropriately for our sense of gendered self. (Is this "manly"? Am I being unladylike?) Studies of work in the household consistently show that when both men and women are employed outside the home, women continue to do a disproportionate amount of the housework. Yet women do not perceive that the division of labor is unfair.[3]

This question of what people *believe* about power is very important to understanding social stratification. If those who benefit from the relationship can convince those who are the losers that everything is fine, then the society appears to be stable, with everyone happy.

But such stability exists only because those who are on the losing end see no other alternative and believe they must accept the pain as their due. When new possibilities are intro duced, the painful relationships may be vehemently challenged. This often confuses and frustrates those on the top, who had always thought everyone was happy! This is certainly what has occurred with women who have begun to challenge all kinds of traditional assumptions about what they should be doing for whom.

In other words, no matter what we believe about power and our position within a stratified system, objective social consequences for these relationships are independent of the individual's beliefs about them.

POWER AND HIERARCHY

American society is highly stratified. In order to understand our system of stratification, we will look at three ways in which negative power is experienced as social pain.

The first and most general negative power relation is **oppression**. This is the general term used to describe groups who fall below, or under, other groups on the ladder. This means that the oppressed group has *less* power, that is, less access to resources and control over the things they need. Oppression can be related to a variety of disadvantages. Obviously, if your group is denied material needs, such as housing, jobs, and health care, you are oppressed. If your group is denied dignity and acknowledgment of your humanity, you are oppressed. If your group is denied political freedoms such as voting rights or freedom of speech, you are oppressed. If your children are made fun of because of their group membership, they are oppressed.

In this book, we use oppression as a word to describe all the ways in which groups, and members of those groups, suffer social pain because of their group membership. Even a wealthy African American may face insults and racist slurs because of his or her ethnic group membership; even a Euro-American who is poor may have to live in a slum because of his or her class membership. And a woman in any class or ethnic group may have her body stared at and joked about simply because she is a woman.

For example, agricultural workers have been oppressed. The housing and sanitary condi tions for such workers are often terrible; they are often exposed to dangerous chemicals; and their children are moved so often they rarely receive good educations. When we look at the social pain of the migrant child who is shuttled from school to school, often sick and underfed, it is difficult to say that child is being directly exploited. Who benefits from his or her condition? But we can clearly say the child is being oppressed, relative to other children in our society.

The second form of social pain is **exploitation**, and it implies that someone has power to use someone or something else for their own unfair advantage. This term is applied when we discuss a benefit that can be observed, and sometimes even measured, by the exercise of power. Exploitation is an exchange relationship that is not equal.

Unlike oppression, which is used to describe the social position of a group and its members, exploitation can be used both to describe the position of a group or of single individuals. We most often connect exploitation of individuals to their group because exploitation is almost always an aspect of oppression. For example, a migrant agricultural worker who does back-breaking work in the fields and is paid less than minimum wage is exploited. The fields are owned by a large corporation, and the principal stockholder of that corporation lives in a large beautiful home with a swimming pool and tennis courts. The stockholder is exploiting the labor of the worker in order to provide himself or herself with a life of luxury. The migrant worker lives in poverty conditions.

Exploitation is not always a direct money benefit. For example, a person can exploit another person's body for his or her own sexual pleasure without providing any pleasure back. A friend can exploit a friend, even if they are in the same group. But whatever the exact nature of the relationship, exploitation involves a person or group using power to take advantage of another person or group.

The third way that social stratification causes social pain is **degradation**. This is the negative use of power as it affects the self-esteem and self-concept of the individual. If I am belit tled and made to feel less of a full human being, I am degraded. We often call degradation "putting down" someone. Social psychology has studied the effects of this on individuals in terms of their **self concepts.** Like exploitation, degradation can happen to an individual because of his or her group membership or degradation can happen because of some particular quality of an individual (e.g. someone who is shy or uncoordinated).

When the children of migrant agricultural workers go to school, they are often degraded. Without hot running water, children cannot take frequent baths or stay as clean. So the other children call them smelly. They may be called "trash" because they are poor. Some teachers may treat them with less respect than the children who are cleaner, who have "better manners," and who seem to be "smarter." If the migrant parents go to the principal to complain about the treatment of their children, they are also degraded. Even a kind principal is likely to talk "down" to them.

Such degradation impacts behavior. Without consciously realizing it, the children will have to cope. Some may become more aggressive and get labeled as troublemakers. Some may become passive and simply withdraw. Most will drop out of school at the first opportunity, rather than continue to stay in an environment that is psychologically painful.

In these examples, I have focused on a group defined by their occupational category—migrant agricultural laborers. As we proceed with the analysis, we see that it is even more compli cated. A great many of these workers in the United States are workers of Latino origin, and many are immigrants.

Thus they are also oppressed and degraded by virtue of their membership in a certain ethnic or nationality group.

The labels, stigmas, and stereotypes we discuss in Chapter 7 are all social mechanisms that act to degrade individuals. Understanding degradation lets us see how structures of social power can actually affect the psychology of an individual.

In this discussion we have talked about the consequences of social power, as it applies to keeping people in their "place." This is different than the idea of **sanctions**, which are the rewards and punishments we get for obeying the norms of our society. A negative sanction may be used as part of positive power. For example, a parent may take dessert away from the child who carelessly crossed the street without looking both ways. The child may *feel* oppressed by the parent, but the parent is enforcing a rule ("look both ways before you cross the street") in order to keep the child safe and healthy. In contrast, a Euro-American parent may take dessert away from a child to punish him or her for playing with an African-American friend. In this case, the parent is using a negative sanction to enforce negative power.

AMERICAN DIMENSIONS OF POWER

In any society, the history and cultural traditions of a people define the exercise of power and the rankings that occur. A small band society in a harsh environment, like the early Innuit (the Eski mo), use power very differently than a complex society like the United States, with its abundant natural resources and diverse people. In this text we are looking primarily at power in American society and therefore have to take into account our own particular history and cultural traditions. At times this book may sound overly critical of the United States. But remember that one could also write different, but still critical, books about the exercise of power in all the complex countries of the world! In other words, other countries have their own "ladders" with different groups assigned to the bottom rungs.

As a society, the United States might be characterized as having a split personality. Ameri cans have a deep-felt commitment to the notion of shared and positive power. The ideas that authority should be based on the consent of the governed and that opportunities for the good life should be equally available are long-standing beliefs in our society. This is what we usually refer to as our "democratic ideals." Whether one examines the Iroquois League of Nation's democracy or the New England town meetings, we can find ample evidence that such ideals were an impor tant part of our historical heritage.

At the same time, American society has been organized in a way that ranked human beings and allowed oppression, exploitation, and degradation to be institutionalized and practiced. Those dimensions are (1) class status, (2) race/ethnicity status, (3) gender status, and (4) environmental status.

At times we look at a single dimension. Most of the time, however, we see that in the real world these four dimensions coexist. For example, the owners of a chicken processing plant in North Carolina had the power to lock the doors of the building, making their workers virtual prisoners. These workers were poor, many were members of minority groups, many were women, and they worked in an unhealthy industrial environment slaughtering and packing polluted chickens. They experienced the social pain of stratification on all four dimensions.

The only reason that their pain was even brought to our attention is that there was a fire in the plant in September 1991. There was no sprinkler system, no evacuation plan, and no fire drills had been practiced. Their escape was blocked by the locked doors. Twenty-five workers at the Imperial Food Products plant in Hamlet, North Carolina burned to death and fifty-five were injured.[4]

Other rankings cause social pain in our society. One is age status. Does our society exploit, oppress, and degrade the very young? the old? We might also include status based on physical appearance. Are you more likely to be exploited, oppressed and degraded if you are disabled? weigh more than the norm? are very short? The answer to all these questions is probably "yes." So it is important to remember that this text is focusing on what I believe are the more important ways in which human beings in our society are exploited, oppressed, and degraded. This focus does not mean that other means of exploitation, oppression, and degradation do not also occur. And at times they are mentioned in the analysis.

POWER AND CONSCIOUSNESS: IS IT REALLY ALL JUST A PLOT?

Human beings have something we call "consciousness." Some psychologists argue that consciousness of self is what distinguishes us from other animals. Religious people might call the same thing our soul or spirit. Earlier we mentioned that all human societies have a sense of right and wrong, or *morality*. We make choices and we can affect what happens to us, because we can think about those choices and consider the consequences. Yet throughout this book, we are going to talk about "society" and how it impacts, influences, and controls individuals—*often without their understanding it.* In other words, social forces can act on you like physical forces—gravity, or germs, or electricity.

Until science finds a cure for AIDS, millions of people will die. Knowing the cause is not good enough; we need to know the cure. But, I doubt anyone has a picture of an evil little virus, meeting somewhere in a cell one day and plotting to create a disease that threatens many of us. We instead think of the virus as originating out of some mutation or other occurrence within nature.

Some people argue that those who control the resources of our society use their power on purpose to create social pain. In other words, they are bad people who plan the bad things that happen to others. This view suggests that those in power conspire against those below them. This perspective is called *conspiracy theory* and is often used to explain the existence of social pain. However, this textbook does not believe that the answer is so simple.

Throughout this book we are going to be talking about things that create enormous social pain—the rape and beatings directed against women, the hate crimes directed against minorities, the wars fought to steal land and exploit cheap labor, the industrial exploitation of our environment. Careful historical analysis reveals that individuals made decisions, over the long run, that led to these things. Yet it is very doubtful that those individuals, at the time, understood fully the implications of their decisions or perceived them as wrong.

If you were born into the family of wealthy slaveholders at the turn of the eighteenth century, you were socialized into the behaviors and ideas of your family, your religion, your nation, and your class. For you, slavery was not wrong, nor was there anything evil about increasing your wealth based on the labor of slaves. You may have honestly believed you had done the poor savages a favor by bringing them to a land of "civilization." The slaves that were whipped were "troublemakers," and you believed that most of your slaves, being subhuman, ac cepted their lots and were happy.

We find such ideas ridiculous today. But we ourselves continue to hold certain ideas that may look equally ridiculous to those who will come several generations later!

This book is an attempt to understand how power came to be in America, how it has worked historically, and how it continues to work today. This means that we must reexamine certain "social facts" in the light of what we know and understand today. This book argues that certain things you have learned are not entirely true, from the perspective of social science. But at the same time, you must remember that the people involved often believed that they *were* true!

The job of science is to show how and why things work; to get at the social laws that govern relationships. When we reveal those patterns, they look logical, and we are tempted to think that someone, somewhere, "conspired" to make it happen. And, yes, that is true—in a way. There were federal bureaucrats who issued orders to give small-pox infested blankets to Native Americans; there were generals who ordered that the women and children left undefended in the Native American villages were to be slaughtered; there were politicians who cut the budgets to the reservations so low that there was no food and the Native Americans died of starvation.

But all these actions were part of a general policy that arose out of the history of this country. That general policy was not the result of any single person or group consciously deciding to commit genocide on somewhere between 6 million and 30 million human beings over a period of 200 years.

Today, homeless people who die on our streets are buried in plain wooden boxes in large trenches. Like the genocide of the Native Americans, we can identify the policies that create homelessness and specific individuals that make specific decisions. Like AIDS, we know what causes it. But we have not found a cure. Finding that cure requires that we go beyond de nouncing the Congress, the president, the slum landlords, or the welfare bureaucrats. A scientific approach requires us to see how the social structure of power created the situation, and ask what kinds of changes in power relationships would be necessary to change the situation of the homeless.

Today, those who hold power still often do not understand the full implications of their decisions. Those who are very wealthy have little or no comprehension of the realities confronting most working people; most men have little understanding of the oppression that women in our society face; white people are ignorant of the discrimination and degradation that minorities con front every day; few of us consider the consequences of our life style for the earth. Those with higher statuses receive privileges from the society that are denied to those with lower status. Rarely do those who have greater privileges voluntarily seek to give them up. Indeed, they may not even understand or perceive the extent to which they receive privilege.[5]

Many law school graduates take well paid jobs with large legal firms representing corporations in workers' compensation cases. Their beginning pay is between $60,00 and $75,000 a year. Their job is to use every legal way possible to save the corporations' money and prevent hurt and disabled workers from obtaining the benefits needed for survival.

These young lawyers only see themselves as doing their job and protecting their corporate clients' interests. But their careers and income are based on keeping less-well educated people from the income they need when they are unable to work. These lawyers may attend church regularly, give generously to the United Way and give time to community activities, but the fact remains: their social class position requires their participation in the oppression of people below them in the system of social stratification.

This textbook is subtitled *The View from Below* because it describes the social reality that is experienced by those who are on the lower rungs of the ladder of social stratification in America. It is a little like going to a birthday party when you were nine or ten. Some of the children who went had a wonderful time. They were dressed in nice clothes and won lots of prizes. They were the "popular" ones. When they came home, they told their parents that it was a *wonderful* party. Then there were the children who didn't have such nice clothes, who were shy, or were in some other way different. They didn't win prizes and they weren't "popular." When they went home, they said the party wasn't fun at all. It was the same party but it was experienced in different ways.

This book does *not* try to give the contrasting view of American society as seen by those who are above. That view is available every day from most of the things we read or see on television. Most textbooks on social stratification present that view. If you are interested in comparing the views you might want to look at a text with an alternative perspective.

This text focuses on the view from below because it is the view that is least understood or accepted by the general society. We are seldom educated in our history classes about how social stratification affects the power we have or don't have. Is that because those who control the most resources don't want us to know fully the extent of social pain created by extreme systems of social inequality? Yet examining the extremes of social stratification is a good way to see the effects of power. In the next chapter we look at two groups in our society that have been ranked at the bottom and discuss the oppression, exploitation, and degradation they have suffered.

SUMMARY

We rank groups and individuals based on the social power they have. Social power is like a glue that holds the ladder of stratification in place. It's a social force, so we can't see it or feel it. But like electricity, we can feel its effects. And we know if it is, or isn't, there.

Social power and stratification exist within our society. They are products of our culture, which in turn is a product of our history. It is not possible to understand or study social stratification and power without taking culture and history into account.

We generally recognize different forms of social power. If power is used to help people and to make people happy we can see a positive form of power. If power is used to benefit one group but hurt another group, it is power causing social pain—or negative power.

Not everyone sees power in the same way. If we belong to a group that ranks high on the ladder and has lots of power, we are likely to enjoy that power and see it as a good thing for us, even if it means that other groups are suffering. In contrast, if we belong to a group at the bottom of the ladder, we may have little power and others may have a lot of power over us. That often means hardship and pain for us, and we see the power of the group over us as a negative force affecting our lives.

Negative power can be looked at in different ways. In this book we look at how groups, and individuals in those groups, experience negative power through oppression, exploitation, and degradation. Just as an individual who is sick with a physical illness like cancer, pneumonia, or a bad cold cannot function to their full potential, so individuals who are suffering the social pain of being oppressed, exploited, and degraded cannot function up to their full potential in our society. The consequences of negative power, then, are felt by the whole society.

American society has understood social power and stratification in ways that arise out of our particular history and culture. We see positive social power in our ideas of democracy and equality—and we are proud of those ideas. At the same time, we have developed ways to put groups into lower positions on the ladder where they are oppressed, exploited, and degraded. The main ways have been race, gender, and class. A fourth way power has been used is speciesism—the negative use of human power over the earth.

Because power is invisible and often taken for granted, people may use it or benefit from it without fully understanding its consequences. This means we are not always conscious of the power in our lives—the power that we have, or the power that someone else may have over us. Other times we are aware, and if power is being used to hurt us, we look for someone to blame. This book focuses on the way that social stratification, and the negative use of social power, has affected different groups in our society. The book's viewpoint, then, is that from "below" on the ladder.

Vocabulary

Social stratification. The ranking of individuals and groups in a society in ways that make some superior and others inferior.

Social power. The social force based on an individual's, or group's, control of resources that can ensure they can do what they want and that they may be able to make others do what they want.

Negative social power. The use of social power by one group or individual that creates social pain for another group or individual.

Positive social power. The use of social power to help other groups or individuals realize their full potentials and contributions to society.

Oppression. The social pain experienced because an individual is a member of a group that is placed in an inferior position in our society and is seen by others in terms of that group membership.

Exploitation. The unequal exchange by which someone (or group) in power is able to take advantage of someone (or group) with less power.

Degradation. The impact that negative social power has on the self-esteem of the individuals involved; the sense of feeling less worthy or not fully human.

Self-concept. The sense of who one is as either a positive or negative person.

Discussion Questions

1. Would you agree that social power is one of, if not the most, important forms of social energy? In science classes we study forms of energy, including electricity. In what classes have you already studied social power and the results of that power? What did you learn about it? If you have never studied it, why not?

2. If you had to draw a picture of the "ladder" of social stratification in America, where would you place yourself? your family? why?

3. Pick a current news event that shows social power being used. What are the different ways to look at that event? Why might people disagree about whether the power is being used negatively or positively?

4. Looking at your own life, can you identify someone or some group that has power over you of which you may not have been aware? Why is it hard to sometimes see social power acting in our lives?

Resources

Video: *Cry Freedom.*

This movie was made before the native people of South Africa were able to gain political power. It is the true story of a brave young African man who spoke out against the social stratification based on race in South Africa (called apartheid). It is also the story of a white newspaper reporter who discovered what power he did, and didn't have, to help his friend—Steve Biko.

This movie illustrates many of the concepts we study throughout this book—social power based on force and fear and the power of organized resistance. It shows how power is a social relationship, and that it can be challenged.

Many people in the United States supported the struggle of the native Africans to have equal rights in their own country. But there were powerful financial and corporate American interests that wanted to share in the exploitation of the African people. So, in many ways, we as a society were involved in South Africa.

The movie stars Denzel Washington and Kevin Kline. Rated PG.

NOTES

Complete citations are provided in the Bibliography.

1. Sandra Harding (1991) is a philosopher of science who has probed the question of how our social location affects our ideas of science and knowledge. See *Whose Science? Whose Knowledge?*

2. "Growing Disparity in Income Verified by Census Analysis." *Wall Street Journal*, 2 Feb. 1992.

3. Berk's (1985) careful study showed that despite lopsidedness in the household contribution, most wives and almost all husbands thought the division of labor in their household was fair.

4. The dimensions of power involved is clearly laid out by Aulette and Michalowski's (1993) study, "Fire in Hamlet: A Case Study of a State-Corporate Crime. "

5. McIntosh's (1992) excellent article "White Privilege and Male Privilege: A Personal Account of Coming to see Correspondences through Work in Women's Studies," clarifies this point.

2

THE VIEW FROM THE BOTTOM

> To do what they [whites] called civilizing us...was to destroy us. You know they thought that changing us, getting rid of our old ways and language and names would make us like white men. But why should we want to be like them, cheaters and greedy? Why should we change and abandon the ways that made us men and not the beggars we became?
>
> —Overtakes the Enemy, A Pawnee[1]

The higher up you are on the ladder of social stratification, the more social power you have. Those who have less power fall to the bottom. Two groups denied the resources necessary to function in society are the homeless and Native Americans. We have already pointed out that power flows from control over the resources that are needed for life. When those resources have to be produced (as in the example in Chapter 1 of the production of energy from oil, gas, and steam) those who control production have that power. When resources are political, then those who control political parties and the government, have that power. This view of power is often expressed by the concept of **control over the means of production.**

This chapter examines the ways in which two groups of people in America have been denied access to control over the resources they needed to survive.

AMERICA'S BOTTOM RUNG: HOMELESS PEOPLE

If you live in a large city, you may have encountered homeless people sitting on top of subway grates for warmth, crowded into a church's basement for a free supper, or standing on a corner asking for quarters. It may have made you nervous to walk by them, and maybe you felt a little guilty.

The homeless are an obvious example of two aspects of social power: (1) that power is based on control over, and access to, necessary resources and (2) that control and access over resources flows from social relationships within the society.

Homeless persons have little or no control over *necessary* resources. They do not have permanent shelter, sufficient income, or health care. Many homeless people work, but nearly half of all new jobs created from 1979 to 1990 paid poverty-level wages. While wages for many were falling, housing costs were rising between 20 and 30 percent. Thus, a job is not enough—the pay must be sufficient to enable you to live on your own. Education is not enough—it must be education that is needed and valued. Physical strength is not enough—if a machine can do the job faster and better. Being a citizen is not enough—you must have an established address in order to vote. Willingness to work is not enough if you do not have a telephone for employers to call or a car to get you to the job.

These examples illustrate the second point: *It is not enough just to have control over resources—those resources must be part of a social relationship that provides power.*

A factory worker in Flint, Michigan, may have left school after the tenth grade. For fifteen years he worked in the car plant, making wages enough to support himself, his wife, and three children. When the factory closed, he could not find another job paying enough to support his family.[2] His wife got sick and he couldn't pay the medical bills. Welfare came and took the children and put them in foster homes. His wife died. He has been left alone—depressed, angry and homeless. Ten years ago the resources he controlled—willingness to work, physical strength, discipline, and love for his family—were enough for him to make it. He is still willing to work, but he cannot survive. What has changed is not him, but the social relationship in which he is embedded as a worker.

The number of homeless in America dramatically increased under government policies in the 1980's that cut back subsidies for housing, funds for construction and maintenance of low income housing, and other welfare programs.[3] It is difficult to count precisely the number of homeless, and those who do the counting may have a vested interest in making the number lower or higher. Some counts have been as low as half a million, while others have argued that the number is closer to 6 million.

James Wright has argued that homelessness is not and cannot be a precisely defined condition.[4] He gives the example of a family living in their truck. A family who sleeps in its pickup truck and has nowhere else to go would be considered homeless. A long-distance trucker, who sleeps perhaps three or four nights a week in the cab of his $100,000 rig when he is on the road and who earns $40,000 a year, would not be considered homeless.

> "Yes, there are new jobs," a minister said. "There's a new McDonald's and a Burger King. You can take home $450 in a month from jobs like that. That might barely pay the rent. What do you do if somebody gets sick? What do you do for food and clothes? These may be good jobs for a teenager. Can you ask a thirty-yearold man who's worked for GM since he was eighteen to keep his wife and kids alive on jobs like that? There are jobs cleaning rooms in the hotel you're staying at. Can you expect a single mother with three kids to hold her life together with that kind of work? All you hear about these days are so-called service jobs—it makes me wonder where American is going. If we aren't producing anything of value, will we keep our nation going on hamburger stands? Who is all this 'service' for, if no one's got a real job making something of real worth?"
> (Kozol 1988,6).

The family forced to sleep in the truck are not on the sidewalk and may not be counted as homeless. There is also a difference between literal homelessness and marginal housing.[5] Those who are literally homeless have nowhere to go except the streets or homeless shelters. The marginally housed have somewhere to go, but they have no choices and what they have is inadequate.

Government agencies have typically counted the literally homeless but have not included the marginally housed. If individuals living in rural shacks without water, sewage, or electricity or urban families living in rat-infested apartments with falling plaster and stopped-up toilets were included, the numbers would be vastly increased. Jonathan Kozol estimates that there are more than 300,000 hidden homeless in New York City alone, and nationwide more than 3 million families are living doubled up.[6]

Despite the difficulties in counting, everyone agrees there has been a marked increase in the number of homeless in America. It is not just numbers that have changed; the kinds of people who are homeless have also changed. One study found that a tenth of the homeless were families—homeless children in the care of an adult parent or parents. Six percent of the individuals in this study were children without any adult caretaker. Looking at children, families, and lone adults, the study found that nearly forty percent of the homeless were women and children.[7]

Nor are all the homeless clustered in the ghettos of northern cities. A survey conducted by the Hunger and Homeless Action Coalition in San Mateo County, California, found that between March 1989 and February 1990 8,655 men, women and children experienced an episode of homelessness in that county alone. This same survey found that 22 percent of the homeless did have jobs, but couldn't afford places to live; that there are four times as many homeless people as there is room for them in shelters; that only one out of four homeless persons had a substance- abuse problem and less than one in five had a mental disability.

Another survey done by the International Union of Gospel Missions in Kansas City, Missouri, of their 119 inner-city rescue missions found that more than half the occupants were homeless less than a year, that men with children made up 3 percent; almost 50 percent were under age thirtyfive; 40 percent of the homeless men were military veterans; 34 percent were women and children and half of the homeless were white.[8]

Sylvia Ann Hewlett describes the end result for infants born on the street or to poverty-stricken parents in New York City:

> [parents] fill out forms to reserve a space in a mass grave. The Health and Hospitals Corporation freezes the tiny bodies, then delivers them unembalmed to the trucks that will take them to New York City's Potter's field. A Catholic priest comes by to bless God's little children, en masse. The wind blew harder. Inmates moved faster. Some boxes contained twins. A few were broken. An inmate cradled one in his arms, much as if things were different. "This is a heavy little baby," he said. In 1986, 1,128 such babies were buried in New York City in this way; in 1989, there were 1,606—a 42 percent increase.[9]

The Health Professions Training Act of 1985 (P.L. 99–129) mandated that the Department of Health and Human Services ask the Institute of Medicine of the National Academy of Sciences to study the delivery of health care services to homeless people. In making the study, the Institute asked the question: Who are the Homeless? The answer given in their report concluded:

> Contrary to the traditional stereotypes of homeless people, the homeless of the 1980s are not all single, middle-aged, male alcoholics. Neither are they all mentally ill people made homeless as a by-product of the policy of deinstitutionalization of mental health care.
>
> The homeless are younger, more ethnically diverse, and increasingly are more likely to be members of families than is generally believed by the public. In most cities around the country, minorities—especially blacks and Hispanics—are represented disproportionately among the homeless as compared with their percentage of the overall population of those cities. *Children under the age of 18, usually as part of a family headed by a mother, are the fasted-growing group among the many subpopulations of the*

> *homeless (emphasis added).* On the other hand, the elderly are underrepresented among the homeless in comparison with their percentage in the general population. There are a substantial number of veterans among the homeless, especially from the Vietnam era.
>
> Homeless people tend to be long-term residents of the city in which they live. The homeless in rural areas, as well as homeless urban families, usually have gone through several stages of doubling up with family and friends before becoming visibly homeless.[10]

It is easy to dismiss the tragedy of homelessness by reeling off statistics and not thinking about the humans involved. Two excellent books that make homelessness real are Kozol, *Rachel and Her Children* (1988), and Liebow, *Tell Them Who I Am: The Lives of Homeless Women* (1993).

The economic and social forces that created this new kind of homelessness are discussed in more detail in Chapter 13. The point here is that power cannot be studied independently of the social context in which it is exercised. Two hundred years ago knowing how to shoe a horse guaranteed an individual a job and a good living. Today that same knowledge and skill is rarely needed. History, technology, and culture all interact to provide the context by which a relationship of power is created.

AN HISTORICAL CONTRAST: THE COLONIAL POOR

How do today's homeless people compare to the very poorest people in America as it was just undergoing urbanization and industrialization? Who were those that might today be the equivalent of today's homeless people—the dirty, smelly persons on the bottom rung?

Howard Zinn has identified the poverty-stricken people in pre–Revolutionary War America as "Persons of Mean and Vile Condition." During the seventeenth century 75 percent of the colonists came as servants; in the entire colonial period more than half of those who immigrated to eastern North America came as servants. These poverty-stricken Europeans signed harsh contracts in order to escape the poverty and oppression of the Old World. Supplying cheap labor to the colonies was big business and unscrupulous shipping companies often misled and lied to prospective immigrants to get their business.[11] English poor laws for the correction and punishment of rogues and idle people were enforced in Ireland, and this led to the wholesale kidnaping of young Irish women and men to supply the labor needs of the colonies.[12]

These indentured servants were those who were at the bottom rungs of the European class ladder, mainly from England but also from Germany and Ireland. They were described as "rogues, vagabonds, whores, cheats, and rabble of all descriptions," raked from the gutter, "decoyed, deceived, seduced, inveigled or forcibly kidnaped and carried as servants to the plantations." They were regarded as the surplus inhabitants of England. Virtually all of these indentured servants came without families.[13]

Under terms of early indenture, the master could beat a servant for the least infraction, rape of female servants was common, and the length of servitude was often extended without good cause. In the early 1600s there was little difference between the condition of indenture suffered by European servants and African servants.[14] Other immigrants came to the New World as convicts and had to work off their sentences. Some peasants spent their entire life savings to pay for passage and arrived penniless.

These descriptions of the earliest immigrants probably describe the ancestors of the vast majority of those of you who are Euro-Americans. In other words, your forefathers and foremothers were not the aristocrats who received the large land grants and arrived in the New World with velvet clothes and their own personal armies. Your ancestors were the hard-working and poverty-stricken peasants who came with dreams and little else.

The cities developing on the Eastern Seaboard in the early 1700s included large slum areas. There were no sewer systems, no public water systems, no welfare, and no public hospitals. The poor lived in miserable shacks in unsanitary conditions. They, like the homeless of today, probably smelled, had poor health, and many drank a lot. They were *less* educated than the homeless of today. Just as today, the better-off looked down their noses at this lowest class and degraded them with stereotypes: "men and women who were dirty and lazy, rough, ignorant, lewd, and often criminal," who "thieved and wandered, had bastard children, and corrupted society with loathsome diseases," the vast majority being "shiftless, hopeless, ruined individuals."[15]

Although a few of the poor became criminals—thieves, gamblers, and prostitutes— most of them found employment. No matter how much the upper classes may have loathed the poor, they needed them and they used them. The poor worked at starvation wages, in dirty and dangerous jobs. An industrializing society needed to have roads built, canals dug, ships constructed and forests cleared. Their social relationship to the society was based on a the resource they had to offer—their labor. It was a resource very much needed by the elite who controlled other resources (money, land, education, technology).

The owners of the land and factories could hire hungry workers at low wages and increase their profits. This exploitation of the poor increased the wealth of the upper class. For example, in Boston in 1687, the richest

1 percent of the population (fifty individuals) had 25 percent of the wealth. By 1770, the wealth controlled by the top 1 percent of the population in Boston had increased to 44 percent. At the same time, according to tax lists, the percent of adult males in Boston who were poor doubled from 14 percent in 1687 to 29 percent in 1770.[16]

In the late 1600s, three-fourths of the land in New York was granted to about thirty people under Governor Benjamin Fletcher. Jackson Main estimates that at the time of the American Revolution, 10 percent of the American population (large landholders and merchants) owned nearly one-half the wealth of the country and held as slaves one-seventh of the country's people.[17]

There is an important difference in the social relationship of power between the urban poor in the 1600s and 1700s and the poor of the late twentieth century. The homeless today, as a group, are oppressed and degraded but they are less needed for exploitation. This is not to say that homeless people are not occasionally exploited. For example, in Philadelphia men at a homeless shelter were made to work a certain number of hours as laborers in farms outside the city to pay back the costs of their upkeep in the shelter. We are arguing that homeless people are increasingly defined as useless. A society using computers and robots to take the jobs of humans no longer needs all its workers. We examine this point in detail in Chapter 13.

AN HISTORICAL CONTRAST: NATIVE AMERICANS

There is a second historical comparison that illustrates this relationship between social status, oppression and power—the Native Americans. Today Native American people are the poorest, least educated, unhealthiest, and worst-housed ethnic group in the United States. Low estimates suggest that there were 3 million Native Americans in North America at the time of Columbus; other estimates place the figure ten times as high—30 million. By 1890 the number of surviving Native Americans had been reduced to 228,000.[18] The term **genocide** describes what happened to the original peoples of North America; they were physically eliminated as a people. Those who remain have been placed in one of the lowest statuses in the American social structure.

The question of Native American genocide is an example of the how figures are altered by their context. For a long time historians downplayed the number of Natives originally in the Hemisphere. In 1910, Mooney estimated that the number was a little over 1 million. Newer studies argued the number might have been as high as 10 million, and in 1984 Dobyns argued the number of pre-Columbian inhabitants could have been as much as 18 million! Whatever the official number, by early part of the twentieth century the "official" number of Native Americans had been reduced to a little over 300,000.[19]

Now that the data *does* suggest a massive death rate, the question is *how* did so many die? C. Mathew Snipp, writing in an official *Census Monograph Series*, admits the high death rate. His study attributes the death rate totally to the effect of disease, especially smallpox.[20] This "official" version is able to sidestep completely the effect that the military campaigns and social policies had on the death rate. Snipp's argument is that the epidemics that wiped out the Native Americans were similar to those of the plague of the Black Death. In this case, the concept of "genocide" would not be correct.

Other social scientists have viewed the death rate in a totally different context.[21] It is true that new diseases can have devastating effects on social structures; it is also true that over time those resistent to the disease re-create their communities. Historical studies show that under normal condidtions human populations make recoveries within several generations. At the time the Native Americans were faced with new diseases, their food supplies were being wiped out, they were under military attack, and the colonial authorities were pursuing policies that encouraged the spread of the diseases and alcoholism. Under *these* conditions, then, the epidemics were turned into genocide.[22]

At the time European immigrants were brought to the cities of the Eastern Seaboard, Native Americans were living in self-sufficient and prosperous villages across the continent. A recent *National Geographic* argued that the standard of living in most Native American communities at the time of Columbus was higher than the standard of living of the average peasant in Europe.[23] The hunting and farming economies of most traditional Native American cultures provided a healthier and more secure life than the disease-ridden, polluted and poverty stricken slums of New York, Boston, or Baltimore in the 1700s.

The power exercised in North American Native American cultures was a different kind of power than that of European society. Social power for Native Americans was far less likely to be based on exploitation, oppression or degradation. The discussion here is limited to Native American cultures of North America. The Native American empires of Central America and South America were clearly examples of highly stratified societies.

The Native American people were organized in smaller communities and states, and social differences were based more on age, gender, and demonstrated skills. In many of these cultures, women dominated agricultural production and held not only high status but also public power.[24] The idea of "private property" as we know it was unknown; the accumulation of material goods and power based on inherited wealth was rarely a major factor in their communities.

> In many Native American cultures, women held positions of equal or even greater status than men.[25] Children were valued, and the elderly were seen as a source of wisdom. Social customs frowned on individual self-gain and rewarded individuals who worked for the gain of the group. Human life was seen as part and parcel of a larger life cycle that involved powerful forces of earth, sky and water:
>
> Governance was through the consent of the governed, and women played a crucial role in family, clan and nation. Food was nutritious, and the Three Sister plants (corn, beans, and squash) would be an inestimable gift to the newcoming Europeans. The Iroquois had few of the sicknesses that plague us, and with herbal remedies close at hand, their life expectancy was greater than Europeans of their day.

Most of all, there was balance, balance with the land, between the sexes, within the political life, in the diet, in the healing arts. Balance and the giving of thanks. Balance that transformed grief into new life, that transmuted even the worst of their people into the best of their leaders, that adopted their enemies and made them brothers. It is a balance that our modern world desperately needs to remember. It is a balance that Iroquois still speak of and, despite the pressures of modern life, that many still manage to find.[26]

In contrast, power in European societies rested on the accumulation of private wealth, professional armies, male dominance, and command over the earth. None of the Native American cultures possessed the rigid and hierarchical social structure to which Europeans were accustomed. Thus, it is not just that the Europeans encountered different *cultures* of religion, art and technological development; the Europeans encountered a radically different *social system* from the one from which they had come. The Europeans saw these differences as proof that the natives were "savages."[27]

This is not to imply that Native American cultures were all the same. There were important differences between them, defined by widely different environments, traditions, and histories. Nor was North America a Utopia. Different Native American groups made war on each other, taking captives and land. But the wars that were fought were very different from those of industrializing Europe. Prior to colonization, there had never been a Native American war of annihilation. Native Americans usually fought for honor rather than killing. Status in many societies was earned through exhibitions of personal bravery. These wars were staged to allow the maximum amount of bravery with the least amount of personal injury; one might say the wars were rigged to keep enemies alive in order that the contest might continue indefinitely.[28]

The cultural rules of warfare changed with the coming of the Europeans. The competing English, Dutch, French, and Spanish provided firearms to the groups with whom they were allied and provoked conflicts between the tribes that fit their political purposes. Modern methods of torture, scalping, and the massacre of women and children were all innovations introduced by Europeans.

Poor Europeans and Africans imported for labor came from socially stratified societies in which exploitation of the lower classes' labor was known. The vast majority of Africans brought over into slavery in the American South came from western Africa—an area in which highly organized feudal kingdoms had produced standing armies, great universities, intercontinental trade, and a complex division of labor.[29] Once here, there was no "home" to which they could escape.

Native Americans, in contrast, could escape bondage, using their knowledge of the land.[30] Once European immigration and the importation of African slaves solved the shortage of labor, the colonial ruling class defined the Native Americans as useless to what they wanted—the land and its resources. The economic system of European capitalism needed to exploit the land, not its native people. It merely needed to get rid of the people.

If one looks at the history of Native Americans from their point of view, they have been brutally oppressed and degraded as a people. They have suffered all the effects of being placed, and held by force, on the bottom of America's social stratification system. Their heroic resistance was met by brutal force. Yet even today the rest of us are unaware of the true history and current social status of Native Americans. Nonetheless, we learned some historical lessons.

These lessons taught us that problems created by the interaction of dissimilar cultures could be resolved by force. The image of the American Cavalry shooting the Indians has taught us that "might makes right." The rape of Indian women and the scalping of Indian children to earn bounties was an historic precedence for today's abuse of children, wife beating, and gang warfare. Rayna Green argues that American society has created an image of the Native American woman that perpetuates the stereotypes and rationalizations of conquest in stories like those of Pocahontas.[31] "America the Beautiful" stretched across a bloodstained fruited plain.

Americans were shocked to hear that American soldiers cut off the ears of their Vietnamese victims. That is because we never learned that after Andrew Jackson and his troops killed eight hundred Creeks (men, women and children) the soldiers made bridle reins from strips of skin taken from the corpses and cut off the tip of each dead Indian's nose for body count.[32] We cannot possibly understand the current level of violence in our society unless we fully comprehend this historical violence. Youth in American schools are taught that Hitler committed genocide on six million Jews, but are still taught that President Andrew Jackson, General Custer, and Buffalo Bill are heroes.

The plight of the homeless and the Native Americans raises serious questions about our democratic ideals and beliefs in equality. Are these simply extreme examples? Or are they part of a larger social stratification system that exploits, oppresses and degrades many groups? The American class system is the fundamental framework by which our society organizes social stratification. The next chapter examines how power in America is distributed by social class.

SUMMARY

If people do not have access to the resources needed for survival in a society, they will be at the bottom of the social stratification ladder. Each society defines what resources are necessary. Those who control those resources have the most power. Those on the top of the ladder who decide how and when these resources are created and who gets them can be said to have control over the means of production.

Today, homeless people are an example of a group that lacks access to the resources needed to survive. As a result they suffer great social pain. Despite the great wealth of America, the number of homeless people has continued to grow. Some of them are sick or mentally disabled; many are women, children, and the elderly.

The very poor who lived in colonial America did not face the same problem. Although they, too, did not have much in the way of material things, they did have a resource that was needed—their labor—and that gave them some power.

Another group that has historically been placed on the bottom of the ladder of social stratification is the Native American. Despite the fact that native people had productive and complex cultures, the Europeans wanted to believe that they had "discovered the land" and could therefore claim it. They saw the natives as only being in the way. Although the natives resisted, the Europeans were able to take their land and largely destroy their way of life. Today, the descendants of these proud people live on reservations and continue to battle to preserve their culture and dignity.

The examples of the homeless and Native Americans raises the question of how social stratification functions in our society. Are these examples extremes that are not typical, or do they illustrate fundamental principles of the way our society operates?

Vocabulary

Control over the means of production. The ability to decide how and when the important resources of a society are created and the ability to decide who gets what; resources can include physical necessities such as houses and food and social necessities such as jobs, political rights, and education.

Discussion Questions

1. Many people assume that if someone is homeless, it is their "fault." What are some of the circumstances under which people make choices to be homeless? What are some of the circumstances under which people are made homeless despite all their efforts? Can you imagine circumstances so bad that *you* might end up homeless? Why or why not?

2. When I was in Tanzania the people there would ask me about homelessness in America. They would say, "Here we have very few homeless. You are the richest country in the world, but you have millions of homeless. Why?" What would you answer?

3. How would you describe the difference between being very poor in colonial America and being very poor today? How does this show the point that it is not just a question of resources, but the social relationship of those resources?

4. I argue that the violence we see in American society today might have its "roots" in the violence against Native Americans. What is my argument? Do you agree or disagree? Why?

Resources

Video: *Revolution*

Most of us study the American Revolution from the point of view of the generals and politicians. But this movie is about an ordinary man who follows his son into the Continental Army, only to discover that the elite care little about the foot soldier or the "cause." If you watch carefully, you will notice that the role of women is accurately portrayed (they often carried arms and actively fought) and that the issue of African American freedom is raised. Al Pacino is the father who decides he should fight for freedom after all.

The movie is somewhat long, but is worth the viewing. Even the role of the various Native American groupings is explored. The scenery is beautiful. And one gets a real feeling of what it must have been like to be a poor and hungry soldier in the American Revolution. Rated R.

Books: Jonathan Kozol, *Rachael and her Children: Homeless Families in America,* and Eliot Liebow, *Tell Them Who I Am: The Lives of Homeless Women.*

Both these books make the problem of homelessness a story of real people facing real situations. It is much easier to understand an issue when we hear it told by those who experience the problem first hand. Both of these books may make you sad, or angry.

Dee Brown, *Bury My Heart at Wounded Knee: An Indian History of the American West..*

Most Americans do not fully understand the true horrors of what "winning the West" meant for those who already lived there. We are more aware of horrors in other places—Nazi Germany or the Russian concentration camps—than of the horror that the U.S. Government committed on the "redskins." This book will shake you up. How could such things happen?

NOTES

Complete citations are provided in the Bibliography.

1. Quoted in Takaki 1993, 104.
2. The social pain caused by the layoffs in Flint, Michigan, were graphically captured by Michael Moore in his movie *Roger and Me*.
3. Cited in Eitzen and Zinn 1993.
4. James Wright 1989, 19.
5. Rossi, Wright, Fisher and Willis 1987, 1336–1341.
6. Kozol 1988, 1, 14.
7. James Wright 1989, 55–61.
8. Reported in *USA Weekend*, January 5–7, 1990.
9. Hewlett 1992, 42.
10. National Academy of Science 1988, 379–380.
11. Zinn 1980, 42
12. Takaki 1993, 54.
13. Takaki 1993, 54.
14. Takaki 1993, 51–78. Also see Jernegan 1971.
15. Abbot Smith, quoted in Zinn 1980, 46.
16. Zinn 1980, 49.
17. Jackson Main, *The Social Structure of Revolutionary America*, quoted in Zinn 1980, 79.
18. Eitzen and Zinn, 1993: 301
19. A summary of this discussion, with citations, can be found in Snipp 1989, 5–18.
20. Ibid.
21. Thornton 1987.
22. Ibid.
23. *National Geographic* 180, no.4 (October 1991); also see Josephy 1993. An excellent description of the oppression, exploitation and degradation of England's poor under feudalism is to be found in the carefully researched novel by Anand 1991.

24. Jensen 1990, 51–65.
25. Jaimes and Halsey 1992, 311–344.
26. Ibid.
27. Takaki 1993, 24–50.
28. Holm 1992, 354–361.
29. Bennet 1982, 3–27.
30. Geschwender 1978, 124–126.
31. Rayna Green 1990,15–21.
32. Takaki 1993, 85.

3

THE LADDER OF SOCIAL CLASS IN AMERICA

> Apparently, the rising tide lifted the yachts; the rowboats foundered.[1]

When we think about social stratification in America, we almost always think of money. Our culture equates money with power and social status—things usually associated with social class. Money alone, however, is not enough for power. If I put several million dollars in a box under my bed, I might be rich but that money would not be a basis for power.

This chapter is a description of how power based on money and wealth is distributed within the population. We all grow up believing the United States is the wealthiest country in the world; we do not grow up understanding the enormous *imbalance* of that wealth. A tiny few receive a large amount of the wealth, whereas the vast majority just manage to get by and even this is getting harder and harder. This inequality is reflected in the social pain experienced by millions of Americans. The exploitation of their labor, the oppression of poor living conditions, and the degradation of their sense of self extracts a terrible toll.

This chapter only describes this inequality. In later chapters we discuss the resistance of people to the conditions that cause that pain and why so many accept the pain as necessary or even justified.

THE ACCUMULATION OF WEALTH

In feudal societies, social status was largely determined by birth. The nobility had a better lifestyle—castles, beautiful robes, and good food and wine. In contrast, an industrializing society required that material goods not be consumed, but *invested*. Early entrepreneurs were often very frugal, reinvesting almost everything they earned. A small fortune, manipulated correctly, could easily become a large fortune. That fortune was not money under the bed but ownership of factories, mines, machines, and land.

These were new ideas. Under feudalism it was not unusual for a king, queen or noble to take a vow of poverty at some point in life. They hoped that such poverty might assure entrance into heaven. In contrast, religion changed during industrialization to teach that wealth was a sign of God's blessing both in this life and the hereafter. Control over productive property became a source of power. The factory owner held control over the labor force. If a landless peasant wanted to make a living, he or she had to go to the owner for a job because the industrialist, or capitalist, owned the machines and could purchase the materials to make products. In other words, the means of production (simple tools, cattle, and looms) had been taken away from those who did the work and transferred into the hands of a different group.

Human beings became part of the accounting of capitalism. Under slavery, workers themselves became property to be exploited. Under wage labor, workers' labor was exploited for a purchased amount of time. Wages were analyzed in the same way that costs for machinery, rent, and maintenance were analyzed. Machines and technology existed, not to make life better, but to increase wealth. The resources of the earth—water, timber, minerals, soil—existed to be exploited for profit. The social theorists of this period believed that capital accumulation and exploitation would lead to the general social benefit of all society. In that sense it is parallel to the "trickle down" theories of today.

According to Pulitzer Prize-winning historian James McPherson, even Thomas Jefferson feared wage labor as a form of dependency that seemed to contradict the republican principles on which the country had been founded:

> Thomas Jefferson had defined the essence of liberty as independence, which required the ownership of productive property. A man dependent on others for a living could never be truly free, nor could a dependent class constitute the basis of a republican government. Women, children, and slaves were dependent; that defined them *out* of the polity of republican freemen. Wage laborers were also dependent; that was why Jefferson feared the development of industrial capitalism with its need for wage laborers. Jefferson envisaged an ideal America of farmers and artisan producers who owned their means of production and depended on no man for a living.[2]

Those who control, use, and manipulate property have the most power and highest social class in our society. Other types of power and sources of power are not acknowledged or seen as serious. Since property is the source of power, rank within relationships is largely based on the nature of the property involved.

This has become more and more apparent. For example, adults are important as long as they can work, but as soon as they retire or become disabled they become "unproductive." Popularity for teenagers is based on what kind of property—clothes, video games, music tapes—they can buy and show off. Marcia Millman's study, *Warm Hearts and Cold Cash: the Intimate Dynamics of Families and Money*, describes how today's family is often characterized by many of the hard but hidden traits of the market, including coercion, game playing, and competition.[3]

Control over property affects all arenas. Winning elections depends on hiring expensive media consultants and buying TV time. Baseball is no longer something fun to do in a sandlot on a summer evening, but a TV production that sells athletic shoes, beer, and cards with the stars on them. To get sexual pleasure, one pays for a 1-900 phone call or buys a personal ad in the newspaper. To impress the neighbors one borrows $50,000 to have a "nice" wedding. The value of the African American subculture does not lie in its contribution to our cultural diversity, but in its ability to sell "X" caps, Mandela T-shirts, and rap tapes. Many doctors and hospitals deliver health care only if there is insurance or the money is put up front.

We have been socialized to believe this is true, necessary and good. Owning more and more "things" has become a way to establish our identity. Materialism has become an important value in our culture. Young people dream of owning fancy cars, big homes and gold jewelry. It is seen as a "good" thing to be very rich. What are the chances that will happen? Let us take a look at the existing patterns of wealth and power in our society.

THE AMERICAN CLASS STRUCTURE

Sociologists have spent many years arguing about how to measure social status. If class position is just a matter of money, then dividing the population into classes is a purely arbitrary exercise. Is an income of $100,000 a year the cutting-off point for upper middle class? But how does one compare a college professor with a Ph.D. who makes $40,000 a year with a union autoworker with a high school education that makes $45,000 a year? Are they in the same class? If we consider power it is easier to analyze because class position is a *relationship*. We are at a given status because we are in a relationship of power to those "above" us and those "below" us. Increasing my power (and improving my class status) is not simply dependent on how much money I earn, but what resources I can manipulate.

It is also important to remember that income and wealth are different. Most of us earn incomes and use that income to pay our bills and maybe save a little for the future. **Income** is money received on a regular basis. People who work get income as a wage or a salary. Disabled persons or those on welfare receive income in the form of a check from the government. Income can also be earned from wealth. **Wealth** is an accumulation of resources that generates some kind of income. If you have a savings account or a CD, you may receive some income based on that wealth.

A person who must work for income is in a very different social position than a person who receives income from wealth. It is easier to understand this by looking at an example. Two white males, Fred and Pete, both earn incomes of $450,000 a year, both have master's degrees and they live in the same affluent neighborhood. The first person, Fred, is chief executive officer of a medium-size corporation. His firm operates in a very competitive environment and there is a lot of stress in his job. He must often bring work home on weekends, and it is not unusual for him to begin work at 7 AM and not return home until 8 or 9 PM. His only outside activity is membership in a local country club, where he gets exercise and interacts with other business people.

Fred has power over other people—he makes decisions that can close down factories, lower or raise the price of stock, and install machines that replace jobs. He earns enough money so that he never has to worry that his bills won't be paid. When Congress considers legislation that would allow cheaper competing products to be imported, Fred has to find time to fly to Washington and meet with lobbyists.

Pete, the other man in the example, had a grandfather who held the patent on making crunchy peanut butter. (This is a fictitious example.) Pete's dad was sent to Harvard for an education. He went into the stock business, investing his family's money and other people's money until he had made a fortune. Pete's income of $450,000 is based on his earnings from that fortune. Pete does not have to work at a regular job.

Pete can live the same lifestyle as Fred but Pete has control over his time. He can choose to run for political office or become the executive director of a large foundation or a patron of the arts. His time allows him to network with other powerful people and use his influence. His large fortune is a source of power with bankers, stockbrokers and politicians. Blocks of stock that he controls can vote CEOs like Fred out of office if he chooses to exercise that power.

Power, then, is more than income. In Pete's case, he cannot spend his wealth without destroying the basis of his income, just as Fred cannot quit his job without destroying the basis of his income. The resources Pete controls gives him more power than the resources Fred controls, although they both earn the same income.

Pete does not *have* to exercise his power. Pete could choose to join the "jet set" and spend his time on the French Riviera, lying in the sun with beautiful women and playing in the casinos. His wealth would give him control over his life, to play, but his activities would not give him much power over the lives of others. Pete would probably delegate that power to a hired consultant, who would look after his fortune (for a price, of course). This consultant, Harry, could attend meetings where he would be respected for the power he wielded. In other words, some individuals attain power that is delegated to them.

One might argue that Harry's power depends upon Pete, who can fire Harry anytime he wants. But if Harry is a clever investor, and Pete doesn't pay any attention to financial affairs, Pete may actually need Harry as much as Harry needs Pete's power base. These examples show that as soon as we discuss power, we must always discuss the social relationships involved.

THE SUPERRICH AND THE RICH

In 1937 Ferdinand Lundberg wrote a book called *America's Sixty Families*. According to Lundberg, "The United States is owned and dominated today by a hierarchy of its sixty richest families, buttressed by no more than ninety families of lesser wealth."[4] Lundberg argued their power was based on their consolidated wealth *as families*. Although all individuals received income derived from the wealth, no single individual within a family could divide and dissipate it. We look more closely at kinship as a way in which families exercise power through networking in Chapter 9.

Lundberg pointed out that because this group is so small in number they do not show up in general statistics. Individuals from this group rarely appear on the lists of wealthiest individuals published by *Business Week* or *Forbes* magazine. Michael Parenti argues:

> a small number of the wealthiest families, such as the Mellons, Morgans, DuPonts, and Rockefellers, dominate the American economy. The DuPont family controls eight of the largest defense contractors and grossed over $15 billion in military contracts during the Vietnam War. The DuPonts control ten corporations that each have billions of dollars in assets, including General Motors, Coca-Cola, and United Brands, along with many smaller firms. The DuPonts serve as trustees of scores of colleges. They own about forty manorial estates and private museums in Delaware alone and have set up thirty-one tax-exempt foundations. The

> family is frequently the largest contributor to Republican presidential campaigns and has financed right-wing and antilabor causes.
>
> Another powerful family enterprise, that of the Rockefellers, extends into just about every industry in every state of the Union and every nation in the nonsocialist world. The Rockefellers control five of the twelve largest oil companies and four of the largest banks in the world. They finance universities, churches, cultural centers, and youth organizations. At one time or another, they or their close associates have occupied the offices of the president, vice-president, secretaries of State, Commerce, Defense and other cabinet posts, the Federal Reserve Board, the governorships of several states, key position in the Central Intelligence Agency (CIA), the U.S. Senate and House, and the Council of Foreign Relations.[5]

At the top of the ladder in the richest country in the world, America's super rich have acquired fortunes that go beyond any other fortunes in human history. To be so rich is never to have to ask "How much does it cost?" There are shops in New York where the dresses are not hung on racks. If you shop there, you tell the clerk what clothes interest you, and they will model them for you. While you observe, you are served champagne. Prices are never mentioned. If you have to ask, you can't afford them. There are restaurants for this class, where the prices are not listed on the menu. There are condominiums where the purchase price includes daily fresh flower bouquets and maid service, an interior decorator, and replacing the drapes and rugs annually.

Most of us watch our budgets and have to make choices based on cost. If we take a vacation, we will not be able to afford a new living room rug. If we choose a job we like better, we may also have to take a pay cut. We cannot imagine living in a world where the price tag doesn't matter.

A discussion of the super rich can easily focus on their money, rather than their power. But without power, they could not keep their money. During the rise of industrial trade unions in the early part of this century, this question of power was the primary one. The left, or "radical," wing of the trade union movement demanded that workers have greater control over their work and working conditions. These early trade union leaders argued that exploited labor originally created the wealth of the super rich. They confronted the source of the owners' power—not their money per se but their ownership of the factories, mines, railroads and other productive resources. The history of that movement is a history of a *power* struggle, which we discuss in greater detail in Chapter 5. The point to be made here, once again, is that it is not

Looking for an apartment to rent in New York?

A Luxury Apartment Hotel Residence
*24 Hour doorman and elevator services
*All Utilities and linens included
*Complete maid and turndown bed service
*Individual climate control
*Full concierge service
*World famous Maxi m's restaurant
*Beauty Salon
*Barber Shop
*Valet Parking and private secured motor entrance
*24 hour message and telephone service
*Room service
*Complete Security

Or how about a mansion in the country?

Greenwich, Connecticut.
Approximately 2.5 acres.
Custom 14 room home suited for both formal and family living. 6 bedrooms, 7 baths, 2 powder rooms, 7 working fireplaces. Spacious rooms have high ceilings and floor-to-ceiling Palladian windows. Pool with spa and waterfall. Easy access to Manhattan. $2,995,000.

These are two typical ads from *The New York Times Magazine*, March 13, 1994.

money alone, but control over productive property, that generates social power in our society.

The wealthy and powerful of our society include more people than just the super rich. Others earn high incomes and are able to wield power based on their access to resources. This group of individuals is largely made up of the executives of the large corporations, banks, stockbroker firms, and legal firms that manage the business of America. These executives have a direct interest in corporate profits. As Parenti points out: "Far from being neutral technocrats dedicated to the public welfare, they represent the more active element of a self-interested owning class. Their power does not rest in their holdings but in their corporate positions."[6]

Business Week ranked the income and benefits of the chief executive officers (CEOs) of America's largest corporations in 1992.[7] The ten most highly paid CEOs and their companies are listed in Table 3.1.

Table 3.1

Chief Executive Officer	Annual Pay (in millions)	Company
Thomas F. Frist, Jr.	$127.00	Hospital Corp. of America
Sanford I. Weill	$67.64	Primerica
Charles Lazarus	$64.23	Toys 'R Us
Leon C. Hirsch	$62.17	U.S. Surgical
Stephen A. Wynn	$38.01	Mirage Resorts
Anthony J.F. O'Reilly	$36.92	H.J. Heinz
Martin J. Wygod	$30.21	Medco Containment
William A. Anders	$29.02	General Dynamics
Ronald K. Richey	$26.57	Torchmark
Louis F. Battle	$24.60	UST

It should be noted that three of the CEOs, including the highest paid, headed companies related to healthcare delivery and service.

Some have argued the high salaries of big businessmen are justified because they work so hard and are worth it to their stockholders. But there are many cases of officers who give themselves far higher raises than the rise in their stock. Critics also point out that large raises are morally questionable when the profits earned have come because the company carried out large worker lay-offs. In an article titled "Gross Compensation? New CEO Pay Figures Make Top Brass Look Positively Piggy," *BusinessWeek,* 18 March, 1996, raises this issue. The article highlights some examples in Table 3.2

The same issue of *BusinessWeek* reports that in the week of 17 February, 1996 there were 382,000 new claims for unemployment compensation, a figure that was 11 percent more than the same week a year ago.

The number of people who control the productive wealth of the United States has not increased proportionally as wealth has increased. In other words, control over the productive wealth in our society has grown more *concentrated.* In 1990, 1.4 percent of the commercial banks in the United States (172 banks out of a total of 12,345 banks) owned nearly 60 percent of all commercial bank assets ($2,019.6 billion). Almost one-third of the top 500 corporations in the United States are controlled by one individual or family. As small businesses have been absorbed by giant corporations, stock ownership has not cut across class lines but has occurred within the owning class itself. One hundred years ago, three families might have owned companies A, B, and C respectively, whereas today all three have holdings in all three companies, giving the elite an even greater community of interest than they had in the past.[8]

Table 3.2 CEO Pay Increases 1995

CEO and Company	Millions	*BusinessWeek* Comments
Robert Allen AT&T	$5.85	The CEO's basic pay didn't climb, but an option grant values at $11 million enraged critics in a year when AT&T announced massive lay-offs and shares rose only 28.9%.
Ronald Compton Aetna Life & Casualty	$6.64	Aetna shares rose 46.9% last year, aided by the sale of its property and casualty unit. But Compton's compensation far out paced that, rising 485%.
Lawrence Ellison Oracle	$14.14	The CEO got most of his 387% pay hike through a $10.8 million gain from exercising stock options. Oracle shares, fueled by the tech-stock boom, rose 44%.
Richard Fisher Morgan Stanley	$11.93	After he doubled return on equity to 16.2%, directors gave him $6.2 million in bonuses and restricted stock—making for a 318% pay hike. Shares rose 36.7%
Roberto Goizueta Coca-Cola	$13.09	A perennial bigtime earner, his compensation rose only 7%. But he also got a 1 million-shares option grant, now worth $25.6 million. Shares rose 44.2%.
Jerry Junkins Texas Instruments	$10.65	After earning $7.7 million on the exercise of stock options, his total pay package climbed 148%; shares rose 50.4%
John L. Clendenin BellSouth	$4.8	Also received an option grant worth $2.3 million. Company has announced job cuts in the past four years totaling 21,200.
Philip J. Quigley Pacific Telesis	$2.4	Pay increase was a 23% rise. Company has laid off 19,000 people during the past four years.
Ronald W. Allen Delta Air Lines	$1.4	Increase in pay of 187%. Company has announced the elimination of 18,800 jobs since 1991.

During the 1950s, the country's largest expansion of the middle class occurred. It was also a time when the number of people reporting more than a half-million dollars in income barely rose, from 842 in 1950 to 1,002 in 1959, a gain of 19 percent. As long as the middle classes were growing proportionately, such concentration of wealth did not seem to be a problem. It appeared that the middle classes were benefitting from a "trickle down" that improved their standard of living.

Because the middle classes were making more money, it was easy to forget that more money was not necessarily increasing their power. Instead, the vast majority of those in the middle class used their increased earning to increase their consumption—nicer homes, more cars, VCRs, and refrigerators that dispensed ice cubes through the front door.[9] Television and magazines urged everyone to do the American thing—buy, buy, and buy some more.

Such goods, however, do not generate more wealth, or are the basis for control over other property. How much more power over your life does a color 27 inch stereo TV-VCR provide than a plain 13 inch black and white?

In the 1970s tangible assets had an annual growth of between 4.2 and 4.3 percent annually. Tangible assets—homes, cars, appliances—are those things that retain some value over time. Both middleclass and rich people have tangible assets, but most middle class people don't have much in the way of financial assets—stocks, bonds, and other investments. Between 1979 and 1989 financial assets—stocks and bonds owned primarily by the wealthy—grew at an annual rate of 2.9 percent. In contrast, tangible assets did not grow at all. Since tangible assets are spread out more evenly than financial assets, their stagnation mainly affected the bulk of the population who are not wealthy.[10]

Several decades ago, most workers controlled some small amount of wealth in their pensions; today, corporations and banks have taken over control of the pension funds. The result is that many of the funds are grossly underfunded and in some cases, have been used as sources of cash by companies making bad investments.[11]

While the middle class took vacations and watched videos on their new VCRs the wealthy were using their power in Congress. In the 1950s, taxable income above $400,000 was taxed at a rate of 91 percent. In 1991, the maximum tax rate for individuals had been cut to 31 percent. That was a tax-rate reduction of 66 percent. Changes in the tax laws for individuals and corporations and the deregulation of commerce created the conditions for an enormous expansion of wealth. Between 1980 and 1989, the number of people reporting incomes of more than a half-million dollars rocketed from 16,881 to 183,240—an increase of 985 percent! That represented the largest percentage increase of wealth in this century, even exceeding the other era of excess, the 1920s.[12]

In 1959, the top 4 percent of all wage earners in the country earned as much on the job as the bottom 35 percent. In 1970, the top 4 percent earned as much as the bottom 38 percent. By 1989 it took the wages and salaries of the lowest 51 percent of the workers ($31 billion) to equal the wages and salaries of the 4 percent at the top (also $31 billion).[13] These numbers deal only with wages and salaries; they do not include interest and dividends, stocks gains and other income from investments.

In the past two decades, this increase in the wealth owned by the rich has been accompanied by a decrease in the middle class and an increase in the poor and working poor.

WHO DO WE THINK IS THE MIDDLE CLASS?

Surveys show that most Americans consider themselves "middle class." A corporate accountant who makes $100,000 a year and a house painter who makes $20,000 a year both believe they belong somewhere in the middle class. In Washington, for example, it is often said that the top of the middle class is whatever salary is earned by members of Congress. That was $125,000 a year in 1992. But that is more money than 97 percent of the households in America earn. Similarly, many families that earn $80,000 in wages and salaries a year consider themselves middle class. But that income actually puts them in the top 6 percent of American households that file income tax returns.[14]

There are several reasons for these perceptions about class. The first reason for believing one is middle class is the great extremes in American society. The existence of welfare is a boundary—a bottom line. It socially defines everyone above it as nonpoor. The welfare system that grew out of the Great Depression was a maintenance system. It kept the poor from starving, but it did not lift the incomes of the poor out of the poverty level. Middleclass people took pride in not depending on the government. The other line at the top is the class of extremely wealthy people. Most Americans see the very wealthy in the same way as they see the very poor—they are the boundaries. The middle class, then, is viewed as people who are neither very rich or very poor.

The second reason for believing one is middle class follows from the first. It may not be possible for the son of the house painter to become a member of the super rich, but it *is* possible that with hard work, luck and good connections, the son of the house painter might become a corporate accountant. Thus, the notion that "everyone is middle class" is based on the view that mobility within this class *is* feasible.

The perception mentioned above is not just a belief. It was a reality of American social structure up until the most recent period. Over the history of this country, with only a few brief exceptions, each generation improved its general standard of living and income.

The daughter of the house painter making $20,000 a year *did* better herself. The son of the corporate accountant was likely to maintain at least the standard of living of his father, or better it. In other words, the general tendency was that more people moved up in living standards than those who fell down. (We discuss in the next chapter how the wellbeing of Americans rested on "invisible" classes outside of the defined society.) It is even possible, in America, for a poor minority child from the inner city to become a star athlete and make $2 million a year, or a bright workingclass kid who plays with computers to invent a new gizmo and start a computer company that makes him rich. Ordinary people can see examples of those like them who did become rich. At the same time, most of these rich do not come close to the wealth and power of the super rich.

Sociologists have struggled to create categories within this large middle sector. Those who rely mainly on income and occupation to define the categories have used terms such as upper-upper, lower-upper, upper-middle, lower-middle, upper-lower, and lower-lower. Other categories rely on the type of work done such as blue collar versus white collar, or managerial versus wage worker. Professionals and small business persons have often been seen as some kind of separate category. Other categories have been "working class" and "petite bourgeoisie."

Donald Barlett and James Steele argue that at the "heart" of the middle class are those wage earners who reported incomes between $20,000 and $50,000 on their tax returns in 1989. Thirty-four million individuals and families filed tax returns reporting incomes between $20,000 and $50,000, and they accounted for 35 percent of all tax returns. If one extended the definition of middle class to include returns between $15,000 and $75,000, that would account for 55 percent of all returns.

Thirty-nine percent, or nearly two-fifths of all tax returns, however, were filed for incomes of *less* than $15,000. While this figures includes returns filed by teenagers working part-time, the overwhelming majority are married couples, single persons, and single parents who represent the working poor.[15] Most of us would not consider someone who is making less than $15,000 to be middle class, and yet nearly 40 percent of all returns fell into this category. In other words, the popular perception that almost everyone in America is middle class is greatly exaggerated.

The confusion as to how to label and categorize obvious differences is also a reflection of the "openness" within the middle class. Some sociologists created categories of class largely on the basis of *how* people lived—not on the basis of real power differences. One social class scale devel oped in the 1950s ranked people on the number of television sets they owned and the number of rooms in their house, as well as their income and educational attainment.

With the explosion of public colleges and community colleges in the 1960s, even higher education failed to make clear distinctions within the middle class. By the early 1980s, approximately half of the country's young adults were receiving education past high school. Some blue collar union workers earned wages greater than college professors or artists. So rank within the middle class was often determined by whether one listened to country music or symphonies; whether one bowled or golfed. Since most sociologists and journalists listened to symphonies and golfed (or certainly did *not* listen to country music and bowl), those activities were given a higher "rank" and earned one a higher social-class status, even with a lower income.[16]

Unions illustrate the role of power in class status. Collective bargaining is a source of power for those who lack power based on corporate wealth. College professors have historically been biased against unions as being "beneath them"—something only bluecollar workers need. Public school teachers, on the other hand, have been much quicker to organize into unions. The result has been that in many states unionized public school teachers have developed the power to protect their wages and working conditions, whereas professors have been powerless to stop the erosion of their salaries. Likewise, strong unions in the industrial sector provided unionized blue collar workers some power vis-à-vis the managers who were "above" them.

The *critical* distinctions of class, then, are the questions of ownership and power. If you are able have a high standard of living without working it means that you are living well off the labor of others. You have a vested interest in maintaining a system of exploitation.[17] You are a member of a class that we will call by several different names throughout this book—the ruling class, the elite, the capitalist, and the owning class.

If you have to work to generate your income and you must spend almost all your income in maintaining a stable standard of living, you fall into the large middle class or the working class. If you do not have control over enough resources to maintain a stable existence you are in the poverty class.

There is a difference between an individual's class position based on real ownership and actual power and the perception individuals have of their power. Those whose incomes barely pay basic bills are much less likely to identify with the interests of the elite. Karl Marx, whose approach to stratification is discussed in Chapter 12, used the concept of **class consciousness** to describe our awareness of our class position in terms of power within society. Those who understand their relationship to other classes in terms of control over, or lack of control over, resources are said to be class conscious.

Those who do not see their powerlessness and identify with the class that oppresses them were said by Marx to have **false consciousness**. Those who are very well paid and have positive futures tend to identify their interests with those of the elite, even though they are working and the elite is not. The recent downsizing in corporate America has been a rude awakening for many well-paid managers, who thought they had power over their lives and awoke one day to find themselves laid off.

For the middle class, the perception of power becomes more a question of how much immediate control we have over our lives. Blue-collar workers are often more closely supervised, have dirtier or more dangerous jobs, and offer fewer chances for upward mobility.[18] This com bination of factors tends to give blue-collar workers lower prestige and status within the middle class, even if they make as much money as white-collar workers.

Jobs in a similar category for women—repetitive, closely supervised, and with low mobility—are usually characterized as "pink collar" because they lack the elements of danger or being dirty. This illusion of safety has recently been questioned with studies that show the adverse affects of radiation from computer screens, carpel tunnel syndrome, and poisoning from office chemicals on women workers.

These large categories do not deny that significant differences exist within each grouping. Later in this book we discuss how the economic crisis affects different groups within the middle class. But first we need to examine the changes that are occurring within our class structure.

WHAT'S HAPPENING TO THE MIDDLE CLASS?

The "middle class" that grew so rapidly after World War II is rapidly shrinking. There are three major aspects to the changes that are occurring.

The first is that the pattern of upward mobility has stopped. Instead, there is a general pattern of downward mobility. A young man entering the labor market today, with a status equivalent to what his father had, will earn *one-half* of what his father earned in real wages. Today's new generation of workers are taking jobs without pension plans, without adequate health insurance, and are facing an uncertain future in terms of their own social security.[19] Even college graduates face an uncertain future. Real wages of college-educated men have slipped 3 percent from 1989 to 1991.[20]

Many individuals who had been upwardly mobile either through increasing earnings or promotions are finding wages frozen or actually decreasing and chances for promotion extremely limited. Large numbers of individuals who thought they were secure are losing their jobs and discovering that *if* they find new jobs, the new jobs have lower pay and decreased benefits. Labor Department data found that blue-collar men suffered a 5.9 percent wage decline over the 1989–93 business cycle, and in the 1991–93 "recovery" this same group suffered a 3 percent wage decline. Male white-collar wages fell 1.2 percent during the decline of 1989–1990 and again in the recovery of 1991–93. Eighteen percent of the new jobs created in 1993 were jobs with temporary help agencies.[21]

A new study by Steven Rose, a Labor Department economist with the government, found that social mobility in the 1980s showed marked differences from social mobility in the 1970s. His research, which followed a nationally representative sample of 5,000 families since 1967, found that mobility is shrinking markedly for minorities, the less educated, the low-paid and for lower-income families.[22] The dream that by working hard and being dependable, one could somehow better one's position, is now no longer realistic. In reporting Rose's results, *Business Week* (26 February, 1996) asks the question in the title of the article: "Is America Becoming More of a Class Society?"

These losses in mobility have occurred at the same time as a dramatic decline in labor union membership. The percentage of the workforce represented by unions fell more rapidly in the 1980s than in the previous several decades.[23] This lowered wages, not only because some workers no longer receive the higher union wage, but also because there is less pressure on non-union employers to raise wages.

The second major change is that the poverty class is increasing. The standard of living previously guaranteed by the welfare system is disappearing. A growing class of people in our society can no longer consume and can no longer dream. After they pay rent and utilities they are still in debt. If they are not already on the streets, they are only a minimum-wage paycheck away. No longer are the poor guaranteed subsidized housing, medical care, and social services. Two decades ago, there were also people who struggled to make it each day, but now there is an important difference. Twenty years ago, there were real opportunities within the social structure, and there was a guaranteed safety net if you could not take advantage of the opportunities. Today, both the opportunities and the safety net are disappearing.

The third major change is the change in the gender and race dimensions of class. The civil rights movements of the 1960s broke down economic social class barriers for *some* women and minorities. Domains in business, education, and government that were previously all white and male have been opened up. The result has been that a small proportion of those in groups historically discriminated against have now been successful. But because these groups have historically been on the bottom, they are the hardest hit by the falling wages and cutbacks in support services. The irony then, is that while a few become success stories, the vast majority are worse off than before.

Today we see more women than ever before becoming lawyers, doctors, and stockbrokers. At the same time, we see more women than ever before heading poverty households.[24] In 1960, families with a female householder and no husband present constituted less than one-fourth of poor families. By 1990, *37 percent* of all families headed by women lived in poverty and 24 percent of all women living alone lived in poverty.[25]

Likewise, although there have been increases in the number of African American and Latinos in professional, political, and corporate positions at the same time, the income gap between minorities and whites has grown, and a greater proportion of minority children live in poverty than ever before. Again, there were openings for upward mobility for just a select few. Many successful African Americans have struggled with the moral dilemma posed by their own success while their brothers and sisters sink further into poverty.[26]

According to Andrew Hacker, the change in income distribution for black families created a larger proportion of families living in poverty. Using 1990 dollars, Hacker compared the proportion of black families to white families in various income groups in 1970 and 1990.[27] Table 3.3 below shows how income was proportionately distributed among black and white families. There were proportionately more black and white families making high incomes in 1990 than in 1970. The chart also shows that in both groups, there were proportionately fewer middle-level income families (from $15,00 to $50,000). The proportion of poor families markedly increased for black families, while there was a slight decline for white families.

Table 3.3

Family Income	**Black Families**		**White Families**	
	1970	**1990**	**1970**	**1990**
$50,000+	9.9%	14.5%	24.1%	325%
$35,000 to $50,000	13.9	15.0	24.1	32.5
$25,000 to $35,000	17.6	14.0	20.8	16.5
$15,000 to $25,000	24.0	19.5	16.9	16.0
Under $15,000	34.6	37.0	14.3	14.2
All income	100%	100%	100%	100%

Many whites blame blacks and other minorities for taking their jobs. Table 3.3 challenges that belief. Both the black and white middle classes have received less income proportionately, but the greater decline is in the proportion of black middle class families. And in that same period, while the proportion of poor black households increased by 2.4 percent, the proportion of poor white households actually decreased by .1 percent. Thus it is clearly not true that African Americans have, in general, benefited while Euro-Americans have been hurt.

These facts are important because many Euro-Americans blame affirmative action and other equal opportunity programs for their declining class status. But if African Americans have experienced a worse decline in class status in the same period, then the problem can be seen as a result of economic changes that are hurting the *entire* middle class—and hurting blacks more than whites despite the equal opportunity programs!

The middle class is possible because a class exists below it. This is the class of Americans who didn't make it. We are often told that people are poor through some fault of their own. Those who have succeeded are told they deserve the better life because they are better people.

THE OTHER AMERICA

The statistics suggest that numbers of poor people in our society are growing. How have the changes in class structure affected the poor? Some sociologists have used the term *underclass* to acknowledge that today's poor are somehow different from the poor of an earlier period. We will look in a later chapter at the concept of underclass. But it is true that the poor in America today have less chance to participate in the American Dream. The ladder of upward mobility is disappearing. Hopelessness, social disorganization, drugs and crime have taken its place. Does the existence of so many poor and oppressed prove that the system is no longer "working"? Or is the existence of a "permanent poor" just one more example of the way social stratification in our society has *always* worked?

The economic history of this country suggests that those who constitute the poorest class are there for reasons far beyond their control. Many are the individuals and families who are caught by temporary misfortune and live in poverty until their luck turns; some were caught in the "cracks" of economic transitions and were never able to recover.

The existence of a poor class has been useful to the owning class because they act as a reserve labor force. They could be hired temporarily when there was a shortage of labor and laid off when the need lessened. A reserve labor force also acted as a "brake" on the power of the regular workforce. Wage and benefit demands from any group of workers could be undercut by the threat to hire the unemployed who would work for lower wages.[28]

Most middle-class Americans know very little about the reality of poverty in the United States. When Michael Harrington wrote *The Other America* in 1963, many comfortable Americans were shocked to discover that so many of their fellow citizens were living in deplorable conditions. Part of the reason for such ignorance is the physical class segregation that occurs in both rural and urban areas. Rich people live in one neighborhood and middle-class people live in another, where they shop, go to church, and attend school. The poor live in their own neighborhoods.

Because many of us rarely actually see poverty, we depend on the movies or television for our information about poor people. The media usually offer stereotypes and sensationalism, which only contributes to our ignorance. Rarely does one find television or the movies offering critical analysis that would help Americans understand the poverty. As Jacqueline Jones pointed out in her 1992 study of both black and white poverty:

> Throughout this period [1960s and 1970s] the federal government and national news organizations continued to manipulate the statistics that measured poverty and, in the process, created the false impression that all black people were poor and that all white people were middle class; the category "Hispanic" conflated data related to race, culture and national origin, further confusing the issue. Dramatically, race came to permeate public discussion of a wide variety of issues, for many whites assumed that African Americans constituted a group apart from 'mainstream America.' Ultimately, the ethnic, regional, and cultural diversity of the poor population became lost in an exclusive focus—more rhetorical than substantive—on black people in the urban North. Americans in a postemanicipation society continued to view poverty through a lens ground and polished in the days of slavery.[29]

Poverty statistics not only manipulate our images of who we think is poor but also manipulate the extent and severity of poverty. The government "poverty level" is set at such a minimum that hundreds of thousands of families who cannot afford medical care, adequate food, or decent housing are not counted among the poor.[30]

The belief that all the poor are unemployed and living on "handouts" is also part of the stereotype. Common beliefs are that welfare mothers have babies to collect extra money, have boyfriends that drive Cadillacs, and lie around all day when they really could work. Such stereotypes degrade those whose circumstances place them on welfare. The society labels them as failures and subhuman. Welfare is not only oppressive in that it fails to provide decent standards of living and opportunities, but it also degrades the individual human beings involved. A *Business Week* (13 March, 1995) summarized a recent Census Bureau report of who was the welfare mother:

> [it] shows that unwed mothers under the age of 18, the prime targets of GOP reformers, make up a tiny slice of the welfare population. When Census did its survey, only 32,000 of the 3.8 million AFDC mothers were 17 or under and unmarried. Their average age was 30, and 53% are—or had been—married. The new data support Democrats' claims that many AFDC recipients could reverse their fortunes with some help. A majority have a basic education: 38% have finished high school, and another 19% spend at least one year at college. Moreover, 15% of AFDC mothers are still pursuing education.

We look more closely at how stereotypes and labels serve the interests of the ruling class in Chapter 7. But we might examine the double standard our society holds regarding government handouts. The failed savings and loans got a government hand out that will come to $500 billion of the taxpayers' money. Stereotypes like lazy, shiftless, and cheater were not applied to the businessmen involved in the scandal. (One of those businessmen was the son of the former president of the United States, George Bush.) Yet a welfare mother who fails to report extra income of $300 earned by babysitting is often cited by the media as evidence of the widespread "fraud" in welfare.

The savings and loan bailout is not even considered part of the accepted subsidies "handed out" to the middle and upper classes. According to former Commerce Secretary Peterson, the government spends $109.8 billion a year on federal benefit programs for those living in poverty; it spends $570.7 billion for those who aren't. And the average benefit going to households with incomes over $100,000 is larger than that going to households with incomes under $10,000.[31]

Most of us picture a black welfare recipient in a northern city ghetto when we hear the words "poor person." Yet census data for 1990 show that poor whites (21 million) outnumbered poor blacks (9 million) by a ratio of two to one. A majority of poor Americans lived outside central cities in the rural areas, small towns, and suburbs. In terms of actual physical want, poverty was greatest in the states of Texas, South Dakota, and Missouri, which together accounted for one-half of the nation's 150 "worst hunger counties." West Virginia, with a 97 percent white population, ranked 48th, 49th, or 50th as the poorest in the country (depending on which statistic is used).

Lawrence Mishel and Jared Bernstein argue that most people pushed into poverty work to get out. Time spent in poverty (a "poverty spell") for most persons is relatively short. There is a small group of between 12 and 14 percent of those in poverty who spend seven, eight, nine or more years as poor. But this also means that more than 85 percent of those who are at sometime in their lives poor are able to move out of a poverty cycle.

Research covering persons in poverty between 1970 and 1982 found that 44 percent of the poverty spells were a year or less and an additional 25 percent were between one and three years.[32] It is probable that persons today are spending longer periods on welfare, due to the economic changes that are discussed in Chapter 13. But the common stereotype that welfare recipients are "stuck" on the welfare rolls forever is clearly wrong.

Research also shows that the main causes for individuals or families to fall into a poverty spell are earnings loss and family structure changes, with the most common cause (for 37.9 percent of families) beginning with a drop in earnings by the family head.[33] Economic changes affect the number of people on welfare and the length of time spent on welfare. It is not surprising to find that the ranks of the poor have increased as real wages have fallen and employment opportunities decrease. The media portray the poor as accepting of their lot, but historical experiences show that poor people who are given *real* opportunities are anxious and willing to lift themselves out of poverty.

Teenagers who refuse jobs are often cited as proof that the poor don't want to work. Jobs such as washing cars, working in a sweatshop, or doing stoop agricultural labor do not offer real opportunities for careers and a stable life. In other words, a job is not enough. It must be a job that provides the individual with the promise of full participation in society

The main increase in the number of poor since 1979 has been among the *working* poor. This increase is the result of declining wages, the increase in working women who head households, and a minimum wage that remained unchanged from 1981 to 1989. Until the economy is able to provide enough good paying jobs with benefits, there will be no real "solution" to the problem of welfare and poverty.

James Wright argues that if poverty in the United States were eliminated, social problems such as street crime, drugs, and homelessness would be largely eliminated. Asking the question, "What would it cost to eliminate poverty?" Wright made some calculations and came up with a figure of $40 billion. Although this sounds like a lot of money, it is small compared to the estimated $500 billion the government haws spent to bail out the bankers and big investors of the savings and loan collapse. According to Wright:

> the fundamental barrier to the eradication of poverty in this nation is not economic, but social and political. We do not seem

> to mind giving billions of dollars to doctors and health-care facilities to provide health services to the poor (that, after all, is what medicaid does) but we do seem to mind giving the same money to poor people themselves so they can purchase their own health care. Likewise, via Section 8, we give several additional billions to landlords to provide housing for the poor, rather than give them the money directly so they can purchase their own housing. We want to increase the food purchasing power of the poor so they need not go hungry. But rather than give them money, we give them food stamps that can only be used for food. The common denominator in all these examples is that we don't trust the poor with our money. The operant mentality seems to be that if we just gave them the money, they would spend it on frivolous things. So we provide them with free services or subsidized services instead. In the process, we make a lot of doctors and landlords rich and we create a vast cadre of middle-class bureaucrats, welfare workers, case managers, and the like to administer our service programs.[34]

This chapter has described how resources and wealth in our society are distributed. I used a lot of figures and statistics. These numbers keep changing, so what is important to remember are not the particular figures but the *trends* that they represent. Perhaps a current, and popular, saying best sums up all the statistics: *the rich are getting richer and the poor are getting poorer.*

Throughout American history there have been many changes in this pattern. We have already discussed the colonial poor, who worked back-breaking jobs to better themselves and the opportunities of their children. We once had a large class of workers who earned nothing at all—they were slaves.

We cannot complete our survey of class in America without considering the groups of people who, like the slaves, contributed to our standard of living but were never granted membership in our society. These are the "invisible classes" of America and we turn next to a discussion of who they have been and what they have done to hold the ladder of stratification in place.

SUMMARY

The power of those on the top of the stratification ladder is based on their control over the resources of society. These resources are usually measured in terms of money, but the real power comes from the way that the money is used. In American society, those with power use their money to control resources that other people need. In earlier societies, other resources may have guaranteed power, but in a capitalistic industrial society, power is determined by control over productive resources.

Social class is a way of breaking the population up into categories based on relationships to society's important resources. One can divide Americans into categories of class based on income and wealth. Research has found that there is a tiny group of families in America who control a very large proportion of the wealth. They have been called the "super rich." Other powerful persons include those who control big corporations, banks and other institutions. Their power is not just based on the amount of money they own but their ability to manage their resources to get their own way.

The proportion of Americans who control great wealth in America has remained concentrated in the hands of a few. Recent data suggest that the proportion is actually shrinking. For many years the proportion of Americans we call middle class seemed to be expanding, but recent data now show that the middle class is also shrinking.

Being middle class is something that most Americans accept. As long as one is not among the dependent poor or a member of the elite, the perception is that one is middle class. If one tries to use income data to define the middle class, we find that 35 percent of all Americans earned between $20,000 and $50,000 a year. Yet many individuals who earn less than $20,000 or as much as $100,000 consider themselves to be middle class!

Those who control less wealth have sometimes increased their power by joining labor unions. This has raised their position on the social-class ladder. Some women and minorities were also able to raise themselves up based on the power of social organization during the civil rights movement—using the power of the vote and other political actions to better themselves. But today, the proportion of workers who benefit from union membership has declined, and while some women and people of color have "made it," a larger proportion have continued to decline in status.

There has always been a poor class in America, but economic opportunities have allowed the children of the poor to better themselves. Today these opportunities are shrinking, and the proportion of very poor is increasing. We are often told that being poor is the fault of the individual, but historical examples show that when economic opportunities exist, the proportion of poor dramatically decreases. We are also told that the poor are people in the inner cities and that they are people of color. In reality, the great majority of the poor are Euro-Americans and the majority of the poor live outside the inner city.

In the past the government provided programs to help the poor. Many citizens feel that these have been unjustified handouts. But when one compares the money spent on the poor to the money spent on hand-outs to the wealthy, the wealthy receive much more help.

Vocabulary

Income. Money received on a regular basis as a result of wages or salaries, benefits, or interest on investment; often spent for living costs, but may be reinvested to increase wealth.

Wealth. A resource (measured in money value) that can be used to produce income or converted into income.

Ruling class/the elite/ capitalist class/ owning class. Those with a high standard of living who do not necessarily have to work but could live off their wealth and control over resources.

Middle class. Those who must work to maintain a stable standard of living and who spend all or most of their income to do so.

Poverty class. Those who control so few resources that they are unable to maintain a stable existence.

Class consciousness. One's awareness of one's class position in terms of power relationships within society.

False consciousness. Mistakenly identifying one's class position with the interests of another class; usually applied to those in the lower class who identify with the interests of those who have power over them.

Discussion Questions

1. We are given mixed messages about money and class. On the one hand, we are told "Every man has his price" and "Just wait til I win the lottery!" Then we are told "Money can't buy love" and "Money is the root of all evil." Discuss the contradictions *you* have been taught. Which do you believe? How do these mixed messages reflect the conflicts in our beliefs about equality and democracy and our beliefs based on racism, sexism, classism and speciesism?

2. To which social class do you think you belong? Why? What about other students in the class? Is there anyone who wants to admit to being poor or a member of the elite?

3. Were you taught that "anyone can make it," and so being poor was that person's fault? Do you still believe this? Why or why not?

4. What's the difference between a government handout to the poor and a government handout to the rich? Does the middle class also get handouts? Can you identify any handouts that you or your family has accepted? Which kind of handout are you most likely to read about or hear about? Why?

5. Why is it so hard to figure out what social classes exist in America? Do they exist at all?

6. I have argued that most Americans live in class-segregated neighborhoods. Is that true for you? Do you know anyone well who is in a much different class than you? If not, why not? Where do you get most of your images of people in classes that differ greatly from your own?

Resources

Video: *Wall Street.*

What is the son of a factory worker and union man willing to do to get rich? This movie answers the question and raises the question for the viewer. We watch as the young man (played by Charlie Sheen) falls under the influence of a powerful and manipulative stockbroker (Michael Douglas). Sheen's actions become more questionable as Douglas tempts him with money, women, and fancy living. The final question is whether Sheen is willing to sell out his father?

I have often asked students how far they would have gone if they had been Sheen. We have had some interesting answers, and arguments, in class about this! The real social pain caused by the actors, however, is suffered by workers in a corporation being taken over. These workers are invisible to the viewer—just as they are to many stockbrokers and corporate managers.

As you watch the movie, note the roles played by the women and the absence of minorities. The large stock brokerage firms remain one of the few institutional arenas in our society where women and minorities have made very few gains.

(P.S. The powerful stockbroker in the movie was based on a real-life junk-bond king who ended up in prison.) Rated R.

Book: Donald Barlett and James B. Steele, *America: What Went Wrong?*

This book is full of facts and figures but they are organized into stories about things that are going wrong in our economy. Barlett and Steele include the consequences for "the little guy," and some of you may know exactly what they are talking about! The two authors are newspaper reporters, so they have a clear and understandable writing style.

NOTES

Complete citations may be found in the Bibliogaphy.

1. Mishel and Bernstein 1993, 271.
2. McPherson 1988, 23.

3. Millman 1991.
4. Lundberg 1937, 3.
5. Parenti 1988. 13–14.; also see Domhoff 1967, 1983; Colby 1985; Collier and Horowitz 1976.
6. Parenti 1988, 14.
7. 26 April 1993.
8. Parenti 1988, 13.
9. Ehrenreich 1989.
10. Mishel and Bernstein 1993, 6.
11. Barlett and Steele 1992, 162–88.
12. Ibid., 1–30.
13. Ibid., xii.
14. Ibid., xiii.
15. Ibid., xiii.
16. See Halle's (1984) discussion of blue-collar culture, 220–330. The question of lifestyle differences as related to class status is explored by Lamont and Fournier 1992.
17. This approach closely parallels that adopted by Parenti 1988, 8–10.
18. Halle 1984, 293.
19. Mishel and Bernstein 1993, 87–91.
20. Mishel 1994.
21. Mishel and Bernstein 1993.
22. As reported in *BusinessWeek*, 26 February 1996, 86–91.
23. Mishel and Bernstein 1993, 187.
24. Goldberg 1990, 17–58. Also Sidel 1986.
25. This rapid shift in the status of women is not confined to American society. Goldberg and Kremen's (1990) study of Canada, Japan, France, Sweden, Poland and European Russia found similar shifts.
26. See, for example, McClain 1992, 120–122.
27. Hacker 1992, 98.
28. Lekachman 1991.
29. Jones 1992, 2–3.
30. Mishel and Bernstein 1993, 275–280.
31. As reported by Alan Murray, *Wall Street Journal*, January 1994.
32. Mishel and Bernstein 1993, 282.
33. Ibid. 283.
34. James Wright 1989, 135–137.

4

THE INVISIBLE CLASSES HOLDING UP THE LADDER

Don't condemn me
For leaving my country,
Poverty and necessity
Are at fault.
Good-bye, pretty Guanajuato
The state in which I was born.
I'm going to the United States
Far away from you.[1]

—Mexican Folk Song

"Give me your tired, your poor,
your huddled masses yearning to breathe free,
The wretched refuse of your teeming shore.
Send these, the homeless, tempest-tost to me,
I lift my lamp beside the golden door!"

—Conclusion of poem inscribed on the Statue of Liberty

Sociologists define **society** as that largest grouping to which people claim membership. Biologically we are all members of the species homo sapiens sapiens, but our society defines our general culture. Most of you reading this see yourselves as Americans, unless you are international students. In that case, you define yourself by your own nationality—Bengali, Brazilian, Iranian, Malaysian, Russian, Venezuelan, Ugandan. (I have had all those nationalities in my classes in West Virginia.)

When feudalism changed into industrialization, a new form of society emerged—the nation- state. Membership in a society based on clan, lineage, or tribe was replaced by membership in a "nation." Our analysis of social stratification in our society is the study of ranking *within* the nation-state of the United States of America.

With few exceptions, Americans know the story of George Washington and the cherry tree. The story has no basis in fact but it is something we all have heard and helps create our common culture.[2] We eat at McDonald's, watch the same TV shows, and share a common president. Part of what makes us members of a society is learning the basic belief systems of that society. Our beliefs in equality and democracy and our ideas about social stratification and power are discussed in Chapter 6.

We also learn that certain things are *Un*-American and certain people and groups don't belong. Our society has boundaries. These boundaries define for us who is, and who isn't, a member of *our* society.

The homeless person sitting on the street corner, the clerk at the department store, and the wealthy golfer at the country club are all seen as members of our society. But the dishwasher at the country club, who is being paid minimum wage for hot hard work, six days a week, and who has held the job for three years, may *not* be a member of our society. She may be an "alien." She fled El Salvador ten years ago and risked her life to come to America. She cannot vote and may be denied constitutional protection of her rights. In some states, her children cannot attend public schools. She was probably not counted in the census. She may be detained without a hearing, without probable cause and has not been provided with a lawyer. To most of us she is "invisible," and yet she lives and works among us.

In this text we are going to use the term **invisible classes** to refer to those groups who are part of the social system supporting our society, but are not *perceived* to be part of it. The term "invisible" implies that you are there, but no one can see you. Other sociologists have explored this relationship using the term "the Other."[3] This concept helps us understand how people who believe in good values for themselves and their own group—not to steal, murder, rape or pillage—can perform those same acts on members of another group. It also helps explain why so many of us confuse blind patriotism with democracy.

In Chapter 2 we identified two groups that were kept at the bottom of the ladder: slaves and Native Americans. They were once defined as outside society's boundaries. Let us look at those historical examples a little more closely.

THE INVISIBLE CLASSES WITHIN

Most of us would never consider our pet dogs and cats to be members of our society. We love our pets and sometimes we joke "they almost act like people!" Yet we put them outside the social boundary. The ideology of racism that defined slavery did the same thing for African Americans prior to the Civil War. Slaves were believed to be "subhuman." The Constitution of this country denied them the vote, constitutional protection, and allowed them to be counted for purposes of congressional representation as three-fifths of a person. Many Protestant churches believed that they did not have souls worthy of Heaven.

Placing slavery outside the boundary of society meant that we also placed the brutality, degradation and exploitation of slavery outside our understanding of our nation. By not *seeing* slaves as real people, the founders of our country who were slaveowners could defend the system of slave labor. This invisibility of slaves explains why we can ignore the fact that wealth gained from the system of slavery was largely the basis of our prosperity after the Revolutionary War.

Most sociologists who do analyses of classes in early American society treat slaves as somehow different from other social classes. If one dates the late 1600s as the point at which major colonial settlements began, there were approximately 200 years in which our society treated African Americans as non-people; yet their labor was absolutely essential to creating the America we know today.

We are only too willing to point out the cases in societies different from our own when a similar thing happened. In the early stages of socialism, Communist Party leaders ruthlessly exploited the labor of prisoners in large camps to build the economic infrastructure of the society. I know of no textbook that acknowledges the parallels between slavery in America and the Soviet forced labor camps. I am sure the Soviet school system taught all about American slavery and, likewise, avoided discussion of its own labor camps. Schoolchildren are taught the horrors of the Holocaust and the attempt by Hitler to eliminate the Jews. *The Diary of Ann Frank* is often required reading. How many schools require the reading of *Bury My Heart at Wounded Knee*, which describes the genocide of the western Native Americans?

Although defined outside the "human" society being created in America, the slaves were perceived as necessary—like cattle and oxen. Native Americans were also defined as outside the existence of our society but were *not* seen as necessary. The "bloodthirsty savages" were pests to be eliminated, like wolves and buffalo.

The idea that the North American continent was largely "empty" and that its inhabitants were insignificant—both in numbers and culture—is still defended today despite overwhelming evidence to the contrary.[4] The legal basis on which Native American land was seized would be undermined if it were acknowledged that there had been a population as large as 15 million persons, living in politically organized states that carried out commerce, utilizing techniques of fertilization and irrigation, and in many ways surpassing the standard of living found in many European societies. As Stiffarm and Lane have pointed out:

> The issue goes to the concept of the "Norman Yoke." The concept, as it was eventually articulated in John Locke's philosophy of Natural Law, held that any Christian (read: European) happening upon "waste land," most particularly land that was vacant or virtually vacant of human inhabitants—assumed not only a 'natural right,' but indeed an *obligation* to put such land to "productive use." Having thus performed "God's will" by "cultivating" and thereby "conquering" the former "wilderness" its "discoverer" can be said to "own" it. It was upon this peculiar doctrine that Chief Justice of the Supreme Court John Marshall, in his 1823 opinion in the *Johnson v. McIntosh* case, based the notion that the U.S. hold "inherent and preeminent rights" over Indian lands. (1992, 28: emphasis in original)

Following the American Revolution, the U.S. government adopted the view that Native Americans were independent nations with whom we negotiated treaties—a view of formal equality combined with actual inequality in power relations. Later, self-interest dictated a shift in policy from viewing them as independent nations to defining them as "dependent nations." This shift gave the federal government ultimate jurisdiction and enabled things like the relocation of the five "civilized tribes" to the West. Later changes in policy followed, including a relatively short-lived attempt to eliminate reservations, disband tribes and make Native Americans into independent American citizens—an attempt to undermine their collective strength.

But whatever the policies pursued the ultimate goals were always the dominance of Euro-American interests over those of the Indians. Cook cites the contradictions faced by the federal government:[5]

> it is one of history's more stunning ironies. The 51.9 million acres in the U.S. reserved for the Indians were lands the white man could not see any conceivable reason to reserve for himself. They were too wet or too dry, too barren or too remote. Now, at a time when the U.S. seems to be running out of practically everything, the 272 federally recognized Indian reservations constitute one of the largest and least known mineral repositories on the continent—nearly 5 percent of the U.S.'s oil and gas, one-third of its strippable low-sulfur coal, one-half of its privately owned uranium.[6]

The examples of the African slave and the Native American are important because they were the first invisible classes in America. The development of democracy in America cannot be separated from the existence of groups whose exploitation, degradation, and oppression were *not* protected by the ideologies of equality and freedom. The very ground on which the ladder of stratification in America stands was owned by the Native Americans and prepared by the labor of slaves—both invisible.

The Civil War freed the slaves and allowed their entrance into American society. They were put on the very lowest rungs of the social stratification ladder. A vicious system of social control called Jim Crow was used to keep descendants of the freed slaves in "their place."[7] Nonetheless, the opening of the boundaries to African Americans allowed them to access certain basic rights—rights they heroically used to resist segregation and fight for *more* democratic rights in what became known as the civil rights movement.

The elimination of Native Americans as a threat, and the termination of slavery, did not end the exploitation, degradation, or oppression of invisible bottom classes. After the Civil War, America moved "west." Like the Native Americans, the Mexican people were also in the way. The story of the Alamo—John Wayne and Daniel Boone fighting to their last breath against Cheeto-chomping banditos with funny mustaches and sombreros—is only another example of our defining a group of people as less than real. (The reference to John Wayne refers to a popular movie from 1960, *The Alamo*. For many Americans their knowledge of this history is based on such biased and stereotypical movies.)

Our schools rarely teach that Texas was taken by military force from the people who had been settled there for years. We never hear the stories of Texan cowboys who used to go hunting to kill Mexicans as a sport, about the Texas Rangers who "executed" 100 to 300 known Mexican residents of border towns without trials or formal charges, or about the lynchings of 114 Mexicans killed in the Rio Grande Valley.

Stan Steiner describes the killing of Mexicans as a "popular game" in his book *La Raza*. So many Mexicans were casually killed around the Pecos River that "Pecosing a feller" became West Texas slang for murdering a man and getting away with it. According to Steiner, in the Valley of the Rio Grande the murder of Mexicans at least equaled, if not surpassed, the lunching of blacks in the South during the late nineteenth and early twentieth centuries.[8]

The vast wealth of the Southwest—the ranches, the oil, the minerals—were taken by the same military force that took North and South Dakota from the Sioux.[9] American armies pushed into Mexican territory, the Caribbean, Central America and the Philippines.

The Spanish-American War was fought for colonies. The United States wanted to be able to control Spain's colonies.[10] Aguinaldo, the great Filipino patriot, led his people against the Spanish. When the Americans landed, he fought the Americans. The American Army subdued the Filipino people with the same ruthlessness that had characterized the Spanish, This included the infamous "water torture" in which four or five gallons of water was forced down the throat of a Filipino captive and then squeezed out by an American soldier kneeling on his stomach. The process was repeated until the captive talked or died.[11]

The Spanish American War was a "Christian crusade" that even the organized Protestant churches saw as another outlet for missionary activity. Union Seminary theologian J.H. Barrows spoke on "The Christian Conquest of Asia" suggesting that "wherever on pagan shores the voice of the American missionary and teacher is heard, there is fulfilled the manifest destiny of the Christian Republic." The Methodist newspaper urged "Every Methodist preacher will be a recruiting officer."[12]

Once the Spanish American War was won, the United States established its economic and political control over a hemispheric area that guaranteed use of its cheap labor force and access to its resources. Guatemalan peasants worked for United Fruit, picking bananas for starvation wages. Filipinos labored in the fields, harvesting pineapple for Dole Fruit Company. The DuPonts invested heavily in the sugarcane fields of Cuba. The hard brutal labor for cheap agricultural produce, once done by the slaves, had been expanded to include the poor of the Hemisphere.

The average American, growing up in the affluent 1950s, was not aware that the cheap fruit on his dinner table had been picked by workers who suffered far greater exploitation, degradation, and oppression than he or she would ever face. This group of people is as invisible to most Americans in the twentieth century as the slaves and Native Americans had been to Americans in the nineteenth century.

The idea that a Guatemalan banana picker is somehow part of the social stratification system of your society may seem strange. Most Americans do not understand the relationship between their country's high standard of living and the oppression of people in poor countries. For example, a group of disabled coal miners from West Virginia were astonished to learn that the passage of a black lung bill in 1970 had had such a "price tag." In a meeting with the miners on 20 May, 1994 Senator Majority Leader Robert Byrd (D-West Virginia) told the group that he had cut a deal with President Nixon back in 1970. If Nixon would not oppose the legislation providing benefits to victims of black lung disease (caused by breathing coal dust), Byrd would not oppose the U.S. bombing of Cambodia during the Vietnam War. One can only wonder at a social system that forces the choice between the health of coal miners or the lives of Cambodian men, women, and children!

You have been taught to see stratification as a reflection of the boundaries your society defines for you. If the slaves, the Native Americans, Mexicans and Guatemalans are outside those boundaries, then you do not have to see them or explain their role in determining how power in your society operates. Indeed, their very presence as an *invisible class* is one of the most important things you need to know in order to understand power in America.

THE LATINO MINORITY[13]

Population experts predict that early in the next century the Latino population will become the largest minority, exceeding the African American population. The average Euro-American may not see or understand how the oppression of Latin America is connected to power in our society, but most Latinos understand it very well. Their grandmothers and cousins, who remain home, working on American-controlled plantations and in American-owned factories understand the connections. The Mexican women, who are working in the Ford auto plants on the border, understand the connection. The Brazilian government official who has had to follow U.S. government orders to roll over his country's debt understands the connection.

Slavery tore African Americans away from their homes and tribal identities. African Americans created a unique national culture that was an amalgamation of African customs of many tribes and the experiences of surviving under the plantation system.[14] In contrast, Latinos in the United States are a diverse group of nationalities.

El Salvadoreans, Peruvians, Haitians, Puerto Ricans, and Mexicans come from their own distinct cultures and historical experiences. In general they share a common language and a common religion, but there are also significant differences. Latinos often retain their connections to their roots through family, travel, and culture. Like many immigrants, Latinos who have lived in this society for several generations have become Americanized and often perceive themselves as very different from more recent immigrants. The general stereotypes fail to make that distinction, however, and all Latinos tend to be subjected to prejudice and discrimination.

African Americans in early America were needed in the colonies due to a shortage of labor. There was also a time when a labor shortage in the Southwest and West meant that Latino immigrants were welcomed. But as the economy has contracted and jobs have become scarce, the flow of immigrants from Latin America is increasingly seen as a threat by many working Americans. On the other hand, employers have often found that "illegal aliens" are easier to exploit because they accept lower wages and are afraid to report employer abuses.

STRATIFICATION AND COLONIALISM

Colonialism is used to describe the relationship between a "mother country" and a geographic area that has fallen under the control of the more powerful country. Ever since human society developed professional armies, some societies have conquered and controlled others. **Empire** is defined as a social system in which one society politically controls others—examples are the Roman Empire, the Empire of Mali, the Incan Empire, and the Mongol Empire. In these earlier cases, the colonies were territories that paid tribute—dancing girls, wine, gold, grain, and silk—to the dominating society. In other words, rather than trade and pay a fair price for goods, the empire could simply take what it wanted.

Industrialization in Europe changed the relationship of colonies to the imperial society. Capitalism as a system required reinvestment, and entrepreneurs whose return on investment was highest were the most successful. The colonies of the industrializing European nations were not just sources of wine and gold—they were part of industrialization.

Complex trading patterns and investments throughout Asia, Africa and North America created the wealth of these European nations. Cheap raw materials—silver from one colony, cotton from another, and coffee from another—were fed into the industrial machine of Europe to make manufactured products that were then sold back to the colonies at high prices. Exploitation of the colonies was a major source of the wealth of the industrializing nations. The greater the wealth they acquired, the greater their ability to militarily defend and control their colonies.

Today we often hear discussion of "developed" nations and "underdeveloped" or "developing nations"—as though development is a characteristic of a nation itself. But just as an individual's social power always rests on a social relationship (who does one have power over? or whose power is one under?), so does the power of countries rest on the relationships between those countries. Many sociologists have fallen into the trap of failing to see how the class structure of the "developed world" was dependent on and intertwined with the masses of poor peasants and workers in the colonies.[15]

The textbooks may say that Britain or France was an imperial power but treats America foreign policy as something different. Perhaps no other society has tried as hard as the United States to hide its imperialism. Beginning as "the thirteen colonies," we were all taught that colonialism was wrong (at least for us). Yet America's economic development was as dependent on cheap raw materials and labor as the development of Europe. Just as the war against the Native Americans benefited the lumber, mining and railroad companies, so American intervention abroad has benefited the big corporations and banks. American marines and sailors have been used to protect "national interests" that were really the interests of the elite.

Colonialism involved the direct administration of a colony and required that the dominating country permanently station bureaucrats to run the country and troops to quell any resistance. Today the process has changed. The dominating country can control through economic and indirect political mechanisms (tariff agreements, loans, and international agencies). When the control over a weaker nation is indirect, that nation is a **neocolony**.

It is hard for many people to admit that Ferdinand Marcos administered the Philippines on behalf of U.S. interests like Dole Pineapple for years and that the revolutions in Cuba and Nicaragua were anticolonial revolutions directed against the United States. When politicians declare "It is in America's interest to ensure that friendly governments stay in power in Latin America," they are making a statement of neocolonialism.

King George III tried to keep a friendly government in the thirteen colonies, and many of our ancestors (including mine) shed blood to throw the British out. On what basis does one country get to decide what government another country should have? Not on a moral basis—because no government has ever been "persuaded" out of office. The protection of a nation's interests has always been a question of *power*—economic power or military power.[16] The question has always been decided on the basis of who is more powerful, not on who is right.[17]

In the spring of 1995 the Mexican government devalued the peso in response to the worsening economic and social conditions in that country. Congress, sensing that the American people did not want to pay for another "bailout," refused to pass legislation that would loan Mexico the money. Yet *Business Week*, in a moment of rare candor, expressed the view that there is a ruling class and it has powerful interests in Mexico—separate from the interests of the American People:

> All that sound and fury emanating from Washington has been sparked by the Clinton Administration's proposed $40 billion in loan guarantees to rescue the Mexican economy. Yet despite the vocal protests, a deal is falling into place—*because the U.S. capital's premier power brokers have joined forces to see to that.*[18] (Emphasis added)

In 1904 President Theodore Roosevelt issued the "Roosevelt Corollary" to the Monroe Doctrine, declaring that the United States was entitled to police Latin America. This Doctrine made official a policy that was already in place. In 1846 the United States had invaded Mexico and took much of the area that is currently Texas, Arizona, and Nevada. A few years later Confederate General Walker went from Mexico into Nicaragua where he set himself up as supreme ruler for two years. In 1898, the United States. fought Spain and annexed the Philippines, Hawaii, Cuba, Puerto Rico, and what is now known as the Dominican Republic.

Puerto Rico today is still occupied by U.S. troops at several island bases, and a naval base is still maintained in Cuba.[19] In 1903 the United States provided the funds and weapons to ensure Panama's secession from Colombia in order to build a U.S.-controlled canal. U.S. troops were sent to Honduras in 1911 to protect American businesses and investments there.

Between 1912 and 1933, U.S. Marines periodically fought Nicaraguan peasant rebels who were demanding unions and democratic elections and the country was actually under U.S. occupation between 1922 and 1924 and 1926 and 1933. While fighting the Nicaraguan peasants the U.S. Army resorted to the first aerial warfare in the hemisphere, strafing and bombing villages—at approximately the same time aerial warfare was attempted in the United States against striking West Virginia coalminers. Before the marines left they were managing Nicaragua's customs, National Bank, and railway and had set up a National Guard that soon placed the dictator Somoza in power.

American troops moved into Haiti in 1915, and the Dominican Republic in 1916, staying until 1924 in order to "reorganize" the economy. In 1916 General Pershing invaded northern Mexico, ostensibly in pursuit of Pancho Villa, but in reality at the requests of those who had interests in the oil in Mexico. U.S. Marines were sent into Honduras and El Salvador in 1924 and the early 1930s. In 1954 the U.S. government helped to overthrow the elected president of Guatemala, calling him a communist because he had taken land from the powerful United Fruit Company and distributed it to landless peasants.

A State Department list presented by Secretary of State Dean Rusk to a Senate committee in 1962 to cite precedents for the use of armed force against Cuba showed 103 interventions in the affairs of other countries between 1798 and 1895. Table 4.1 is a sampling from the list, with the exact description given by the State Department:[20]

In 1961, the United States invaded Cuba. In 1965 and 1966 23,000 U.S. Marines invaded the Dominican Republic to help put down a sugar workers' strike. In 1973 the United States played an active role in the assassination of Salvador Allende, the elected president of Chile, and helped install a fascist government. Allende had been elected on a pro-socialist platform that advocated nationalizing the copper mines owned by large American corporations.

In 1983 U.S. armed forces invaded Grenada to prevent loss of control over an important airstrip. In 1989 the U.S. forces invaded Panama and kidnaped the president, Manual Noriega. In 1994 the U.S. sent troops to Haiti.

Table 4.1

1852–53	Argentina.	Marines were landed and maintained in Buenos Aires to protect American interests during a revolution.
1853	Nicaragua	To protect American lives and interests during political disturbances.
1853–54	Japan	The "Opening of Japan" and the Perry Expedition. [The State Department does not give more details, but this involved the use of warships to force Japan to open its ports to the United States.]
1853–54	Ryukyu and Bonin Islands	Commodore Perry on three visits before going to Japan and while waiting for a reply from Japan made a naval demonstration, landing marines twice, and secured a coaling concession from the ruler of Naha on Okinawa. He also demonstrated in the Bonin Islands. All to secure facilities for commerce.
1854	Nicaragua	San Juan del Norte [Greytown was destroyed to avenge an insult to the American Minister to Nicaragua.]
1855	Uruguay	U.S. and European naval forces landed to protect American interests during an attempted revolution in Montevideo.
1859	China	For the protection of American interests in Shanghai.
1860	Angola, Portuguese West Africa	To protect American lives and property at Kissembo when the natives became troublesome.
1893	Hawaii	Ostensibly to protect American lives and property; actually to promote a provisional government under Sanford B. Dole. This action was disavowed by the United States.
1894	Nicaragua	To protect American interests at Bluefields following a revolution.

(The Dole mentioned in 1893 is the Dole of Dole pineapples and bananas.)

U.S. intervention is sold to the public in terms that will garner support: "protecting freedom," "saving American lives," and "ensuring democracy." There is no chance that the public would support an invasion designed to "protect sweatshops for U.S. companies" or "ensure Chase Manhattan Bank's loan."

Today the social class structure of most Latin American societies consists of a wealthy elite and the masses of poor. The middle class is very small, if it exists at all. Without the promise of social mobility, the majority of the population does not give its consent, and the stratification of these systems is maintained largely through military dictatorships or repressive civilian regimes.

These are societies where people consistently live near starvation. The conditions we associate with the homeless—shacks, begging, and disease—are ordinary circumstances for many millions in Latin America. These poor living conditions are the forces that push some to come to the United States—legally or illegally. Such immigrants tend to accept low wages and bad working conditions because, compared to what they had, anything is better. These same conditions also explain the attractiveness of Mexico, Brazil, and other Latin American countries as places in which to build new U.S. factories.

As the world economy has deteriorated, and the marketplace has become more competitive, companies have been forced to seek cheaper and cheaper labor. If a Mexican woman will accept $2.17 an hour, why pay a unionized Detroit worker $10.34 an hour? These figures are "average industrial wages" in the two countries.[21] LaDou states that factory wages in Mexico average about $5.40 per a nine-hour day, or 60 cents an hour![22]

The rights that are granted and protected by norms of democracy in the "mother country" are not extended to "the natives"of a colony. They are invisible to us. While workers in the United States of America were granted the right to form unions in the 1930's, the workers in Guatemala who were attempting to form unions were ruthlessly repressed by U.S. Marines in the 1950s. Citizens of the U.S. would be outraged if some other country's government made the decision as to who would be our political leaders. Yet an Associated Press article of 18 February, 1996 discloses that President Ferdinand Marcos of the Philippines was placed in power by the United States and literally dumped years later when the people were rioting in the streets:[23]

> "Senator, what should I do?" asked Ferdinand Marcos, under siege by hundreds of thousands of Filipinos who were camping out in Manila's streets to support military defectors backing his election opponent, Corazon Aquino. Marcos was appealing to Sen. Paul Laxalt, R-Nev., President Reagan's special emissary for the Philippines crisis, for Washington Help in arranging some kind of power-sharing arrangement. Laxalt's reply was blunt, void of diplomatic niceties. "Cut—and cut cleanly. The time has

> come," he told Marcos. There was a pause that Laxalt later said seemed to last minutes. He asked if Marcos was still on the line. "Yes," Marcos whispered. "I am so very, very disappointed."[24]

As workers in Detroit, Chicago, Cleveland, and San Diego lose jobs to workers in Monterey, Sao Paulo, and Santiago, the lower wages paid mean cheaper products. These cheaper products flood the U.S. market for the consumer. As consumers, workers, *and* taxpayers, then, the average American is connected to a group below it—"invisible," yet real. From the Chilean grapes in the grocery store to the Brazilian leather shoes sold in the Penney's catalog, our society reveals its relationship to Latin America.

The fact that the dominant society tries to hide the exploitation, degradation, and oppression of its "invisible bottom class" does not make the existence of that class less real. The ruling classes that held power and grew wealthy from slavery and the genocide of Native Americans are the same classes that grew wealthy from the land grab of Texas and the expansion into Central America. But the "people" of America *also* benefited. The Euro-American settler who supported the genocide of the Native American received cheap land as a reward. This is important. When politicians declare "it was in our nation's interest" they are speaking for a middle class whose standard of living was based on the continued exploitation and oppression of other peoples.

Cheaper consumer goods, free land, and better wages were all a result of our society's pursuing its interests at the expense of others. We, as a people, were convinced that it *was* in our best interests to maintain starvation wages in Guatemala—it ensured cheap bananas. The United States imports 7 *billion* pounds of bananas a year from Central and South America. The author of the article citing this fact in a food magazine also includes a number of recipes using bananas but makes no mention of who owns the plantations or who picks them. In other words, the bananas arrive in the grocery stores, but the social forces that put them there are invisible.[25]

When Catholics with ties to the Latin American churches raised the moral issue—that 80% of the children in Guatemala suffer brain damage as the result of malnutrition—their pleas were largely ignored. The Guatemalans are invisible to most Americans, who are busy making car payments, buying VCRs, and making banana cream pies.

This discussion has focused on the particular relationship of American society to Latin America. With the exception of our historical ties to Africa through slavery, the most important cross-cultural power relationships of U.S. society are with Latin America. This, however, does not mean that other power relationships are not also important.

Asian immigrants, particularly the Chinese, were exploited as cheap labor in the dangerous job of building the railroads across the West. Treated like animals, they died by the thousands. Efforts to protest their working conditions were brutally repressed.[26] The companies importing the Chinese did not pay to bring the men's families. The result was a flourishing international trade in women (often called sexual slavery) by which girls from poor families in China were kidnapped or lured away and resold for high profits in the United States. Approximately 85 percent of Chinese women in San Francisco were prostitutes in 1860, and 71 percent in 1870. Subjected to constant physical and mental abuse, the average prostitute did not outlive her contract terms of four to five years.[27]

Like the Chinese, Japanese immigrants played a crucial role in developing the West. At the onset of World War II, many Japanese Americans had lived in the United States for three or four generations. The racism in American society still projected them as the "enemy," and despite years of good citizenship, thousands of Japanese-Americans had their constitutional rights taken away, and were placed in concentration camps during World War II.[28] History books rarely discuss the fact that local Anglo-American businessmen were able to buy up the confiscated Japanese farms and businesses at bargain prices. Finally, a generation later, the Supreme Court ruled that the seizure of the Japanese American assets was unconstitutional and granted restitution.

Our exploitation of foreign labor continues. Go to your closet and check out your shirts and sweaters. The tags on your clothes will prove the existence of a worldwide invisible class producing affordable goods for you to wear. Nepal, Bangladesh, Macao, and the Dominican Republic are all poverty-stricken countries where people work for starvation wages to make the clothing we wear. Without health and safety standards, the right to unions and in many cases the right to vote, these workers support our society but are granted none of the rights which we take for granted.[29]

When people from countries that are colonized come to the United States they are seen as outside our boundaries—they must have their national identity prefixed before "American" (Mexican American, Japanese American, African American, Filipino American). Immigrants from a European society, however, lose that prefix as soon as they become Americanized. My ancestors were Celtic, German and Swedish immigrants. When people look at me they see an "American." My ancestors did not come from countries with a colonial status; my ancestors were always within the defined boundaries of what was U.S. society.

It is probably obvious that every group with a prefix is also a people of "color." The ability to define, and rationalize, the oppression of such groups is tightly connected, then, to the ideology of racism. Not only is the United States a more powerful nation, but as a "white" nation, we see ourselves as more civilized and more able to take care of those who are like "children."

CONCLUSION

Those of us who are standing on the ladder of social stratification in America rarely look down to see the ground upon which our ladder is standing. The "base" of the ladder is invisible to most of us. Yet when that base shakes, the whole ladder trembles. If colonial peoples accepted their starvation and poverty, our society would not have to use military force to maintain "friendly" governments. But when peoples are completely denied access to democracy and a decent standard of living—the things we hold dear—they resist and rebel. The wholesale violation of human rights in countries like Haiti, Guatemala, El Salvador, and Brazil are reflections of unpopular governments that do not rule with the consent of the governed. Their people can be controlled only through secret police, torture, kidnappings and with the occasional aid of U.S. troops.[30]

The base of the ladder has been shaken many times in American history. The descendants of slaves are no longer an invisible part of our class structure because an earthquake known as Abolition destroyed the base of the ladder called slavery. The Abolition movement is one example of a social movement that challenged the ladder of stratification and changed it.

Social movements that challenge the distribution of power require a different kind of power, because they flow from below and cannot be based on wealth. They are instead based on the organization of people, acting together for change. In Chapter 5 we turn to a discussion of how several major social movements in our society changed our history, and the distribution of power.

SUMMARY

Our culture defines our nationality. We are "American." But throughout our history, there have been groups who contributed to our society who were not allowed inside the circle of acceptance. Two of these earliest groups were the enslaved African Americans and the Native Americans. The rules and laws that made democracy work for Euro-Americans were denied to these groups.

As the United States expanded west other groups who were equally "invisible" made major contributions while being brutally exploited—the Mexicans, the Chinese, and the Japanese. American corporations soon sought out the cheap labor and resources of groups outside American boundaries. Peasants in places like Guatemala, Haiti, and the Philippines did not want to be exploited by American corporations and resisted. The U.S. military had to be used to "protect" American interests against the resentful ("troublesome") natives.

The American middle class benefited from the oppression and exploitation of these groups. Consumer goods and resources imported from these areas were cheaper. Most people were unaware of the hunger, disease, and repression that were required to provide them with cheap bananas and grapes. They were told that these were "simpler" people who did not mind lower standards of living. Such explanations of differences for people who were of color was and is an aspect of American racism.

The United States continues indirectly to control the economies and politics of a large number of Latin American nations. American interests, however, are not confined to Latin America. U.S. corporations and banks have investments throughout the world and often pressure our government to act to protect those interests.

Vocabulary

Invisible classes. Those groups that are part of the social system supporting our society but are not perceived to be part of it.

Colonialism. The relationship between a militarily powerful nation and a geographic area that has fallen under the economic and political control of the more powerful nation.

Empire. A social system linking a more powerful society with societies it controls.

Neo-colonialism. The relationship between a militarily powerful nation and a nation that is controlled indirectly by the more powerful country.

Discussion Questions

1. Most of us are "decent" people, but our tax dollars are used to provide instruments of torture for repressive governments in Latin America. How does the concept of "invisible classes" help explain why decent Americans allow their tax dollars to be used this way?

2. I have argued that the United States has had, and continues to have, colonies. How is it possible that a country that is "democratic" can have colonies?

3. How many different "invisible" groups are present in your classroom? Check the labels on your blouses, sweaters and shirts. How many different countries are represented?

4. In the Chapter 4 it was pointed out that $40 billion would be enough to bring all poor Americans above the poverty line. But we are told it is "too

expensive" to do this. In this chapter it was pointed out that the U.S. government was able to loan $40 billion to Mexico. Why is it possible to do one and not the other? Do you think the $40 billion of your money loaned to Mexico helped the poor peasants? Why or why not?

Resources

Videos: *The Alamo*

This is an old and bad movie. But it is useful to watch to understand how we learn that it is all right to take land away from other people. John Wayne is brave and the "good guy," while the Mexicans are greasy, treacherous and stupid. The assumption is that the Mexicans are responsible for the violence. If someone arrived at your house and declared that they were simply taking it and forcing you to leave, what do you think you or your parents would do?

Salvador

This movie is based on real events that occurred in El Salvador in 1980-81. James Woods plays an American journalist who tries to investigate the relationship between the American government and the repressive Salvadorean government. The movie is violent, but so were the actual events. Rated R.

Missing

What would you do if you were a parent and one of your grown children "disappeared" in a country known for its violation of human rights? Jack Lemon plays the father in this true story of a man who naively assumes that the U.S. government will help him find his son in Chile, after a repressive military junta has taken control of the country. I had visited Chile a year before the military coup and can attest to the accuracy of the film. Chilean friends who had gone to graduate school with me were imprisoned in the stadium, and many were killed.

This is a moving film, because most of us can identify with the father—we don't want to believe that *our* government would support such things! Rated R.

Book: Leon Wolff, *Little Brown Brother: America's Forgotten Bid for Empire Which Cost 250,000 Lives.*

This is a gruesome but fascinating book of how the U.S. government took the Philippines and the heroic resistance of the Filipino people. Wolff wrote the book in 1970 in hopes that it would help educate the American people about the consequences of our involvement in Vietnam. If you have trouble believing that America has taken colonies, you must read this book. Stanley Karnow's book *In Our Image: America's Empire in the Philippines* (1990) brings the story up to date with the political crisis of Ferdinand Marcos and the corruption of his regime. Karnow's book is good but drier and harder to read than Wolff's.

NOTES

Complete citations are provided in the Bibliography.

1. Davis 1990, 8.
2. Shenkman 1988, 40.
3. This theme of "the Other" is part of the analytical framework used by Anderson and Collins 1992.
4. Jaimes 1992.
5. Cook 1981, 108.
6. The 1992 film *Thunderheart* bases its plot on this point.
7. Jacqueline Jones's (1992) history of the poverty class in America after the Civil War identifies both the freed slaves and the poverty stricken white southerners as "The Dispossessed." This terminology is more accurate than the current popular term underclass.
8. 1970, 359–60.
9. Barrera 1979, 7–33.
10. Karnow 1990.
11. Wolff 1970, 253.
12. Ibid., 84–5.
13. Official government agencies use the term *Hispanic* but many persons from Central and South America prefer the term *Latino*. *Chicano* or *Chicana* is used for someone whose ancestors were part of the land seized by the United States and was made a citizen by conquest or a person of Mexican ancestry born in the United States. (Takaki 1993, 177–90).
14. Rawick 1972.
15. Rodney 1982. The research and writings of sociologist Immanuel Wallerstein in the past two decades has done much to raise these relationships within sociology.
16. Muñoz 1993, 53–65.
17. The clearest analysis of the relationship between the United States and the less powerful countries in which the United States has "interests" has been made by Williams 1972.
18. "Washington to the Rescue. Now, About the Price," *Business Week*, 30 January 1995, 47.
19. Melendez and Melendez 1993.
20. Cited in Zinn 1980, 290–91.
21. Mishel and Bernstein 1993, 134.
22. LaDou 1991.
23. Thurber 1996.
24. Briscoe 1996.
25. Raichlen 1993.
26. Takaki 1993, 196–98.
27. Yung 1990, 195–207. Also see Hirata 1979, 224–44; and Hirata 1979, 3–29.

28. Matsumoto 1990, 373–86.
29. Grieder 1994, 43–45.
30. Amnesty International 1993.

5

SHAKING THE LADDER—SOCIAL MOVEMENTS FOR EQUALITY AND DEMOCRACY

"Power concedes nothing without a struggle;
it never has and it never will."

—Frederick Douglass

At the time the Constitution of the United States was written, only *6 percent* of those who today are eligible to vote could have voted. In 1789 you had no vote if you were a Native American, a slave, a woman, not literate, under twentyone, or did not own land. How did the vast majority of Americans win voting rights, union rights, civil rights, and generally increase their well-being in just two hundred years? How did some "invisible" groups gain access to the rights and protections granted other Americans? Were they merely the passive recipients of wise and good leaders? Or did they have to fight every inch of the way for what they got?

The answer to that question is complex. In order to understand how social power and social stratification in America has changed we have to first understand social movements. A **social movement** is a group, or collective, conscious attempt to promote or resist social change. An individual may try to change his or her own social situation, but that attempt will not change the larger society. If a large number of individuals get together and work for change, however, their efforts can change the society. In this chapter we focus on social movements that tried to change the social stratification of the society—social movements that challenged the way social power was distributed and used.

Social movements are as American as apple pie. A social movement that organized, protested and disrupted was responsible for the Bill of Rights—

those ten amendments guaranteeing our freedom of assembly, speech, religion, and press. Those amendments became the legal basis upon which all subsequent social movements in our society could express their dissent. The abolition of slavery, women's right to vote, legal unions, open admissions to public colleges and student aid, and Head Start are all changes in our society that were won through social movements.

LEARNING THE HISTORY

American history is traditionally taught in a manner that downplays or even omits our country's great social movements. The impression left by most history books is that George Washington supported the Bill of Rights; that Abraham Lincoln wanted to give slaves citizenship; and that Franklin Roosevelt was the one who personally gave workers Social Security and the right to form unions.

None of the statements above is accurate. What most people know about George Washington is designed to make him a myth or a "superhero." While children are taught he cut down the cherry tree and could not tell a lie, they are not taught that his military career was made in western Virginia, killing Native Americans and buying up land, eventually becoming the richest man in America.[1]

We are all told that important names are the names of the Presidents. Most students forget the names of Daniel Shay, Frederick Douglass, Sojourner Truth, Mother Jones and Tecumseh almost as soon as the history course is over (if they learned them at all).[2] Those names are not attached to anything exciting or important—after all, they are just the names of a New England hick farmer, an ex-slave, a black woman, a working class-widow and an Indian.

The story of Tecumseh challenges the stereotype of the "dumb Indian." Advanced to warrior status by the age of twelve, Tecumseh's intelligence and charisma made him a leader of the Shawnee by his early twenties. It was Tecumseh's knowledge that enabled the Shawnee to win the greatest Indian victory in history over any American military force. He organized a regional alliance of Native Americans against European settlement. He drew together combined Native American forces that played a decisive role in the capture of Detroit and the taking of 2,000 U.S. soldiers during the War of 1812.[3]

Without knowledge of past social movements, it is much easier to make an emerging movement look "un-American." Students who protested the war in Vietnam were labeled communist sympathizers. Few Americans knew that even before socialist countries were founded, Mark Twain and Eugene Debs had spoken for, and led, large social movements that protested American involvement in wars that benefited only the upper classes. The women in the 1960s who protested gender discrimination were called "bra burners." There was little public awareness of women one century before who had also been labeled, and still fought on, or of the women *two* centuries before who had been ridiculed for advocating women's rights and still fought on.

We learned that Betsy Ross made the flag and Molly Pitcher delivered water to the men. We did not study the women who carried arms in the Revolutionary War and collected military pensions. We know only that Abigail Adams was the wife of President John Adams. We don't learn that she was a militant feminist who protested loud and long over the mistreatment of women in the new "democracy." In a letter to her husband in 1776, Abigail Adams wrote:

> By the way, in the new code of laws which I suppose it will be necessary for you to make, I desire you would remember the ladies and be more generous and favorable to them than your ancestors! Do not put such unlimited power in the hands of husbands. Remember all men would be tyrants if they could. If particular care and attention is not paid to the ladies, we are determined to foment a rebellion, and will not hold ourselves bound by any laws in which we have no voice or representation.[4]

Because we have not fully learned about such movements we have been denied the lessons of those movements. For example, why did Irish immigrants bitterly protest the draft for the Civil War, when abolishing slave labor would be in their interest as wage workers? Studying the splits between white and black women and middle-class and poor women in the nineteenth century would help us understand the social forces pitting women against one another in the women's movement today. We might want to understand why the predominantly white labor unions of the North failed to organize unions in the South and across the border to Mexico.

History should provide us with the data for this kind of study; sociology should provide us with the analytical framework that would allow us to draw conclusions and learn the lessons. But giving such knowledge to the general public might be dangerous for the ruling elite. If new generations are taught beneficial changes for the majority come "from below," it suggests that protesting exploitation, degradation and oppression is a good and positive thing. Such movements have been essential to protecting and expanding the important and cherished heritage of our democracy and equality. Without them, we would still have the stratification system described in Chapter 2.

THE ORIGINS OF SOCIAL MOVEMENTS

Individuals who suffer social pain often resist, even heroically. The way that individuals resist their own oppression, exploitation and degradation is an important topic in its own right, and one that is not often studied. But in this book, we are more interested in how individuals *come together*, identify their *common* exploitation, oppression, and degradation, and then act to make social changes to better their lives.

For a social system to work, the members must share ideologies. An **ideology** is a *system* of ideas and beliefs that helps explain the world to you. Ideas about power are one of the more important ideologies in any society. A social movement is not just a group of people challenging the system through their actions; it is also a group of people who challenge the ideas and beliefs of the system. We examine the major ideologies in American society in detail in Chapter 6.

Slavery and the struggle to end slavery provide us with an excellent example of the role of social movements in changing power relationships. Simply being oppressed, exploited, and degraded is not necessarily enough for the beginning of a social movement. Although there were a number of significant slave rebellions prior to the Civil War, some historians have asked why were there not more?[5] When one considers that the average length of life for a slave in the Deep South was seven years, it seems that slaves would have had little to lose and much to gain from rebelling.

George Warwick, in his study of the American slave community, makes this point about the need for a community base of resistance:

> The mechanisms of individual acts of resistance, as well as those of collective actions, become clear if we focus upon the slave community. People do not individually resist in any significant degree without some sort of support and social confirmation from a community. There must be way whereby individual acts of repression become known throughout the community, ways whereby individuals learn from each other that resistance is legitimate, and ways whereby individuals learn from each other of particular ways to resist. In order for large numbers to resist with any degree of success, the slave had to know that other slaves resisted and how this was accomplished.
>
> At the center of any community is a network of communications and social relations. The slave community, like other communities, was not composed of individuals living in a vacuum. The existence of the 'bush-mail' or what West Indian blacks today wryly call the 'niggergram' is a central part of slave resistance.[6]

Slaves did develop complex systems of resistance and covert rebellion. Work slowdowns, sabotage, and poisoning the owners were all accepted and common practices. A communication system including coded music (spirituals) and coded church sermons provided information that linked plantations and African Americans in the North and South. The Underground Railroad provided one escape route; many slaves also escaped into the southern swamps where they were given refuge by, and accepted into, the Seminole and other Native American communities.[7]

It was not clear to the slaves what the alternative arrangements would be if they were to revolt openly. Unlike the slaves in Haiti, who rebelled and were able actually to take control of the island, it was obvious that African Americans would not be able to take over the United States. Successful rebellion for people of African descent held in bondage required a goal or plan and allies in the larger society. The social movement we call Abolition provided those allies.

The challenge to slavery came from two important ideologies—the rights to life, liberty, and the pursuit of happiness promised during the American Revolution and the belief in human worth that could be found in the Christian tradition. Ironically, the resistance to Abolition also claimed to come from the same two sources—the right that the U.S. Constitution gave to own property (slaves were property) and the interpretation of the Bible as making people of color "cursed of God." The Abolitionist's appeal was by far the broader one, and over several decades, beginning with newsletters, small group meetings, and limited petitions, the northern Abolitionists created an avalanche of sentiment in America.

History books tend to portray Abolition as largely a white movement, with a few exceptions such as Frederick Douglass. This is not true. Abolition was essentially based in the black community and was at all times dominated by free African Americans. The movement depended on black support for its continuation; Abolitionist lecturers were usually lodged in black homes, spoke in black churches, ate food prepared by black women, and traveled on monies in part donated by blacks with little money themselves.[8]

Many whites who had no particular liking or respect for "Negroes" could be convinced the continuation of slavery undermined free labor and their own economic interests. The moral argument that a loving God would not want human beings kept in slavery also had a mass appeal. Opposition to slavery did not necessarily mean that Euro-Americans were ready to accept African Americans as equals; several generations of socialization into racism certainly could not be overcome in a short period of time.

The Abolitionists proposed giving freed slaves both the right to vote and the right to land. "Forty Acres and a Mule" was a slogan that stood for the creation of an independent Black farming class in the South, which could become self-sufficient if they were provided with land and the basic tools to work that land. This solution made sense to the majority of Americans, who themselves dreamed of owning land and the independence it would provide.

Abolition was one America's greatest social movements and played a critical role in freeing the slaves. Yet Abolition illustrates another important point—once a social movement begins, its success does not necessarily mean the end of social stratification. Fifty years after the Civil War, the majority of the freed slaves in the South were trapped in a vicious system of debt called sharecropping, and held in second-class citizenship by discriminatory Jim Crow laws. Beatings and lynchings by the Ku Klux Klan replaced the beatings and killings by plantation overseers.

A similar pattern can be seen in the movement for women's suffrage. In the early nineteenth century the suffrage movement culminated in thousands of women chaining themselves to the gates of the White House, only to be arrested and replaced by more protestors. The jails of Washington and then Baltimore were filled to capacity.[9] For women, the right to vote was the key to achieving political power and equality. That right was won in 1920. Still, in 1993 there were only six women out of one hundred members in the U.S. Senate and that was the highest number ever in American history! And today, as Chapter 3 pointed out, vast numbers of women head households that live in poverty.

Abolition and women's suffrage were both based on the ideologies of democracy and equality, yet both movements failed to realize their goals fully. Indeed, the fight for racial equality had to spawn a new social movement in the 1960s, as did the fight for women's liberation. In order to understand both the success and failures of these and other American social movements fighting for greater democracy and equality, we must go back to the question of allies in the struggle.

Power in America has never been exercised along a single dimension—that will be the argument throughout this book. Ordinary people are controlled in *different* ways in their everyday lives; the mechanisms of this control varies, depending on their relationship to color, gender, class and environment.

Exploitation, oppression, and degradation took many forms in early nineteenth century America. The slave in the South was clearly marked by his or her color. A German immigrant worker toiling long hours in a New England factory under dangerous conditions for starvation wages did not see his problem as race or color; she or he was probably the same color as the factory's owner. That worker saw exploitation as a question of class. The middle-class woman confined to her home and corset as a "lady" was oppressed by neither class nor color, but was oppressed by gender.[10] Children with tuberculosis from factory pollution and sewage in the cities were killed by the degradation of environment, regardless of color or gender. In all these cases, the individual was maintained within a system of social stratification, but experienced oppression, exploitation, or degradation in different ways.

When those in social movements for democracy and equality identified the *common* elements of exploitation, oppression, and degradation they shared, they found allies in their fight for equality and democracy. But when one group fought only in terms of their own particular problems, their struggles were perceived as irrelevant, or even detrimental, to other sectors of American society.

Takaki develops this argument in his historical analysis of how the poor in America have been "pitted" against one another, often consciously. He contends that the greatest fear of the emerging elite in America was that the "giddy multitude" would unite.[11] According to Takaki, the ruling elite understood this threat well and consciously divided oppressed groups by giving slight advantages to one over another.

The relationship between the movements for Abolition and women's suffrage provide a good example of the point made above. Women of the early nineteenth century believed that extending democratic rights to former slaves should be coupled with the extension of democratic rights to women. Women were the "foot soldiers" of Abolition and although Frederick Douglass and William Lloyd Garrison are the names most often repeated in history, the activities of the Grimke sisters and women like Lucretia Mott and Sojourner Truth were absolutely essential to the education and mobilization of the American public in favor of Abolition.[12]

White men in the North saw no threat to themselves if slaves were freed, and indeed saw the end of slavery as a means of protecting wage scales. But these same men were threatened by the idea that women would challenge their authority in the home and their power in public. The northern churches led the attack on women who dared to speak out in public on either the issue of slavery or women's rights. To the majority of churchmen these women represented an un-Christian assault on the social order and the sanctity of home and family. The result was that the social structure of slavery was defeated but women's oppression remained firmly in place for another half century.

Freed male slaves received the right to vote; freed female slaves remained bound in the oppression of gender.[13] In other words, the struggle to free the slaves did not lead to a general movement for all human liberation; it was limited to a specific struggle to end only one kind of exploitation, oppression, and degradation for only one group. The further irony of Abolition is that many freed slaves looked west for land that was being taken from the Native Americans.[14] African American Civil War veterans, organized into a contingent called the "Buffalo Soldiers," also joined the efforts of the U.S. Calvary in the war against the Native Americans. Thus, while African Americans had struggled for their own rights, they had not linked that struggle to that of the Native Americans. The vote was granted to the slaves in 1870 but the *original* inhabitants of this country were not granted the right to vote until 1924!

Neither social movement—Abolition nor women's suffrage—addressed the class issues of economic rights and control over one's labor. Yet class interests were very much a factor in the history of this period. We have already mentioned that many northern white workers realized that slavery undercut their ability to raise or even maintain wages. Slavery was also a threat to the upper classes of the North. A system of wage labor industrialism based on a home market was incompatible with a system of slave labor plantation agriculture based on an export market.[15] Laws such as tariffs and tax credits for investment would hurt one system and help another.

Thus the Abolitionists were supported by the upper classes of the North who wanted to open the South to their kind of system—capital investment, industrial development, and cheap wage labor. In other words, the social movement called Abolition coexisted with a division within the ruling classes over national policy. This division was reflected, politically, by the formation of the Republican Party and the election of Abraham Lincoln.

Could the Abolitionists have succeeded without a section of the ruling class as their ally? Could the northern financiers and industrialists have succeeded without the Abolitionists and free labor as their ally? The answer to both questions is no. In that historical period both interests were intertwined and inseparable.

What happened after the Civil War? For a decade after the war, the promises of freedom burned bright. African Americans built schoolhouses, formed social welfare associations and elected local, state and even national representatives. An African American senator and congressman were elected in 1870. But there were deep divisions within the elite as to what should happen in the South.[16] These political differences were settled by the Hayes-Tilden agreement in 1877. The government withdrew the protection of federal troops, and the hard won gains of freed slaves were driven back by a new vicious form of social control.[17] The forces for freedom were abandoned by their allies in the upper classes, who had gained what *they* wanted.

The exploited labor of sharecroppers living in poverty became a source of cheap food for the industrializing north. Poorly paid pulpworkers and lumber workers provided the housing materials for the growing population of the North. Although slavery had been ended, the racist ideology continued. Stereotypes of African Americans in stories, cartoons and then movies promoted the picture of a childlike character happy to be eating watermelon and living in a shack.[18]

Poor whites living in the South could not raise their living standards as long as racism prevented them with uniting with their natural allies—poor blacks. The infamous convict labor gangs of the South were used to build the railroads, canals and roads of the "New South," in effect becoming a new form of slave labor for wealthy farmers and industrialists. Poverty-stricken whites, as well as blacks, were caught in this legalized cheapening of labor.[19]

There were attempts to organize the southern workforce across the lines of color, but few were able to endure successfully under the brutal repression of the Ku Klux Klan dominated South.[20] The labor movement emerging in the North failed to understand this contradiction, and the South remained divided by color and oppressed as a region.

The Civil War is also associated with the rapid growth of industrialization in the United States. Prior to the war, most workers operated as "craft" workers, even if they were in a factory. War production gave impetus to the steel, railroad, and coal mining industries and gave rise to a new form of production. The worker in the factory was no longer practicing a craft. The associations that craft workers had formed to protect their interests could not adequately protect the industrial worker, and industrial unionism was born. The Congress of Industrial Organizations (CIO) is most often recognized as the major form such organizing took, but it was preceded by the Knights of Labor and the International Workers of the World ("Wobblies").

The workers who organized and struck around workplace issues in this period were acting against the law. The Constitution was interpreted to make industrial unionism an "illegal constraint of trade" (i.e. unconstitutional). This legitimated employers' use of police, state troopers and the National Guard. Like the early Abolitionists, the labor movement combined tactics of education, mass protest, and armed self-defense. The need for self-defense was made painfully clear during the Colorado miners' strikes. In the strike of 1903-4 for the eight- hour day, 42 men were killed, 112 wounded, 1,345 arrested and imprisoned in bullpens or military concentration camps and 773 deported from the state.[21]

The willingness of the government to use violence in support of the companies was made painfully clear in the march on Blair Mountain in West Virginia in 1921. Thousands of armed union coal miners (many of whom were World War I veterans) marched across the mountain to confront armed guards hired by the company and deputized by county officials. A firefight ensued and the miners won. The company asked the U.S. government for help and the National Guard was called, along with the a squadron of army airmen.[22]

This was the first time in American history that U.S. Government air forces were called upon to bomb American citizens. They did not succeed.

Six of the planes got lost and crashed in the mountains. However, county officials borrowed an airplane and dropped a homemade bomb near the battlefield.[23]

By 1919, 4 million workers in the North, Midwest and West were actively involved in the movement, and massive strikes and shutdowns paralyzed industry.[24] The powerful union move ment in the North made significant gains that have benefited millions of Americans. Unions established the principles that workers had certain rights within the workplace. Union contracts set precedents for standards of living that included health care, paid vacations, and pensions. The dream of equality—where all could access the good life and opportunities for one's children— seemed to many Americans to have been won.

Yet, once again, the struggle by one group to gain greater power and control over their lives (this time in terms of improved wages and working conditions) was often limited only to their own particular interests. The unions' bureaucratic leadership largely ignored the poverty stricken southern worker—black or white. Many of these leaders defined labor's goals only in terms of more money and benefits and ignored other issues of social hierarchy—women's oppression, environment, and racism.[25] Those who did raise such issues were "red-baited"—accused of communist sympathies because they wanted to raise the broader issues related to class unity. The United Mine Workers of America were a notable exception to the general racism of the northern union movement. The UMWA not only forbade membership in the Ku Klux Klan but had an affirmative action policy to ensure that African Americans could be elected to local union positions.

William G. Domhoff's study of the strength and weaknesses of the union movement in the 1930s lays out the political and legislative implications for the failure of the North to organize the South:

> The emphasis on the split in the ruling class is another way of saying that the political power of the southern segment of the ruling class is demonstrated very graphically by comparing the legislative histories of the Wagner Act and the Taft-Hartley Act. When the southerners acquiesced in the New Dealers' solution to capital-labor conflict in the North, the act could pass. However, once they turned against the act, thereby uniting the three major segments of the ruling class, the handwriting was on the wall for organized labor due to its inability to organize in the South.[26]

Several decades later the garment industry, television industry, and other factories moved south to take advantage of cheaper, nonunion labor, especially women. Ellen Israel Rosen, in her study of blue-collar women in a New

England factory town, analyzes the complex feelings that working women had regarding the union:

> Women expressed a good deal of anger at unions and at particular union leaders they felt had not done enough to protect their rights; this was especially true for those women who lost jobs due to plant closing or employment declines. Yet if unions are weakened and allow bosses to violate workers' rights, women feel, in their justified anger, that even in the breach, they do have rights. Even in the context of declining wages and job losses, they often feel a sense of security; the union gives them the right to express their anger when they feel they are not being treated with justice or dignity. Should they have a problem the union will be there to back them up.[27]

SOCIAL MOVEMENTS AND WAR

This brief historical review above suggests that social movements are often accompanied by violence. We do not normally think of war as part of a social movement but it may be. Attempts to change power relationships almost always begin peacefully, but if the ruling classes refuse to change, or meet demands for change with violence, social movements may become violent. The extent of violence is directly related to the challenge that is occurring. If the challenge does not attack basic power relationships, it may be met with resistance but not with violence. If the challenge threatens a basic relationship necessary for the maintenance of power, it is met with violence and sometimes results in civil war or revolution.

The American Civil War was the bloodiest war in the history of humankind up to that time. In one battle, Antietam, there were more American casualties in one day than American casualties in the entire Vietnam War. The war was a truly horrible and devastating wound for America and serves to remind us of the terrible price paid for the extension of democracy and equality.

Abolition "caused" a war because it challenged the right to private property and the power generated by control over that property (the slave). An entire social system in the South rested on that control. The Civil War was started by the South not just in an attempt to keep slaves but to protect a way of life based on property. In other words, abolishing slavery did not just reform the agriculture of the south, it transformed it.

Southerners had been socialized for generations in an ideology that rationalized and justified their system. They did not see themselves as bad people, or did they necessarily even see slavery as good. But they did see their way of life as familiar and predictable and they were afraid of changes that would leave them powerless and vulnerable.[28] To them, the North was attempting to subjugate them and take away their own local control. It is important to remember this point. Their resistance may seem backward and stupid to us. But those beliefs were powerful motivators and helps explain why ordinary people went to war or donned a white hood.

In 1860 only 5.5 percent of southern whites actually owned slaves. From a purely economic point of view it is not clear why poverty-stricken whites who were economically competing with slave labor joined the Confederate army to defend a system that did not directly benefit them. This can be understood only if one analyzes the white person's belief that what little prestige or status they possessed was because the slaves were "under" them. This belief was supported by the southern legal and social system which granted poor whites privileges that slaves did not have.[29]

The South's resistance was apparent long before the Civil War. Small farmers settling in Kansas wanted it to be a free state. But they were attacked by vigilante groups from the South that killed their livestock and often the farmers themselves. The vigilantes were southerners who wanted to frighten freeholders off the land so the territory would vote itself into the Union as a slave state. The small farmers organized to fight back against these terrorists. They needed a leader and asked a militant preacher named John Brown to come help them establish their defense. John Brown came to Kansas and led the fight against the southern vigilantes.

October 16

Perhaps
You will remember
John Brown.
John Brown
Who took his gun,
Took twenty-one companions
White and black,
Went to shoot your way to freedom
Where two rivers meet
And the hills of the
North
And the hills of the
South
Look slow at one another—
And died
For your sake.
Now that you are
Many years free,
And the echo of the Civil War
Has passed away,
And Brown himself
Has long been tried at law,
Hanged by the neck,
And buried in the ground—
Since Harpers Ferry
Is alive with ghosts today,
Immortal raiders
Come again to town—
Perhaps
You will recall
John Brown.

Langston Hughes, 1959

Kansas stayed free. But once again it must be pointed out that "free" meant freedom for the small farmers. The proud Native Americans, who had once hunted and farmed that land, were being herded into reservations that resembled concentration camps, where they died in astounding numbers.

John Brown is one of the most important persons in our country's history. He was a Euro-American, a dedicated Christian, who was willing to give his life in the battle to end a system that he saw as evil. He had no illusions that those who held power over the slaves would peacefully give up that power; he understood they would use their power, violently, to protect that system. Brown also believed that the slaves themselves would rise up in resistance when they were given goals and a plan for success. Brown's plan was visionary. He argued for the redistribution of land in the South to insure that wealth would be fairly redistributed to those who had labored to create it—the freed slave and poor white.

John Brown carried out a military raid he knew would fail. His goal, however, was not simply to obtain arms at Harper's Ferry, but to make a statement to the country that the issue could no longer be resolved by talk or votes. He knew the South would secede and he knew the North would go to war. Brown was hanged for the crime of attempting to take arms that could be given to slaves.[30] In the eyes of the elite, however, Brown's real crime was his vision of property redistribution in the South. The northern ruling class was less threatened by Brown's abortive raid on Harper's Ferry than by his plan for southern reconstruction.[31] Two years later thousands of human beings picked up arms for the very same cause.

The history books often portray Brown as either crazy or a fanatic. The African American Abolitionist leader, Frederick Douglass shared many of Brown's views. Douglass is portrayed as a wise and great leader. The lesson that is drawn from these contrasting pictures is that if you are a member of the oppressed group it is expected that you will fight militantly against your oppression. But if you are *not* a member of that group (Brown was white), then you must be *crazy* to fight against the oppression of someone else! In other words, many historians twist Brown's understanding that *any* oppression was wrong into a mental illness on his part!

CONCLUSION

It is tempting to look backward in history and see those who defended slavery, shot down union workers, or imprisoned women who voted as "the bad guys." But such a view reduces history to a question of motives. In almost all the cases we have been discussing, individuals saw the protection of their power as a necessary and right thing. History can only give us a perspective.

One hundred years from now students will look back on the America of the late twentieth century and see that violence continues to mark the social life of our society. Our cities burned in the late 1960s and Los Angeles burned again in 1992. We have the largest per capita prison population in the industrialized world and the highest rate of rape. Our inner cities are currently at war—drug wars and senseless drive-by shootings are an everyday occurrence. We continue to deploy our troops abroad in the "brushfire" wars that are erupting all over the world. We are dying by the hundreds of thousands of AIDS and cancer.

The great social movements of America's history have not solved all our problems. Indeed, we have had to repeat struggles that at one time appeared to have been won. Why do people have so much trouble learning and understanding the lessons of history? Why can they not clearly see the consequences of oppression, degradation, and exploitation for others as well as for themselves? To answer those questions, we must look at not only where people are in the social structure, and what people have done, but we must examine what people *think* and *believe*.

SUMMARY

At the time the United States became a nation, the vast majority of people had very few rights. The elite held both economic and political power. We cannot understand how oppressed groups in America were able to better their position on the ladder without understanding social movements.

A social movement goes beyond individual resistance to oppression, exploitation, and degradation. It unites many individuals into action that challenges the way the ladder of stratification is organized. Usually history books give the impression that the elite made the changes that helped the lower classes. But it was massive social movements, involving thousands, sometimes millions, of people that were responsible for many of the changes that extended democracy and equality in America.

The Abolition movement was one of the most powerful American social movements. It challenged the part of the stratification ladder called slavery. It also challenged the ideology of racism, which justified slavery. The Abolitionists offered a new ideology—one that extended the idea of equality to everyone, regardless of color. Likewise, the suffrage movement challenged gender stratification. The suffragettes wanted to end the ideology of male supremacy.

In studying social movements we can see that people often organize around changes that will benefit only their group. Male Abolitionists did not want to extend their struggle to include rights for women; some white women did not want to extend their struggle to include rights for black women; and many workers fighting for union rights did not see their struggle connected to questions of gender, race, or environment.

John Brown is an example of an individual who, although white, fought to the death for the rights of black people and for economic rights for the poor. Yet many history books have called him "crazy"! Brown understood that power in America has never been exercised along a single dimension. Those on the lower rungs of the ladder are controlled in different ways depending on their relationship to color, gender, class, and environment.

When social movements seriously challenge fundamental power relationships in a society, those in power will respond with force in order to maintain their power. Thus, what begins as a social movement can become an insurrection, a civil war, or a revolution. Abolition was a challenge to basic power structures in the South and the result was a civil war. The Northern elite, however, had an interest in changing power relationships in the South, but for different reasons than the Abolitionists. Thus, twenty years after the end of the war and the end of slavery, most Southern African Americans, and many poor Euro-Americans, continued to be held in poverty through debt bondage. The oppressive structures of slavery had been replaced by informal oppressive structures like the Ku Klux Klan.

These historical examples help us understand that although a social movement may be successful in making a specific change in social structure, it may not be able to end the systemic stratification of the society.

Vocabuary

Social movement. A group's collective attempt to promote or resist social change.

Ideology. A system of ideas and beliefs that helps explain the world; ideologies are organized around the general aspects of our lives—religious ideologies, political ideologies, economic ideologies, etc.

Discussion Questions

1. Most history emphasizes what the elite did and downplays the role of the ordinary people in making social change. Why is it important that we learn one and not the other? What difference does it make for us today?

2. One of my African American students told me that until he learned about John Brown in my class, he never knew that there was a white person who had fought and died for the rights of black people. Why isn't John Brown a major American hero?

3. Harriet Tubman is known by most people as a woman who led slaves to freedom on the Underground Railroad. Very few people know that she earned the rank of general in the Union Army during the Civil War and was responsible for organizing guerrilla activities behind Confederate lines

(including blowing up bridges, burning supply houses, and assasination.) Is our lack of knowledge about her wartime activities related to the fact that she is a woman? Discuss.

4. The text argues that violence occurs in social movements when fundamental power relationships are challenged. In the example of the march on Blair Mountain by the coal miners, the two opposing sides were literally "armies." What fundamental power relationship were the miners challenging? Could there have been a more peaceful resolution? Why or why not?

5. The 1960s are often called the decade of social movements—the women's movement, the civil rights movements, the antiwar movement, the student movement. What did you learn about those movements in school? (If you are an older student, what do you remember about those movements?) Did they accomplish their goals? Why or why not?

Resources

Videos: *Glory*

A wonderful and inspirational film about the first African American regiment that fought in the Civil War. This is one of the few movies about the Civil War that allows you to see it through the eyes of those most oppressed by slavery. The movie also portrays the class divisions within the African American regiment.

Watch for Frederick Douglass and his part in supporting the regiment. Unfortunately, the moviemakers chose to ignore the fact that Harriet Tubman had dinner for the officers of the regiment shortly before their fateful attack on the fort. (Don't ask me why they could not have included a least one strong woman character!) Stars Denzel Washington and Morgan Freeman. Rated R.

Buck and the Preacher

A marvelous film—funny, sad, and educational. The historically based plot revolves around a group of freed slaves who hire Buck (Sidney Poitier) to guide their wagon train west. He must also protect them against the vigilantes—terrorist gangs hired by plantation owners who want the freed slaves to stay in the South as cheap labor. Harry Belafonte plays the role of the opportunist preacher who hooks up with Buck to save his own skin and ends up helping the settlers.

One of the best things about this film is that it confronts the contradiction between the freed African Americans and the Native Americans, whose land they are now crossing. There is one scene where a Native American woman leader confronts Buck with his hypocrisy—he wants the Native Americans not to attack his wagon train, but why did he ride with the U.S. Calvary and fight the Indians? she asks. Good question.

This was one of the first "Westerns" (1972) to be directed by an African American (Poitier). Also stars Ruby Dee. Rated R.

The Autobiography of Miss Jane Pittman

This made-for-TV movie follows the life of a single woman from her early childhood memories of the Civil War, the Jim Crow period of the South, moving west, and finally the civil rights movement. This is not only a film about an African American but very much a film about a woman. Although a strong person, as a woman she cannot officially lead. So she expresses her leadership as a teacher, profoundly influencing the lives of several young men who then become overt leaders.

Matewan

The massacre at Matewan preceded the march on Blair Mountain. This movie reconstructs the story of the massacre and was filmed in West Virginia near the actual site of the massacre. This is the early twentieth century, before the union is legal, and men go into the mines as children, and die early. The Appalachian miners go on strike so the company brings in African Americans from the South and Italian immigrants to break the strike. Each group is suspicious and afraid of the others. But the union organizer is able to convince them to work together.

This movie eloquently raises the issue of violence in social movements. The organizer is opposed to shooting back; the miners are adamant that they must, in order to win. After you watch it, ask yourself—with whom would I have sided in that argument?

The movie played to packed theaters in West Virginia, as miners and the sons and daughters of coal miners came to learn a history that they had never been taught. It stars James Earl Jones and is rated PG-13.

Hoffa

This is another good film about the social movement that built American unions. It also illustrates the point in the text about allies in the movement. Oppressed and exploited workers follow the charisma and bravery of young Jimmy Hoffa. But it is not enough to win against the power of the big companies. Hoffa makes the decision to accept help from the Mafia, who he sees as the lesser of the two evils.

Jack Nicholson plays Hoffa and Danny DeVito plays the friend through whose eyes the story is told. Watch for the very unsympathetic portrayal of Robert Kennedy as attorney general. Rated R.

Book: *The Autobiography of Frederick Douglass*

One of the greatest figures in nineteenth-century America, Douglass possessed the intelligence, spirit, and skills to lead a massive social movement.

Born a slave, Douglass writes frankly about his feelings of oppression, his perceptions of whites, and his own doubts and fears. It is difficult for us to imagine what it must have been like to be a slave, but reading books like this helps us understand. It also gives us a glimpse into an exciting historical period.

NOTES

Complete citations are provided in the Bibliography.

1. Schwartz 1987.
2. For an interpretation of American history that argues individuals such as those were the ones who shaped our country, see Zinn 1980.
3. Eckert 1992.
4. L.H. Butterfield, ed.,"The Adams Papers," Series 2, *Adams Family Correspondence*, cited in Hymowitz and Weissman 1978, 36.
5. Huggins 1990, 1978.
6. Warwick 1972, 107.
7. Katz 1986.
8. Rawick 1972, 109–116.
9. Hymowitz and Weissman 1978, 266–84.
10. Ibid., 64–75.
11. Takaki 1993.
12. Hymowitz and Weissman 1978, 156–75.
13. J. Jones, 1986.
14. The movie *Buck and the Preacher* portrays this contradiction both realistically and with sensitivity.
15. Keller 1983, 15–50.
16. Geschwender 1978, 259–59.
17. DuBois 1992.
18. The classic example of such stereotypes can be found in D. Griffith's 1915 movie, *Birth of a Nation*. The first "epic" movie ever made, it was enormously popular and dramatically reinforced the racism of EuroAmericans for a generation. This was followed in 1939 with *Gone With the Wind*, again abounding in racist stereotypes. Both films are listed as the most popular film of their decade.
19. J. Jones 1992, 148–55.
20. A heroic attempt was made by timberworkers in the South between 1911 and 1913. Green 1976, 21–29.
21. Boyer and Morais 1977, 142.
22. Lee 1969.
23. Williams 1976, 147.
24. Boyer and Morais 1977, 204.
25. The complex history of the Taft-Hartley law and the 14-B amendment outlawing the closed shop are key to understanding how this happened. See Domhoff 1990.
26. Domhoff 1990, 104.
27. Rosen 1987, 75.
28. For a recent historical interpretation of the consciousness of the southern ruling class see Genovese 1992. Also Takaki 1993, 51–76.
29. Takaki 1993, 51–76.
30. Most Americans did not even know that free African Americans and ex-slaves were part of the Union Army until the release of the movie *Glory*. Also see McPherson 1982.
31. Zinn 1980, 180–82.

PART II

WHAT DO WE THINK ABOUT STRATIFICATION?

The first five chapters made an argument that significant stratification exists in America, even though we do not always like to admit it. We want to believe that we have a good country. It is hard to explain why so many people are poor, or why we have so many social problems. In other words, social stratification is not just something that exists out there, it is also a part of what we *think*. This part of the book looks at how we think about social stratification and tries to figure out why we think that way.

- **Chapter 6** examines the origins of the major beliefs about power and social stratification in America. Where did the beliefs come from that rationalize why it is necessary for some people to be on the top and other people to be on the bottom? We identify four major belief systems used to keep people in the places: male supremacy, racism, classism, and speciesism. At the same time, our society has held beliefs that contradict the ideas justifying social stratification. It is those beliefs—in democracy and equality—that Americans have historically used when they challenge the stratification ladder. This chapter shows the historical roots of these beliefs—where they came from and why.

- Learning the beliefs about social stratification is part of our socialization. **Chapter 7** looks at the ways we are taught to accept our places as we are growing up. Children on different rungs of the ladder learn different things. People we trust who are in authority tell us certain things. It is easy to accept these things and believe they are right, and were always meant to be. So we learn to go along with the way things are and sometimes even come to believe that we belong on the lower rungs!

- **Chapter 8** looks at what happens to us if we *don't* accept our places. If what we are taught is "good" really creates social pain for us or other people, we may begin to question what we are told. And when groups on the lower rung begin to question and act to change their position, there are attempts to control them, to keep them in place. These are direct social controls, and often they are very effective ways of keeping the ladder stable. But in the long run, these controls often create more and more violence. This chapter looks at how these controls work and don't work.

As you read these chapters you will be able to see things that *you* were taught, and maybe even believed in. What these chapters suggest is that there are things designed to keep you in your place. How was it that you came to accept some of these things as "true?" And if you begin to question certain things, what kinds of social punishments can you expect? Do you dare to be called names? to be moved even farther down the ladder? to make people upset with you? As you try to answer these questions, you will see why it is so hard to change social stratification.

6

BELIEVING IN THE LADDER—THE ORIGINS OF IDEOLOGY

"They would all take America away from me if they could.
But I won't let them.
If I have to, I'll stop them in their tracks.
Just as I stopped Amy.
How do you stop someone in their tracks?
By not believing them."

—Evelyn-Tashi in *Possessing the Secret of Joy*[1]

We have been discussing power and social stratification as though they exist outside ourselves. But social structures also exist in our heads. If we go back to the example in Chapter 1 of the police officer who stops you when you speed, we ought to be able to predict what will happen.

You have been going 59 in a 45-mile-per-hour zone. You see a flashing blue light coming up behind you. You look down at your speedometer and know you were speeding. You are not surprised to see the police. The officer expects you to pull over when you see his light. If you do not see the light, he will sound the siren. When you pull over you expect the officer to approach your car and politely ask for your license and registration. He will say something about going too fast. You will make a lame excuse. You will get a ticket.

The officer has the power to punish you for breaking the rule. You believe the speeding laws are good laws—they are meant to keep the roads safe for everyone. You have consented to a social structure in which officers have power to enforce those laws. You even support politicians who talk about the need for "law and order."

The situation described above is the "normal" situation. Hundreds of thousands of times a day, individuals are caught speeding, pay their fines, and try to drive slower next time (or at least avoid the speed traps!) However, let us look at a different situation.

Let us say you were doing 59 in a 45-mile-per-hour zone, you are driving a beat-up old Chevy because you are working a minimum wage job, and you are a Chicano teenager. Let us also say that you have seen police officers hassle your friends for just standing on street corners and that your uncle was severely beaten by police when he was arrested for drunkenness. Police officers have called you a "dirty wetback." You believe that had you been white and driving a nice car, the officer would not harass you. In other words, you don't trust the officer and you don't trust his power.

The white officer following you (the Chicano teenager) also sees this situation differently. Two days ago he helped arrest a Chicano teenager for selling cocaine. The suspect was heavily armed and dangerous. The officer has no personal friends who are Chicano and all Latinos tend to look alike to him. They call him "honky pig" and resent his presence in the neighborhood. The officer just can't understand why "they" don't go out and get decent jobs. He's also angry because a relative recently applied to the police force and didn't get the job. Instead a young Chicano who scored slightly lower on the test was given the job and the personnel office said it was because of affirmative action.

The officer in the second example does not *expect* you to behave as you would in the first example nor do *you*, in the second case, expect the officer to behave as the officer in the first case. In other words, in the second situation, the power of the police officer does not rest on your consent to his power over you; you see the situation as another case of racist harassment. Likewise, the officer approaches you, the Chicano teenager, as a potentially dangerous individual whereas in the first case the officer approaches you as a decent average citizen who has made the mistake of driving too fast.

This example illustrates how social relationships of power are affected by individual beliefs.[2] In the first case, the beliefs of both parties enabled the process—giving a ticket—to go smoothly. No force was needed. In the second case, it is possible that force will be involved. There may be bad language, shoving, and even beating. Both individuals actually expect it to happen.

We discuss "self-fulfilling prophecies" in Chapter 7. It is a sociological concept used to describe how we often act in the manner that others *expect* us to act. The teenager expects the officer to be abusive; the officer expects the teenager to be surly and violent. Both individuals have actual experiences in their background; they do not hold these ideas without a foundation.

This example is also useful in another way. In the spring of 1992, the United States was shocked by news that Los Angeles police officers who had been videotaped beating an unarmed African American motorist were acquitted of charges of excessive force. The reaction to those acquittals was the most serious urban rebellion in this century. Outraged citizens in the poorer sections of Los Angeles responded to the news by burning and looting. Scores of people were killed, over 2,000 were injured, 12,000 were arrested, and almost a billion dollars' worth of property was destroyed.

The "normal" power relationships between these citizens and police in Los Angeles had broken down. Inner-city minority residents believed the police were an oppressive force. Residents knew they were exploited by many inner-city merchants who charged higher prices for inferior goods. They felt degraded by the schools, politicians, and the police. They no longer believed in the system.

A recent study found that young teenagers in the inner city are far more disillusioned and cynical than formerly expected. The report from the study "Reaching the Hip-Hop Generation" concluded that those surveyed even rejected mainstream black culture and African American role models such as Jesse Jackson and Magic Johnson.[3]

When those with power have the consent of those below them we say the power is **legitimate**; in Los Angeles, tens of thousands of people rejected what many Americans believe is the legitimate power of the police.

Most middle-class Americans, like the driver in the first example, have never personally experienced police harassment or brutality. They have no real idea of what it is like to live in an area where oppression, exploitation and degradation are constant reminders that you are on the bottom of the ladder.

Ideas in our head about power—who we trust, who we believe, what we think is right—are both personal questions *and* questions of social structure. Individual beliefs about power are not easily measured. But we can surely measure the number of blocks burned and the lives lost. This is important. Throughout this book we continue to make the point that what individuals believe and do are important parts for understanding large social events—wars, rebellions, crime, and social movements.

One key aspect of keeping ladder rungs in place, or knocking them down, is ideology. In Chapter 5 we defined ideology as a system of ideas and beliefs that help explain the world to you. We have already seen the role of ideologies in the social movements in our history. For a social system to work, the individual members must share ideologies—the belief and idea systems of the society.

Shared ideologies of power legitimate the power of those who exercise it over others. This is called **ideological social control**, the control of individuals by controlling their minds. Ideologi cal social control is the most effective glue because it convinces people the rung they are on is "where they belong."

Social relations of power require two kinds of glue to keep the rungs of the ladder in place. That's ideological social control. If that doesn't work, then people must be kept in their place on the ladder through threats, intimidation and physical force. In large sections of Los Angeles in 1992 the first kind of power relationships had disintegrated.[4] Even the most minimal kind of "reward" for believing in the system—employment—had been taken away. Over the decade preceding the rebellion, over 100,000 jobs had left the Los Angeles area. The unemployment rate in these communities was double and triple the national average. Social order could be reestablished only through the massive deployment of force—police and the National Guard.

But before we look at how power is used forcefully, we must first examine how power in used by getting us to *accept* what others do to us.

IDEOLOGIES OF POWER

We are taught in school that power in America is based on democracy—of the people, by the people, for the people. We are taught every citizen is given equal protection under the law. We believe that everyone should have an equal opportunity to achieve a good life.

If we you took a poll in your class at this moment, and if everyone were honest, how many would say you *really* believe the average citizen has power in this country and the system works the way it is supposed to? Most of us would say we had little or no power. We might name a few rich persons, or a handful of politicians, or maybe some small group as having *real* power in America. In other words, we are taught ideologies that legitimate power, that those who exercise power over us do it with our consent and for our benefit. We are taught that democracy provides a positive way for power to be exercised. But our everyday experiences, and other things we learn, lead us to believe that this ideal norm of power rarely functions in real life.

While we are taught the ideology of equal, shared democratic power we are also taught other, contradictory, ideologies. Chapter I identified democracy and equality as a fundamental belief system in our culture. We also identified four dimensions of power—racism, classism, sexism, and speciesism—that allow exploitation, oppression, and degradation to occur.[5] Where did these ideas come from, who do they benefit, and why do we believe them? Let's examine first the origins of the democratic ideals of American society.

THE IDEOLOGY OF DEMOCRACY AND EQUALITY

Everyone is taught the story of the first Thanksgiving—how the Pilgrims were saved from starvation by Indians willing to share food. We are rarely taught that early European settlers, coming from countries where power was held by elites, were deeply impressed by the way the Native Americans used power, resolved disputes, and managed their internal affairs. The natural inclination of many European settlers moving into a strange territory was to make friends with and learn from their neighbors who had lived there a long time. Some of the educated and powerful Euro-Americans, like Thomas Jefferson, saw the League of Nations of the Iroquois as a democratic model for a confederation of states.[6] Thus, one of the first sources of ideas of democracy can be attributed to the cultural contact between the Native Americans and the early European settlers.[7]

At the same time, European beliefs in the superiority of their own culture prevented the settlers from truly accepting the natives.[8] As the flood of settlement threatened the Native American's ability to survive, and government policies encouraged genocide, Europeans were pitted against the natives. But we are only taught that whites and reds on the frontier were *always* busy shooting and scalping.[9]

Among the European settlers, there were two very different views of power. As discussed in Chapter 2, the vast majority of settlers were either very poor or independent peasants who wanted the freedom to make a living and raise a family farming the land. These immigrants came to escape the terrible conditions of life they had faced in Europe. To them, kings, queens, nobility, and factory owners represented hunger and exploitation. These settlers carried a dream of a different social system in which no class or group could dictate your beliefs and dreams.

The kings, queens, nobility, and factory owners saw the New World in a very different light. To the ruling classes of Europe, North America represented cheap natural resources and a way to make a quick fortune. It mattered little to them that the fur trade destroyed the indigenous economies of the eastern natives or disrupted the wildlife ecosystems.[10] For the European investors, the fur trade was an immediate source of great wealth that could be reinvested back into land speculation and be used to pay more soldiers to kill more Indians.

These aristocrats expected to establish the same kind of stratified system in North America that benefited them at home. But the ideologies used to maintain their power in the Old World were not going to easily work in the New World. There was no single king that one's parents, grandparents, and great-grandparents had served; there was no one church that collected tithes, controlled land, and backed up the royalty.

This was a land where the Irish settled next door to the English; where Prussians sold produce to the Dutch. There were almost as many religions as there were groups of people fleeing religious persecution. If you didn't like living in one town, you could move to the next, because there was always work, even if it was hard and underpaid. If you had a little money, you could pack up and head west where no one could tell you what to do. The majority of the European settlers were not going to agree to, and participate in, a social system that put them back in the same social status they had held in Europe—exploited, oppressed and degraded. They were demanding a new kind of system that guaranteed their opportunities and recognized the achievements of each individual.

Some of the wealthy and well-educated were also "enlightened." Leaders such as Patrick Henry, Thomas Paine, and Abigail Adams had been influenced by ideas about democracy and individual liberty. These thinkers and writers gave us the cultural commitment to what *we* identify as "Life, Liberty, and the Pursuit of Happiness."

According to some, the founding fathers themselves did not embrace the modern idea of democracy. Richard Shenkman, in his book *Legends, Lies & Cherished Myths of American History,* points out:

> Historian Charles Beard writes that most of the drafters of the Constitution viewed democracy as something rather to be dreaded than encouraged. Well into the nineteenth century, he insists, he word was repeatedly used by conservatives to smear opponents of all kinds. Even so stout a defender of the people's rights as Jefferson never publicly identified himself as a democrat. Throughout his long life he preferred to call himself a republican, and he used that term even after many of his own supporters had begun to call themselves democrats.
>
> So controversial was the word "democrat" that it does not appear in any of the famous documents associated with the birth of the country—not in the Declaration of Independence, the U.S. Constitution, or any of the state constitutions. That the founders believed in equality is no more true than they believed in democracy. The Declaration of Independence may say it, but the founders didn't believe all men created equal. They apparently believed all men are created equal in the eyes of the law, and that was all. They did not believe men are socially or economically equal and didn't believe they should be. Put another way, the all-American founders didn't believe in the all-American concept that any all-American boy can grow up to be President.[11]

Shenkman goes on to point out that only when President Wilson needed to rally the American people to go to war against Germany was the term democracy (as in "This is a War for Democracy") widely used.

The society that endorsed the saying "We hold these truths to be self evident, that all men are created equal" was the same society that believed in enslaving people of color, treating women as children, slaughtering the Native Americans, and taking from nature without regard to consequences. In order to understand this apparent contradiction, we must understand the *other* ideologies that have been so important in our culture.

THE IDEOLOGY OF MALE SUPREMACY

Male supremacy is the oldest ideology of oppression, exploitation, and degradation in human society. Beliefs that men are superior to women, that men should have power and control over women, and that women should serve men are part of male supremacist ideology. A social system in which power and gender roles are defined by this ideology is known as a **patriarchy** and it is a specific kind of social stratification.

Smaller human societies were not patriarchies. With the development of more complex and larger societies patriarchy emerged. When and how gender and sex roles become part of social stratification is dependent upon the particular nature of the culture involved. In societies where women were responsible for the major food production, as in the Iroquois culture, they controlled the major resources and therefore had a major source of power. But by the time societies had reached the stages of feudalism or industrialization, patriarchy was the dominant form.

Immigrants from patriarchal societies—the Europeans, the Chinese, the Japanese, the western Africans—brought their ideas of patriarchy with them. The New England churches, which fought for religious freedom and individual liberty, also viciously persecuted women who dared to assert their rights. Women who questioned male power in the church or the community, were driven from their communities or burned at the stake as "witches."[12]

The frontier was the exception to the rule. On the frontier Euro-American women were in short supply, their labor was needed, and shared power in the family made more sense in the homestead. The territories of Wyoming and Utah gave women the vote in 1870. It was fifty years before the other states were forced to follow suit. Patricia Nelson Limerick suggests that not all the western women were the silent sacrificing mothers of *Little House on the Prairie*. The general shortage of females on the frontier created a demand for prostitutes, and large numbers of women went west for such employment.[13]

The relative freedom of Euro-American women in the West did not negate the brutal treatment meted out to Native American women. In the Indian Wars, the women were usually raped before they were mutilated and killed, and once the Native Americans were "pacified" the Native American woman continued to be treated as fair game for Euro-American men.[14]

The Catholic missionaries who attempted to convert Native Americans in the Southwest also brought the idea of witches with them. The indigenous cultures already had persons who controlled magical spirits, but who were *not* witches (i.e., evil). The missionaries altered that definition to make these women something to be feared. Irene Isabel Blea argues that the end result was similar to that of New England—it was a social-control mechanism over women:

> I contend that the roles of bruja and curandera were assigned to women who could not be socially controlled and that the bruja role was attributed to women who were defined as anti-social and as not fulfilling feminine roles according to cultural prescription.[15]

The full story of the torture and murder of women in New England or the burning and flogging of women by missionaries in the Southwest is not taught in our schools. If "witchcraft" is taught at all, it is presented as a problem of religion, not as the brutal result of patriarchy.

Under European patriarchy women were perceived as the property of men. If a woman earned wages, they belonged to her husband. Any property a woman brought to a marriage automatically became the man's. A woman had no right to refuse sexual intercourse or refuse to bear a man's child. If a woman did not perform her proper role, a man was expected to punish her. "The rule of thumb" refers to the general rule that a man should use a stick, no larger than the circumference of his thumb with which to beat his wife.

Women in the larger society were not allowed to speak in church and generally not allowed to speak in public. They were not allowed to pursue higher education. Women in the lower classes who worked for wage labor were expected to perform sexually for their male bosses and had no protection against sexual harassment and exploitation. Women in the upper classes were expected to live lives of useless luxury, as status symbols for their successful husbands.

Patriarchy also characterized the cultures of other immigrant groups. Some Asian immigrants came from cultures in which girls were held in such low worth that they might be killed at birth—female infanticide. The feet of Chinese girls were bound and stunted so that they could only hobble and never be able to run away from an abusive husband.

Many forced immigrants from Africa also came from patriarchal societies in which women were subjected to the brutal practice of genital mutilation. The conditions of slavery undermined the African American male's power over the female. Power was held by the slave owner who was free to force intercourse on any slave, or breed any woman, at his will. Today we would identify such forced intercourse as "rape," but by the rules of early America, it was perfectly legal and even expected.[16]

Not only is patriarchy the oldest form of oppression, exploitation, and degradation, but it is perhaps the most difficult to recognize and change. A recent movie about a battered wife was titled *Sleeping with the Enemy*. This suggests that patriarchy is the most intimate power relation ship. Women are taught to "love" the person whom the system allows to oppress them.[17]

Throughout this analysis we will see that ideas of male supremacy and the structure of patriarchy interact consistently and at all points with other forms of domination in our society. Go back to the example of the police officer and the speeder in the beginning of this chapter. The officer was referred to as a "he." The speeder was identified as a Chicano (the male adjective). If the example were changed, and we were to make the Police Officer a woman, or the speeder a woman, or both women, how would that change the power relationships in the example?

Slavery illustrates the way in which different forms of power domination mixed and interacted. The sexual assault on female slaves was a reflection of patriarchy but also a reflection of racism. Although patriarchy is the oldest form of social domination, the ideology of "race" is critical to understanding the particular character of stratification in American society.

ORIGINS OF THE IDEOLOGY OF RACE

This analysis argues that the various ideologies of domination in American society have interacted and mutually supported the ladder of stratification. Others have argued that particular ideologies are primary. For example, Andrew Hacker states that race is the most important division in American society: "So America must be seen as two separate nations. The separation is pervasive and penetrating. As a social and human division, it [race] surpasses all others—even gender—in intensity and subordination."[18]

Racism is the ideology that superiority is based on membership in a group that is physically and culturally distinct from other groups. Racism does not necessarily have to involve the particular characteristic of skin color, although that is the main form it has taken in America. There are numerous examples in history of race being defined on the basis of physical characteristics other than color. Hitler attacked Jews as an inferior race, although Germany's Jews were white. There are racial animosities between the Japanese and Koreans and yet both have similar skin color. Anthropologists have found cultures in which racism was defined by such characteristics as hair texture, fingernail shape, and height.

According to the ideology of racism, members of the superior race have the right to oppress, exploit, and degrade those who are "by nature" inferior to them.[19]

Unlike patriarchy, which was an ideology from European tradition, American racism was to a large extent a cultural creation of the new society. As mentioned in Chapter 2, the earliest forms of bondage in American society, indenture and slavery, were very similar. From a legal standpoint, it was hard to distinguish the status of the first African slaves from the European indentured servants.[20] Conditions changed and the two statuses—slavery and indenture—grew further apart. There were several reasons for the distinction between the two kinds of exploitation.

The first had to do with labor shortages and working conditions. As the economy of that region changed from individual yeoman farmer to large plantations, the need for workers increased.[21] European immigrants did not have the disease resistance to the hot, humid and disease-ridden plantations of the South, particularly of the Deep South. If an indentured white worker fled to the North to escape his servitude, it was difficult to find him or her because an indentured worker didn't look different than a free worker. A slave, on the other hand, was better adapted to the climate. If slaves tried to escape, they were marked by colorand could more easily be identified.

Second those in power feared possible alliances between poor whites, slaves, and Native Americans. There were numerous times in early colonial history when slaves, poor whites, and Native Americans threatened to band together and challenge existing power relationships.[22] If poor whites were given more privileges, it would then be in their interest to maintain slavery and support taking the land of the Native Americans.

As the wealth of the new nation grew, this bribe was increasingly given. The living standard of poor whites, especially food, was subsidized by the exploitation of the agricultural laborer in the South—the slave. The poor whites' future hope—a homestead of their own—was possible if the "Indian threat" was removed. Economic development made possible the promise of a better life to the poor of European origin—*if* they would agree that their lot lay with being a "white American" against the savage red man and the black slave. As Euro-Americans moved West they encountered a complex mixture of ethnicities. Racism was then directed not only against Native Americans but against African American settlers, Mexicans and Chinese.[23]

A third reason was the need to create cultural identity and national unity. The thirteen colonies had been founded by people of different European nationalities, different religions and vastly different cultural traditions. In Europe, Serbs had killed Croats, the English had enslaved the Irish, and the Swedes had conquered Norway. How would all these differences and historical hostilities melt together to create a single people? What did they all have in common? The answer, really, was quite simple. They were all "white." The African was "strange" and unfamiliar.[24] All Euro-Americans stood to benefit if the slavery of African people and the removal of Native Americans was successful.

Clearly, no group of people gives consent to being enslaved, having their land and food supply taken from them, or being harassed and mistreated. In other words, the power that Euro-Americans used against Africans, Mexicans, and Native Americans had to be brute, naked force. There is no way to disguise it.

Most Americans are well aware of the fact that the Native Americans fought back. But slaves are often pictured as passively "accepting their lot." This was certainly not historically correct. Not only did slaves unite in widescale rebellions, but everyday life on the plantation was marked by subversion, covert resistance, and guerrilla organization, as pointed out in Chapter 5.[25]

If the "winning of the West" is taught as a glorious adventure, the Native American, Chinese American, and Chicano or Chicana student sees the lesson as a lie. If the "winning of the West" is taught as the slaughter of men, women, and children who were defending their land and culture, the morality of White supremacy is challenged. *Maintaining American identity, as we know it, requires maintaining the ideology of racism.* This is one of the reasons why the interpretation of history, and how it is taught, has become such an important issue today. The struggle for power over curriculum in our schools is addressed in Chapter 15.

Most Americans did not understand the complex relationships that oppressed the Native Americans, Asian Americans, and Mexican Americans in the West.

Pulitzer prize-winning author Toni Morrison argues that race has functioned as a metaphor necessary to the "construction of Americaness." In the creation of our national identity, "American" has been defined as "white."[26] That's because *real* Americans are white. If, on the other hand, you are black, brown, red, or yellow, you are an AfricanAmerican, a HispanicAmerican, a NativeAmerican, or an Asian American. (Ironically, whites are not "white." They are peachy pink!)

Patterns of racism appear logical and it is tempting to assume that someone conspired and plotted to make racism as a national identity "happen." There were certainly individuals who were conscious, at any given time, of aspects of these processes. But this analysis is not asserting that the ruling class sat down somewhere sometime and decided to create racism to forge national unity. We *are* asserting that their desire to preserve their power and privilege led to certain decisions and actions that had these end results.

The slave plantations exhausted the soil of the Deep South, and planation owners looked to the West. The genocide of Native Americans opened the West to the lumber interests and the mining interests. Always, the view of the Europeans was expansion to new lands and the exploitation of those lands.[27] The earth was for taking.

THE IDEOLOGY OF SPECIESISM

European ideology saw human beings as having control over the earth. Euro-Americans built canals and dumped sewage into them, cut down timber and denuded mountains, spewed factory pollution into the air and said this was "progress." Unlike the Native Americans, whose religions required them to ask the permission of the gods to use Wind, Rain, Earth and Wildlife, the Europeans had no sense that the planet was a living thing that could be harmed and damaged.

The relationship between racism—seeing the foe as less human than you—and the degradation of land is clearly pointed out by Chiksika, elder brother of Tecumseh, in a letter to Tecumseh on 19 March, 1779:

> When a white man kills an Indian in a fair fight it is called honorable, but when an Indian kills a white man in a fair fight it is called murder. When a white army battles Indians and wins it is called a great victory, but if they lose it is called a massacre and bigger armies are raised. If the Indian flees before the advance of such armies, when he tries to return he finds that white men are living where he lived. If he tries to fight off such armies, he is killed and the land is taken anyway. When an Indian is killed it is a great loss which leave a gap in our people and a sorrow in our heart; when a white is killed, three or four others step up to take his place and there is no end to it. The white man seeks to conquer nature, to bend it to his will and to use it wastefully until it is all gone and then he simply moves on, leaving the waste behind him and looking for new places to take. The whole white race is a monster who is always hungry and what he eats is land.[28]

Modern science is now discovering what the Native Americans understood. Earth scientists are now using the concept of Gaia as the notion that natural feedback mechanisms involving life maintain the conditions that life requires automatically. Thus, despite volcanic eruptions, sunspot explosions, and massive meteors hitting earth, the planet survives and is hospitable to life. The question is that of human interference in those natural feedback mechanisms.[29]

Christianity taught "responsible stewardship" of natural resources *given to Man by God*. There was no sense that humans were only part of a web of life; that they had no right to destroy other species or the balances of nature in pursuit of ever higher standards of living. But to the Euro-Americans settlers, minerals, water, and wildlife were there only to be exploited by humans.

Speciesism is the ideology that justifies human domination of the earth. It asserts that humans are above the laws of nature. It defines the immediate needs of human society as more important than the needs of future generations. Speciesism claims humans have more value than other living things. Even today, most ideas of conservation and responsible use of resources reflect speciesism. One is merely trying to more intelligently exploit. For example, timbering large tracts of land, and then replanting with trees, still reflects the idea that the forests have no use except to serve the needs of humans.

Speciesism was given its main impetus by the Industrial Revolution. The application of science to the production of goods for market and profit created an outlook that has been called Utilitarian. The first question one asks is "How can this be used for *my* needs?" The push to maximize profits undermined any ideas about considering long range consequences. Science and technology were seen by the industrialists as ways to conquer and control nature and became a cornerstone of modern thinking. We often speak of "conquering" polio or "controlling" the weather, for example.

The destruction of the Native American culture removed any philosophical constraints that might have existed in American society, and industrialization was given free rein.[30] Slaughtering Native Americans and slaughtering buffalo were both necessary to secure the land for railroads, ranches, and mining. It is ironic that a generation of Americans who today deplore the destruction of the Amazon's rainforests have little understanding of the speciesism in their own cultural heritage.

The social costs of speciesism, like those of male supremacy and racism, are high. Today we are paying for the ideology of our parents, grandparents, and great-grandparents. We can no longer safely go out in the sun; we can no longer safely eat the fish we catch in many streams; and we cannot dispose of our sewage and sludge because it is contaminated. We have degraded the landscape with litter and advertising, destroyed the habitats of our songbirds, and scarred the mountains with strip mining. We have oppressed our generation and future generations by undermining the quality of life.[31] A society that justifies the domination of male over female, and whites over people of color, also provides an ideology to justify the domination of humans over the earth.[32]

Enormous wealth was created by the exploitation of our natural resources, but the profits from the mines, the railroads, the factories were not equally shared. Land taken from the Native Americans by force and products created by the labor of slaves and indentured servants enriched a few at the expense of the many. Justifications for the unequal distribution of the products and services of a society are the ideologies of class.

THE IDEOLOGY OF CLASS

Technology, environment, and historical background shape the form that classes take in different societies. In some cultures, control over valued resources is based on religious status; in some cultures control over resources is based on knowledge of magic and technology; and in some cultures it is based on birthrights. Class status may also be a combination of several of these factors. If a society allows individuals with particular talents or achievement to move upward into the higher classes, we characterize that society as having **social mobility**. If a society draws class lines that individuals are not allowed to cross, we can speak of a class system that has a **caste** within it. Slavery in the United States, when differentiated from indenture, was a caste.

Class systems, by definition, create inequality. Those in the upper classes control and use more of the valued resources of the society than those in the classes below them. When a few receive greater benefits than the many, some ideology is required to explain the inequality. Thousands of years ago, peasants asked, "Why should a King, surrounded by beautiful dancing girls, drink fine wine and eat roast pig, while I labor in the rice paddy from sunup to sundown and only have rice, one egg, and a turnip all day?[33] If I am convinced the king is necessary for my survival and if I believe his rule is a good thing for my community, I will labor. But I must be convinced!"

If the lower classes accept inequality as necessary, and even beneficial, the higher classes will have their consent—i.e. they will exercise power through authority. Class ideologies exist to explain and justify why those who have it, have it, and why those who don't, don't.

The Industrial Revolution, both in Europe and America, required an ideology that allowed entrepreneurs to accumulate capital. The economic system we call capitalism created a class of individuals (capitalists) who made a profit that was used to expand and innovate production. Without accumulation, investments into productive resources and innovative technologies were not possible. These "Captains of Industry" saw themselves as necessary for progress.[34] Without their efforts the gains in productivity and technology we associate with industrialization would not have occurred.

But if you were the person working fourteen hours a day, six days a week, in a polluted and dangerous workplace for starvation wages, you might ask, "Why do I get stuck with the dirty work? Why does the owner get to live in a nice house and I'm stuck in a filthy tenement? He eats meat, vegetables and potatoes every night and his children go to school. I eat rotten potatoes at night and my children have to work in the factory alongside me." Like the person working in the rice paddy for the king with the dancing girls earlier in the discussion, if you are going to give your consent to this social arrangement, you have to be convinced that it is right.

The economy in early America expanded rapidly, fueled by the rapid population growth, exploitation of the natural resources, cheap land, and the profitability of slavery.[35] A few ordinary people were able to "get rich quick." The idea that your own effort and hard work determined your class status was already part of European ideology called the Protestant Ethic; in the United States this idea of **individualism** became an important part of class ideology.

According to the ideology of individualism, if you remained poor, it was your own fault. What happened to people was determined by their own efforts, fate, or God, but certainly not by social forces like power and stratification. This ideology helped "explain" class stratification by suggesting that those who had accumulated great wealth had worked harder, or God felt they were more deserving. These beliefs were part of the ideological social control of class.

Sociologists call those characteristics over which we, as individuals, have no control **ascribed attributes** while those characteristics that we earn by our own efforts are called **achieved attributes**. The ideology of individualism claimed that social mobility in our society was based on each person's own effort—our class status was an **achieved status**. But this perspective denied the reality that a person of color, a poor person, a disabled person, or a woman could not equally compete because of **ascribed status**. In other words, persons were assigned positions on the ladder because of ascribed attributes and then were told that they held that status because they had failed to achieve!

Many people believe that American society is characterized by "open" mobility and that succeeding generations were able to better themselves. Historian Susan Boyle argues that it is difficult to prove assertions about mobility:

> Sociologists were the first to study the subject in depth. From the beginning they concentrated on methods and measurements but seldom analyzed mobility within a historical perspective. Thus they made unwarranted assumptions about the degree of opportunity available in past times. Historians were quick to point out the

> fallacy of comparing twentieth-century mobility rates with the alleged unlimited opportunity available during the nineteenth century or even before. Indeed, later research has tended to suggest few Americans experienced dramatic changes in socioeconomic status before 1900.[36]

For the purposes of understanding American ideology, however, what is important is that people *believed* it to be true.

For many Euro-Americans, however, the society did reward hard labor and frugality. Despite terrible working conditions many saved a small amount of money and were able to move west. When the government asked them to pay taxes for the wars to kill Native Americans, most were willing. The rich—owners of the railroads, mining companies, and land speculators—became richer, but the "little guy" also benefited. In the first half of the nineteenth century, the average income in the United States rose 102 percent. The average wages for workers increased somewhere between 40 and 65 percent. Although most of the wealth was going to the upper classes, the lower classes were still prospering.[37]

The slogans of that time, like "Go west young man," "Anyone can get rich who really tries," and "Manifest Destiny," all explained and rationalized the American class structure.[38] "American Democracy" was made synonymous with capitalism, industrialization, and the movement west. The benefits of the expanding U.S. economy were "trickling down" and that trickle was the reward to lower class white Americans for believing in the system and giving consent to the rule of the upper classes. It was difficult for the average American to see or understand the invisible classes that were helping to make his or her prosperity possible, as we discussed in Chapter 4.

The lower classes did not always buy into the justifications for the exploitation, oppression and degradation of early capitalism. The more brutal the conditions, the less the probability that any ideology could possibly justify it. Slaves who worked the plantations in the Deep South had an average length of life of seven years. Women were unable to bear children because the labor was so hard and living conditions so harsh. The true story of this kind of slavery has yet to be told. The TV series *Roots*, which defined slavery to most Americans, was set in the "Upper" South—those plantations that bred the slaves subsequently sold "down river." Although conditions on those plantations were also hard, life was better. The theme of being sold Down River running through the poignant songs and poetry of early black America has its basis in the slave consciousness that this was a drawn-out death sentence.

Class relationships under slavery could not be legitimated when individuals assigned to a caste knew there was no hope to improve their status.

There was no promise of opportunity or future reward. Thus, a large army of whip-yielding overseers, road patrols to catch runaways, and severe punishments for breaking any rules were required to maintain slavery.

Slavery was a capitalist relationship—a highly efficient exploitation of labor under existing plantation technology. The thirteen colonies could not have paid for the weapons and aid they received from France and other European nations during the American Revolution if they had not been able to sell cheap cotton, tobacco, and other products from the South. The very Revolution that set forth humankind's most articulate ideas of liberty was based on the most severe exploitation of human labor known up to that point in human history!

The discussion above has implied that ideology is not enough to control those who do not benefit from the power relationships. Those who have no hope within the system will not give their consent and ideological social control will not be sufficient. Thus, ideologies that keep people "in their place" are supported by an intricate system of rewards and punishments that sociologists identify as **sanctions**. While we are growing up we learn, often unconsciously, what happens to us if we break the rule and we learn what rewards we can expect if we are "good."

The ideas and beliefs that make up ideologies and our knowledge of society's rewards and punishments are all learned during our socialization. The next chapter examines in greater detail how we were socialized to accept our place on the social stratification ladder.

SUMMARY

Social stratification exists in our beliefs and ideas as well as in our social relationships. Individuals carry ideas about who belongs where on the ladder, and what they can expect in a social interaction.

Our ideas about social stratification are part of the ideologies we are taught. One of the most important of these is the ideology of equality and democracy. Early settlers embraced these beliefs because they wanted to escape the oppressive stratification of aristocratic Europe. At the same time, however, they placed slaves and Native Americans in a subordinate position to themselves—creating a particularly American ladder of stratification.

Immigrants also brought with them the ideology of male supremacy—beliefs that men were stronger, wiser, and more capable than women. Women were denied basic economic, political or social rights. This way of organizing society—patriarchy—was reflected in the witchcraft trials in New England and the persecution of witches in the Southwest. Native American and slave women were often raped and brutalized. When there was a shortage of women, however, as in the frontier, women were able to gain greater power and equality.

Poor immigrants, debtors and petty criminals were often brought to the New World as indentured labor; Africans were brought as slaves. In the beginning both groups were viciously oppressed and exploited. But the elite were frightened by the threat of Native Americans, African Americans, and poor Euro-Americans uniting against them. They changed laws and policies to make conditions of servitude for whites on the lower rungs less harsh. The explanation used was racism—the ideology that explains the power of one group over another as based on some "racial" characteristic. In the United States, that has most often been skin color. This ideology was also used to justify the killing of Native Americans and the dispossession of Mexican people in taking their land. Later on, racism was used against immigrants of color from China, Japan and other countries. Immigrants from Europe, however, were allowed to "melt" and become just plain Americans.

Taking the land also meant exploiting the land itself. European society believed the earth existed for the purpose of human use. This ideology that humans have the right to dominate and exploit the earth is speciesism. In contrast to other ideologies that give sanctity to animal life and forces of nature like the wind, water, and soil, speciesism sees only how those things can be used by humans. Speciesism fails to see that all parts of the ecosystem are equally valuable and necessary if a healthy life is to be maintained. Today we are suffering the results of three centuries of speciesism.

The exploitation of labor and the land created great wealth. In early America, this wealth was distributed unevenly. The Native Americans got none, the slaves got the rags on their backs and a bowl of grits, and the "Captains of Industry" gained unheard-of riches. The ideology that justified these class divisions was individualism. These beliefs said that those who sat high on the ladder deserved their place as individuals—they had worked hard, or "earned" it in some special way. If you were lower on the ladder, it was your own fault—not the fault of the system of social stratification.

Vocabulary

Legitimate Power. Social power granted by the consent of those below.

Ideological Social Control. Control over individuals by using their beliefs that it is good and right that they should be controlled.

Male Supremacy. The ideology that men are superior to women and should have power and control over women.

Patriarchy. A system of power in which control and access to resources is determined by one's gender; this is justified by the ideology of male supremacy.

Racism. The ideology that superiority is based on membership in a group that is physically and culturally distinct from other groups.
Speciesism. The ideology that justifies human domination of the earth.
Social Mobility. The movement of individuals or groups up or down the ladder of social stratification.
Caste. The assignment of a position lower on the ladder of social stratification that cannot be changed.
Individualism. The ideology that one's class position is only the result of that individual's behaviors or actions.
Ascribed Attribute. Something about an individual over which she or he has little control—skin color, gender, height, who your parents are, etc.
Achieved Attribute. Something about an individual that is the result of that individual's own actions—learning to play football, studying hard to get an A, etc.
Ascribed Status. A position an individual holds on the ladder of stratification over which she or he has little control—you are born poor, or a woman.
Achieved Status. A position an individual holds on the ladder of stratification due to actions or behaviors of the individual—you have earned a college degree and improved your class status.
Sanctions. The system of rewards and punishments used to make sure individuals obey the rules, and hold the beliefs, of the society.

Discussion Questions

1. Can you identify persons and groups that have legitimate power over you? Can you describe the ways in which ideological social control is used to convince you their power is legitimate? Would you agree that often that power is a positive power—for example, the power your parents had over you to raise you and protect you as you were growing up? Can you name persons or groups to whom you have given consent that may actually be exercising negative power over you? Why is that so much harder to recognize?

2. I argue that all the different ideologies of domination in American society interact, and that all are negative (i.e. cause social pain). Do you think that there is one that is more important, or is the "cause" of the others? Which of these negative ideologies most affects *your* life?

3. We rarely think of human domination over the earth as a form of social stratification. Why do I argue that it is? Do you agree? Can you describe a way of thinking about our use of food, land, water and air that is *not* the ideology of speciesism?

4. Is your position on the ladder of stratification largely determined by your ascribed or your achieved characteristics? Can you distinguish which is

which? Is it possible that some of your achieved statuses are originally based on your holding an ascribed status? Give an example.

Resources

Video: *Fried Green Tomatoes*

Although this movie focuses mainly on the ideological social control experienced by women, it also touches the ideologies of class and race. It is the story of a proper middle class white girl (Mary-Louise Parker) raised in the early part of the century who rejects what she is taught about being a woman. She also challenges that ideas of race (which gets her into trouble with the Ku Klux Klan) and helps out the poor. Her life is seen through the eyes of a modern woman (Kathy Bates) who is struggling to find her own identity. One can clearly see how the different ideologies of domination interact when viewing this movie. Rated PG-13. (*Note*: The book on which this movie is based, *Fried Green Tomatoes at the Whistlestop Cafe*, is even better than the movie!)

Books: Toni Morrison, *Beloved.*

This novel won Toni Morrison a Pulitzer Prize for literature. It is the powerful story of escaped slaves, and how the trauma of the slave experience follows them, even into freedom. I have found no other book that expresses so clearly the human pain and suffering of slavery as this.

Alice Walker, *Possessing the Secret of Joy.*

Alice Walker exposes the contradictions of gender and race by comparing their impact on both American and African woman in this insightful and beautifully written novel. Her characters transverse Africa, France, and America in their search for self and love. Throughout the story, Walker uses myths to show how we are affected by ideological social control. Otherwise, why would a woman voluntarily allow herself to undergo genital mutilation or do it to another woman?

NOTES

Complete citations are provided in the Bibliography.

1. Alice Walker 1992, 164.
2. Some sociologists have studied the perceptions of power in social interaction. See Thomas, Franks, and Calanico 1972, Weitz 1975, and Franks 1985, 1989.
3. Juzang 1993.
4. Rubenstien 1992, 319–24.

5. A detailed and scholarly examination of the roots of these ideologies can be found in Jean Delumeau 1990.

6. Grinde 1977; also Takaki 1993, 47–50.

7. For a more general discussion of the influence that Native Americans had on American culture see Weatherford 1991.

8. Takaki 1993, 24–50.

9. One exception is the movie *Dances of the Wolves* which shows how one EuroAmerican came to respect and understand Native American culture. The movie, however, focuses only on one individual's experience. And when the hero falls in love, it is with a Euro-American woman who had been a captive, not with a Native American woman. The historical fact is that large numbers of Euro-American male settlers did marry, or partner, with Native American women.

10. Grinde 1977, 24–25.

11. Shenkman 1988 32–33.

12. Hymowitz and Weisman 1978, 16–20.; also see Harris 1989.

13. Limerick 1987, 48–52.

14. Hymowitz and Weisman 1978, 181. Brownmiller 1975, 140–153) notes that rape committed by men of either group was seen as an attack upon the men of the other group.

15. Blea 1980, 181.

16. Although there has been extensive historical documentation of this reality, the best understanding of what this degradation meant to the women is gained in reading Morrison 1987. See White 1990, 22–33. Also see Hymowitz and Weisman 1978, 40–63.

17.There is a saying: "A man's greatest fear is that his woman will laugh at him; a woman's greatest fear is that her man will kill her."

18. Hacker 1992, 3.

19. See Takaki 1993 for an excellent discussion of the way racism as an ideology evolved in America; also Hacker 1992.

20. Takaki 1993, 51–76. Also Jernegan 1971.

21. Geschwender 1978, 116–128.

22. Zinn 1980, 53–58; also Takaki 1993, 51–76.

23. Limerick (1987) explores the way in which EuroAmericans settling the West used racist ideology to rationalize their settlements.

24. This "strangeness" was the basis on which the earliest settlers were able to construct their ideology of racism, according to Takaki 1993.

25. Rawick 1972, 95–121; Huggins 1990, 1978.

26. Morrison 1992, 47.

27. For a discussion of the relationship between environmental degradation and racism, see Bullard 1993.

28. Eckert 1992, iii.

29. Gibbon 1990, 43.

30. Mander (1991) does a well-written and powerful critique of the ideology of speciesism.

31. The full, and frightening, implications of the greenhouse effect are discussed by Gribbin 1990.

32. Obviously there is a different view that says we *can* rationally dominate the earth and that the concerns expressed in this text are "radical" and "overkill". Dixie Lee Ray's recent book *Environmental Overkill: Whatever Happened to Common Sense?* represents this line of thinking. The cover of this book carries an endorsement by Conservative commentator Rush Limbaugh!

33. Societies that reached the point of being kingdoms were almost always patriarchies. It is for this reason that royalty is by definition patriarchal (the king, then his first-born son, etc.) The famous queens of history exist only because the King was killed or left without a male heir.

34. Josephson (1934,1962) captures the mentality of America's early financiers and industrialists.

35. See McPherson (1988, 6–46) for a well written description of this rapid expansion.

36. Boyle 1989, 4.

37. McPherson 1988, 10.

38. The difference between the myth of the "frontier" and its reality is explored in Linmerick 1987.

7

STRATIFICATION AND SOCIALIZATION—GROWING UP ON THE LADDER

Then again, from below, in the great heavy stack,
Came a groan from that plain little turtle named Mack.
"Your Majesty, please...I don't like to complain,
But down here below, we are feeling great pain.
I know, up on top you are seeing great sights,
But down at the bottom we, too, should have rights.
We turtles can't stand it. Our shells will all crack!
Besides, we need food, We are Starving!" groaned Mack.

—Dr. Seuss, *Yertle the Turtle*

Chapter 6 discussed the origins of the major ideologies in American society related to power and stratification. We all learn these ideologies, and we all learn what could happen to us if we challenge them. This chapter looks at *how* these belief systems are learned and how we learn about the sanctions that accompany them.

We are all subject to social control. For example, you have probably recently bathed and used a deodorant. You don't want to "smell bad." Several companies make millions of dollars because we believe it is a bad thing to smell human and a good thing to smell like spice or daisies. Visitors from other countries have remarked that many Americans smell like drugstores. Why do we care so much about how we smell? The answer to that question is simple: we know what would happen to us if we had B.O. (body odor). We would be subject to snide jokes, we would be perceived as poor or ignorant, and pressure would be put on us—as one advertisement intones, "Why don't you try Dial?"

This illustrates how everyday social-control functions to make us behave in certain expected ways. The agreement that our natural body odor is offensive and that smelling like chemicals is agreeable, is arbitrary. Anyone who has spent time in a tropical country knows that in cultures with intense heat, everyone sweats, and *everyone* has what we call "B.O." I taught for a year at the University of Dar Es Salaam in Tanzania, close to the Equator. I can say from personal experience that I had B.O.! The smell of sweat should not be confused with cleanliness. The Tanzanians made the same distinctions that we do between someone who is dirty and someone who is clean.

This norm also functions to enforce social stratification. The children of the agricultural worker mentioned in Chapter 1 may not have had access to hot water or even clean running water. Soaps, shampoos, and deodorants are expensive and cannot be purchased with food stamps—they are nonfood items. When the kindergarten teacher kindly asks "How many of you had a bath today?" and a child doesn't raise his or her hand, that child is acutely embarrassed. The teacher is trying to give a lesson in hygiene, but in reality the child is being degraded. The child who "smells" is placed in a lower social status in that classroom.

We rarely recognize the extent to which such norms control our lives. Many of us can't imagine *not* taking a shower every morning, using breath-freshening toothpaste, washing our hair with perfumed shampoo, applying our deodorant, and putting on clothes that smell like spring because they have been washed in Tide.

Social control is necessary to ensure that individuals obey the rules. No society can exist unless human behavior is *ordered*. We must be able to predict in a general way what other people are going to do and they must be able to predict our behavior. None of us would want to live in a society that lacked social controls. If everyone could drive on just any side of the road, if there were no stop lights and no speed limits, we would not be able to drive.

We assume the rules that order driving are fair rules—everyone equally obeys and everyone equally benefits by having safer highways. Yet in an earlier discussion we analyzed a situation in which a police officer stopping a speeder is not only enforcing traffic laws but may also be enforcing rules of social stratification. If the son of a wealthy state legislator is stopped for reckless driving, will he receive the same treatment? We all know the answer to that question. Thus, social stratification affects *which* rules are applied to *whom* and *how*.

Many police officers *try* to enforce the rules fairly and it may be higher in the system where rules are unfairly administered. Police officers themselves are subject to the rewards and punishment of existing systems of power. Often they do things they would rather not do in order to keep their jobs, get a promotion, or just stay out of trouble.

In this study we are most interested in norms that distribute social power and maintain patterns of social stratification. Learning and accepting these norms begins when we are children. Rules could not exist without rewards and punishments—sociologists call these **sanctions**. By starting with the individual member of society we are beginning with a **microsociological** analysis. Later on we examine social control exercised by the larger social structures of society—a **macro sociological** analysis. It is important to remember that we can separate the two levels (micro and macro) in a discussion like this, but in the real world they are tightly linked.

SOCIALIZATION

Socialization refers to how we are taught to be members of our particular society. Socialization starts with the way we are raised. Parents usually teach the norms of social control as necessary and good. (It's a good thing to use deodorant, say "please", etc.) We will look at four different kinds of norms that we learn in our socialization: egalitarian norms, dominant group norms, arbitrary norms, and culturally imperative norms.

Egalitarian norms are the rules that allow us all to get along. They make society safer and more predictable without giving advantage to any particular group. If speeding laws were administered fairly, they would be an example of this type. Laws that protect the personal security of individuals are egalitarian norms; no one would want to live in a society where it was all right for someone to beat you up, rape you, or murder you. Courtesy norms that make life easier and simpler for everyone, like opening the door for someone whose arms are full of packages or waiting your turn in line, are also egalitarian norms.

In contrast, **dominant group norms** allow a dominant group to exploit, oppress and degrade others. These rules maintain the ladder of social stratification. Rules from our past, like those that forced African Americans to sit at the back of the bus, are obvious examples of dominant group norms. A current example of laws that are dominant group norms are the income tax laws that give tax loopholes to millionaires, who then pay little or no taxes.

Arbitrary norms are a result of cultural consensus to agree on social meanings. We don't know why we made red the color of stoplights, but once we all agreed, the rule works. Stoplights could be another color, but it would work only if we all agreed. Right now, the United States does not use the metric system of measurement even though it is more efficient scientifically. We don't because we have a cultural tradition of inches, feet, acres, and quarts. Of course, we have no idea whose foot was used for the original measure or why. But we have agreed on these measures for many years and we're all used to them. There is no "good reason" for these standards.

Many of our lifestyle customs are arbitrary norms. The agreement that men should not wear skirts is an arbitrary norm. Scotsmen wear kilts; in centuries past, men wore flowing robes. No one would be hurt if a man wore a skirt; it is simply that we have all agreed men should not. Traffic would not stop if men wore skirts, but traffic *would* stop if we simply allowed anyone to drive on any side of the road or to run red lights.

Arbitrary norms can also be used to maintain social stratification. In the example at the beginning of the chapter, it was pointed out that we agree not to smell like humans. When that agreement is translated into degradation and oppression of those who cannot afford deodorant, perfume, and expensive soaps, it becomes a means of putting others down. In the last section of the book we see how the ruling class uses differences in these arbitrary norms to divide us by pitting groups at the bottom against each other. People from cultures who have different arbitrary norms, or persons whose lifestyles have rejected certain arbitrary norms, are portrayed as dangerous to our "way of life."

A society has a certain amount of choice as to how it will be organized and what its rules will be. But there are limits to those choices. Rules related to the existence and survival of cultures are known as **cultural imperatives**. An imperative is something you *must* do, and so a cultural imperative is a rule a society must obey if it is to continue to exist.

For example, before the discovery of the atom bomb, societies could choose to resolve conflict through large-scale warfare. With nuclear weapons, it now becomes impossible to use major weapons to resolve disputes *if we want to survive as a human race.* Likewise, societies obey the rule against incest because close intermarriage among kin creates genetic weakness and can lead to a people dying out.

Cultural imperatives limit social stratification. If the gap between the very rich and powerful the very poor and powerless becomes too great, the tensions created will destroy that society. Many historians believe that is what happened to the Roman Empire. Thus, dominant group norms create privilege and benefits for some and hurt others. But eventually those norms could act against the cultural imperatives and destroy everyone, including the dominant group. We look at how dominant group norms in our current society violate cultural imperatives in Chapter 14.

With few exceptions, we are simply taught "the rules." Children rarely understand whet her the rule they are learning is for everyone's benefit (egalitarian), a rule that allows another group to exploit, oppress, or degrade (dominant group norm), a rule that could really be anything else as long as all agreed (arbitrary), or a rule necessary for survival (cultural imperative).

These rules are handed to us at birth. We are born into an existing culture and into a particular status. We are supposed to learn and obey the rules that apply to our status.

If we are born "American," we are taught both the ideologies of our society and the rules that go along with them. This is not to ignore the fact that a significant percentage of our population is *not* born American, but immigrated. Nevertheless, their children are expected to be socialized into the American culture and its ideology.

Obviously, any one of us is capable of challenging the rules—we do it all the time. Sometimes we get caught and sometimes we don't. When individuals, for their own personal reasons, act outside the norms, society perceives them as **deviant** and calls their behavior **deviance**. If that individual's deviance is a protest against a dominant group norm, we can identify it as **resistance**.[1]

All through American history, individuals have heroically resisted what they see or believe to be unjust dominant group norms. But individual behavior doesn't change the rules. In other words, if I refuse to pay my taxes because the rich don't pay their fair share, my action is unlikely to change the tax laws. But, when large groups of people decide to challenge the ideology that justifies certain rules it is possible to redefine the norms. Behavior that was called deviance can then become a new norm.

For example, if Rosa Parks had simply sat in the front of the bus in Montgomery, Alabama in 1955, she would have been arrested for her deviance. But because her resistance was part of a planned bus boycott to force a change in the rules, her behavior was an important part of the civil rights movement. We have already discussed how such social movements in American history challenged dominant ideologies and changed some of the dominant group norms into egalitarian norms. In this chapter, however, we are going to assume the dominant groups norms as given, and analyze how it is we come to learn them and often accept them as "good."

LABELS, STIGMAS, AND STEREOTYPES

Social stratification orders people and thus creates ranked groups. Those groups may be large categories, such as "people on welfare" or very specific categories, like "those people who live on Maynard Street." A **stereotype** exists when society describes a group with a set of characteristics and teaches that all members of that group have those characteristics.

Stereotypes are important social mechanisms for keeping groups in their place on the stratification ladder. They "explain" why that particular group belongs where they are. For example, the stereotype that African Americans are better athletes but not so smart is used to justify African American domination of some sports and the lack of representation of African Americans among the doctorates in the natural sciences and mathematics.

Such stereotypes can affect official behaviors and social policies. One example was the racist myth that blacks were predisposed to the addiction of cocaine and that this made their skin impervious to the impact of the .32 caliber bullet. As a result of such unfactual beliefs, police departments around the country adopted the .38 caliber weapon as the appropriate gun for blacks. Accompanying this myth was the belief that the so-called propensity to cocaine addiction stimulated black male sexuality, thus making white women vulnerable to black rape.[2]

Negative stereotypes explain to us why some group is lower, or inferior. Who wants to be known as a dumb jock, a slut, or an alcoholic? These types of terms are called **stigmas** because they make membership in the stereotyped group a social disgrace. We all work very hard to be respected, and no one wants to be stigmatized.

Stereotyped stigmas are punishments. If a young woman obeys the gender norms in her high school, she may be rewarded by being placed with the "popular" group and positively stereotyped. If, however, she sleeps with whomever she has a date, she may be punished with the stigma of "slut." Because men occupy the dominant status, if a young man sleeps with his dates, he is likely to be called a "stud," which for men is a positive label. The norms regulating sexual relations in our society are dominant group norms. Thus, the behavior (sleeping around) is the same, but the differential labels reflect the dominant status of men.

Not all stigmas reflect dominant group norms. Some stigmas enforce norms of equality. For example, the stigma of "racist" is used for those who have refused to accept the ideas of racial equality. Most of us who agree with the norms of racial equality see nothing wrong in calling someone who belongs to the Ku Klux Klan, or who discriminates against minorities, a racist. One hundred years ago, that label was not a stigma. But today it is used to enforce egalitarian norms.

In contrast, the stigma of the word "nigger" arose out of the slave status and the oppression of African Americans under slavery. It is more than a label; it also represents a historical status with a specific meaning in our culture. When the term nigger is used, we see it as a stigma because it reinforces dominant group norms that degraded minorities and gave higher prestige and privileges to Euro-Americans.

When I was growing up, I was not allowed to use the word nigger to refer to African Americans. But even though my parents were attempting to teach me egalitarian norms, my society was teaching me something else. For years I called the large dark Brazil nut a "Niggertoe" and my first learning of the nursery rhyme "Eeny Meeny Miney Moe" was followed by "Catch a Nigger by his toe. If he hollers, let him go. Eeny Meeny Miney Moe."[3]

Stigmas are used to place an individual in a group that is undesirable. If society accepts the stereotype, then we who want to be respected work hard to avoid behaviors that would makes us like the people in that stereotyped group!

A young girl may not want to be a cheerleader; she may want to play baseball. But she will be told being a cheerleader will make her popular (a positive label in her school) and being a baseball player will make her a tomboy (a stigma in her school). A boy may not want to play football; he may want to play flute in the band. But again, his peers will inform him that playing a flute is sissy. By the time he reaches high school he may be called a "band fag."

Thus, the behaviors appropriate to the status of female (to cheer the males) and appropriate to the status of male (to run around and knock down other males) are rewarded; the behaviors that challenge the dominant group norms are stigmatized. Euro-American girls who date African American boys are stigmatized as "nigger lovers"; rural white kids from poor homes are labeled "rednecks"; children who challenge their teachers are called "troublemakers."

To understand how children learn dominant group norms that degrade, oppress, and exploit, we have to understand the powerful role that stigmas and stereotypes play in socialization. Children lack both the life experience and the strong self-concepts to make judgments independent of the group around them. They must rely on their social environments for definitions of what is acceptable and moral.

Sociologists who study the process of labeling have shown that stigmas often lead to **self-fulfilling prophecies**. These are events that occur because they were socially predicted. The prophecy is confirmed because people alter their behavior to conform to the prediction. The child who is stigmatized gets the signals and responds as expected.

For example, "troublemakers" may be identified by teachers, who *expect* them to misbe have when they get into their class. Or a child who is perceived as "dumb" is told by test scores and adults' attitudes that she or he cannot perform. No one is surprised when the child then misbehaves or does not perform well. The child fits the stereotype and ceases to be a unique individual. The teacher does not ask if the behavior is a result of domestic violence in the home or whether the lack of performance is the result of a hearing loss or a learning disability.

Stereotypes, like labels and stigmas, exist in the social environment. They define a group's status relative to other groups. Almost all children in America are raised to believe that "Eskimos" live in igloos and rub noses and that all Mexican men wear sombreros and have handle-bar mustaches. These are example of ethnic stereotypes.

I have lived for twenty years in West Virginia—an area where an ethnic group, the descendants of the Celts, are subjected to exploitation and oppression by the large coal, timber and natural gas industries. The poverty of West Virginia (one of the poorest states in the nation) is rationalized by the hillbilly stereotype. What do most of you reading this know about West Virginia? You have been taught that they feud (the Hatfields and McCoys), make illegal liquor (moonshine) and marry their cousins (which makes them feeble minded). The hillbilly stereotype has been reinforced by the mass media through the comic strips *Lil' Abner* and *Snuffy Smith*, such television shows as *Beverly Hillbillies* and *Hee Haw,* and by the movie *The Beverly Hillbillies*.

Likewise, the vast majority of Americans do not know that the slaves of Haiti were the first people to carry out a successful revolt against modern slavery, or are we taught that Haitian soldiers fought on the side of the Patriots in the American Revolution. Instead, we are taught the stereotype that they are "boat people," have a high rate of AIDS, and are all poor.

There are labels, stigmas, and stereotypes for all the ideologies of domination we have been discussing—class, gender, race and speciesism. You might want to think back over your own socialization and analyze how stereotypes and stigmas acted as social controls on you. If you are a male, and your friends were making lewd remarks about a woman who was a friend, did you keep silent because you didn't want to be "square?" How many times have you made crass remarks about "dykes" and "fags" in order to prove that *you* were a "real" male? How many Euro-Americans have kept quiet when someone made a "Pollack" joke, a "nigger" joke, a "wetback" joke? How many of you really believe the stereotypes of welfare mothers as lazy women who have extra babies to make money?

These are general things that we all learn as we grow up. But our socialization also reflects the particular groups into which we are born. *We are taught how to think, and how to behave, in order to be kept on our particular place on the ladder.*

Every one of us is immediately placed somewhere on the ladder as soon as we are born, even before we are born. As soon as we are conceived the effects of our social status are felt. If a mother is uneducated and does not have proper nutrition or prenatal care, the growing fetus may be affected. If the mother lives in an area that is highly polluted or eats foods that are contaminated with unsafe preservatives, the fetus may be affected. If the mother is placed under unusual stress from home life or work, the fetus is affected. A March of Dimes study cites battering of women as the leading cause of birth defects and infant mortality.[4]

It is *not* true, then, that all babies are "born equal." A baby's physical condition—certain disabilities, diseases, and predispositions—may be the result of one's social status before birth.

Socialization occurs in different ways for people on different places on the ladder. We now look at the way we are taught, depending on where we stand within the power structure of America.

GENDER

A baby's sex is a physical thing. How society treats that physical attribute is how **gender** is created. The baby's gender immediately assigns the child to a status. A baby girl is wrapped in pink blankets, a bow is pinned on her bald head, and her cheeks are pinched while the relatives coo. A baby boy is wrapped in blue blankets, a little baseball hat is placed on his curly hair, and when he grabs the relatives' fingers, they say "What a strong boy he is!" Right from the beginning the rules of gender status—the social controls to ensure we behave as "men" or "women"—are laid down.

The norms that regulate "girls' colors" and "boys' colors" are arbitrary norms but are another example of how arbitrary norms can also be used as dominant group norms. A mother who wrapped her baby boy in pink would be accused of trying to turn him into a "sissy"!

Our gender self-concept is probably the most basic and fundamental idea of self we are taught. It is certainly the first one. Obviously, males and females *are* different, and it is not surprising that society should acknowledge those differences.[5] In American society, however, those differences are used as the basis for unequal power relationships and become part of the system of patriarchy that keeps women in a subordinate position.

Little boys are taught that it is OK for them to be "rough and tough" and little girls are taught to be "ladies." When little boys don't have to wash dishes but their sisters do; when teachers encourage boys to study math and girls to take keyboarding; when boys are encouraged to play team sports and girls are encouraged to be cheerleaders; and when dirty jokes are shared by dad, the sons, the male teachers and even the male principal—the lessons are being taught.

Little girls are given Barbie dolls with which to play. Barbie comes with a "Ken"; the female doll requires a male doll to be complete. There are no little boy toys that require a female toy to be complete! These lessons are reinforced by television, magazines, and music. The ultimate sanction—the punishment for refusing to play your gender role—is the stigma of homo, fag, fairy or dyke.

We continue to stigmatize people who have no control over their sexual orientation. They are not homosexuals or gay and lesbians—they are "sinners" and repulsive. We continue to reward women who have thin bodies and to stigmatize plumpness as a personal failure. The result is the punishment of a huge proportion of our society's population who are homosexual or tend to be heavy. By the time they are ten children in this culture learn the stigmas and the stereotypes associated with being a "fag" or "fat."

It is hard to estimate the terrible costs in mental illness associated with anorexia, bulimia, or denying homosexuality that individuals suffer in trying to avoid undesirable labels. Such negative labeling can have devastating personal consequences. A high proportion of teenage suicides, perhaps as many as half, can be traced to fears by gay and lesbian youth of being found out. The impact of homophobia in school and in education is discussed by Richard Friend in "Choices, Not Closets." He quotes a gay teenager:

> I'm 16 and I'm gay but I never felt comfortable in school. If they just had someone who knew, understood or even tried to understand it would have helped. The subject was never mentioned; nothing about homosexuality or gays. It seemed as if it was bad, wrong or against morals of everyday society. I thought " Do I have a disease? Is it a sickness? How did I catch it?" In time I realized it was O.K. for me to be gay but in school I had to be straight and played a straight role, I left school early every day because I was afraid of someone finding out. I wish someday the schools would have a program to help young people find the answers as to who they are and it's O.K. to be gay.[6]

Early on, boys learn that women exist to please them, cheer them on, and serve them. Women who do this are rewarded; women who do not are punished. Punishment may not be overt. For example, a teenage girl in high school may refuse to play the required games that are necessary to attract the boys (de-emphasize her own intelligence, laugh at stupid male jokes, etc.) Her punishment will be a lack of dates, which translates into lack of "popularity" in American high schools.

By the time we are adults, these dominant group norms and their sanctions are fully in place. The belief that men have the right to possess and use women is not limited to the home. The rate of rape and sexual assault in American society suggests that *any* woman is "fair game." Some social observers have argued that violence against women is increasing because as women break the rules of expected behavior, men feel that they must be "put back in line" or punished.[7]

The American Medical Association estimates that nearly a quarter of women in the United States will be abused by a partner at some point in their lives, and 30 percent of all women murdered will be murdered by husbands or boyfriends. The situation has become so serious that the AMA is recommending that doctors begin to question women patients routinely in order to detect battering and abuse. The definition of domestic violence used by the American Medical Association is "a pattern of coercion that can include repeated battering and injury, psychological abuse, sexual assault, progressive social isolation, deprivation and intimidation."

From this viewpoint, the "traditional" happy home of American society is one in which men have power and privilege and women exist to support and ensure that power and privilege. It is hardly surprising that studies show that husbands benefit more than wives from marriage, that marriage protects men from death more than it does women, and marriage gives men better psychological well-being.[8] Berk's study of the division of household labor between men and women who were both employed showed that women continue to do a disproportionate share of the housework. When asked if such a division was "fair," 94 percent of the men and 70 percent of the women reported that it was. In other words, many men and women *did not perceive* an in equity.[9]

It is important to understand the full implications of gender socialization for social stratification and power in the society as a whole. The very idea of who one is, as a male, is based on the notion that you are able to command, control, and be aggressive. In order to carry this out, there must be someone to command, control, and aggress on! The very idea of being female, on the other hand, is based on the idea of nurturing, pleasing, and taking care of someone stronger than you.

In other words, half of our society's population is raised to believe that one's personal identity is dependent upon having power OVER someone else. The other half of the population is raised to believe that one's personal identity requires "taking care of" (being subordinate to) someone else.

Many men support the movement for women's equality because they do not *want* to act out the dominant group norms; they would prefer a supportive and equal relationship with women. Men who are supportive of women are examples of individual resistance to dominant group norms. But no man can escape his place in a patriarchal social structure. Thus, men who defend women's rights and challenge their masculine gender roles risk being called "wimps," "henpecked," or "sissy."

Gender socialization supports patriarchal structures in all the institutions of our society, including government, the economy, education, and religion. Women have always constituted a group that was more exploited than men and whose work was less valued in terms of social prestige and status.

Women received the vote later than any other major group in our society and continue to be grossly underrepresented in our "democratic" government bodies. Women artists face far more difficulty in having their works displayed or performed, and women educators continue to be a small minority in the higher ranks of learning. The most prestigious fields of science continue to be largely closed to women.

Although both gender and race status are based on dominant group norms, there is an important difference between early childhood socialization based on gender and that based on race. Men and women live together; women are placed in the subordinate position within the home *as well as* in the larger society. There are fewer opportunities for women, as women, to gather and develop a response to their subordination. They are isolated within their oppression. If a woman also happens to be of color, her position is one of "double jeopardy."[10] Again, it is clear that the dimensions of power are not exclusive but intersect.[11]

RACE

What is the difference in socialization between a child born to Euro-American parents in a white community and a child born to African-American parents in an black community? By our ideals we would say, "They are both Americans with the same opportunities. They should be treated the same!" Most Euro-Americans have little realization of how skin color and ethnicity constantly affect one's daily life because, for them, that effect is not negative. Without realizing it or understanding it, they learn to accept the privileges that come from being white in our society.[12]

While Euro-American children learn the dominant group norms and ideology that benefit their group, children of color are supposed to learn the dominant group norms and ideology that oppress them! We can immediately see how dominant group norms operate in a situation of a "mixed marriage"—the child of one white and one black parent is assigned membership into the lower-status group. She or he is "black."

Parents of minority children, therefore, must raise their children to live in a society where they are stereotyped and stigmatized by an ideology and its dominant group norms.[13] They must prepare children to deal with insults, threats, and discrimination. They must teach their children that there are certain stores, restaurants, and neighborhoods they cannot enter without problems.[14] They must give them coping mechanisms to respond to a teacher, principal, or police officer who is racist.[15] They must explain why commercials show almost all Euro-Americans, and the few African Americans,

Latinos, or Asian Americans they do see are very light skinned and have European-like features. They have to answer the early questions of "Why are all the presidents white?"

We know that small children don't see color as particularly important. Their games are governed by egalitarian norms. If you watch kids from different backgrounds play, you can see that the most important things are personal characteristics—who throws the ball best? who runs fastest? who can sing? Why should a different shade of skin be any more important than the difference between blondes and brunettes, tall and short, or having to wear glasses and not having to wear glasses? In other words, ranking by race has to be taught. It is socially transmitted knowledge that comes from the ideology of our culture because it maintains social stratification.[16]

A group in society may be said to constitute a **subculture** when their system of beliefs, norms, and behaviors distinctly vary from the larger culture. Subcultures are similar to the larger culture in general ways but possess specific cultural characteristics that also set them apart. Minority communities develop their own subcultures as both a defense against the degradation faced in the larger society *and* as a means for creating positive responses and reinforcements for their members.

The existence of a "black subculture" means that an alternative identity and socialization process can occur.[17] Nonetheless, the minority community remains a part of the larger culture. Jones makes this point clearly when she states: "in their commitment to formal education, to family, and to hard work, African Americans have adhered to values shared by other Americans regardless of race, class or regional identification."[18]

The African American janitor who quietly does his work during the day, accepting his degradation by the businessmen who treat him like a "boy" becomes something very different at nights and on weekends.[19] He becomes an aggressive and creative deacon of his church. He helps plan youth activities, leads services, and helps raise money. He is respected and valued in his community. Those white businessmen who just see him as "Joe" would not recognize him in his own milieu.

But Joe's African American church does not allow women to become deacons. Joe's degradation as a racial minority in the larger society does *not* automatically mean that he understands patriarchy and the oppression of women. Joe is also socialized by the culture as a male. Indeed, if the larger society oppresses and degrades him, it may be even more necessary for Joe to act "macho" within his own community in order to "keep his self-respect." Likewise, Joe may be prejudiced against Vietnamese "gooks" or "dirty Mexicans." In other words, the general social dynamic by which members of our culture are socialized to perceive *their* status as being dependent upon putting *others* down, continues to operate.

Minority children can "act black" or "be Mexican" at home but also learn to "act white" or "Anglo" when they have to. African American children who embrace white behaviors may be called "Oreos" or "Uncle Toms" at home in their own subculture, but will be rewarded in school and in the larger society for their "proper" behavior.

Euro-Americans, on the other hand, learn only to be white. If a Euro-American youth tries to act "black" she or he is stigmatized as a "wannabee," or "nigger lover." Most sociologists who study race relations focus on the minority community. Very few social scientists have seriously discussed or analyzed how Euro-American children learn to be "white."

When Crayola crayons created a "flesh" colored crayon of a pinkish hue, they were really telling children that it is *white* people who have flesh! (Band-Aids and "nude" stockings continue to do this.) If you are white, this country and culture belong to *you*. You are not part of the "others" who are trying to change and redefine things. When we discuss what is "normal" in American society—the normal child, the normal family, normal behavior—we are usually saying "white."

Unlike racial minorities, who understand how racism blocks their opportunities, poor Euro-Americans cannot blame their skin color. If the society is open to anyone who is white (since it is *thei*r country), then the failures of poor whites are the most serious of all. Even before the Civil War, well-to-do southerners had labeled poor southern whites as "white trash," "wool hats," "sandhillers," "claybeaters," "crackers," and "clodhoppers."[20] Many poor Euro-Americans do not understand the social controls of *class* that keep them at the bottom of the social structure because failure in our society is so closely linked to color.[21]

CLASS

Just as the "normal" family in America is white, so the normal family owns a three-bedroom house, two cars, a dog, a dishwasher, two televisions, a nice yard, and has money in the bank. Children who grow up lacking these things are often degraded. For some reason, they learn, their parents have not been "successful." The ideology of class in America teaches children that anyone can make it. So if you don't, it's your own fault or something is wrong with you. Conversely, if you are born into wealth, it is because you deserve it or you are better than most people.

Every child is given a class status at birth. A child's caretakers (parents, adopted parents, relatives, or foster parents) will be able to provide a certain level of resources to the child. These resources are not just money. They include the formal and informal education parents pass on to children; they include learned coping mechanisms; they include the physical environment.

If the family is wealthy, the child may be cared for by a nanny who will do all the real work (changing diapers, burping) while the parents concentrate on other parts of childrearing. But a single mother who works three part-time minimum-wage jobs and takes long bus rides to work may face long periods of time in which she has no time or energy for her child. If her child gets an ear infection and she has no health insurance, the child may end up with a hearing loss. Undetected, this may result in the kindergarten teacher deciding the child is "slow" (a stigma with devastating consequences) and placing the child in special education (which are stereotyped and called "speds").

In other words, access to resources lays the basis for a child's future opportunities. In the case of the wealthy family, the nanny may have been hired because she speaks German or French. By the time the child is five or six, she or he can speak two languages. The child will be given private music lessons if she or he shows talent. Private tutors will be hired if the child has difficulty with reading and a private school that will specifically reflect the child's needs will be chosen. High school for the child of a wealthy family will be an expensive boarding school, where the young adult is prepared to assume the role of his or her class.[22]

A child is taught the beliefs and behaviors necessary to act correctly in a certain class status. Just as boys learn to play with trucks, and African Americans learn to rap, so a child of wage-working parents is socialized to that class status. The "work ethic" and "learning to take orders" are important aspects of working-class socialization. When parents begin a lecture by saying, "If you want to get anywhere in life, you ought to" they are usually talking about norms related to class status.

Children in low income families learn very different beliefs and behaviors about money and consumption than do children in high income families. The struggle to "make ends meet" puts greater stress on marriages. Komarovsky's study in 1967 of working class families showed that one-third of the marriages were perceived as unhappy. She argued that there were class-linked factors that helped explain marital happiness. In her preface to the second edition Komarovsky points out that subsequent research that did examine working class families had borne out her conclusions.[23]

Children in a family with secure employment never have to learn to deal with the insecurities and stresses that children learn in a home where parents are frequently unemployed. Children raised in homes where support is derived from a support check (welfare, social security, etc.) learn the behaviors and beliefs necessary to survive under those conditions. Since the dominant group norms do *not* operate in their benefit, they may learn behavior that allows them to circumvent the rules.

Lack of material resources and worries about economic survival create stresses that are sometimes acted out in the family.[24] Children often bear the brunt of their parents' worries and concerns. At the same time, they are learning that these are the coping mechanisms for stress and may, in turn, act out the same behaviors when they become parents. Such stresses cut across class lines. A wealthy father, fearful of not being promoted to an executive position, may be as likely to lash out at his child as a poor father who has just lost his job. By failing to see the economic stresses behind child abuse and neglect, our society focuses on the symptoms, not the cause.

It is very difficult for someone who has always had a good job and enough money to understand what it is like to live on extremely limited resources. One hears upper-middle-class persons saying things like "I just can't understand why those people don't keep themselves cleaner" without understanding that a poor person may not have a washing machine and dryer, bus fare to the laundromat, or a closet full of clothes into which to change. In many cases in our society, the social distance between the well-to-do and the poor are as great as the distance between whites and people of color.

Just as minority groups developed social structures to cope with the oppression of their status, so have lower-class Americans learned various survival mechanisms. The key protection for those with minimal resources is the family. By sharing, cooperating, and pooling resources, families are able to provide support that individuals alone cannot provide. The fear about the "break up of the family" that is so often expressed in today's society is an expression of this reality.

Individuals in the upper classes, on the other hand, do not need the extended family as an economic backup. The family, in the upper class, is not a survival mechanism, but a networking mechanism that makes connections to help further careers, consolidate money, and assure one's social status. (We discuss networking in greater detail in Chapter 9.) Children in the different classes, then, learn very different meanings for the importance of family.

ENVIRONMENT

A child is born into a physical, as well as social, environment. Will a child be raised in a crowded building owned by some big real estate firm downtown that refuses to fix toilets or repair broken windows? Will she or he have to share a bedroom with several brothers and sisters? Will this child play on the street because there are no safe parks nearby? Will the air stink and the sewers overflow? Will everything in this child's experience be run-down, dirty, and owned by someone who doesn't care? This child will learn that she or he has no control over her or his environment and that needs for space, cleanliness, and beauty are irrelevant. The rules that govern his or her physical space are dominant group norms that do not benefit this child.

Children who live in "nice" neighborhoods also learn rules related to the environment. It is "progress" when lovely old trees are cut down to clear space for another 7-11 or Speedy-Mart, with plastic flags and black-topped parking lots. Toxic chemicals on the grass make your lawn look better than your neighbor's. You can build your *own* pool because the lake or the ocean is now too polluted to swim in. If Mom overeats, she can make chemical milkshakes for breakfast to lose weight fast. In other words, the dominant group norms of speciesism sets up the expectation that environment can be "managed" to serve our own ends.

Children learn early that the world around them is something to be used and exploited in the interest of those in power. The decisions to build super-highways through a neighborhood or wetland, or strip the mountain in order to mine coal, are all part of that process. Eating off styrofoam is OK as long as you put it in a trash can and don't litter; discharging chemical emissions that foul the air and cause cancer is OK as long as jobs are provided.

The same lessons that children are taught regarding the earth can be applied to their bodies. Diet pills, sleeping pills, laxatives, and antacids are a manipulation of the natural rules that govern our bodies. Television tells children that all these drugs are normal. This is the *real* "drug edu cation" in America. Likewise, caffeine, alcohol or tobacco can make life nicer, regardless of what they do to your liver, lungs, or brain. It's not a very big step from this to drugs like cocaine and heroin.

Children are taught that comfort and our standard of living requires the exploitation and degradation of the earth. Those who fight for the environment are stigmatized as "ecology freaks" and "tree huggers." Respect for one's physical self and one's physical surroundings is not part of the ideology of speciesism.

A class society makes ownership of property a high value. Children are taught that they must own more clothes and gold jewelry, have the latest video games, and drive the fastest car. The dominant group norms that support speciesism are consumption and waste.

REWARDS AND PUNISHMENTS

The discussion above has emphasized the major ways in which individuals in our society, especially children, are taught to see the world in terms of ranking. They are supposed to learn the rules of society, including the dominant group norms often used to keep them down. Why should we obey rules that hurt us? What are our rewards for accepting degradation, oppression,or exploitation? There are very few. One cannot say to the child of poverty, "If you don't study hard, you won't get to Harvard" when this child knows that he is not even expected to finish high school! Thus, the lower one goes on the ladder, the greater the use of coercion, or force, as the punishment.

The next chapter examines how violence and coercion are used to keep the ladder in place.

SUMMARY

The different ideologies that encourage or discourage social stratification are taught and learned in a variety of ways. Our socialization into society includes learning these ideologies and the sanctions used for rewards or punishment. Our acceptance of these ideologies is based on our following the social rules, or norms, of social stratification.

There are different types of norms. The egalitarian norms are used to promote positive social power. The dominant group norms are used to promote negative social power. The arbitrary norms can be used either way. Cultural imperatives, however, are social rules that a society is required, over the long run, to obey if it is to survive.

When individuals are ranked, those on the groups on the lower rungs are often subject to stereotypes, labels, and stigmas. These mechanisms are particularly effective for teaching children "their place."

The experience of learning these rules and ideologies differs from group to group. Gender role behavior is the first ranked status that individuals learn. From the time the baby is expected, social reactions differ between "Is it going to be a boy?" to "Is it going to be a girl?" Gender is used in another way to create ranked difference. Those who are heterosexual are assumed to be better (more "normal") than those who have a different sexual orientation.

Many individuals first learn domination in a family that is patriarchal. The widespread incidence of domestic violence that cuts across ethnic and class groups suggests that our society teaches that violence is an acceptable way to resolve differences and that those in power may use violence when challenged.

Another early socialization around ranking occurs with one's racial identity. Minority subcultures must teach the individual coping and response skills to deal with the discrimination and prejudice she or he is likely to encounter. Euro-Americans do not have to be taught these skills. Instead, they are taught to accept as natural the position of privilege they occupy in the social structure.

Class also affects our socialization. Families are deeply impacted by the extent to which they can access the resources of the society. Lower class families develop coping mechanisms and teach the specific skills that are necessary for survival on the bottom rungs of the economic ladder. Likewise, upper-class families take for granted their access to resources and the power that it gives them.

We learn how to relate to our physical environment, as well. Our culture teaches us that nature is controllable, and that humans can dominate it. Rather than learn rules of natural order in diet, exercise, and care of the environment, we learn that we can do damage and then fix it by taking pills, drugs, or a "clean up."

Vocabulary

Microsociological Analysis. Studying individual behaviors and beliefs in relationship to the larger society; looking at how individuals have an impact on the social structure.

Macrosociological Analysis. Studying the ways in which society is organized and the social forces over which individuals have little or no control; looking at how the social structure as an impact on the individual.

Socialization. How we are taught to be members of our particular society.

Egalitarian Norms. Rules that allow all individuals to participate equally in society without giving advantage to any particular groups.

Dominant Group Norms. Rules that allow a dominant group to exploit, oppress, and degrade others.

Arbitrary Norms. Traditional rules that are the result of cultural consensus. May be used as an egalitarian norm (it's to everyone's benefit that we agree to stop at a red light) or may be used as a dominant group norm (only those with adequate incomes can afford the perfumes and after-shaves that make us smell "acceptable").

Cultural Imperatives. Broad general norms that a society must obey if it is to survive over the long run.

Deviant. An individual who acts in violation of the social norms.

Deviance. Those acts that break the social norms and are punished by social sanctions.

Gender. The social meanings that society assigns to persons of different sex.

Resistance. An act by an individual against a dominant group norms that is oppressing, exploiting, or degrading them.

Stereotype. A description of a group's characteristics that assumes all members of the group will share those characteristics.

Stigma. A label applied to an individual to punish them for breaking social norms.

Self-fulfilling Prophecy. Individual actions and behaviors that occur because they have been predicted for that individual, the individual believes the prediction, and acts to make it become true.

Subculture. A group that is part of the larger society but has a system of beliefs, norms and behavior that distinctly vary from the larger culture.

Discussion Questions

1. What things can you identify in *your* upbringing that prepared you for your gender status? your racial status? your class status? your status in the environment? How aware were you of this preparation? how accepting? Why?

2. Some of my male students have said that I was "too hard on men" in this book. They argued that a new generation of males is being socialized into more egalitarian norms. Do you agree or disagree? If this is true, why does it appear that the rate of domestic violence in America is increasing, not decreasing?

3. African Americans, Latinos, and other minorities of color are very conscious of their physical appearance. Why is it that very few Euro-Americans are conscious of being white?

4. To what extent are you subjected to dominant group norms? Can you describe times that you have broken those norms as a form of resistance? At the time, did you understand the source of your resistance? Why or why not?

Resources

Videos: *The Long Walk Home.*

A sensitive portrayal of how southern whites are socialized into racial prejudice and the story of one woman's struggle to overcome her prejudice. Sissy Spacek plays Miriam, an upper-middle-class housewife who struggles to deal with her maid's (Whoopi Goldberg) decision to participate in the Montgomery bus boycott. The movie touches on all the elements of stratification: the patriarchal husband that tries to control his wife; the privileges of the middle upper class while the working class tries to make ends meet; and the power of the real estate developer to build wherever he wants. Rated PG.

Mr. and Mrs. Bridge.

This movie portrays patriarchy in the upper class. Paul Newman is the businessman husband who cannot understand why his wife (Joanne Woodward) is desperately unhappy. An excellent view of the failure of communication that arises out of gender socialization. Rated PG-13.

Philadelphia

Tom Hanks won an Academy Award for his role as the gay lawyer who develops AIDS. Afraid of the stigma, he tries to hide the disease and his sexual orientation from his conservative partners. When he is fired, he files a lawsuit and hires Denzel Washington to represent him. Washington has his own prejudices, and this is as much a movie about how a straight African American male learns to overcome his stereotypes of gays as it is about a brave and dying individual who must face society's condemnation.

Note the scene in the movie where Hanks dances with his partner, Washington watches, and the opera music is about love. This is the critical point where Washington realizes that the issue is love and not just sex.

NOTES

Complete citations are provided in the Bibliography.

1. Collins (1990) made the concept of resistance a key element in her analysis of black feminism, and I have drawn from her perceptions.
2. Musto 1988.
3. For a discussion of the important role played by language, see "Racist Stereotyping in the English Language," in Anderson and Collins 1992, 317–29.
4. Meir and Zoeller 1995, 60.
5. Hubbard, a feminist biologist, analyzes the social construction of sexuality in her (1990, 130–40) study and raises some startling questions!
6. Harold, a personal communication, 27 July 1985, quoted in Friend 1993.
7. See Faludi 1991. Also, Hall 1992.
8. Gove, Style, and Hughes 1990; Ross, Mirowski and Goldstein and Messeri 1989; Litwack and Messeri 1989.
9. Berk 1985, 192–93.
10. Amott and Matthaei 1991.
11. The clearest exposition of this intersection is that in Collins 1990.
12. McIntosh 1992.
13. Boykin and Toms 1985; Peters 1985; Harrison 1985.
14. Edelman 1985.
15. Bruce Wright (1987) who served as a judge in New York City's Criminal Court, Civil Court, and eventually the New York State Supreme Court poignantly describes how he learned to cope with being "black."
16. Cohen (1993, 289–308) analyzes the way in which African-American youth learn to be "black."
17. See Stack's (1975) excellent study of "The Flats."
18. Jones 1992, ix.
19. This is an actual characterization of one of my neighbors, although the name is not his.
20. Ibid., 54.
21. One of the best studies of the intersection of class and race in America is by the historian Jacqueline Jones (1992). Her comparison of the statuses occupied by poor whites and blacks during the period of Jim Crow and the subsequent migrations of the poor to the industrial North is excellent.

22. Cookson and Persell 1985.

23. Komarovsky 1987, vii–x.

24. Rubin (1976) remains one of the better studies of this interaction between economic stress and family life.

8

KEEPING THE BOTTOM RUNGS IN PLACE—DIRECT SOCIAL CONTROL

"The Elders sit beneath the tree, and argue til they all agree."

—East African Saying

"It is the function of police to exercise force, or to threaten it, in execution of the state's purpose, internally and under normal conditions. It is the function of armed forces to exercise force, or the threat of it, externally in normal times and internally only in times that are abnormal . . . The degree of force which the state is prepared to apply in the execution of its purpose . . . is as much as the government of the day considers it necessary or expedient to use to avoid a breakdown in its function and a surrender of its responsibilities."

—General Sir John Hackett[1]

The two previous chapters looked at how we learn the ideas and beliefs that glue us into our places. We called this ideological social control because it uses the individual's own mind to regulate social behavior. Thus, if women are socialized to accept their degradation, they "willingly" model for magazines in which they are judged by the shape of their buttocks and breasts and not by their capabilities as full human beings. Women are not "forced" to become nude models for men's magazines.

This chapter focuess on **direct social control**—coercive and sometimes violent sanctions used when individuals do not accept the ideologies and norms of society. All of us would prefer to not use force and violence. At the same time we would agree that sometimes it is necessary. But we often confuse two very different types of direct social control. The first is that necessary to enforce egalitarian norms; the second is that necessary to enforce dominant group norms.

No anthropologist has discovered a society where everyone obeys every rule. Indeed, one of the more interesting parts of cultural anthropology is the study of how different societies handle the problem of deviance. Deviance occurs when individuals violate the expectations of their society. In order for society to be predictable, everyone is supposed to act as expected. Thus, social order requires protecting the group against the individual deviant. When an individual breaks an egalitarian norm, he or she equally threatens order for everyone in the society, whereas obeying the rule benefits everyone in the society. We can use the example of drunk driving. Anyone—a family including small children—can be killed by people who break the rule against drunk driving.

Societies in which most norms are egalitarian norms are very different than societies in which most norms are dominant group norms. This difference is reflected in the two quotes at the beginning of this chapter. In a society marked by great inequalities, such as the United States, dominant group norms often supersede egalitarian norms. Because individuals resist dominant group norms, the society must commit enormous resources to the enforcement of these norms.

Business Week magazine calculated the total cost of crime in the United States as $425 billion a year in 1993.[2] Their breakdown of the costs includes:	
Spending on police, courts, and prisons	$90 billion
Spending on alarms, private guards, and security systems	$65 billion
Urban decay with costs of lost jobs and fleeing residents	$50 billion
Value of stolen goods	$45 billion
Medical costs of treating crime victims	$5 billion
Economic value of lost and broken lives due to crime	$170 billion
Annual Cost of Crime in America	$425 billion

It costs $30,000 annually to place a young person in a juvenile offender facility. For that amount, the young person could be given a high-quality college education! Imprisoning a twentyfive-year-old for life costs a total of $600,000 to $1 million.

Theft—stealing the property of another—should be an egalitarian norm equally applied to all. In a stratified society, however, theft is defined by a "double standard." For example, under slavery a slave who stole a pumpkin or a chicken from the master might be brutally beaten. But the master was allowed to take the labor of the slave without any payment and it was never called theft. The taking of land from the Native Americans was not called theft, it was called "westward expansion." Exploitative relationships that benefit the dominant group are not *seen* as theft; they are redefined to be legitimate.

A contemporary example of this same discrepancy is found in the act of "looting." During the Los Angeles rebellion in the spring of 1992, there was widespread looting. Looting is defined as theft. The looters, however, did not necessarily see their activity as wrong. The stores they looted were often targeted because they were the most oppressive and exploitative merchants. People who cannot afford cars are unable to take advantage of competitive shopping. They must buy groceries and other necessities from local stores. The result is that these stores can charge much more than stores in the suburbs for goods of lesser quality. Stores owned by merchants who treated customers fairly and who had invested back into the community were often not looted.

This example is important because it illustrates the role of direct social control. Most of us cannot imagine looting. If you are from the middle class, and all your life you have been rewarded for your hard work with a "good life," you give your consent to the system. You do not feel that anyone has exploited you or taken unjustly from you. If you were in an area of rebellion, you would not join in the looting. Society's ideological social control has taught you it is wrong, and you have no reason to question those teachings.

But suppose all your life you had lived in a neighborhood where no matter how hard people worked they never were able to get ahead; where there was not enough money for medical care and education; where everything cost much more; and where the garbage was picked up only every two weeks instead of every week, like other neighborhoods. You might feel differently about the rules. You would obey the rules because you didn't want to get caught, not because you believed the rules were right. The direct social control of police patrols and the chance of prison might prevent you from stealing. At the point you knew you could get away with it, you would take back from those who had, over the years, exploited you.

This is not to suggest that looting is the way to solve the inequalities that exist in the inner cities. The point is that without a social movement that organizes people to make demands on the system for greater equality, individuals *will* attack the system in less constructive ways. And the elite are less threatened by looting and crime than by large-scale organized resistance.

Even well-to-do educated African Americans are able to understand the dilemma of looting because they, too, face the effects of racism. Joseph N. Boyce, a senior editor of the *Wall Street Journal*, describes the hidden costs of racism that he has personally experienced as "the black tax." In an editorial entitled "L.A. Riots and the 'Black Tax'" Mr. Boyce points out:

> The black tax was also a source of the L.A. rage. Korean merchants were central targets for the rioters. Growing racial animosity has been offered as an explanation. But the hostility of many of the blacks (and Hispanics) participating in that kind of unacceptable carnage was due more to economic reasons than racism.
>
> The inner-city riots of the 1960s and early 1970s resulted in the pillaging of many white-owned businesses in the ghetto. Like today's Koreans, those whites served a community where crime rates were high and amenities like chain supermarkets, department stores and bank branches were virtually absent. For some, it was a change to exploit people by overcharging. Dollars spent by poverty-stricken customers were seldom recirculated in the community. Folks who couldn't afford to travel to cheaper venues paid the black tax.
>
> The answer is not to force out Koreans—they have a right to be there. Blacks analyzing Los Angeles argue for direct infusions to black-owned business in cities. They're on the right track. But that's not likely to work of black entrepreneurs continue to be deprived of financing, insurance and other support. A level playing field is the best way to ensure that L.A. and other cities never again experience events such as those of recent days.[3]

The unemployed teenager who has been degraded throughout school and dropped out has a lot of anger and bad feelings inside. If she or he steals, does drugs, or gets in fights, we label these behaviors as wrong. These behaviors *do* threaten the order and stability of our ordered society. But it is a society that is ordered in such a way to keep that teenager on the bottom. In other words, the order is not benefiting that teenager. It is unlikely that the teenager thinks about or understands why she or he is behaving badly. *But the deviance that results from resisting dominant group norms is a predictable response, even if it is not understood by the individual involved.*

Most people believe that deviance is the fault of the individual and that punishing the individual is the way to "cure" the problem. William Ryan called this process "blaming the victim." The ideology of individualism teaches us to punish those who resist oppression, degradation, or exploitation, rather than change the conditions that gave rise to the resistance.

Sometimes we hear people say "We will not lower the teenage pregnancy rate until we provide better opportunities for teenage women and stop teaching them that their bodies and sex is what they have to offer", or "We won't get rid of drugs until everybody has a decent job." Those kinds of statements *do* reflect an understanding that if the *rewards* of the society were more equally distributed, then the deviance *against* the society would decrease.

Unless there is a social movement that can channel and organize that resistance, it is expressed individually and often destructively, as in looting. Crime is not the only way in which individuals reject their exploitation, degradation or oppression. Suicide, mental illness or just plain "giving up" are other ways in which individuals act out their resistance to inequality.

It is easier to understand why someone who is poor or directly oppressed may want to "escape" the reality of existence through alcohol, drugs, or mental illness. But it is also true that individuals higher up on the ladder may also want to escape the pressures that their status places on them. Judges who must punish but have no power to prevent the social pain they see; businessmen who must lay off trusted long-time workers; men who are pressured to act tough and "macho"—are all examples of those in dominant power positions who also feel the stresses of inequality.

Chapter 1 used the example of how high-power voltage may "seep" into our environment and have effects that are difficult to trace directly. Likewise, it is extremely difficult to "prove" that alcoholism, drug use, mental breakdowns, and crime are "caused" by social inequality. At the same time, we can look at other societies in which the inequalities have been less and such social problems have been significantly less. Indeed, the United States, the most highly stratified society in the world, also ranks among the highest in a number of areas of such stress.

The list below reveals the different ways in which our society "pays" for the extreme social stratification under which we live:

- According to figures from the San Francisco-based independent non-profit National Council on Crime and Delinquency . . . by 1989 the national murder rate had reached more than 30,000 per year. If you are a young black man in America, you are more likely to die by homicide than in any other way. If you are a woman, you have one chance in five of being raped in your lifetime, and once chance in three that you suffered sexual molestation as a child.

- 1990 figures published by another independent research group, the Sentencing Project, reported that the U.S. prison population had passed the 1 million mark. That represented a higher per capita rate of incarceration than any country in the world. (South Africa was second; the Soviet Union was third.) If you add to these figures the number of people in the United States in juvenile detention or on parole, or in other controlled situations such as halfway houses, the total figure is nearly 1.5 million.

- As has been widely reported, suicide and drug use in the United States, especially among young people, are at epidemic levels and growing. In 1990, the National Institute of Mental Health (NIMH) reported that suicide was the third leading cause of death among young people ages fifteen to twentyfour.

- The economic costs of alcohol abuse were estimated to be $98.6 billion in 1990. In 1988 it was estimated that 15.3 million Americans exhibited symptoms of alcohol abuse or alcohol dependence.

- And the Public Citizen Health Research Group reports that about 25 percent of American hospital beds are filled by mental patients. The National Institute of Mental Health's Office of Scientific Information reported in March 1990 that 28 million American adults over eighteen years old, suffer some mental disorder during a given six-month period. About 16 million suffer anxiety disorders, 10 million suffer depressive disorders, and about 2 million are classified as schizophrenic.[4]

DIRECT SOCIAL CONTROL AND VIOLENCE

The data listed above reflect two social facts. One is that the exploitation, oppression and degradation of our society lead to objective consequences. The second is that our society tends to respond to all of these consequences with *increased* coercion. We put more police patrols in poor neighborhoods (we do not increase job opportunities); we jail welfare mothers if their children do not attend school (we do not provide family counseling and job training for the mother); police are sent to "sweep" the public parks of homeless people and to burn their shelters (we do not increase low-income housing).

This is not to say that there are not attempts in all these examples to respond humanely. But if you talk to anyone in social services, you will find that the programs to help disadvantaged people reconstruct their lives are pitifully funded and staffed in comparison to the coercive agencies—the courts, prisons, jails, and police.

The police are an obvious institution of coercion. The democratic ideal of equal justice under the law assumes that police, courts, and prisons are independent of social stratification. Research indicates the opposite. Judges are largely white males from well-to-do backgrounds. As a result, judges are more inclined to send poorly educated, low-income persons to prison and less likely to give them suspended sentences or probation than better educated higher-income persons *convicted of the same crimes.*[5]

Only 18 percent of white-collar embezzlers go to prison for an average of fifteen months and many have their sentences dropped. But 89 percent of working and poor people convicted of larceny spend an average of ten and a half years in prison.[6] If the offender is a businessman or corporate executive who is responsible for injury or death in the pursuit of making money, the behavior may not even be viewed as illegal, or the fine is paid by the company.[7]

The police and courts are charged with upholding the legal norms of society—the laws. But as we have already discussed, many dominant group norms are not laws, and the direct social control used to enforce those norms occurs in a different way. Let us look at another institution of the American culture—one that is not normally seen as an institution of coercion—the family.

VIOLENCE AND THE FAMILY

In some families, the adult partners work out shared responsibilities and both benefit from the relationship. In these cases of egalitarian rules within a partnership direct social control is not needed. But in many cases, family relationships are not based on egalitarian norms and one of the partners, usually the woman, feels trapped, angry, and helpless. In many families a husband decides if and when a wife should get pregnant and may beat the wife if he finds out she is "sneaking" birth control. Some men will complain if dinner is not on time, if the kids are dirty, or if the house is not clean. Many men expect to have their sexual needs met and often care little about a woman's sexual needs.

In patriarchal relationships, partners are acting out the roles they learned from society—roles that are "expected" of them. And within that relationship it is understood that the man has the right to punish the woman if she questions her proper place or fails to perform her proper duties. Slapping one's wife, an occasional beating, withholding money from her, and keeping her isolated from friends and family are sanctions that are not only used but expected. When the male accepts the ideology of male supremacy, he becomes the agent of direct social control over the woman. And social controls exist to support him in that role, for a man who washes dishes and permits his wife to argue may be stigmatized by his friends or coworkers as "henpecked."

We have no idea how many women died from beatings fifty years ago because the idea of domestic violence was not part of our understanding. Just as no court heard the cases of violence against slaves who resisted, no courts heard the cases of violence against women who resisted. Today we are beginning to know—and the extent of this "hidden" violence is hideous. Women who do not benefit from a family relationship can only be held into it by violence or coercion, just as a slave was kept as a slave only by the road patrol and the whip of the overseer.

We also know that children who watch their caretaker being beaten are being taught that human relationships are based on dominance and force. Just as women were seen as the property of men, to serve them, so were the children. Patterns of child abuse and incest, which we now condemn, are the logical outgrowth of these power relationships of patriarchy. Carole Sheffield calls such social control "sexual terrorism" and argues that American society has condoned five forms: rape, wife assault, sexual abuse of children, sexual harassment, and sexual slavery (the international traffic in women and prostitution).[8]

The "traditional" family, then, is a miniature stratification system. Usually, the male head holds power over the other members. Women, tied down by childcaring and homemaking responsibilities, cannot then compete with men for positions in the larger society. Whatever power women had was exercised within the limited space inside the family and always under the control of the male. The direct social control necessary to enforce these power relationships cuts across all social classes and race and ethnic groups.

Even today many women continue to believe that if they are beaten they somehow deserved it. Few women will admit that their bruises or black eyes are a result of domestic violence. "Oh, I slipped on the stairs going down to the laundry room" they say. Some begin to drink silently and others go into depression. In the 1950s, the euphemism for a woman who failed to cope with her status was a "nervous breakdown." There were even lobotomies performed—removal of the front part of the brain, which is the base for creative and independent thinking—to cure women of any tendency to rebel against their roles.

It is not surprising, then, to find that women resist inequality differently than men. While more men commit "crimes" and make up the largest proportion of our prison population, women are more likely to become "mentally ill."[9]

Violence follows women out into the larger society. Rape and other forms of sexual assault are only extensions of the idea that a woman's body is the property of the man who is "powerful enough" to take it. Women do not have freedom of movement in our society; a woman must constantly ask herself if she can safely walk to her car or through the park. Women are considered proper targets for degrading jokes or comments. Men who would be outraged if someone talked to their mother or daughter in certain ways will yell the same comment out to a strange woman. And women are constantly told through advertising that their personal worth depends on the shape of their bodies—with the social diseases of bulimia and anorexia the result.

The violence against women in our society is a highly personal violence. Gang warfare implies large groups engaged in violence; a crazy man with a submachine gun who kills several people in a downtown restaurant is a visible and public enemy. But an accounting of the brain damage, injured eyesight, mental illness, broken bones, and beating deaths that occur singly and regularly in American society rarely makes the front page. Despite the obvious fact that such violence in the home has a deep and scarring influence on a whole new generation of children, it is still treated as a "woman question."

Closely connected to the violence aimed at keeping women "in their place" is the violence related to keeping everyone tightly bound to their gender role. Because "men are supposed to act like men, and women are supposed to act like women," those who step outside those traditional roles are often subjected to violence as well. **Homophobia** is the fear that arises in individuals who feel personally threatened by homosexuals. Only recently has there been a documentation of the hate crimes fueled by homophobia. "Gay bashing" has long been considered a sport for men who were needing to prove that they were "real men." Gays and lesbians in our society are not only called names and made fun of, but are also subject to violence—beatings, rape, and even killing.

Two groups of you have read the paragraphs above. Some of you came from happy homes in which adults acted on egalitarian norms and despite occasional arguments, no real violence ever occurred. You may have trouble accepting what is said above because your own experience does not bear it out. Others of you have come from homes in which such violence marked your everyday life or the lives of relatives or friends close to you. The chances are you have never shared many of your feelings about the beatings you saw or the abuse that was suffered. You may have even tried to forget that it ever happened. In either case, the violence of patriarchy still remains largely unspoken.

Those who talk about saving the American family and its "traditional values" rarely specify which of the values they are talking about. If they are talking about family values in which each individual member is shown respect and equally valued and cared for, then most of us could agree. But if they are talking about the traditional family where some members are subordinated and dominated by others, where those with a different sexual orientation are taunted and despised, then a return to that family means a continuation and deepening of the violence. We discuss this campaign to "return to traditional family values" in Chapter 15.

We would all agree that the family is important; it is in the family that children learn the first and most important lessons of their lives. If children in a family learn that disagreements are settled by force, then they will practice those lessons in the larger society. One could argue that all forms of human violence—gang warfare, hunger, rebellions, and wars—will never be eliminated as long as patriarchal families teach the first lessons of dominant group norms and direct social control.

RACIAL AND ETHNIC VIOLENCE

The civil rights movement opened the eyes of many Americans to the direct social control used to enforce segregation—lynchings, beating, and assassinations. Although the movement challenged the ideology of racism, it did not eliminate it. The dominant group norms of racism are useful to the ruling groups in a stratified society. By blaming black, Latinos, or other minorities, those in power can focus anger over unemployment or poverty away from the system. Frustrated middle class taxpayers can be convinced that their high taxes are due to minority women on welfare having too many babies and that crime is the caused by minority teenagers.

Thus, racism's ugly head is continually raised. Residential segregation, for example, keeps certain "kinds" of people out of neighborhoods. If an African American or Vietnamese American family moves into such a neighborhood, they may receive threatening letters, rocks through the window, a cross burned on the lawn, or their house may be firebombed.[10] In 1986 the country was shocked to learn that young African Americans who had stopped to get a pizza in Howard Beach, a "white section" of New York City, were brutally assaulted and one killed because they had dared to come into white territory.[11] Thirteen white teenagers, armed with sticks and baseball bats and chanting "Niggers get out of the neighborhood" carried out the assault.

Many Americans are aware of organizations such as the Ku Klux Klan and their attacks on African Americans. But most people believe that such attacks occurred in the past and that such organizations are no longer around. The opposite is true. The Southern Poverty Law Center reported in October 1994 a monthly total of 179 documented cases of racial hatred—including assaults, arsons, clashes, threats, cross burnings, intimidation, harassment, vandalism, legal convictions, leafletting, marches, rallies and meetings.[12]

Their published reports were only a sampling of hate crimes committed in the United States. In summer 1996 the media carried stories of the burning of numerous black churches, predominantly in the south.

Nor are hate crimes directed only against African Americans. The Montana Advisory Committee to the U.S. Commission on Civil Rights observed that "Indian nations located in the Pacific Northwest have been the target of increased hostility from right-wing and extremist groups. They have had to contend with racial attacks, organized efforts at political de-stabilization, and increasing incidents of individual harassment, destruction of property and public misinformation."[13]

The box on page 156 is the text of an announcement recently found by members of the St. Croix Band as well as pinned on the bulletin board of Tombstone Pizza, Medford, Wisconsin.

In many parts of the country, a young adult who dates someone of a different color will be called names and even physically threatened. Pressure will be placed on the parents of the couple. Everyone will say "a mixed marriage is more difficult" when what they really mean is that the "white" partner will lose their privileges. Many of the social rules that maintain segregation between racial groups are really rules designed to prevent individuals from falling in love and marrying.

The school systems begin *socially* to separate African American, Latino and Euro-American children as they reach the dating age. Falling in love is an egalitarian process—we are all equally open to doing it. While the textbooks may talk of a democratic society, the youth are learning that freedom does not extend to dancing with, dating, and marrying whoever you want. An important part of the ideology of racism is that "white blood" must remain pure and that somehow there is something wrong in "mixing" blood. People will say things like "God meant you to marry your own kind." These beliefs justify and rationalize the discrimination and violence that occurs as "necessary" to keep intermarriage from occurring.

In my years as a teacher I have had white students frequently come to me, puzzled by their parents' reaction when they begin to date an African American student. "My parents raised me as a Christian," they say. "I was taught to love everyone and that we were all equal in God's eyes. Now they told me I have to stop seeing him or her. Why?" These students are often subjected to direct social control. Parents will threaten to kick them out of the house, stop paying their tuition, take away their car, or even beat them.

The student's parents *do* believe the ideology of equality and love. So how is their reaction to be explained? The answer lies in the reality of "white privilege." The children of a "mixed marriage" are assigned the status of the subordinate group. The parents are reacting to the fact that their son or

First Annual Indian Shoot

TIME: early spring, beginning of walleye run
PLACE: Northern Wisconsin lakes
RULES: Open shoot, off hand position only, no scopes, no sling, no tripods and no whiskey for bait!

OPEN TO ALL WISCONSIN TAXPAYING RESIDENTS

Residents that are BLACK, HMONG, CUBAN or those on WELFARE, ADC FOOD STAMPS, or any other GOVERNMENT GIVE-A-WAY program, are not eligible. (Don't complain about discrimination, you'll have your own shoot later.)
SCORING: Wisconsin rules apply. Points system will be used.

PLAIN INDIAN . . . . 5 POINTS
INDIAN WITH WALLEYES . . . . 10 POINTS
INDIAN WITH BOAT NEWER THAN YOURS . . 20 POINTS
INDIAN USING PITCHFORK . . . . 30 POINTS
SOBER INDIAN . . . . 75 POINTS
INDIAN TRIBAL LAWYER . . . . 100 POINTS
(Does not have to be spearing)

JUDGES:Governor Tommy Thompson, Rev. Jesse Jackson

PRIZES: Fillet-O-Fish sandwiches and six packs of treaty beer

SPONSOR: Society Helping Individual Taxpayers Own Nothing: (Known as SHIT ON)

ENTRY BLANK:

I ______________________________ will attend shoot
I _______ will _______ will not be taking scalps.

I BELIEVE SENATOR ROSHELL IS:
___ HONEST ___ CORRECT
___ ACCURATE ___ A SAINT
___ ALL OF THE ABOVE

I am enclosing $ _______ for his re-election.

Bumper stickers reading "SAVE A FISH-SPEAR AN INDIAN" only $5.00 each. "T" shirts with same message only $10.00 each.

daughter and grandchildren will lose this privilege.[14] Parents, after all, want what is "best" for their children!

As long as racism creates powerful sanctions to maintain inequalities, individuals will be subject to its direct social control. "Learning to love each other" is not enough (although it helps); the problem will be solved only when there is no longer an unequal power status based on minority group membership.

Like domestic violence, much of the violence that occurs as the result of racism—beatings, verbal abuse, rape and murder—is not identified as such. The institutionalized rape of black women has never been as powerful a symbol of black oppression as the spectacle of lynching. Darlene Clark Hine argues the combined influence of rape (or the threat of rape), domestic violence, and economic oppression is key to understanding the culture of resistance developed by African American women.[15]

The courts and the police are generally under the control of the dominant group in society and laws are often unequally enforced. There is overwhelming statistical evidence that people of color are more likely to be arrested than white people for the same behaviors; that Anglo American men who sexually assault African American women are far less likely to be punished than African American men who sexually assault Anglo American women, and that people of color are far more often sentenced to prison, and for longer terms, than Anglo Americans who have committed the same crimes. Latinos charged with crimes face similar discrimination. Author Alfredo Mirande, who studied the legal system's treatment of Latinos, called it "Gringo Justice."[16]

In 1990 the U.S. census classified the American population as 80.3 percent white, 12.1 percent black, and 9 percent of Hispanic origin. In that same year, of all inmates in the country's jails, 46 percent were white, 43 percent were black, and 14 percent were Hispanic. New York Supreme Court Justice Bruce Wright pointed out that in the state of New York there were 3,500 judges of which no more than 80 were black.[17] The bureaucracy that is the judicial system—from police departments to prosecutors to courts—remains largely in the hands of well-to-do white males and reflects the ideologies into which they are socialized.[18]

The call for "law and order" that is frequently raised by politicians is often a cloaked appeal to racism. Americans are being exposed to a television and movie campaign that identifies street crime, drug dealing, and gangs with people of color. "Race" is seen as a cause, rather than poor schools, minimum-wage jobs, and police brutality.

Direct social control based on racism takes not only the form of police. Addictive drugs are themselves a form of social control. Unemployed youths strung out on heroin or cocaine are not going to organize any kind of social movement that challenges the power of the ruling classes. Indeed, their addiction will turn them into threats to the order and stability of their own communities.

In the time that I lived in Detroit I heard numerous eyewitness accounts of how addictive drugs had been used a social control in the auto factories. At that time, the League of Revolutionary Black Workers was organizing African American autoworkers as a caucus within the union. They had run candidates for union offices and were beginning to have some success in their demands for better working conditions and an end to racism in the plants. At the same time, addictive drugs became widely available and were often openly distributed within the factory without any interference from management.

Drugs are not confined to minority communities. Throughout the society, drugs (legal and illegal) appear as an alternative and an escape to anyone who feels more threatened, more frustrated, and more angry . The Children's Defense Fund, pointed out:

> The deadly, quick violence of guns takes an American child's life every three hours and the lives of 25 children—the equivalent of a classroomful—every three days. Nothing more graphically reflects what Lee Atwater on his dying bed called the "tumor" growing on the American soul than our acquiescence in the senseless killing of innocent children.
>
> Do you believe that the top military power in the world—with a $1.1 trillion arsenal and 1.7 million active duty military personnel; with 800,000 federal, state, and local law enforcement officials; 1.2 million national guard and reserve personnel; and a purported $8 billion war on drugs—is helpless to keep young children safe to, from, and in school? Is our social and moral development so arrested that we cannot see, hear, feel, and respond to the killing and injuries of our children or curb the gun- and drug-driven violence blanketing America?[19]

THE VIOLENCE OF CLASS

In discussing the violence involved in direct social control we have focused on the traditional idea of what is "violent"—personal physical force. But there is a broader definition of violence. When a child goes hungry because welfare payments are not enough to feed him or her, is this not violence? Is the pain of a hungry stomach the same as hitting or hurting the child? If an elderly person becomes sick with pneumonia because the slum landlord did not repair the heating in the apartment building, is the landlord guilty of violence against that elderly person?

If we accept this broader definition of violence, then we can immediately see that the violence of direct social control is closely related to class status. Without the resources to ensure shelter, food, medical care and education, the poor suffer the violence of want. The ideology of class says that they are being punished for being poor. According to the Children's Defense Fund, the slow grinding violence of poverty takes an American child's life every 53 minutes.[20]

One of the most powerful forms of direct social control related to class is the power to take someone's job away. One cannot survive in our society without a job with decent pay. Thus, a worker told to perform a task that might cause injury or illness may do the work in order to keep the job. If joining a union may threaten employment, workers are afraid to join. But without union protection, the working poor are far more likely to suffer illness and injury on the job and are far less likely to be able to afford to pay for proper medical care. Parenti pointed out:

> Every year more than 14,000 workers are killed on the job; another 100,000 die prematurely, and 400,000 become seriously ill from work-related diseases, such as black lung and cancer. Five million on-the-job injuries occur each year. About 20 million Americans work with chemicals that can damage the nervous system, even in small does. All told, one out of every four workers suffers from occupationally connected disease.
>
> Industrial work may always carry some risk, but the present carnage is due mostly to inadequate safety standards and lax enforcement of codes.[21]

As more and more companies "downsize" and good jobs become more scarce, the threat of unemployment becomes an even more powerful form of direct social control. The government and companies can now reduce wages, cut pensions, and extend working hours, and employees are afraid to protest.

VIOLENCE AGAINST THE ENVIRONMENT

A powerful rule of industrial capitalism is that profits must be maximized as quickly as possible. If one corporation is able to increase profits more quickly, it will be at a competitive advantage and may drive other companies out of business. To stay in business, owners and managers must use their power for profit, not for social good. If the two coincide, that is fine. But if there is a conflict, then profit must come first.

The drive for the maximization of profit has overridden the need to protect and preserve the earth's ecology. Even with laws that now regulate toxic chemical disposal and emissions, any company that can find a way to circumvent the costs of those laws will have an advantage. If there is pressure from environmental groups, the companies can retaliate with powerful weapons of direct social control—they can threaten to close the plant and relocate.[22] The threat of the loss of jobs and the tax base to a local community is often enough to make local politicians side with the company against the environmental groups.

The long-range impact of such corporate power is to increase the violence visited on the rest of society. The carcinogens dumped into our air, water, and food supply contribute to millions of slow painful cancer deaths. Pneumonia, emphysema, allergies, and arthritis are all exacerbated and related to environmental pollution.

These consequences are just those suffered by humans. We know that fish, songbirds, and many smaller animals are in danger of extinction as the carcinogens in the environment cause their sterilization, poison their habitats, and destroy their food supplies. The ideology of speciesism rationalizes the violence to other species; the ideology of class rationalizes the violence to humans.

If today is a typical day on planet Earth, we will lose 116 square miles of rainforest, about an acre a second. We will lose 72 square miles of land to encroaching deserts. We will lose 40 to 100 species. We will add 2,700 tons of CFC's and 15 millions tons of carbon to the atmosphere. We will add 220,000 more mouths to the population, yet 35,000—most of them children—will die of starvation and malnourishment, despite adequate but maldistributed food supplies. We will burn 800 billion barrels of oil—all nonrenewable-despite the fact that two thousand times our total global energy consumption arrives free from the sun each day. Add to this picture the extraction of thousands of pounds of raw minerals, the production of tons of toxic and solid wastes, and all of this on a planet where the top 20 percent of the population controls and consumes 80 percent of the world's wealth, while spending $1 billion a day on armaments.[23]

CONCLUSION

The violence of direct social control in our society is based on all the dimensions of social hierarchy—race, class, gender, and environment. We can see that the deepening of such violence threatens the cultural imperatives of our society, and world.

A *Wall Street Journal* headline picks up this growing realization: "Widening Rich-Poor Gap Is a Threat to the 'Social Fabric,' White House Says."[24] Crime "spreads" into the affluent neighborhoods; people of all statuses must breathe the air; cocaine is sold to the son or daughter of the corporate executive as easily as to the minority youth. And riots and rebellions burn up millions of dollars of goods and threaten thousands of lives.

We began this chapter by arguing that there is a difference between deviance from egalitarian norms and deviance from dominant group norms. We have suggested that the second type of deviance requires greater and greater levels of direct social control in order to insure the maintenance of inequality. As American society closes down opportunities and denies more and more of its members not only the benefits, but even the most basic necessities of life, the need to use violent social control will grow.

If labor is no longer needed, and large sections of the population become more and more difficult to control, is it possible that the most violent of all solutions—genocide—will once again be practiced? Can one argue that the flow of drugs into the poor and minority communities will increase rather than diminish? These questions are discussed more fully in Chapter 14.

Before we look at the answers to these questions, we need to examine how the dominant groups themselves are organized. Those who possess the power to stand on the highest rungs of the ladder have ways to keep themselves there. In the next part of this book we look at how those at the top use networking, control bureaucracies—especially the bureaucracies of ideological social control—and manipulate science.

SUMMARY

All societies face the problem of making people obey the norms that order and predict life. But there is a difference between societies in which almost all the norms to be enforced are egalitarian and societies in which many of the norms to be enforced are dominant group norms. Dominant group norms are more likely to be resisted and therefore there is greater deviance in societies marked by great inequalities.

The United States has always been a society of great inequalities and direct social control. No slave "willingly" labored for no pay and a lousy hut—she or he had to be driven by the threat of the whip. Native Americans did not "willingly" give up their land and way of life. Poor people do not "willingly" live in apartments with rats and broken toilets.

Dominant group norms can define an act as deviant when committed by those lower on the ladder and acceptable if it is committed by those above.

Slavery was a "legal" system of property ownership; taking Native land was legally justified; and the slumlord legally allows his property to run down while making profits and taking tax exemptions.

According to egalitarian norms, the police and the courts' use of direct social control should be equally applied. Research, however, shows that the judicial system reflects social stratification. Deviants high on the ladder are often not punished at all, or punished lightly.

The ideology of individualism teaches us that when people are deviant, it is their fault. The solution is to punish the individual. This prevents us from seeing the conditions that caused the deviance. Although we may lock one person up, the conditions are still there, and other individuals continue to be deviant. More and more direct social control is then needed.

Direct social control is also practiced in families. Parents may discipline children for their own good—positive social power. But in patriarchal families, children and women are often punished because they have resisted dominant group norms. The result is a high rate of domestic violence and child abuse.

People of color in our society are kept in "their place" through direct social control as well. After slavery, the lynch rope was used as a threat. Minorities' homes may still be firebombed or stoned if they move into a Euro-American neighborhood. Hate literature and beatings continue. The courts and legislatures continue to be dominated by Euro-Americans, and it is more difficult to prosecute such crimes.

Individuals are also kept in their place on the lower rung through the direct social control of class status. The threat of being fired is powerful coercion. The loss of credit, being evicted, or having a benefits check cut are all direct mechanisms of social control.

Threats and coercion are also used against the environment. People are told their jobs and tax revenues will be lost if they do not allow a factory to pollute the air or water. The consequences of such environmental degradation is suffered by all—increased cancer rates, breathing problems, and loss of wildlife and natural beauty.

Vocabulary

Direct Social Control. The coercive and sometimes violent negative sanctions used when in dividuals do not accept the ideologies and norms of society.

Homophobia. Undue fear of homosexuality and homosexuals; prejudice against them.

Discussion Questions

1. In the text I argue that those who "loot" may have reason to do so. Most of us are socialized to see looting as a deviant (and wrong) act. Am I arguing that it is "all right" to loot? How are our ideas about looting a reflection of the ideology of individualism?

2. I also argue that the elite would rather that individuals loot, take drugs, or become suicidal than to organize into social movements of resistance. Why do I say that? Do you agree or disagree? Why?

3. One of my classes wrote an assignment about their own experiences with domestic violence. Of the nineteen students in the class we found the following results: 5 had no experience with violence; 2 women had directly experienced male violence; 7 had experienced male violence in the family; 3 had experienced male violence with close friends; 1 woman had experienced coerced rape; 1 had experienced female violence in the family; 1 had experienced female violence with a close friend. They were surprised by the extent of violence revealed by the survey. Are you? If you were to take an anonymous survey in your class, would the results be comparable?

4. There is controversy today over whether parents should "spank" children as a form of discipline. Using the analytical framework of the past chapters (socialization, positive and negative social power, egalitarian and dominant group norms, and direct versus ideological social control) discuss what you think the best sanctions are for parents to use to enforce norms. (No one will argue that we should let the kid run into the street in front of the truck so that she or he can learn from "experience" what will happen to them!)

5. Do you know of any incidents of direct social control in your community directed against racial or ethnic minorities? violence in families or against homosexuals? directed against individuals because of their class status? directed against the environment?

Resources

Videos: *The Color Purple.*

This movie could be used for a number of the chapters in this book. It is the story of how one woman (played by Whoopi Goldberg) could overcome the oppression, exploitation, and degradation of her gender, class, and race and walk away proud. Watch closely for scenes in which she, and the other women, encourage one of the men to beat his wife (played by Oprah Winfrey). Why do people actually enforce the dominant group norms used to oppress them? Can you identify all the various forms of both ideological and direct social control used in this movie? Rated PG-13.

Platoon.

Although this movie is often cited as one of the best war movies ever made (it won an Oscar), it is also a movie about a group of men being forced to do something that they do not understand, or particularly want to do—kill Vietnamese. How are decent young American men convinced to go out and kill? And what happens when they begin to question the role they are given? Charlie Sheen plays the young idealistic soldier who ends up in a war he doesn't understand. This movie is very difficult to watch. But if you ever thought that war might be glorious, this will shatter your illusions. Rated R.

NOTES

Complete citations are provided in the Bibliography.

1. Quoted in Clancy 1990, iii.
2. *Business Week,* 13 December 1993, 72–80.
3. Boyce 1992.
4. This list is adapted from Mander 1992, 27–28.
5. Reiman 1979.
6. Parenti 1988, 129.
7. Hills 1987.
8. Sheffield 1987, 175–84.
9. Chesler 1972, 312–22.
10. Klanwatch Project of the Southern Poverty Law Center.
11. Hynes and Drury 1990.
12. Southern Poverty Law Center, "For the Record," *Intelligence Report.* , October 1994, No. 75, 9–15.
13. Southern Poverty Law Center, "The Hidden Victims: Hate Crime Against American Indians Under-Reported", *Intelligence Report* October 1994 No. 75, 3.
14. See McIntosh's (1992) listing of what such white privilege consists.
15. Hine 1990, 292–97.
16. Mirande 1987.
17. Wright 1987, 84.
18. Wright 1987.
19. Children's Defense Fund 1992, xi.
20. Children's Defense Fund 1992, xi.
21. Parenti 1988, 114.
22. Barnett 1995.
23. Ladd 1994.
24. *Wall Street Journal* 15 February 1994.

PART III

HOW THE TOP GROUPS STAY ON TOP

How can just a tiny group of people stay at the very very top of the social stratification ladder while millions of us are stuck on lower rungs? Is it just that they get us to believe it? Is it just our fear of being punished? If we are so many and they are so few, why don't we just all get together and make some changes?

This part of the book tries to answer those kinds of questions by looking at how the groups at the top are *organized*. It is not just their money. If tomorrow, every American who owed on their credit card decided to stop making payments, the economy would collapse! But it would take a massive organization of millions of people all agreeing to do the same thing. And it would take an organization with ideas of how to restructure the economy once it collapsed.

Obviously, the key is organization. Societies must be organized to get things done. Our society is organized through social stratification. If we toppled the ladder, who would know what to do? Without the ladder, how would we be organized?

- **Chapter 9** examines the ways in which the ladder is organized, both laterally and hierarchically, through networking. In this way, important resources get distributed. Of course, some get more and some get less. These networks are present everywhere in our society. Families are usually networks, and so are small churches. Political parties form the basis for networks, and so do golf courses. Because these networks control resources, they are sources of power. And so they act to help hold the ladder in place, although networks can also be used as a source of power to challenge social stratification.

- **Chapter 10** looks at a more obvious form of organization in our society—bureaucracy. We focus on bureaucracies as sources of social power and look at the ways in which they help maintain social stratification in our society. As bureaucracies have increased in size and in the scope of their activities, they have also increased their power. This has concentrated social power into the hands of a smaller and smaller group of people.

- **Chapter 11** examines three such bureaucracies of our society—education, media, and religion. These are bureaucracies whose main task is to teach us what to think, and therefore they are the primary sources of the ideological social control discussed in the previous section. New technologies such as videos, satellites, and the Internet have made it easier for these bureaucracies to reach us and have helped concentrate the power and control these bureaucracies have over us.

- These new technologies arise out of a bureaucracy we call science. **Chapter 12** looks at how science has been organized to maintain social stratification. Scientific results that threaten or challenge the ladder are often ignored or suppressed. This is because science, like the other bureaucracies, is organized to support the interests of those at the top of the ladder. This includes social science, and sociology as well. Thus, there is a tension between social scientists, such as myself, who write books like this criticizing the system, and the bureaucracy of science, which does not want to acknowledge what I have to say.

9

WEBS ON THE LADDER—NETWORKING

"It's not *what* you know, it's *who* you know."

The preceding chapters have discussed the unequal distribution of power in American society. We looked at the ways people on the lower rungs have resisted as individuals, and organized as social movements to increase their power within stratified America. But we have not really examined how the dominant groups organize and act to hold on to, or increase, their power. The next four chapters look more closely at how those on the top of the ladder stay there.

This chapter looks at a social mechanism called **networking**. Networking describes the informal relationships that allow individuals to tap into, and share, resources. Members of networks can then access not only the resources they control but the resources of others. This pooling of resources increases the possible power of all members of the network.

Since networks are by definition informal, they represent access to resources over and above the official, and formal, resources an individual may have. Networks often link formal organizations as well. Male coaches, for example, may belong to the local Rotary or Kiwanis whereas a female coach may have no such network of support. The result may be similar to the situation that occurred in the small community in which my college is located. The businessmen got together a number of years ago and established a private fund to support scholarships for football and men's basketball. There is no such equivalent support for women's sports at the school. Because the fund is private, it is not regulated by federal laws regarding equity.

Networking describes social interactions linking persons who have shared interests. Those interests may be a result of history ("our families have lived in the same town for generations,") common activities ("we both like to golf,") or recognition that the relationship is mutually beneficial ("when I play golf with him, I give him stock tips and he tells me about what's going on in city government.")

Networking almost always reflects the given patterns of interaction in our society, that is, men are more likely to network with men, whites with whites, the wealthy with the wealthy, and so forth. In other words, African Americans or Latinos do not belong to networks in white suburban communities; few women are members of networks that link powerful New York stockbrokers; blue-collar workers do not go to the country club and drink martinis with corporate executives.

The box presented on page 169 describes a network that connected drug dealers to bankers and politicians. Relatives are also involved, since kinship is a very important basis for networking. The network discussed in that quote shared resources—money, political protection and influence, and information. Individuals who were able to cut past the corners of legality and rely on their "friends" to make a fast buck controlled the savings and loan Industry. The regulators within the federal bureaucracy were not able to stop them because of the power of these networks. They were only "stopped" when they had made their millions, the Savings and Loan (S&L) banks collapsed and the American taxpayer was left with a clean-up bill of over $500 billion.

Many politicians (in both major parties) were involved in these networks and benefited from low-cost loans and lucrative investments. As a result the S&L scandal has *not* been an issue in political campaigns and politicians rarely talk about the relationship between the huge federal deficit and the scandal.

Networking is not confined to just the upper levels. In Chapter 5 we discussed the ways in which social movements used existing networks. The early union movement, for example, often began within the networks that early immigrant groups brought with them—mutual assistance associations, religious organizations, and kin groupings.[1] Likewise, the powerful African American civil rights movement of the 1960s skillfully utilized the network of black churches that already existed.

Jones's study of the poor in America discusses how rural black migrants to the northern cities organized networks. These networks included kinship, informal and formal associations and provided the new city dwellers with a certain base of power in urban politics. In contrast, her research showed that poor white migrants in the North were less likely to develop such networks. She suggests that poor whites believed they could "make it" in the system whereas African Americans understood the racism they would encounter and therefore became better organized.[2]

Miami banker Ray Corona hungered after a bank of his own. So Corona, Fernandez and Samos cooked up a scheme to buy a bank. The money would come from Fernandez's drug smuggling and would be funneled to Corona through Samos's wife in May 1978, Corona won permission to buy Sunshine State bank in Miami. After Fernandez was indicted and then kidnaped to Colombia, he sold his shares in Sunshine to Corona federal examiners were expressing concern about lending practices there, citing insider abuse and insufficient collateral for loans. Corona cultivated politicians. One of Sunshine's directors was Howard Gary, the Miami City Manager, who borrowed $95,000. Another stockholder was South Miami Chief of Police Sal Vizzini. And a big borrower was Lazaro Albo, the right-hand man of former Miami mayor Maurice Ferre. But the politician who most helped the Coronas was Florida Comptroller Gerald Lewis, whose office continually frustrated the efforts of the Federal Deposit Insurance Corporation (FDIC) to remove the Coronas or shut down the bank. Lewis also presided over the failure of E.S. M. Government Securities that caused the failure of Marvin Warner's Home State Savings in Ohio. Gerald Lewis is Warner's second cousin.

Sunrise Savings in Boynton Beach, Florida was one of the first big S&L failures in the country, at a cost to citizens of about $680 million. Among the borrowers at Sunrise were Ray Corona [who] owed $5.4 million. During the 1989 criminal trial of several top Sunrise executives, there was incredible testimony about then-Vice President George Bush's interference into Sunrise's federal oversight. Berkovitz testified that in 1984 Sunrise CEO Robert Jacoby met with Bush...Vice-President Bush called a lady who was in a position underneath the head of the FSLIC (Federal Savings and Loan Insurance Corp.) and told the unidentified woman to back off from Sunrise, Berkovitz stated.

from *The Mafia, CIA & George Bush*

LATERAL NETWORKS

In this chapter, however, we are looking specifically at the ways in which the dominant groups of society use networks to both protect their power and privilege and to control those below them. There are two major types of networks: lateral and hierarchal. **Lateral networks** link persons in similar statuses and with similar levels of resources. One could think of a lateral network as a sharing that goes across and around the network, rather than going "up and down."

We first examine kinship. We then examine the more general types of lateral networks used to organize, coordinate and consolidate their power.

Finally, we will look at the hierarchical networks that the elite use to control those below them.

NETWORKING AMONG THE ELITE: KINSHIP

Kin networks exist at all levels of our society. For those on the lower rungs, family networks may be the only means for survival. If you make only minimum wage, keeping your job depends on having an uncle who fixes your car, a lady in the church who is willing to babysit for you, and parents who buy the kids their winter coats. Kinship for those on the higher rungs of the ladder has a different function. It provides a way to network wealth, power, and influence.

Human societies have always used kinship as a way of giving individuals status. In smaller societies occupation, place of residence, and marriage partner were determined by kinship—not by a person's choice. The family or clan gave people their identity. If you have taken a course in cultural anthropology, you have already learned how important kinship was in determining the social structure of smaller-scale societies.

In American society we stress individual achievement and choice instead of kinship for many statuses. We no longer have government leaders whose first-born son will be the next leader; we no longer have priests whose sons or daughters will automatically be the next priest; we no longer have customs that force a woman of one family to wed a man of another family. There remains one important exception. Property (wealth) in our society continues to be transmitted through kinship. Class ideology justifies and rationalizes the belief that children are automatically entitled to the wealth acquired by, or inherited by, their parents.

This particular fact of kinship is not very important for the vast majority of people. Today when a middle-class person dies, and the family has paid the medical bills, the nursing home bills, and the funeral bills, there is not very much left. The few things of real value—some of Grandma's jewelry, some good furniture from the old house, and Grandad's guns or tools—have more emotional value than financial value. Today more and more families are finding that the loss of the elderly leaves nothing but debt. A pension, Social Security , and savings were not enough to cover the costs of chemotherapy, home health care, and doctors' bills. Since women outlive men, more and more middle class women are finding that they approach old age not only as widows but also in poverty.[3]

The transfer of property through kinship, then, becomes a significant issue only for those with wealth beyond that needed to meet the costs of living and dying. Inheritance of wealth is a lifetime guarantee to members of the upper class. The socialization of their children requires training on how to maintain and protect that wealth and the status it secures.

The elite private schools that serve these children do not offer budgeting classes that teach how to use grocery coupons and how to figure credit card interest charges. These private schools teach students how to invest wisely in the markets, how to purchase paintings, jewels, and futures that will increase in value, and how to organize assets professionally and efficiently.[4] Networking is one of the ways to do that, and kinship networking is one of the most important.

Marriage either increases or decreases wealth. If two individuals who will inherit wealth marry, the marriage consolidates two sources of wealth. If a person with wealth marries someone without wealth, then the wealth is dissipated. In other words, it is to the benefit of this class to ensure that their children, who inherit wealth, will marry someone who will also inherit wealth. The selection of marriage partners for the young adults of this class requires that their dating be networked among those of their same class.

The expensive private schools, the custom of debutantes and "coming out" balls, and the exclusive fraternity and sororities of the wealthy all act to ensure that the children of the elite will mix with, and choose someone, from their own class and race. There are exceptions, of course. In some cases, the son or daughter of a wealthy family may marry "new" wealth—someone who has made a great deal of money on their own rather than inheriting it. But in general, one finds that the system that interlocks and consolidates existing wealth works well.

Television shows such as *Lives of the Rich and Famous*, *People* magazine, and books about Sam Walton (founder of Wal-Mart) tend to concentrate on particular individuals who have "made it." Rarely do we read stories or see television shows about those who inherited great wealth, who pass that wealth on to their children as well as passing on the knowledge of how to manage and maintain that wealth. These are not wealthy individuals—these are wealthy *families*. Their power lies not in them as separate people but in the pooling of their resources and connections. Any one of the richest individuals in America becomes poor in relationship to the power and wealth that these kin groupings can exercise.

A Case Study: Kinship in Detroit

The inheritance of wealth is a historical process. This means that class status and the control of resources are dominated by the same families over generations. Kinship provides networks that may not even be specifically known—that is, an individual may not even be aware of exactly how they are related to someone else.

In 1970 I began a study of the ruling class in the city of Detroit.[5] My hypothesis was that I would find several small circles of people who were kin-related and who held common economic, political, and social interests. I began by looking at 471 directors of the forty-one largest economic units with headquarters in the Detroit area at that time. This included 25 industrial corporations, 5 retailing corporations, 6 banks, 3 utilities, and the 2 largest savings and loan associations. There were a total of 471 individuals who were members of the boards of directors of these firms.[6]

These 471 directors held a total of 507 positions in the 41 firms studied. Obviously one way that they controlled their interests was through **interlocking directorates**—sitting on more than one board. But such interlocking directorates are official parts of the bureaucratic structure of corporate America. I was interested in the informal interlocks—the networking between these individuals that went beyond the official channels.

To examine these networks I looked at the extent to which these individuals belonged to the same clubs, served in the same civic organizations, and were related to each other by descent or marriage. Many of these individuals belonged to a small group of prominent country clubs. Many served on the same boards of directors for community organizations. But the most interesting finding was the way in which a key group of individuals were networked by kinship.

There were a total of fiftyfour directors related. Twenty-eight of these were related only to one or two other directors—usually to a wife or son or daughter on the same board. But twentysix directors who were all related to each other! My hypothesis had been wrong. There were not several family groups that held concentrated power and control—there was only *one*.

In examining these twentysix individuals I found that they were among the most powerful of all—linking the banks, industrials and utilities; belonging to the most exclusive clubs; and sharing positions in the most powerful community organizations.

This kin grouping was not the result of twentieth-century industrialization, although it included members of the Firestone family, the Ford family, and the Stroh family. The ancestors of these individuals were the original aristocrats who had received land grants from the French and British Kings, who had brought their European fortunes with them, and who had stolen land from the Native Americans and made fortunes in speculation selling land to the early settlers. Indeed, of the twelve wealthiest families in Detroit in 1860, eight families had descendants who were directors of the firms studied between 1900 and 1970.

The kinship chart presented here shows only a portion of the kinship network that was discovered in the study. (The complete kinship chart took eight pages in a foldout in the original report of the study.) This charts shows how the historical links, the social links, and the economic links are connected to kinship for several of the more noted Detroit families—the Morans, the VanDykes, the "chemical" Fords, the Joys, and the MacNichols.

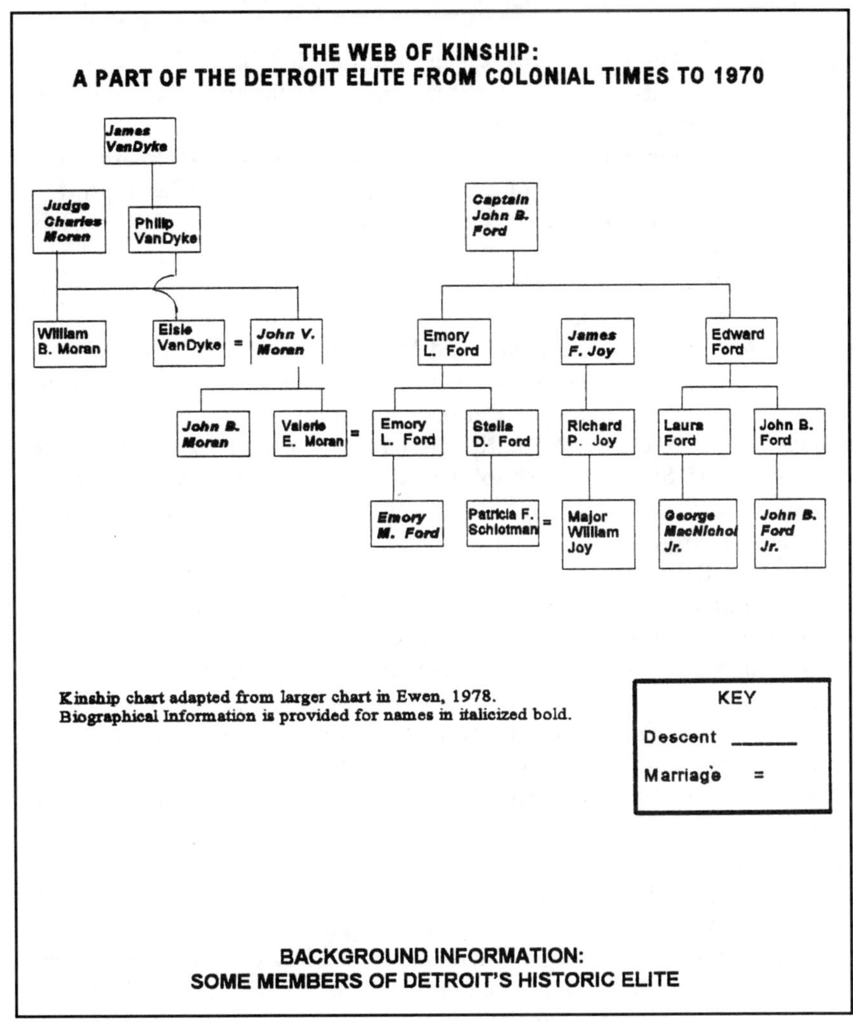

***Judge Charles Moran*:** Owner of the third largest original estate

James VanDyke: Attorney for the Michigan Central Railroad; City Attorney of Detroit, 1835, 1839; Prosecuting Attorney of Wayne County, 1840; Chairman of Ways and Means Committee, City Council, 1843; Mayor of Detroit, 1847; member, Detroit Board of Water Commissioners, 1853; President of Detroit Fire Department, 1847–1851.

John V. Moran: Director, Merchants and manufacturers Exchange; organizer and Director of Gale Sulky Harrow Company; organized American Banking and Savings Association and the American Trust Company, a director and trustee of both; President of Peninsular Lead and Color Works.

John B. Moran: Organized a real estate firm; founded Gray Motor Corporation and the City National Bank; at time of death, 1953, held directorships in 20 different companies.

Emory Moran Ford: Director, Manufacturers; National Bank; Advisory Board, United Foundation; trustee, Jennings Memorial Hospital; member, Grosse Pointe Club, Country Club of Detroit, Yondotega Club, Detroit Club.

Capt. John B. Ford: Founded Libbey-Owens Ford, Pittsburgh Plate Glass, and Michigan Alkali Chemicals (became Wyandotte Chemicals)

James F. Joy: Attended Dartmouth and Harvard Law School; joined Porter law firm—litigated case with Michigan Bank and invested in Michigan Central Railroad; organized Chicago, Burlington, and Quincy Railroad; purchased 800,000 acres in Kansas territory considered "neutral" and used United States Cavalry to clear homesteaders and Indians; owned 750,000 acres in Michigan; President of Michigan Central Railroad; controlled Jackson, Lansing, and Saginaw Railroad; organized Detroit and Bay City Railroad; bought out Detroit, Lansing, and Northern Railroad; in partnership with Buhl, Shelden, McMillan and Newberry built the Detroit Union Depot and Station Grounds.

George MacNichol Jr.: Director, Wyandotte Chemicals Corporation, Wyandotte Transportation Company, American Standard Inc., Columbia Gas System, Ohio Fuel Gas Company, Columbia Gas of Ohio, Libbey-Owens Ford, Ohio Valley Gas Company, Johns-Manville Corporation; Vice-President and Trustee, Toledo Museum of Art; Honorary Trustee, Toledo Hospital.

John B. Ford Jr.: Director, National Bank of Detroit, Parke Davis, Wyandotte Chemicals Corporation; Director and Executive Vice-President, Lanston-Aubrey Gas Company; Trustee, Henry Ford Hospital; Advisory Board, United Foundation; Chairman of the Board, Detroit Symphony Orchestra; member, Detroit Club, Yondotega Club, Country Club of Detroit, Gross Pointe Club.

Biographical information is given for some of the key members of the families. Viewed from this perspective—from "below"—these individuals are not the wise and generous leaders of our past and present, but individuals who were born at the top and did whatever was necessary to stay there. If one looks at James Joy, for example, we see a man who was not only economically powerful but was willing to use deadly force against the little person—the homesteader. George MacNichol Jr. was a director of Johns-Manville Corporation, a company that has now admitted it knew that its asbestos would kill thousands of people but kept on using it anyway.

This kind of research dispels the myth that the rich in America got that way simply by working hard, being smarter, or being lucky. Although that myth may apply to a few of the very wealthy, *most of America's wealth is controlled by individuals who inherited it.* Kinship, then, is one of the most important ways that those who have power, and sit on the top rungs, keep that power.

We have already argued that such power can be challenged. The power of slaveholders in the South was challenged by the Abolition movement. The power of factory owners was challenged by the union movement. And the power of the rich over the lives of people has also been challenged.

An 1810 map of the private claims in Michigan Territory surrounding the small settlement of Detroit shows 45 claims, varying from 2 acres to 309 acres. Of the 45 claims, 24 are held by individuals whose descendants are identified as still actively involved in the ruling class of Detroit.

The connections between contemporary members of the ruling class and the early ruling class is graphically illustrated in the exceptional story told by John Bell Moran in his memoirs:

"Some years ago I completed the sale of the last piece of property held by our immediate family from the old Charles Moran farm. The deal was ready to close. The money was in escrow, everything was satisfactory except that the buyer's attorney had not yet approved the abstract...he discovered the transfer was being made by the heirs, of the heirs of the heirs of Claude Charles Moran, who, as I have explained in the chapter dealing with him and his land holdings, owned the property fronting on the river at what is now Hastings Street extending North for about three miles.

What baffled the lawyer was that the property seemed to have been held by one owner for over a hundred and fifty years. He could not believe it. He phoned me. I explained to him that the property was part of a French Land Grant made first by Cadillac, then by Beauharnois for the French King. The Grant was confirmed to Charles Moran, as owner, by the United States Government in 1817,

How did the Morans get it? Why that was easy. The family in the beginning just took it from the Indians. They didn't need it and the French government okayed the deal." (Cited in Ewen 1978.)

In 1967 Detroit experienced a large-scale urban rebellion. Those who held official power (the mayor, police, city council) appeared unable to maintain order. Similar to the Los Angeles rebellion of 1992, the Detroit rebellion demonstrated that large sections of the community no longer gave their consent to the system. The city government, which could no longer govern, went into crisis.

Those with the *real* power, who actually control the resources of the city, could no longer stay in the background and let those they had hired or approved run the city. Thus the "leading citizens" stepped forward to form an organization called New Detroit to temporarily run the city and figure out how to solve the crisis. Who were these people? Simply concerned wealthy citizens? Or were they a network of people—networked by common financial, industrial, social, and kinship interests? Using the research from my study, I found that the key individuals who stepped forward to deal with the crisis were either members of the powerful kin grouping or socially closely connected.

The New Detroit Committee was supposed to be a "power-based, yet truly representative, action-oriented committee able to call its own shots, identify its priorities and targets and set its own timetables."[7] But the ruling class organized the committee, appointed its leadership and provided the organization's resources. *Then* it claimed it would create a representative organization. Shortly after its formation, black organizations that did represent grassroots community efforts withdrew from New Detroit, charging that New Detroit's monies had too many "strings."

What New Detroit did make clear was that in time of real urban crisis the hollow governmental forms elected "democratically" did not really represent power in Detroit. The real holders of power, in order to ensure their continued control, had to step forward. The government bodies supposedly serving the people could not preserve the stratification system that existed in Detroit. The *class* of people who benefited from that system had to step forward to save it.

Other social scientists had already demonstrated that the ruling class is linked through common financial and social positions.[8] What the Detroit study illustrated was the extent to which kinship underlay and organized all the other connections.

KINSHIP AND PATRIARCHY

Women of the wealthy class have not escaped the oppression of patriarchy. They are not exploited, as are working class and poor women, but they continue to be seen as wives and mothers first. While the men of the upper rungs are U.S. senators, corporate executives, and the presidents of elite universities, their wives are expected to organize cocktail parties, oversee the children's education, and make necessary social connections at the charity fund raisers—all to facilitate the work of the men.

The woman of great wealth who lives in a mansion with twenty bedrooms, a spa, an outdoor and indoor swimming pool, a horse stable and tennis courts, and servants' quarters is actually doing the work of a full-time hotel manager. Her luxurious lifestyle requires that she oversee a staff that includes stable boys, gardeners, chauffeurs, maids, maintenance personnel, and household accountants. She is expected to attend the opera, the art shows, and to help raise money to benefit the Children's Hospital. She is given primary responsibility for the networking that occurs within this elite class.

A wealthy woman's socialization, of course, prepared her to do all this. But in certain ways, she may be as "trapped" in her gender role as the middle-class housewife who is home mopping the floor for the third time in a week. If she had wanted to be an artist herself, or be an engineer, rather than attend horse shows, she may even be resentful and angry. It is possible that she may be physically abused. The woman's movement" would have a certain appeal to her.

Wealthy socialite Leila Eliott Burton Hadley Smitter Musham Luce gave an interview to the magazine *Town and Country* in which she described getting married to her first husband:

> I met him when I came out, in 1943, at the Junior Assemblies—darling, I was a *glamour deb*—and a year later I married him, at St. Thomas's Church. The reception was at the Colony Club. I was 18. He was the grandson and namesake of the thirteenth president of Yale, and the son of the eponymous Hadley in Milbank, Tweed, Hadley & McCloy—Morris Hadley, my first father-in-law—and the godson of Archibald MacLeish. I was made by Arthur's mother to go to a well-known society gynecologist, Dr. Richard Pierson, to be deflowered—so the Hadleys could be sure, number one, that I was a virgin. And, number two, so Arthur could have an easy—a non-traumatic—time on his wedding night. *My* mother was Scottish; she was vague about this sort of thing. Mummy cared about antiques, Mummy cared about Scotland, Mummy cared about genealogy, not gynecology, so she let Mrs. Hadley, who was on the board of Vassar, arrange all the practical details, among which was—*this*! (emphasis in original)[9]

There is an important difference, however, between the oppression of an upper-class woman and those in the lower classes. Her life of luxury is based on the lower wages of her servants, gardeners, cleaning women and chauffeurs who are often persons from minority groups. Her wealth is created by working men and women whose access to medical care, quality education, and recreation is substantially below hers. She will never have to worry about losing her home because the house payments had to be missed, or not having surgery because there was no insurance. Her class status will mitigate her oppression. In popular culture, this contradiction was personified by Sue Ellen in the TV soap opera series *Dallas*. Sue Ellen was married (several times) to a lying, scheming, selfish character named J.R. They hated each other, and he mistreated her. But she wanted to be rich. So she kept coming back to him.

KINSHIP AND THE EARTH

Native American ideology believed the earth's resources should be available only as needed by the community. In feudal society, the ownership of the land was based on a relationship of the church (which held it as God's trust) and was controlled by noble families who held that right through birth. Only under capitalism did land become titled and legally denoted as "private." Thus, the earth—land, mineral rights, waterways, and agricultural produce—could be inherited just as any wealth. Not only could the king "give away" large tracts of land in colonial America, the children of the nobles who inherited the land were automatically given the rights to the land, whether they cleared it, farmed it, or even came to live on it!

Again, the relationship of kin to class status becomes important. The average middle class family owns the house in which they live, their yard and perhaps one or two rental properties as part of their old-age security. Many families who consider themselves middle class spend their entire lives paying off their homes and become landowners very late in their lives. This ownership of land is directly related to personal use and needs. There is pride in taking care of what you own. One rarely finds a homeowner who allows rats to live in his basement and the heating system to fail.

Among the very wealthy, however, large amounts of the earth are held as "assets" which they as individuals will never personally use. Pieces of paper in their stock portfolios say they own copper and coal assets, steel plants, and hold the mortgages on other people's houses. This is a different type of personal property. They never have to mine the family's coal or work at the blast furnace in the steel plant. If the air conditioning in the furnace room of the factory breaks down, they will not experience the heat.

Today those who legally own the earth's resources are far removed from the realities of their ownership. Their investments are spread throughout the economy. Although they and their children receive the benefits of the exploitation of the earth's resources and the use of the land, they may not even know which coal mine, which shopping center, or which dam on which river is part of their wealth. *This in itself is a network—a vast network of legal ownership that obscures direct responsibility yet functions to funnel continuing wealth to the owners.*

Back in the days of slavery, the ownership of slaves was a clear example of exploitation. The plantation owners lived in large mansions while working their slaves to death. Likewise, the individual who owned the sweatshops where immigrant men, women, and children worked in crowded and unhealthy conditions could live in a mansion off the profits from their labor. Today it is much more difficult to see these relationships. Ownership is spread through "mutual funds" and complicated stock ownership schemes. But, in reality, little has changed. There is still a class of people who continue to get richer and richer because they own while others, who labored or are laboring, receive almost nothing.

The Constitution of the United States guarantees the right to private property, including the resources of the earth. But like the norms in earlier discussion, the laws protecting this ownership break down into dominant group norms and egalitarian norms.

Laws that protect our rights to own the land on which we build our homes are egalitarian, perceived as beneficial laws to all. The laws that allow one individual, family, or corporation to strip the earth to mine coal, removing homes and causing landslides and floods, is a very different kind of law.

In Appalachia, the people who actually live on the land, farm on the land, and hunt on the land, consistently speak of "Our Mountains." It has been estimated that 80 percent of the land in the state of West Virginia is owned by large out-of-state corporations. The ownership of these corporations is part of the wealth that has been historically transmitted from generation to generation.

The Native Americans, and African Americans Celtic farmers and loggers who originally lived in the mountains had no understanding of "mineral rights" or the economic potential of the coal and gas that lay under their land. When speculators in the early late 1800s and early 1900s offered them $500 for the mineral rights, they eagerly accepted what seemed like an enormous amount of cash. Of course they did not understand that what they had sold was at that time worth millions and today has reached billions. In this way, the Appalachian people can be compared to the Native Americans, who "gave away" land for cloth and whiskey without understanding the legal, economic, or social consequences under capitalism.

The governor of West Virginia from 1988 to 1996, Gaston Caperton, comes from a family whose ancestor, Hugh Caperton, used military force to take land from the Native Americans in what was then Virginia. During the Civil War Sam Caperton served in the Confederate Congress and, after West Virginia seceded, became a legislator in the new state. Wealth made under the slave system was then invested into coal properties, and the next generation made wealth through the Slab Fork Coal Corporation. That wealth was then invested into insurance, including health insurance. As the costs of health care have skyrocketed, so have the profit margins of the "health care industry." Gaston Caperton, a multimillionaire, had never held a political office in his life. But when he decided he wanted to be Governor of West Virginia in 1988, he was easily able to raise $1.5 million from his own pockets and networks to purchase the election.

Caperton is a close political ally of West Virginia Senator Jay Rockefeller. An outsider, Rockefeller decided to make a "political career" in West Virginia. When he ran for governor, he spent more (in terms of per capita expenditure per population) than any candidate in the country had ever spent. The Rockefeller family, of course, hold key ownership of the world's largest energy corporation. Thus it was not surprising that a Rockefeller was interested in a state with major energy resources.

This kind of political leadership has certainly not benefitted West Virginia. In 1993 and 1994 it had the highest unemployment rate in the nation. In 1995 it had the highest death rate of any state and in 1995 had the lowest median income in the country. The state also has the lowest percentage of college graduates in the country. The valuable resources of the state have been exploited by a network of families that have combined control over corporations and control over politics to run the state in their own interests.

LATERAL NETWORKS AND RACE

Lateral networks function essentially through generalized reciprocity—you do this for me, and when you need something I'll pay you back. Over time, it is supposed to balance out. What makes networks different, for the purposes of our analysis, is the amount and type of resources that are involved and how that affects power in our society. Since different racial and ethnic groups occupy different positions on the ladder, they have access to different kinds of resources.

When sociologists and political scientists do "power structure research" in communities, they look for the leaders within those networks who exercise authority, and with that authority, power. But those leaders are usually very much like the people they are leading, and their power is based largely on consensus. This confusion between lateral and hierarchical networks helps explain the different conclusions drawn by Robert Dahl and William G.

Domhoff in their analysis of the power structures of New Haven, Connecticut. Dahl examined only the lateral networks while Domhoff asked the types of questions that revealed the hierarchical networks.[10]

The networks that one finds in a small rural community—the local farmer's cooperative, the churches, the local Rotary, the PTA, and the local NASCAR club—are more than organizations. The people in them went to school together, intermarried, worship together, drink together, race together, and fight with each other. As an example, we might look at the different networks available to the white middle sectors of a small town versus the networks available to the agricultural workers who are not only a lower class but a different ethnicity.

If that small rural community (white and Protestant) is like the one in which I was raised in upstate New York, there are also people who are almost entirely outside the town's networks. For example, in Penn Yan, New York, there were Latino migrant laborers who came to pick the fruits and vegetables in the summer. Largely Catholic and Spanish speaking, they were not invited to the local Protestant churches. They were not invited to join the Kiwanis or Rotary Club, serve on the volunteer fire department or go to the local bars for a drink. They were poorer, and they were "different." For many people in the town, they were the invisible class, although the local merchants gladly took their money on Friday nights.[11]

If a migrant child got sick, the parents could turn only to the networks they possessed *within* the small migrant community. If the child had to be taken to the local hospital, the parents were at the mercy of a formal and impersonal bureaucracy. They were not related to any of the doctors and nurses. No one who worked at the hospital owed them any favors. Without these connections, the migrant laborers with the sick child had far less access to resources—they had less power.

In comparison, if the child of a local farmer was sick and taken to the hospital, a number of networking factors might come into play. One of the doctors might be married to the farmer's cousin's wife's sister. The mother may have graduated from high school with several of the nurses and the hospital administrator. The Baptist Women's group might volunteer to help sit with the sick child, or watch the other children while the mother stays with the sick one. These are all resources that go beyond the formal organization of help that a hospital officially provides. Although the farmer is only middle class, these networks will provide a critical kind of support in time of need.

This contrast shows how the resources of a network are based on the type of resources available to the people who make them up. Although the local farmers were certainly not at the top of the ladder in our society, they were still far more able to access resources than the migrants who were at the bottom. The example also illustrates how networks function within race and ethnic groups. The earlier example, of a male principal networking to get money for sports, also points out that networks can have a gender base.

The very wealthy are different. Although they may use networks for personal ends—to obtain information that protect's one's company or obtain stock tips—they do not need to turn to networks to provide services and goods they can purchase. The sick child of very wealthy parents can be flown to the most advanced clinic in the country, where expensive specialists will provide the most advanced care. Nannies will watch the other children. No one will need to hold a bake sale, Gospel Sing or rummage sale to raise money to pay the parents' hotel costs while they are with the child.

Individuals are often born into networks and rarely are *formally* taught how to use and protect their networks—it is just simply something that you do. Women's status in the home has traditionally isolated them from creating their own independent social networks. Recently, women have begun to research and analyze "good old boy networks"—the ways in which men organize themselves to exercise power and keep women subordinate. The response by women has been consciously to organize networks that can compete with male networks and end their dependence on men's networks. Getting jobs, raises, good recommendations, and information are all network functions, and women in the workplace have begun to use one another as support for these functions.

Likewise, as minorities have entered previously all-white areas of society, they have learned to create networks in new arenas. In all these cases, informal social networks are part of the struggle for power—to improve one's access and status in terms of the rewards of society.[12]

Chapter 3 pointed out that a small segment of the African American community has entered the upper classes as a result of the openings created by the civil rights movement. Because racism continues to function even when one has wealth, the black elite have themselves formed networks. *Business Week* in 29 November 1993 identified what it considered to be key players "Inside the Black Network" and drew a diagram to show their connections. Some better-known members of this network include "Magic" Johnson (former basketball star), Ron Brown (the late secretary of commerce of the United States), Spike Lee (filmmaker), David Dinkins (former New York City Mayor), General Colin Powell (former Chairperson, Joint Chiefs of Staff), Michael Jackson (singer), Betty Shabazz (widow of Malcolm X), and Bill Cosby (television star). Lesser-known players included a variety of black businessmen and investors.

The article described how these people operated "behind the scenes" to access influence and money for their goals: "as black businesspeople create strong beachheads in fields such as communications, entertainment, and consumer goods, networking provides leverage that would otherwise be lacking.

Working together, African Americans are forming pools of capital and new opportunities that are helping to overcome traditional barriers to success."[13]

The question remains whether such networks will operate in ways to benefit the entire African American community, including the unemployed youth of the inner cities. Or will the money earned off "gangsta rap" and other "ethnic enterprises" be seen as a lucrative source of greater and greater wealth for the few?

LATERAL NETWORKS AND POLITICAL POWER

Those who control the great wealth of our society are a tiny minority. Lower status groups (the poor and disappearing middle class, women, minorities, etc.) resist and continually challenge elite control with their ideas of equality and democracy. Thus the upper-status groups must constantly use networks to protect their power and social status. In other words, since they cannot really justify their privilege and since they cannot outnumber the oppressed, they must be better organized. They must create and sustain active lateral networks that continually assess the political situation and provide ways for them to maintain their power. They must also actively work to prevent lower level networks from developing into social movements that challenge their power. (This is discussed later under hierarchal networks.)

Three staff writers for *The Indianapolis Star*, newspaper of Indiana's state capital, wrote a five part series detailing the corruption of that state's legislature:

> Something was missing from the Indiana General Assembly last year. Oh, the lawmakers were there, all right. The lobbyists were out in force. And so was big money.
>
> Nowhere in sight?
>
> Democracy.
>
> Or at least the spirit of democracy—the expectation that public servants will make laws with the good of everyday Hoosiers in mind. That was hijacked by a coalition of powerful special interests that had poured millions of dollars into election campaigns, then drew up its own legislative agenda and rammed it through.
>
> An extraordinay coalition of about 40 big-business interests, led by the Indiana Chamber of Commerce, aligned itself with the sympathetic Republican majority to win virtually everything it wanted.[14]

The formal structure of government in the United States of America is supposed to give power to "the people." Most Americans are committed to the ideologies of democracy and equality. No politician can run for office by proclaiming, "If elected, I promise to protect the interests of the big banks and the oil companies, cut back on aid to middle-class college students, eliminate job training for the poor and provide subsidies to corporations to install robots that replace workers." How many of us would vote for a politician who campaigned on that platform?

Yet, in reality, the vast majority of politicians in this country vote in a way consistent with our hypothetical politician and the Indiana legislators described above. How is it possible for those who hold formal power in a government based on the vote of the people actually to end up representing only the interests of the tiny elite? A large part of the answer lies in the way the lateral networks in our society are used by the elite to wield far greater power than their numbers would suggest.

C. Wright Mills was the first major American sociologist to raise such a question in his book *The Power Elite*.[15] But the first real study of how networks operated within the structure of American politics was provided by William G. Domhoff's *Who Rules America*?[16] Domhoff researched the way that powerful people were connected through their membership in influential organizations, social clubs, and social activities. His research was structural—he did not explore *how* they used these connections—but he showed that the connections existed. In a more recent book, Domhoff chose several important political issues as case studies and showed, indeed, how groups that represent the networks of the elite are able to impact and largely determine the shape of decision-making within government.[17]

Mills and Domhoff were using a theoretical perspective similar to that of this book. They believed that the informal powerful networks of the elite were undermining democracy and the chances for those of lower status to achieve greater equality. Other authors, whose perspectives were far more conservative, asserted such networks were used as a "conspiracy" to undermine the republican form of government.[18] Because such writers were not in favor of labor unions or civil rights, they tried to link such networks to plots by Jews in collusion with labor and "black militants." This ideology of the right wing has its own network. In the current period, it is largely identified with the "Religious Right." We discuss the power of this network in more detail in Chapter 15.

Despite such obvious differences, both types of studies demonstrated the existence of a vast, well-organized network of political power in America that is largely invisible to most citizens and is certainly not talked about in most high school "social studies" classes!

The networks of power in America, then, consist of more than kinship and golf games. The *New York Times*, for example, described the Young Presidents' Organization in the following manner:

> The YPO is a little like the CIA. You know it exists, but you're never quite sure exactly what it's doing or who's in it. Like the spy agency's staff, the membership roster of the Young Presidents' Organization is carefully guarded, and its 7,000 or so members are fiercely protective of one another. Even spouses aren't allowed to know who participates in certain meetings, let alone what is discussed.
>
> But chances are, if you know someone who's youngish (average age 42), male (97 percent) and head of a substantial business (average sales $35 million) that person belongs to the YPO. In many ways, the Texas-based not-for-profit YPO is a curious phenomenon for the s—an unapologetic old-boy network with a youthful cast.
>
> . . . Apart from the three universities (weeklong study junkets in idyllic settings for some 5000 YPO couples), the monthly chapter meetings, and weeklong courses at the country's best business schools, it is the closed-door monthly forum meetings that members mention as the most impressive part of the organization. For all this, they pay about $2,000 in annual dues plus varying local dues that run as high as $4,000 in New York. In these four-hour session, eight to 12 members discuss professional and personal problems and issues.[19]

Note that no mention is made of ethnicity or race, but it is highly probable that the organization is all or almost totally EuroAmerican.

The lateral networks of the elite in American society may be networks that link formal political power to other organizations that protect business interests. In the example above of the black business network, the late Secretary of Commerce Ron Brown and former General Colin Powell represent the interests of that network in the official bureaucracy of government.

There are numerous and detailed studies of how various business networks have influenced, bribed or corrupted government.[20] When Bechtel Corporation wanted to get involved with nuclear reactor manufacturers in 1953, they turned to an organization called the Business Council, whose primary purpose is to network corporate interests with government. McCartney describes in detail the way in which Steve Bechtel was able to approach the president and vice-president of the United States, the chairperson of the

Atomic Energy Commission, senators and congresspersons, and officials of the Central Intelligence Agency.[21] The box at the beginning of this chapter is another example.

Other networks transcend specific business interests and act, instead, as general bodies to network the wealthy as a ruling class. In other words, despite particular differences, those in power share a common concern that their right to power not be questioned, and that they are able to maintain their power.

One such organization is the Trilateral Commission. The organization describes itself in the following way: "The Trilateral Commission was formed in 1973 by private citizens of Western Europe, Japan, and North America to foster closer cooperation among these three regions on common problems. It seeks to improve public understanding of such problems, to support proposals of handling them jointly, and to nurture habits and practices of working together among these regions." In other words, the "global economy" that is now so widely accepted was planned and organized beginning in 1973.

The first chairperson of the commission was David Rockefeller, chairperson of Chase Manhattan Bank and a member of the elite and powerful Rockefeller family. John D. ("Jay") Rockefeller III is currently senator from West Virginia and a member. The rest of the membership consists of the chief executives of the largest global corporations and banks, other powerful politicians and heads of state from England, Japan, France, and Germany, professors from some of the most elite universities in the world, and top leaders of major international labor unions.

Researchers such as myself have no access to the internal documents or discussions of such a powerful and elite group. One can only surmise the processes that occurred, using the consequences that flowed from certain activities. An example is the inclusion of Georgia Governor Jimmy Carter in the Trilateral Commission several years prior to the presidential election of 1976.

If we remember our history, 1976 was a low year in American politics. Kennedy was assassinated in 1963 and in the next several years the scandal surrounding the Warren Commission report of the assassination increased. Many Americans believed that something more was involved than a lone crazy gunman named Oswald. Lyndon Johnson chose not to run for reelection to the presidency several years later. Information soon surfaced regarding Johnson's connections to companies that made huge profits from the Vietnam War as well as his personal and social connections to individuals involved in the Kennedy assassination. Martin Luther King and Bobby Kennedy were both assassinated, and questions regarding the assassins, the FBI, and the CIA continued to surface.

Then the Watergate Scandal broke. As Richard Nixon's network of spies, blackmailers, and extortionists was revealed by the press, public confidence in the government of the United States was at an all-time low. When Nixon resigned, there was no vice-president (the elected vice-president, Spiro Agnew had been convicted of Mafia-related kickbacks). So Jerry Ford, former University of Michigan football player and president of the Senate, became president of the United States.

Like the breakdown in confidence that occurred in Detroit following the rebellion, the elite of American society realized that they had to intervene directly to restore credibility to a leadership that had been exposed as rotten to the core. Where did they turn? The U.S. Senate picked Nelson Rockefeller (brother of David) to be vice-president of the United States. He occupied the office for only six months and carried out only one major task—chairing a commission to reform the CIA. When that was done, he resigned. One could hypothesize that the ruling class realized they had to bring the CIA under their control and away from drugs and gun-mob influences.

But the American public were cynical and disillusioned. A presidential candidate that would inspire trust was needed. A well-to-do peanut farmer who had worked his way up through the Democratic Party of Georgia suddenly became a front-runner for the Democratic nomination for president of the United States. His smiling face appeared on the covers of *Time* and *News week*. Jimmy Carter, as governor of Georgia, had developed close connections to Coca-Cola Corporation, a huge multinational corporation headquartered in Georgia.

Someone somewhere knew that this politician, with his down-home smile and religious beliefs, would appear clean and appealing to a cynical American people. But Carter had no foreign policy experience. What to do? By August 1975 this relatively obscure state politician had become a member of a powerful global network—the Trilateral Commission. One can only assume that Carter's rise into membership was part of a grooming process necessary to teach him the ruling class perspective on the problems of the world.

One of the "problems" referred to by the commission's description of purpose in 1973 were the massive social movements sweeping the Western world. Simply put, the Trilateral Commission needed to meet the challenge of movements demanding greater equality and democracy. Carter's ascent to political power coincided with the peaking of these social movements of the 1960s. Not only were the elite concerned about the credibility of the government, they were concerned about the very stability of American society. The Trilateral Commission hired three prominent political scientists to study the problem. The results were published in 1975 as a book titled *The Crisis of Democracy: Report on the Governability of Democracies to the Trilateral Commission.*[22]

The following quotes are from the Trilateral Commission's study of the United States. Emphasis has been added to the points which reveal their elite orientation and their basic hostility to the extension of democracy.

> Unlike Japanese and most European societies, American society is characterized by a broad consensus on democratic, liberal, egalitarian values. For much of the time, the commitment to these values is neither passionate nor intense. During periods of rapid social change, however, these democratic and egalitarian values of the American creed are reaffirmed. The intensity of belief during such creedal passion periods leads to the challenging of established authority and to major efforts to change governmental structure to accord more fully with those values. In this respect, the democratic surge of the 1960s shares many characteristics with the comparable egalitarian and reform movements of the Jacksonian and Progressive eras.
>
> *. . . some of the problems of governance in the United States today stem from an excess of democracy*—an "excess of democracy" in much the same sense in which David Donald used the term to refer to the consequences of the Jacksonian revolution which helped to precipitate the Civil War. Needed, instead, is a greater degree of moderation in democracy.
>
> *. . .democracy is only one way of constituting authority, and it is not necessarily a universally applicable one. In many situations the claims of expertise, seniority, experience and special talents may override the claims of democracy as a way of constituted authority.*
>
> Second, the effective *operation of a democratic political system usually requires some measure of apathy and noninvolvement on the party of some individuals and groups*. This marginality on the part of some groups is inherently undemocratic, but it has also been one of the factors which has enabled democracy to function effectively. *Marginal social groups, as in the case of the blacks, are now becoming full participants in the political system. Yet the danger of overloading the political system with demands which extend its functions and undermine its authority still remains.*
>
> The vulnerability of democratic government in the United States thus comes not primarily from external threats, though such threats are real, nor from internal subversion from the left or the right, although both possibilities could exist, but rather from the internal dynamics of democracy itself in a highly education,

> mobilized and participant society. We have to recognize that there are potentially desirable limits to economic growth. *There are also potentially desirable limits to the indefinite extension of political democracy.*[23]

HIERARCHICAL NETWORKS

Networks also function to link individuals and groups that have a higher status to individuals or groups on rungs of the ladder below them. These are **hierarchical networks**. These are hierarchical because the exchange is *not* equal. Those on the top of the network get more out of it than those on the bottom. Nonetheless, something "trickles down" to the bottom, and those receiving it often believe they must stay in the network to receive anything at all.

Unlike bureaucratic hierarchies, hierarchical networks are unofficial. In many organizations, a manager or officer will use an informal network to get information or exert influence on those below him or her or on those with less power. These networks circumvent official organizational channels and are used either when official channels are not working well or something is needed that cannot be done officially. For example, a manager may invite the local union president to be a member of the local business organization with the argument that it will help the union to have "the connections." At the same time, the union president is being offered the prestige of membership and the feeling of hanging out with important people. Although the union person might have been offended had she or he been offered a bribe, the manager is bribing in a more subtle, but just as effective, way.

The example above is often described by the term **cooptation**. The is the social process whereby a leader or spokesperson for one organization or network is brought over, or into, a competing organization or network. When individuals are coopted they cease independently to represent the interests of their own constituency; they now are compromised by their involvement with the competing constituency. Militant women or minorities are often offered promotions, with the price tag that they moderate or stop representing the demands of their group. Community leaders who organize the poor are often given comfortable positions through government or foundation grants and become bureaucrats instead of leaders.

A coopted individual often serves to connect a lateral network (his or her neighborhood, union or church) to another, more powerful network. The coopted leader is given credit for "getting" the jobs, donations, or contracts from the more powerful network. But in turn, the co-opted leader is expected to "deliver" his or her constituency (their votes, their agreement on a contract, their support of a policy.) The coopted leader is also expected to defend the interests of the dominant network if any independent leaders emerge who call for changes not in the interests of the dominant group. In the African American community, leaders believed to have been coopted by dominant white interests were called "Uncle Toms." In the union, they are called "sell-outs." But those below do not always clearly see who, or who, they have become the inferior part of an hierarchical network.

The presence of important labor leaders among the membership of The Trilateral Commission is one example. Of course, labor leaders would argue that their memberships promote cooperation and that their members benefit from their participation. But as the global plan for a world economy has been actualized, the workers of the world have suffered greater and greater unemployment and lower and lower living standards. This suggests that such "cooperation" has not benefited the labor leaders' members.

Hierarchal networking is most prominent in politics. The two major political parties—Democrat and Republican—both rely on networking to carry out campaigns, patronage, and raise money. Legal *and* illegal political activities (bribes, vote fraud, bureaucratic harassment) are car ried out almost entirely within these informal networks. Only a tiny percentage of the American people actively participate in a major political party, other than registering and voting. Yet the parties act as major brokers of power—through their hierarchal networks. How candidates are selected, who gets the blessing of "the machines," who gets the government grants, the lucrative contracts, and the good jobs are all a function of the networks.

If a local political contact "delivers" his or her ward or precinct to the chosen candidate, then there will be money the next summer for jobs for teenagers or money for a recreation program, or the streets will be paved. If the local political contact acts against the chosen candidate, an informal telephone call may suggest that such benefits will be denied to the area. These networks deliver votes, volunteers, and money and link poor and working-class neighborhoods to middle-class and wealthy neighborhoods within a single party or behind a single candidate.

The examples above show the exchange function of networks—if you do something for me, I'll do something for you. If the network is lateral the exchange is likely to be reciprocal—that is, the rewards to each side will "balance out" over the long run. But if the network is hierarchal, the exchange is not balanced.

A poor community that gets a playground for supporting a certain candidate is still without a health clinic, a good school, or decent housing. They have traded a precious resource—their votes—for a token return. Because they were not a part of the lateral networking that selected the candidates, made the major contributions, or got the important government jobs, they can do very little except exercise a possible "negative" power—"If you don't give us something for our votes, next time we might vote for the other guy."

The notion of such powerful networks, of course, runs counter to the idea that candidates are selected for their stand on "issues." Many voters do indeed take the issues into account. But one cannot underestimate the power of the networks, and any candidate who wants to make a serious bid for political power must either use the existing hierarchal networks, or create his or her own.

COMPETING NETWORKS

There are often different and conflicting interests within the elite itself.[24] In other words, networks can represent the special interests of particular groups as well as the broader interests of a class or dominant ethnic group. Those who argue that the "people" in America have the real power usually are describing the process by which various factions within the elite will appeal to the public for support of *their* side in some issue. This is called *pluralism* and has to do with the competition between special interests within the ruling class.

For example, several years ago there was a fierce battle between those who favored a treaty giving Panama greater control over the Panama Canal and those who opposed that treaty. The television and newspapers were full of arguments from businesspeople and politicians who were taking sides one way or the other. Meanwhile the vast majority of people who were trying to pay their bills, obtain medical insurance, and keep their jobs were asking "What difference does it make in *my* life who controls the canal?" In other words, no matter who "won" that argument, most average Americans would not find their situation changed.

A more recent example is that of NAFTA—the North American Free Trade Agreement. Certain banks and industries stood to benefit from open trade, others stood to lose. Both sides appealed to the average American. The question remains: if there are any benefits to NAFTA, will the average American on the street receive those benefits or will it go into the pockets of those who are already wealthy?

Both of these are examples of a power struggle *within* a given class grouping. It is easy to confuse what appears to be real political competition in American society with what is really just competition between groups within the ruling class. Stephen Wildstrom fails to understand this distinction in his review for *Business Week* of two recent books on lobbying. *The Lobbyists: How Influence Peddlers Get Their Way in Washington* describes the tax-and-spending debate of 1990. Wildstrom says this book demonstrates democratic politics because it shows how the power of some lobbyists are checked by the power of other lobbyists. He is very critical of the other book, *The Lobbyists*, which purports to show the dominant power exercised by corporations over the political process. Wildstrom calls these arguments "silly." He misses the point. The first book is analyzing the struggle between lobbyists themselves, which is indeed a competitive process. The second book is analyzing the effect of corporate lobbying on the general wellbeing of citizens, which is the issue of class.[25]

In contrast to the somewhat unconscious and hidden nature of the informal networks, the organized networks of our society—the bureaucracies of government, business, religion, education and other institutions—function openly as channels of communication and power. The way these bureaucracies use power to maintain social stratification is the next subject of discussion.

SUMMARY

One major source of social power is through networking. This chapter looks at how networking is used to maintain the ladder of social stratification in America. Networking is often ignored in studies of social power since it is informal, and often not readily recognized.

People network within their own groups. The higher the group is on the ladder, the more resources they will be able to access within their network. These groups may be based on gender, class, kinship, or ethnicity—or some combination of those.

Lateral networks link individuals who are on the same rung of the ladder. For the elite, kinship is one of the most important lateral networks. Wealth is inherited in America and kinship is the key to that inheritance. Despite popular myths, much of the great wealth of America's richest families can be traced back hundreds years to original land grants from the European kings. Research showed that in the city of Detroit, the wealthy elite linked by kinship were also those in key positions of economic and political influence.

The wealthy intermarry to protect their wealth and privilege from dissipation. Women in the elite groups are expected to play a role that insures that continuation of the family wealth and the proper socialization of children into the network.

The inheritance of wealth in a capitalist society means that owning groups may control resources that they do not personally use, but rather exploit. This ownership is no longer direct, as in the days of the direct exploitation of the slave or immigrant laborer. Instead, it is mediated through a complicated layers of stocks, bonds, mutual funds and other papers that obscure the results of the oppression, exploitation, or degradation that may be going on.

Lateral networks may also be based on race or ethnicity. Many different immigrant groups in America used their networks to survive in a new culture. The more a group is discriminated against by the dominant groups, the more that group is likely to create its own networks. As individuals—such as women and ethnic minorities—have been able to enter previously closed arenas, they have discovered that they still need to create their own networks. They may be formally and officially integrated, and still be kept outside the informal networks that are often the real sources of power.

Networks also operate within and around the government. Since democracy is based on the premise that the majority rules, the elite minority must find others ways to protect its interests. One way is to be highly organized. Another way is to coopt the leaders of the networks that might challenge their control. The third is to create hierarchical networks, where control of those below them is based on allowing a small amount of resources to "trickle down" in exchange for the support of those on the lower rungs. The two most important examples of hierarchical networks in American society are the networks that operate within the Republican and Democratic parties.

Networks can also be in competition with one another. When different groups within the elite have conflicting interests, they will often appeal to other networks for support.

Vocabulary

Networking. The informal relationships that allow individuals or groups to tap into, and share, resources; members of networks can access not only the resources they control but the resources of others.

Lateral Networks. Networks that link persons in similar statuses with similar levels of resources; a network based on reciprocity—the assumption that you will get back approximately the same amount that you put in.

Interlocking Directorate. When boards of directors are connected by one or more individuals who serves on more than one board and provides that basis for networking.

Hierarchical Networks. Networks that links individuals and groups with a higher status to individuals or groups on rungs of the ladder below them; the exchange within the network is not equal.

Cooptation. A social process whereby a leader or spokesperson for one organization or network is brought over, or into, a competing organization or network.

Discussion Questions.

1. In the spring of 1995 the nation was shocked by the bombing of a federal office building on Oklahoma City. It was believed that the bombers were members of a militia who felt that there was "a conspiracy" by the elite to "sell out" America. People who believe this conspiracy theory often cite the existence of the Trilateral Commission as proof. What is the difference between viewing social power as a conspiracy and seeing the exercise of social power through networks? Would you characterize the Trilateral Commission as a conspiracy or as a form of network? What difference does it make for our understanding when we analyze it in these two different ways?

2. Can you describe lateral networks to which you belong? What kinds of power do you derive from being a member of those networks? Are you a member of a hierarchical network? Are you on the receiving or losing end of that network? Discuss.

3. Can you identify networks that exist in your workplace, school, or neighborhood to which you are *not* allowed to belong? Can you sociologically analyze why?

4. We are often taught how our government is "supposed" to run. Rarely are we taught about how congressmen, judges, and other officials are members of powerful networks. Why are we not taught this?

5. We are taught that we shall be judged on the basis of our individual merits and achievements. (Many students think *this* is what "individualism" means.) How do networks prevent individuals from being assessed fairly on their merits? Does someone who is *not* a member of a controlling network have to work two or three times harder to get a promotion than someone who is a member of the network? Can networks actually hamper or hurt the success of a company, university, church or other organization?

Resources

Videos: *All the President's Men*

Based on the best-selling book by the two reporters who "uncovered" Watergate, this movie tells their exciting story. What appears to be a two-bit burglary soon is discovered to be connected to a complicated network of Nixon campaign workers, government officials and even CIA agents. Woodward (Robert Redford) and Bernstein (Dustin Hoffman) investigate the connections in a series of articles for the *Washington Post.* Richard Nixon is not the only president who rose to power using networks but surely he mastered the techniques of networking! Rated PG.

Boyz 'n the Hood.

This movie is about a much different kind of network. Trapped in an inner city neighborhood of Los Angeles, the young men in this movie form a network that shares friendship, protection, drugs, and women. The human drama, and tragedy, that is played out reflects both a microsociological view (how does the concept of "self-fulfilling prophecy apply to Doughboy?) and a macrosociological view (listen closely to Furious Style's speech in front of the billboard). This is the story of what it means to network close to the bottom of the ladder. Starring Ice Cube and Larry Fishburne. Rated R.

NOTES

Complete citations are provided in the Bibliography.

1. Takaki 1993.
2. Jones 1992, 123–24, 237, 252–54. Also see Stack 1975.
3. Sidel 1986.
4. Compare the description of education of elite schools given by Cookson and Persell (1985) with the description of education for the working class and the poor given by Apple and Weis (1983) and Kozol (1991).
5. *Corporate Power and Urban Crisis in Detroit* (Princeton: Princeton University Press, 1978).
6. For a more complete description of the methodology that was used, see the original study.
7. "Progress Report," New Detroit Inc., cited in Ewen 1978, 210.
8. Mills 1956; Domhoff 1967, 1983; Parenti 1988.
9. Aronson 1993, 78.
10. Dahl 1961; Domhoff 1983, 157–97.
11. When I was a teenager, our church youth group visited the migrant camp to put on some kind of program to "do good." I don't remember what it was we did, and I doubt we did much good. But what did happen was that for the first time in my life I *saw* the invisible class of Americans, who picked my food and kept the prices cheap so my family could live a better life. I was appalled at the living conditions in the camp and learned something no schoolroom had ever taught me.
12. Perucci and Potter 1989.
13. *Business Week* 29 November 1993, 71.
14. Janet Williams, et al 1996..
15. Mills 1956.
16. Domhoff 1967. Domhoff expanded and updated the study in 1987.
17. Domhoff 1990.
18. Allen 1990.
19. *New York Times* Service, 8 November 1992.
20. One example is Brewton 1992. This book looks at the savings and loan collapse and bail out. Others are Potts, Kochan, and Whittington 1992; McCartney 1988.

21. McCartney 1988,106–12.

22. Crozier, Huntington, and Watanuki 1975.

23. Ibid., 112–15.

24. Domhoff's (1990) careful study of the power struggles that occurred around the passage of the Social Security Act of 1935, the Employment Act of 1946, and the National Labor relations Act of 1935 looks at the networks within the government and the lobbying organizations. His conclusion is that such power struggles must be viewed in their contexts — the historical period, the state of the economy, and shifting competing interests within the elite itself (pp 29–104).

25. Wildstrom 1993.

10

RED TAPE AND GOBBLEDYGOOK—BUREAUCRACIES AND POWER

How soon, sugar, the terrible becomes routine. We've all got this dangerous built-in talent: For turning horrors into errands. You hear folks wonder how the Germans could've done it? I believe part of the answer is: They made extermination be a nine-to-five activity. You know, salaries? Lunch breaks? And the staff came and did their job and went home and ate supper and slept and woke and came back and did their job and went home and at their supper and slept and woke and came back and did their job.
—That's partly how you get anything done, especially a chore what's dreadful, dreadful.
—Honey? we've all got to be real careful of what we can get used to.

—Lucille, in *Oldest Living Confederate Widow Tells All*[1]

The previous chapter discussed informal networking. In this chapter we examine how formal organizations, particularly bureaucracies, interact with social stratification. A **bureaucracy** is a system of administration characterized by specialized roles, explicit rules, and a hierarchy of authority. Formal organizations, and bureaucracies in particular, standardize "channels" on the assumption that clear and known relationships are more efficient for carrying out organizational tasks. If you have studied Max Weber's theories of a bureaucracy or organizations in a business management course, you are already familiar with the way they are *supposed* to function.[2]

Bureaucracies are a form of social organization and thus they reflect the society in which they exist. The extreme inequalities and the ideologies that justify them can be seen in our bureaucracies. In this chapter we are going to look at the way social stratification has an impact on bureaucracy. We will also examine the ways in which bureaucracies themselves become a source of social power and a tool for maintaining stratification. This is a different emphasis from the formal study of bureaucracy or organization.

American society is dominated by bureaucracies—both government and private. Our very existence depends on the bureaucracies that supply electrical power, deliver the mail, put food on the grocery shelves, and pick up the garbage. We often complain when these bureaucracies become inefficient or the channels don't work. Sometimes we vehemently disagree with the decisions made within a bureaucracy and carried out by it. But it is difficult to contemplate what life would be if there were no bureaucracies.

Bureaucracies in American society function within the parameters of the economic system of capitalism. They are part of a system that generates profit for the benefit of the upper classes. Bureaucracies have existed in other societies. In medieval Europe, the bureaucracy of the church was organized to benefit those in the highest positions of the church hierarchy. The kings, barons, and lords who supported the bureaucracy were rewarded with land grants and titles.

During most of the twentieth century the bureaucracies of Eastern Europe, the former Soviet Union, and China were structured to meet the goals of central planning and to provide jobs. Ultimate control over resources in these socialist societies was not held by those who owned capital but by those who sat on the top of the large bureaucracies—of the state and of the party.

Social scientists have argued about the relationship of social class, patriarchy and racism to bureaucratic structure. Do bureaucracies serve the higher-status groups, or do bureaucracies themselves control and determine who has higher status? These arguments are not very useful because they set the question up as either/or. It is not that a ruling class, patriarchy, or dominant ethnic group uses and manipulates bureaucracies only in its own narrow interests; it is not that monolithic powerful bureaucracies only override the interests of the dominant groups. What we argue is that there is an *interaction* between the ideologies that justify and rationalize inequality, the power of the elites, and the bureaucratic structures of society.

BUREAUCRATIC SUPPORT FOR DOMINANT GROUP IDEOLOGIES

Class ideology justifies organizing society in a way that benefits the upper classes. In general, government bureaucracies and private corporate bureaucracies function to subsidize the profits of the upper class. Businessmen do not see anything wrong with this. It is automatically assumed that what is good for business is what is good for government. One can find many examples of this at both local and national levels.

City governments can condemn low-income housing areas in order to provide cheap land so that mall developers can make money. When the New York Yankees threatened to leave town unless their stadium was refurbished, the city expended $28 million on the job and granted the Yankees a lease on very favorable terms. More than a decade later, the city was still servicing a multimillion-dollar debt and the Yankees were enjoying handsome profits.[3] With $3 billion of the taxpayers' money, the government took over the failing Penn Central Railroad and six others and built it back up to profitability with cash reserves of $800 million. In 1985 President Reagan, with the support of Congress, sold Conrail to private stockholders at less than half its value.[4]

Bureaucracies also function to support other stratification ideologies in our society. The basic assumptions of patriarchy assume that positions that organize and direct important resources outside the home should be held by men. Thus, at the highest levels men continue to control the most important bureaucracies. The ideology of racism defines the organization of resources in the best interests of "white America." Again, one finds the highest levels of important bureaucracies to be controlled by Euro-Americans. And the beliefs of speciesism assume that bureaucracies control natural resources for the exploitation and incidental use of humans. Americans are so used to these assumptions that they rarely think about or question them.

The people who hold the highest positions in these bureaucracies are persons who have already been socialized and molded by dominant group ideologies. They already hold a class, gender, and ethnic status when they come into the bureaucracy and have the training and the beliefs of those statuses. A top-level male manager raised in a wealthy suburb, who went to a private all-white exclusive male prep school and who now lives in another wealthy suburb reflects his own experiences and beliefs. He brings into the position his networks in corporate, financial and government circles. His ideas about what is good for the company, the country, and the earth are shaped by what is good for men, for whites, and for his social class.[5]

In contrast, the woman who works in the mailroom of that same company for minimum wage brings into that position her socialization as a woman, as a member of the working class, and as a member of her respective ethnic group. The hierarchy of the company is now superimposed on the already existing social hierarchies that make up social stratification in America—class, race, and gender. The groups that have power over her in the general society also have power over her in the bureaucracies that control the labor force.[6]

Bureaucracies are social structures and as such they are organized to use resources for social ends. If the production of paper requires dioxin for bleaching, and the waste must be dumped, the question of the bureaucracy is one of efficiency, cost and profit. Left alone, the bureaucracy will not raise questions about the environmental impact of cutting down trees to produce more and more paper or dumping toxic wastes in a local river. In other words, just as race, class, and gender affect the distribution of power within the bureaucracy, speciesism dictates that the bureaucracy views itself as having power over the resources of the earth.

The distribution of power in bureaucracies is not simply the result of individuals who hold ideologies. Dominant group norms are **institutionalized**. This means that the very structure of the organization enforces the attitudes and behaviors identified with class, race, and gender. These processes are called **institutionalized racism**, **institutionalized sexism** and **institutionalized classism**. Because a bureaucracy is a system that has its own rules of functioning, the individual who tries to act in an egalitarian way is likely to be isolated, punished, or simply made ineffective. For example, many social workers truly want to help the poor but the very way that welfare bureaucracies work actually prevent them from carrying out what they would really like to do.[7]

WAYS IN WHICH BUREAUCRACIES EXERCISE POWER

Bureaucracies obviously exercise the power for which they have been designed. For example, Ford Motor Corporation has the power to manufacture cars and make money; the police have the power to arrest criminals; the university has the power to schedule and cancel classes. Bureaucracies attempt to combine physical resources such as land, buildings, and machines with human resources such as administrators, scientists, technicians, and laborers in the most efficient and productive way to get their task done, whether that is building cars for a profit (General Motors), delivering mail (the U.S. Postal Service) or educating students (the university). But there are two major limitations in looking at only the obvious functions of bureaucracies.

The first is in looking only at the formal channels and approved hierarchies. This prevents one from seeing the many ways in which informal networks inform and control important resources. These are the networks we described in the previous chapter. The best management techniques in the world may not help a woman who moves into an administrative position over an informal network of older white males who resent her authority and use their network to ensure her failure.

The second problem with seeing the bureaucracy in only its own terms—what it's *supposed* to do—is that it removes the bureaucracy from its place in the already existing power relationships of the larger society. Again, knowledge of good management is not necessarily the knowledge an administrator needs to join the country club networks, attend cocktail parties with legislators, or subtly offer bribes.

Because our focus is on the relationship of bureaucracies to social stratification and power we are not going to analyze how they act to carry out their more obvious functions. Instead, we examine the three main ways in which bureaucracies interact with the social stratification system in our society.

BUREAUCRACIES AS A SOURCE OF POWER

The first is the way in which bureaucracies themselves become a source of power. If an individual or group can "grab control of" a bureaucracy, it can become a source of power. The larger the bureaucracy, and the more resources it commands, the greater the power that can be derived from control of it.

Perhaps the best example of this in recent American history was J. Edgar Hoover, director of the FBI. According to Epstein,

> in theory, six presidents, from Franklin Roosevelt to Richard Nixon, had the power to fire J. Edgar Hoover as head of the FBI, but in each case he had the power to retaliate by revealing illicit activities that occurred during their administrations (as well as information about the private lives of the presidents). This potential for retribution by government officials is compounded by the fact that in the vast complexity of the executive branch a president cannot be sure where embarrassing secrets exist, and he must assume that most officials have developed subterranean channels to journalists, who will both conceal their sources and give wide circulation to the "leak."[8]

Those in control can use the power of the bureaucracy to impose their own view of reality on others. As sociologist Charles Perrow argued in his study of complex organizations, "the power of the rich lies not in their ability to buy goods and services, but in their capacity to control the end toward which the vast resources of large organizations are directed."[9]

An incumbent governor running for reelection can give away state jobs, contracts, and deliver community services as part of winning votes. The governor can also threaten to withhold operating licenses or threaten safety inspections in order to create pressure on businesses for financial support.

Throughout American history politicians skillful in manipulating bureaucracies have worked their way up the political ladder, not because they were individually wealthy, but because they could use whatever bureaucracy they controlled as a base of power which in turn allowed them to control even larger bureaucracies. President Lyndon Baines Johnson was one example of a politician who skillfully used power within the bureaucracies of the State of Texas and the federal government to reach the highest political post in the country.[10]

Those who control the bureaucracy have this power because those of us outside it need the resources the bureaucracy controls. This is their source of power over us. The bureaucracy may have the power to deny us what we need, delay what we need, or make us accept something other than what we want. If we complain, we may find ourselves lost in "red tape"—filling out forms, staring at confusing computer printouts, or having phone calls transferred and put on "hold." Trying to get insurance claims adjusted, trying to get a refund on a faulty product, and trying to obtain Social Security disability benefits are all examples of plunging into society's bureaucracies. Of course, if you play golf with the insurance commissioner, you can access an informal network to resolve your problem. But the vast majority of people must plod through the official, and confusing, channels.

Confusing and misleading corporate reports may allow directors to take expensive golf trips and buy yachts instead of purchasing new machinery that is needed. Insurance companies have found that complicated claims forms and frequent challenges of claims discourage people from filing claims. State programs of welfare assistance can reduce the amount of money spent by requiring welfare recipients to make frequent trips to the welfare office to report. Many recipients cannot afford the bus or taxi fare, or cannot find child care while they are gone, and miss their appointments. The result is that they are dropped from the rolls.

Bureaucratic red tape may actually increase the power or benefits of a particular individual or group while interfering with the actual delivery of a product or service. The owners of the insurance company pocket greater profits if the number of claims in reduced. The governor of the state may be reelected by proving that he has "cut the welfare rolls." The stockholders reading the misleading reports will probably receive less dividends for their investment.

In other words, when the bureaucracy fails to function efficiently, the question must be asked—efficient for whom? Demands to make the bureaucracy function more effectively may be against the special interests of those who control the bureaucracy.

Another example can be found in the bureaucracy of the court system. It might be assumed that the function of courts is to dispense "justice." But if judges perceive the court as an avenue for career advancement, then the function is very different, as Wright points out:

> Under our system, judges who dispose of the greatest number of cases in the shortest possible time are the ones most favored. Justice in such hands becomes a numbers game, in which questions of humanity are disposed of summarily. Put bluntly, success in the game meant disposing of as many black and Hispanic bodies as possible. This was done by exacting pleas of guilty or by conducting speedy trials. Prosperity in such statistics wins one a promotion as an acting Supreme Court justice. That temporary glory results in an increase in pay and prestige, those indispensable symbols of American success. The increase in pay and prestige, not to mention power, served as powerful goads to comply with the system's rewards for such conduct.[11]

The examples above concern bureaucracies whose public, or agreed-upon purpose is the delivery of goods and services. According to egalitarian norms, delivery of bureaucratic goods and services should be impartial and available to all who satisfy the rules. What we have pointed out is that bureaucrats have the power to deny, delay, or alter the services or resources one needs. In these cases, the public is asking that the bureaucracy do better those things it is supposed to do.

HIDDEN BUREAUCRACIES

A second way in which the existing stratification of American society is maintained is through the "hidden" bureaucracy. If the actual purpose of a bureaucracy is to increase the power of the elite, then that bureaucracy may be concealed from general public view or its exact functions obscured. These are the bureaucracies that are masked from the public view but exert vast power over our lives.

William Greider describes one such bureaucracy, the Federal Reserve System, and argues that it is the most powerful bureaucracy in America:

> The American system depended upon deeper transactions than elections. It provided another mechanism of government, beyond the reach of the popular vote, one that managed the continuing conflicts of democratic capitalism. It had the power to resist the

> random passions of popular will and even to discipline the society at large. This other structure of American governance coexisted with the elected one, shared power with Congress and the President, and collaborated with them. In some circumstances, it opposed them and thwarted them. The community of elected politicians acquiesced to its power. The private economy responded to its direction. Private capital depended on it for protection. The governors of the Federal Reserve decided the largest questions of the political economy, including who shall prosper and who shall fail, yet their role remained opaque and mysterious. The Federal Reserve was shielded from scrutiny partly by its own official secrecy, but also by the curious ignorance of the American public.[12]

The power of the Federal Reserve, which includes the right to raise or lower interest rates, has an impact on the lives of all Americans in profound ways. For example, raising interest rates widens the gap between the rich and the poor. Because the top 7 percent of households own 60 percent of the nation's bonds and 31 percent of all other interest-bearing assets, taxpayers in the top 7 percent rake in nearly 40 percent of all interest income. Whereas the poor and the middle class, who have proportionately higher debts and less income assets, experience losses.[13]

Other powerful bureaucracies are rarely exposed to public scrutiny. In many localities, utility rates are fixed by commissions that are appointed. No one can avoid the consequences of rising electric, gas, phone, and water costs, but very few Americans have any idea of how those rates are fixed and whether that power is exercised in their own interest as consumers or to protect the profits of the large utility corporations. Pension funds worth hundreds of millions of dollars are administered by bureaucrats who have almost no accountability to the workers whose money is invested in the account. City and state government bodies invest their revenues in bond markets controlled by bureaucracies of which the average local politician has little, if any, understanding.

The existence of powerful bureaucracies that act largely in the interests of the elite and control our lives in largely invisible ways runs counter to our ideas of democracy. "The curious ignorance of the American public" noted by Greider is a reflection of our ideology of democracy that teaches us to believe *elected* officials exercise the most power. Our schools do not teach youth about the power of the Federal Reserve System, or organizations such as the Trilateral Commission because such information about the real world does not fit the myth of what our society is supposed to be. How many of you reading this ever learned much about the Federal Reserve?

BUREAUCRACIES AS INSULATORS

Bureaucracies interact with the system of social stratification in a third important way—by creating an "insulating" layer between elites and the lower classes. The massive bureaucracies of social control pay the wages of an important segment of the American population. It is often their job to enforce the unfair rules and unequal distribution of goods and services. These "middle layers" believe their positions on the ladder require supporting the ladder.

The police officers who are called on to protect the interests of banks in the inner city or corporate demands to break a picket line of workers are themselves members of the working class. Even though they are told they are to enforce equal justice under the law, they rarely act against the slum landlord or the sweatshop operator who uses illegal child labor. There are police officials who would very much like to enforce more egalitarian laws. But if they act too vigorously, they will discover that the slum landlords and sweatshop operators have powerful friends "downtown" in the city council or state legislature.

Of course, the socialization of police officers during their training does not help them to understand their role as enforcers of dominant group norms. Thus it is difficult for them to understand why poor and ethnic communities are so hostile to their activities. This is reflected in current rap music in which inner-city musicians portray the police as an occupying force within their communities. As pointed out earlier, when material benefits such as jobs, education, and good housing are not available, compliance with the dominant group norms of society must be done by force.

Police officers are the persons who are asked to bear the brunt of the outrage of those who have no stake in the current system. Too often the result is that the officer becomes bitter and hostile and the vicious cycle of abuse and hostility begins. It is also possible that the role of "enforcer" may attract the kind of individual whose socialization has made him or her need to dominate others.

Other government bureaucracies enforce other kinds of dominant group norms over less powerful individuals. When a social service agency deems that unemployed parents are "unfit" to care for their children, force may be used to remove the children from the home. In many cases, the problems in the home could be solved if parents had intensive counseling, if steady employment at a decent wage were available, and if the social workers were able to spend the time and resources necessary to help the family. But, like the police officers, the social worker is not given enough tools to help, so ends up punishing.

Thus our society creates an enormous layer of bureaucratic workers—school principals and teachers, administrative law judges for Social Security and workers' compensation , inspectors for environmental protection agencies. All these workers enforce bureaucratic roles that often protect the privileged at the expense of those on the bottom. Bank employees who repossess from those who default on their loans and hospital intake workers who decide who can afford medical care are workers who implement and enforce dominant group norms and in exchange are given jobs and a marginal "stake" in the system.

Edna Bonacich describes this middle class sector as the "sergeants" of the system:

> We professionals and managers are paid by the wealthy and powerful, by the corporations and the state, to keep things in order. Our role is one of maintaining the system of inequality. Our role is essentially that of controlling the poor. We are a semi-elite. We are given higher salaries, social status, better jobs, and better life chances as payment for our service to the system. We middle class people would like to believe that our positions of privilege benefits the less advantaged. We would like to believe that our upward mobility helps others, that the benefits we receive somehow "trickle down." But this is sheer self-delusion.[14]

The result is that anger against the ruling class is often deflected against some lowly bureaucrat. A frustrated and pain-ridden worker who is denied workers' compensation may take a gun and try to kill the bureaucrat that sent the notice of denial.

Violence by employees of the U.S. Postal Service markedly increased after the decision by Congress to "privatize" it. Instead of indirectly subsidizing corporate profits, the Post Office became a profit-making enterprise. Thus, tremendous pressure was now placed on employees to work faster and under more rigid rules. After several postal service supervisors were attacked and killed by outraged employees, management was finally forced to acknowledge a serious problem. But instead of looking at the speed up of working conditions and the capricious and arbitrary practices of management, the higher-ups decided to test all future employees for personality traits of aggression!

BUREAUCRACY AND SOCIAL CHANGE

Social pressure for bureaucratic change has usually been exerted by social movements. The reason is quite clear. As structures of the status quo, bureaucracies are conservative stabilizing forces. A bureaucracy is a form of organization based on rules, traditions, and common practice. Bureaucracies continue to do things in the old way, unless subjected to pressures for change. Groups who *like* the "old ways" that things are done are more likely to be represented by, and within, bureaucracies; groups seeking change are more likely to be "outside agitators,"and usually are seen as threatening the bureaucracy itself. One good example is the impact of the woman's movement on bureaucracy.

The woman's movement, as it was labeled in the 1960s, was largely a reform movement. Many women who were involved understood patriarchy as one of the fundamental ideologies shaping power in American society. But the question of how the structures that supported patriarchy should be changed was less clearly understood and certainly not agreed upon.

Most women approached the question of change as an issue of discrimination. In other words, women fought to have equal access to the positions formerly occupied by men. They felt that if the rules that kept women out of bureaucracies could be changed, then the bureaucracies themselves would change in their relationships to women. Women fought hard to open the bureaucracies that controlled education, science, corporations, and government to full participation at all levels. Women entered politics and began to run for offices, on the assumption that as political policy makers they could help overcome bureaucratic gender discrimination.

After three decades of intense political and social struggle, can we say that the woman's movement changed bureaucracies? The answer is yes *and* no. There have been some remarkable successes. Several professions formerly dominated by men—including law and medicine—now include a large proportion of women. At the local and state levels, the number of women elected to political office continues to increase. Women's consciousness around issues such as domestic violence has been raised, and women have created alternative bureaucracies to lobby, network, and provide services.

But the efforts and the successes only serve to make the failures all the more visible. Despite intense pressures, women are still struggling to change bureaucratic structures:

1. *Women still have to "crack" the glass ceiling.* Bureaucracies have allowed women fuller participation at lower levels. But the highest levels—the positions with the greatest power—have remained closed. The executive boardrooms, the partnerships of the most powerful law firms, and the U. S. Senate still hold only a token representation of women.
2. *Women still have to alter the media bureaucracy's manipulation of the images of women.* "Feminism" is still used as a media stigma to discredit women. Advertise ments continue to use female bodies to sell. Stand-up comedians continue to make women the butt of their jokes.

Movies continue to portray women in stereotyped roles and glorify violence against women. Simultaneously, the media continue to perpetuate dominant male stereotypes.

3. *Women still have truly to impact the male work climate of the bureaucracy.* Sexual harassment continues, and may even be escalating because the fundamental ideology of male supremacy has not been altered. The Tailhook incident in the U.S. Navy is an outstanding example. Women who had fought hard to achieve officer rank became the butt of sexual jokes and physical harassment from fellow male officers at a party and then the men at the highest levels of the navy bureaucracy tried to cover up the incident.
4. *Women still have to create an alternative role that allows women to be feminists and still be accepted.* In most bureaucracies the message is very clear—to be accepted by the "good old boys" you have two options: you can either act like us or you can act like a lady should and take the consequences. In the first case, women are supposed to act masculine—a requirement that includes laughing at male supremacist jokes and not questioning male supremacist behavior. In the second case, women are supposed to be pretty, coy, and not too aggressive. As desirable objects they are supposed to expect and handle the sexual advances that they will (through their "own fault") encourage.
5. *Women still have successfully to link women's struggles against patriarchy with the other forms of power domination in American society.* Some women managers have been more exploitative of lower-paid secretaries and janitors than male managers. And many women who have succeeded within bureaucracies have not spoken out in defense of the environment. Many white women continue to pay low wages to the minority women who clean their houses while they pursue successful careers.

Zoe Baird was a recent example of the contradictions within the women's movement. The Senate confirmation hearings for her appointment as Attorney General revealed that she had used the services of an undocumented worker for whom she had failed to make Social Security payments. Many women pointed out that no one had previously raised questions of male candidates about their household workers. Nonetheless, the unfairness of such exposure does not erase the fact that as an upper-class woman, Baird had climbed the career ladder exploiting the labor of poor women who were vulnerable as undocumented workers.

The organized women's movement succeeded in many cases because individuals within bureaucracies agreed with the democratic goals of equality and were willing to try to make changes. But the failures reflect a reality about bureaucracies that cannot be denied. Individuals within bureaucracy attempting to challenge the traditional power hierarchies discover resistance that is more subtle and more difficult to handle than government regulations or the demands of the marketplace.

Any politician who has taken office with ideas for cleaning out government bureaucracy quickly discovers two things. First, that she or he in certain ways depends on that same bureaucracy for information and access to services or goods, which gives those who have power *in* the bureaucracy *over* the politician. Second, orders from "the top" can be undermined and circum vented if they go against the interests of key persons in the bureaucratic structure. When Bill Clinton ran for president in 1992 his campaign criticized government "gridlock." But once in office, Clinton became as locked in by that gridlock as any other politician who succeeds by playing by the rules of the bureaucracy.

Director Oliver Stone argued in his movie *JFK* that John Kennedy's assassination was a result of the resistance by a powerful military network within the federal bureaucracy. This is an extreme example of the point above, but an example nonetheless. The president of the United States is supposed to be the commander in chief of the armed forces. Channels of authority in government allow the president to give orders that even the highest ranking generals must obey. Others beside Stone have argued that Kennedy's foreign policy decisions angered certain powerful industrial interests, particularly those that manufactured weapons and had strong informal links to high-ranking military decision makers.[15] If this hypothesis is true, then the military networks within and outside government were so powerful that they were capable of circumventing government bureaucracy, removing even the president of the United States and covering up their actions.

This analysis again raises the question of "conspiracy theory" and its relationship to any discussion of power in America. Most of our lives we are taught the way that bureaucracies are supposed to perform. Congress is *supposed* to draft legislation, not powerful elite groups operating behind the scenes. Politicians are *supposed* to represent the people, not powerful and wealthy campaign contributors. Church bishops are *supposed* to be loving and ethical and are not supposed to use church connections to make profitable investments and have mistresses. University researchers are *supposed* to be searching for scientific answers and are not supposed to slant their findings to assure that they can get more funding.

In all these examples, there is a gap between what is the proper and expected behavior and what actually happens. In none of these examples is the behavior actually illegal. In other words, if an individual is placed in a position in a bureaucracy, particularly if that position carries some power, many of us assume that the individual will act in the best interests of the bureaucracy—and ignore his or her class, gender, and other status interests and networks! When some individuals are discovered using networks that give them power beyond what they are supposed to have, there is a tendency to see this as a "plot" because those who are outside the networks can see a pattern and see ulterior motives.

Those accused of conspiracy, however, usually see themselves as only "doing what we had to do" given what they saw as their interests.[16] When businessmen chat informally on the golf course about the need to defeat a prounion candidate in November; when women gather in the church basement and discuss ways to prevent the minister from being reassigned to the church; when several deans have coffee and discuss who should receive the research grants—the individuals involved rarely think of themselves as "conspiring."

But when the prounion politician sees an orchestrated and well-funded advertisement campaign against him or her; when the church minister finds his or her support in the church evaporating; when the researcher discovers the grant monies have dried up, she or he may well argue that there has been a conspiracy against him or her! What we are describing are predictable and knowable social relationships and forces.

At times, individuals may actually see themselves as plotting. *But how they see themselves must be placed in the context of the results of their behavior.* No matter how much the bureaucrats rationalize their behavior as being for the "general good" the consequences may be the exploitation, oppression or degradation of some segment of the population. The decisions by bureaucrats under the Reagan administration may be seen in this context. Many of those who cut funding for public housing may have believed the effects in the "market economy" would be beneficial. But those cuts are directly responsible for the appearance of approximately 3 million homeless people on the streets of America within a decade.

All bureaucracies that exist within the general system imperatives of our society share certain characteristics. This means that bureaucrats who work for a corporation have little difficulty moving into a government bureaucracy; university administrators have little difficulty taking jobs in a corporation; media journalists have little difficulty working in a private public relations bureaucracy. As long as the bureaucrats share the dominant group ideologies, they will "fit in."

THE CONCENTRATION OF BUREAUCRATIC POWER

American society has not always been so highly bureaucratized. Indeed, one of the hallmarks of the post-World War II age has been the rapid growth of bureaucracies into larger and more concentrated organizations. Not only have corporations and banks merged and interlocked until a few giants control most of the wealth and resources of this country, but other areas of society have also come under the control of monolithic bureaucracies. *As these structures have become larger the power that lies in the hands of those who control those structures has markedly increased.*

We have already discussed the concentration of wealth in Chapter 3. But power in our society is more than just money. Other social structures that have power over us have also become larger and more powerful. The bureaucracies of religion, the media, and education also reflect the trend toward concentration of power.

The bureaucracies of the media, religion, and education are *not* socially separate. To a large extent those who own and control these bureaucracies are networked in ways described in Chapter 9. Kinship and country clubs connect newspaper editors to church bishops to university presidents. Such powerful individuals are not only linked by their shared social characteristics—overwhelmingly male, white and upper class—but by their shared ideologies. It is not a "conspiracy," then, when one finds the appointment of the state superintendent of schools to be a close personal friend of the publisher of the largest metropolitan newspaper in the state. Such connections have always existed; today, however, the bureaucracies being connected are larger and more powerful than every before.

For example, in 1922 there were four major daily newspapers in the city of Detroit. There were also 276 periodicals being published in the city, and that figure does not include company house magazines, specialty journals, religious publications or publications in the areas surrounding Detroit, but not in the city.[17] In other words, different ethnic groups, local neighborhoods, and unions all had their own newspapers and magazines. An individual living in Detroit had many different sources of news and analysis from many different perspectives. Today Detroit has only two daily newspapers and it is one of only forty-one cities in the country that still has two competing dailies. There are only a small handful of periodicals still published.

Detroit reflects the trend in the country as a whole. In 1900 there were 2,226 daily newspapers in the United States with an average circulation of 15,000 each. In 1992 the number of daily newspapers had been reduced to 1,570, but the average circulation was over 60,000. Concentration is also reflected by the fact that many city newspapers are no longer locally owned; they are owned and controlled by chains and dependent on other chains for access to national and international news.

The twenty-largest newspaper chains account for more than 57 percent of all daily circulation in the United States. Fifty years ago the news received by people around the world came from their own local radio stations and newspapers. Today the entire world watches or listens to just a handful of news sources. Ninety-eight percent of all American homes have television and over 60 percent have cable. Nearly 59 million people can now get their news from one single cable company, CNN.[18]

A similar concentration of bureaucracy and power has occurred in education. In the early 1900s there were small local schools in every town and city. Control of those schools was in the hands of the local citizens, teachers, administrators, and parents. Today, the small local school is being consolidated into large, impersonal schools where teachers, administrators, students and parents are strangers to one another. Policies are now dictated by countywide or even state boards of education, as well as the federal government.

The power (and salary) of the district superintendent of a large school system today would have been unimaginable a hundred years ago. The recently fired superintendent of the third-largest school system in the United States was making $200,000 a year and overseeing a system of 410,000 students. The Chicago Board of Education fired him, according to news reports, because of high costs and low achievement scores.[19]

In the early 1900s, small local churches printed their own bulletins, developed their own Sunday school lessons, and hired their own ministers. Today, millions of people receive their religion from a single preacher over a television set, and many more go to churches with millions of members where the church bureaucracy provides the bulletins, the Sunday school lessons and the minister. In 1989, 336 television stations and 1,485 radio stations in the United States were owned by religious organizations. Schuller's "Hour of Power" had 1.6 million viewers and record donations in 1989.[20]

Fifty-seven million Americans belong to the Roman Catholic church, 14 million belong to the Southern Baptist church, and 8 million belong to the United Methodist church. Even the lesser-known denominations boast large memberships. More than 2 million people belong to the Assemblies of God, almost 2 million people are Greek Orthodox, and the Church of the Nazarene and United Pentecostal Church International both have memberships of over half a million. The large denominations not only publish their own media but hire lobbyists to influence government and provide support for political candidates that agree with their views. Smaller independent churches without national affiliation continue to exist, but because they are small and have minimal resources, they have limited power.

The shape and structure of these bureaucracies of ideological social control have also been shaped by the new technologies. Satellites, computers, and robots make worldwide news reporting possible. Computers can now keep grade and attendance records for thousands of students in a single school system. Fiber optic cables now make it possible to transmit entire books across the country in seconds. The Reverend Billy Graham's evangelistic tours could be viewed simultaneously across the country as well as throughout the world.

But the new technology requires large capital investment. The small-town newspaper of fifty years ago could be financed as a small business investment requiring basic machinery and some skilled labor. Today newspapers require hook ups to international and national news services, expensive laser scanners and printers, computerized printing, and sophisticated marketing departments. Schools require expensive laboratory equipment, computers in all the classrooms, and satellite hookups to receive educational programs. A successful evangelist requires his or her own public relations (advertising) team, production of videos, and access to publishing. It is becoming increasingly difficult for an individual or group to compete with the large, well-financed bureaucracies that control ideology in our society.

The organizations that informed, taught, and preached a hundred, or even fifty years ago were smaller, more diversified, and more dispersed; today a handful of individuals can make decisions as to what the entire country should hear or know as "news" or "the truth." *The question is not just whether one agrees or disagrees with the content of the ideology being sold by the media, taught by the schools, or preached by religion. The point is that today whoever has access to these bureaucracies of ideological control wields enormous power.*

CONCLUSION

This chapter has argued that bureaucracies perpetuate and reinforce the social stratification of inequality and the concentration of power in the hands of dominant groups. It is important to remind the reader that the negative perception of bureaucracies in our society cannot be separated from the highly stratified society in which these bureaucracies arose and function. In a society where egalitarian norms overrode dominant group norms, would bureaucracies function in a more positive manner? One would assume so.

The three bureaucracies discussed in the latter part of this chapter—the media, religion, and education—are largely responsible for providing us with information, knowledge, and beliefs. Those who can control those bureaucracies have the ability to influence the ideas and beliefs of the vast majority of Americans. In other words, they are bureaucracies of ideological social control. The next chapter examines more closely the content of that ideological control.

SUMMARY

Bureaucracies are the formal organizations of power. American bureaucracies reflect the social stratification of our society, organizing resources and persons to get things done in a way which reflects the ideologies of culture. Since capitalism organizes the economic system, American bureaucracies are part of a profit-making system. Those who control these bureaucracies have been socialized into the norms of the society, and reflect the larger social stratification ladder. Thus, the largest and most powerful bureaucracies continue to be run by wealthy Euro-American men who perceive that humans should dominate nature.

Bureaucracies are part of the systems that enforce the norms of society. When we see racism, sexism, or classism being practiced by a bureaucracy, we say that it has become institutionalized. It is very difficult for an individual within such a bureaucracy to change or challenge those practices because they are a part of the functioning of the bureaucracy itself.

Bureaucracies are related to social power in three major ways. First, they are themselves a source of social power. A bureaucracy controls resources that other persons and groups want, or must have. They can decide who and when those resources are delivered or not delivered. Often those decisions are made in the form of what we call "red tape." While an outsider may charge that the bureaucracy is failing to perform its function, persons in control may only be protecting their individual or group's interest.

A second way in which bureaucracies exert social power is to remain "hidden." Thus, we may be very knowledgeable about the way the U.S. Congress operates and know almost nothing about the way the Federal Reserve Board functions. Yet some have argued that the Federal Reserve Board actually has more power!

Third, bureaucracies act as insulators to protect the elite from those below who are the most oppressed, exploited, or degraded. Workers within the bureaucracy—police officers, social workers, teachers, and other low-level officials—are the ones who must enforce the dominant group norms of the society.

Efforts to change bureaucracies almost always come from outside. There have been attempts by social movements to change bureaucratic structure and functioning. The women's movement has had some successes in changing American bureaucracy, but there are still many problems.

As technology has grown more complex, bureaucracies have also grown larger and more powerful. Whereas a hundred years ago, many more small bureaucracies ran our society's schools, newspapers, churches, and government, today there are fewer, but larger, bureaucracies that do the same things. Thus, more power has been placed into the hands of a smaller group of people.

Vocabulary

Bureaucracy. A formal organization characterized by specialized roles, explicit rules, and a hierarchy of authority.

Institutionalization. The process by which social norms become part of the bureaucracy, and therefore acquire a "life of their own" apart from the specific individuals that make up the bureaucracy.

Institutionalized Racism. The patterns of behavior and belief incorporated into the practice of a bureaucracy that perpetuate racism.

Institutionalized Sexism. The patterns of behavior and belief incorporated into the practice of a bureaucracy that perpetuate sexism.

Institutionalized Classism. The patterns of behavior and belief incorporated into the practice of a bureaucracy that perpetuate classism.

Discussion Questions

1. A bureaucracy is one of the social structures of our society, but not all social structures are bureaucracies. How is your family an example of a social structure that is not a bureaucracy? What social structure do you work or live in that *is* an example of a bureaucracy? Discuss the difference in trying to change people's attitudes and beliefs in (a) your family, (b) the bureaucracies to which you belong.

2. Some people say, "You can't fight City Hall," meaning that you cannot change bureaucracies. Do you believe that is true? Why or why not? If you could change the bureaucracy of the school you were currently attending, what would you do? Why hasn't it been done?

3. Many of you watch television news or read a newspaper for the news. Many of you attend church. And if you are reading this book, you are probably attending a college or university. So what difference does it make that those things listed above (watching the news, going to church, getting an education) are controlled by more powerful and larger bureaucracies than those that affected your parents or grandparents?

4. Can you identify persons who as members of a bureaucracy have power over you? Would you argue that they act to enforce dominant group norms? Why or why not? Is it possible that officials of a bureaucracy could be enforcing egalitarian norms? Can you give examples?

Resources

Videos: *And the Band Played On*

This made-for-HBO movie is now available on video. It is a fascinating true story of one bureaucracy, the Centers for Disease Control (CDC), as it struggles to find out how AIDS is spread and to stop the epidemic. The CDC is part of the federal government bureaucracy, and so politicians who have their own agendas try to manipulate and control the CDC efforts. The CDC must also confront the profit interests of another powerful bureaucracy—the American Red Cross. Despite growing evidence, the Red Cross refuses to test the blood and as a result thousands of hemophiliacs are infected with the deadly virus. This movie is also good for comparing the efforts of bureaucracies to the efforts of the networks of victims who have to form a social movement in order for their voices to be heard. Stars Matthew Modine, Alan Alda, Richard Gere, and Steve Martin. Rated PG-13.

Article 99

What happens when some angry Vietnam vets team up with some idealistic young doctors (one of which is played by Kiefer Sutherland) to challenge the massive government bureaucracy called the Veterans Administration? This is a funny, and sometimes sad, story of ordinary people getting together to fight the stupidity and rigidity of government officials—one particularly pompous bureaucrat in particular. The story is not totally believable. But the issues that the movie raises are very believable. Rated R.

JFK.

If you are too young to remember Kennedy's assassination—or even if you do—this is a mesmerizing account of what one director, Oliver Stone, thinks *really* happened. Be warned that Stone believes there was a government cover-up and he makes liberal use of the research by investigators who questioned the Warren Commission report.

The cast is star-studded—Kevin Costner, Sissy Spacek, Joe Pesci, John Candy, Jack Lemmon, Walter Matthau, Edward Asner, Donald Sutherland—but it is the story that holds you to your seat. Is it really possible that the political bureaucracy in which we are supposed to place our trust is controlled by a shadowy network of powerful persons with their own anti-democratic agenda? And who *did* kill Kennedy? Be warned that it is difficult when watching the movie to distinguish between those scenes that are based on fact and the few scenes where Stone enacts events that he *thinks* may have happened. Rated R.

(*Note*: For those who are interested in other, and competing theories, of the assassination, you should look at the books suggested in note 15 and listed in the Bibliography.)

NOTES

Complete citations are provided in the Bibliography.

1. Gurganus 1989, 319.

2. Weber's classic study was *The Theory of Social and Economic Organization* (1947).

3. Parenti 1988, 257. Fainstein and Fainstein 1980.

4. *New York Times* editorial, 20 May 1986.

5. Edna Bonacich's (1992) discussion of the Chicana who was fired from her job as an assistant cook by the Marriott Corporation is a good example of the intersection of race, gender and class within bureaucracy.

6. Amott and Matthaei (1991).

7. An excellent historical overview of how social welfare policy and organizations have acted to maintain patriarchy in American history can be found in Abramovitz' (1988) study.

8. 1990, 1–2; also see Theoharis 1993.

9. Perrow 1979, 13.

10. Divine 1987.

11. Wright 1987, 113.

12. Greider 1987, 11–12.

13. "Who's Hurt by the Rate Hikes? Hint: It's Not the Rich" *Business Week*, 21 November 1994, 71–2.

14. Bonacich 1992, 106–7.

15. Stone based much of his movie on the arguments made by former Louisiana Attorney General Jim Garrison (1991) and popularized by author Mark Lane (1992). Many other theories also posit cover-ups and hidden networks. See, for example, Shawwith and Harris 1992; Oglesby 1992; and Hurt 1985.

16. Some sociologists have attempted to understand and explain how individuals can act in a questionable way and still defend their behavior. C. Wright Mills described these rationalizations as a "vocabulary of behavior" including the individual's own idea of his or her motives. This is "a complex meaning, which appears to the actor himself or to the observer to be an adequate ground for his conduct. A satisfactory or adequate motive is one that satisfies the questioners of the act." (Mills 1972, 396) Lyman and Scott (1968, 33) also analyzed such rationalizations, calling them excuses and justifications.

17. Burton, Stocking, and Miller 1922.

18. A history of how control over television became more concentrated is given in Chapter 2 of Douglas Kellner's (1990) study, pp. 25–68.

19. Associated Press report, 30 January 1993

20. Applebome 1989; *U.S. News & World Report* 1989.

11

TEACHING US WHAT TO THINK—BUREAUCRACIES OF IDEOLOGICAL SOCIAL CONTROL

A popular government without popular information or the means of acquiring it is but a prologue to a Farce or a Tragedy; or perhaps both. Knowledge will forever govern ig norance; and a people who mean to be their own governors must arm themselves with the power which knowledge gives.

—James Madison, *Fourth President of the United States*

Chapter 7 described our socialization into the ideologies that explain and justify the use of social power. Chapter 8 described what happens to us (the punishments) if we refuse to believe the dominant group ideologies. But those descriptions did not answer a fundamental question: if the ideologies of equality and democracy would be of greater benefit to the vast majority, *how* is it that so many people seem to believe in, and accept, the ideologies of racism, classism, sexism, and speciesism?

How is American society structured to ensure that ideologies benefiting the dominant groups are the ideologies we are taught? How are we prevented from learning history, current events, and the thinking skills that would let us criticize the dominant group ideologies? This chapter attempts to answer those questions by examining three major bureaucracies responsible for ideological social control in America.

This chapter focuses on three important means for teaching and maintaining our ideas and beliefs—education, religion, and the media. Within sociology, there are entire courses that study the larger roles of education or religion or media in our society. Our focus here is only on how education, religion, and the media are organized in U.S. society to preserve existing power relationships and prevent competing ideologies from emerging.

THE CONTENT OF IDEOLOGICAL SOCIAL CONTROL

All stratified societies practice ideological social control. Philosophies justifying caste in ancient India, classical Greek rationalizations that slavery was necessary for "democracy," or the current Serbian Government's arguments for the "ethnic cleansing" of Muslims are all examples of ideological social control. Hierarchies based on exploitation, oppression, and degradation cannot occur without persuading and manipulating the consciousness of the ruled. The content of this manipulation and persuasion varies according to the history and culture of a society.

The cultural tradition of the United States is based primarily on an industrial capitalistic economy that places a high value on the accumulation of material goods and emphasizes property relations between human beings. *All* of the ideologies of American society that reinforce hierarchy are based on two main ideas: the power of certain groups of individuals to accumulate and control property at the expense of others; and the right to evaluate the worth of others based on what they own and consume.

If a woman is the "property" of a man, then she is expected to serve him by keeping his house, raising his children, and servicing his sexual needs. If American culture is the property of Euro (white) Americans, then those from African, Latin, or Asian cultures have fewer ownership rights in the system—to education, jobs, or citizen participation. If property ownership is the mark of power, achievement, and quality then the rich are more worthy and the poor are the failures. If control over resources is necessary for success and progress, then the cutting of forests, the pollution of streams, lakes, and oceans, and the elimination of species is justified.

We often call our culture a "consumer society." This means you are judged by the clothes you wear, the car you drive, and the house in which you live. The economic structure of society requires that individuals participate as consumers. Industry has even been accused of creating "planned obsolescence"—making things so the consumer will buy a replacement as quickly as possible. This can occur by building items that wear out or break down quickly, or this can occur by using advertising to create new fads and fashions that make perfectly useful items "out-of-date."

This demand for goods drives the market, which in turn creates profits for the ownership class and jobs for the workers. Theoretically, all of this should create a "balance" in which the general needs of everyone are met.

But the premise of the system remains—it works only if everyone is driven to want more and more.

Gordon Ghekko, the manipulative stockbroker in the movie *Wall Street,* gives a speech in which he praises "greed, greed and more greed" as the founding principle of this country. Ghekko is referring to the way in which we are socialized always to want more. To the ruling class it means more in the way of wealth and the power over others that this wealth brings. When we say the word "greed" everyone understands that this is what we mean.

For the lower classes this means more in the way of consumer goods—cars, stereos, computers, clothes. A line from the song "Sixteen Tons" that was popular a generation ago was "I Owe My Soul to the Company Store." This referred to the way in which southern mill workers, coal miners, and other rural industrial laborers were kept in constant debt. Today, the Visa and the Discover cards do the same thing. A worker who is deeply in dept has fewer options in terms of looking for alternative work, going back to college, or considering a strike.

If I were to say that I was greedy for knowledge, or for appreciation of the arts, you would know what I meant, but you would not really understand me. Why would I want to be greedy for knowledge? What good would it bring me? If I said I was greedy for justice or equality, you would think I was some kind of radical kook. In other words, our culture tells us what we should be greedy for. We are supposed to want those things that will give us more power in the social hierarchy. Knowledge, appreciation of art, or love of justice will not raise me on the social ladder. Martin Luther King, who was greedy for human brotherhood and sisterhood, was punished by death.

The "need" to accumulate more and more material things, wealth and power are part of our socialization. We are also taught that this need for accumulation is "human nature"; that our interpretation of greed is "natural." *But we are taught these ideas; we are not born with them.* Other cultures in human history have not assumed that it is natural to always want more and more.

We now turn to an examination of how the institutions of our society teach us these dominant group ideologies.

THE SCHOOLS

Most of us take public education for granted. Yet true *public* education is less than a hundred years old. Schools in the colonies and in the first half of our country's history were private and only the rich could afford to send their children. Children in the lower classes may have become apprentices to learn a trade, if they were lucky. What limited opportunities existed to learn trades were open only to boys. Very few girls in the lower classes were allowed to attend any kind of school. Slaves and immigrants of color were denied any educational opportunities at all.

Until recently, most children were needed to run the farm, help with housework, or work in the factory or mine. Children earned the little more that was necessary to keep the family going. Factory owners could keep wages for adults low if the adults knew the additional wages could be earned by their wives and children. Thus, whether on the farm or in the city, early American families needed their children to work and children's labor was often more exploited than adult labor. The family where Mom stays home, takes care of children and bakes cookies was *never* a possibility for most women. This option was possible only for a significant minority of women in the two decades of the economic boom following World War II.

Two of the earliest demands of the American labor movement were for laws to eliminate child labor and for a public school system. These laws could not be passed as long as adult wages were not enough to support the family. The trade union movement began to link the demand for public mandatory education to a living wage for adults.

At the same time that the unions were demanding public education, the composition of the workforce was radically changing. The massive flow of immigrants into the country to meet the labor shortages of a rapidly expanding economy in the late 1800s and early 1900s was posing a serious social problem. These immigrants came with their own languages, religions, political ideas and cultural traditions. They had to be Americanized—taught the values, myths, and beliefs of the dominant Euro-American culture—if they were to fit into, and support, the existing power structures.

A public education system was needed to teach how the Puritans and Indians had celebrat ed Thanksgiving together. Certainly it would *not* teach that the Dutch introduced scalping and by 1703 the Massachusetts Bay Colony was offering $60 for each native scalp. (There was a sliding scale—adult male scalps were worth the most, then female adult scalps, then children's scalps.)[1] *All* American children had to learn how George Washington cut down the cherry tree and then could not tell a lie. Chinese children, Italian children, and Puerto Rican children needed to understand that wise white wealthy men were responsible for America's economic strength (and *not* the forced labor of African slaves, indentured Irish servants, or exploited Chinese laborers).[2]

These two social forces, the emerging labor movement and a movement for a national system of education to ensure a "melting pot," merged with a third social force—industrialization. In the early 1900s the country was shifting from a rural agricultural and craft-based economy to a factory industrial economy. The skills taught on the farm or in the small shop were in less demand. The rapidly growing industries of America needed blue-collar workers who could read machine manuals, write production reports, and understand basic mechanical functions. It needed white-collar workers who could keep accounts and manage a workforce. Industry required a school system that could prepare millions of new workers to enter this new kind of workplace.

The following are selections from the Rules and Regulations of the Budd Company as published in the 1968-1971 National Agreement with the United Autoworkers. Although electronics was beginning to be introduced at this time, this factory was typical of mass production industrialization in America.

The discipline imposed by many of these rules is remarkably similar to that in the classroom.

- When an employee wishes to take any of his personal effects from the plant, he must obtain a Package Pass from his foreman and also obtain the approval of the Tool Crib. This pass will be taken up by the plant guard at the gate.
- If for any reason an employee has to leave the plant during working hours, he must secure an "Employee's Gate Pass" from his foreman and turn it in to the guard at the gate.
- Regularity in attendance is required by The Budd Company. Employees must be at their machines or branches, ready for work, before starting time. Employees shall not leave their work places before quitting time.
- Clock cards must be left in the rack assigned to them and must not be altered or defaced in any way. Handling another employee's clock card or ringing his time, IN or OUT, will result in disciplinary action up to and including discharge.
- In the event no clock card is in the rack, the employee must get his card from the time-keeper. No time will be paid for unless registered by the clock, or approved by General Foreman. Employees failing to ring IN or OUT will be penalized one-half hour.
- Discipline: Sleeping on the Job. 1st Offense—3 days off; 2nd Offense—Discharge. Two offenses must be within twelve month period. Records cleared every twelve months.
- All paper and rubbish must be placed in the waste cans provided throughout the plant for this purpose. Spitting on the floor or in cutting compounds breed disease and is strictly prohibited.
- Absentee Control Policy: First Step. If an employee has 3 days of unexcused absence during any 60 day period, he will be given a DISCIPLINARY NOTICE and warned that continued poor attendance may result in disciplinary time off at his own expense. This NOTICE will be prepared by the Personnel Division from the daily absentee reports, will be signed by the Foreman and handed to the employee on the job.

(There are three more steps, each increasingly more complex.)

The result of these forces can be seen in the changes in the American public school system as it emerged in the twentieth century. Classrooms were organized on the basis of factory discipline—students signed in and out, requested permission to go to the bathroom, obeyed the authority of the teacher (foreman), were punished for questioning authority, and learned what they were told was important—*not* what they may have wanted to know.

History, geography, and "social studies" presented equality and democracy as ideal ideologies but in actuality reinforced sexism, racism, class, and speciesism by leaving out the history of women, minorities, and labor and never questioning the rape of the land. It was *not* a country that had been built on slavery, committed genocide on Native Americans, burned women at the stake, and destroyed aquifers (underground water tables). By keeping such "negative" information out of the curriculum, the image of our leaders as wise wealthy white men is not challenged. Eitzen and Zinn identify this facet of education as the "hidden curriculum."[3]

The skills taught were those necessary for industrial production, not for participating as citizens. Lower-class students learned to run cash registers but not how to run for the legislature; students learned basic principles of science but not basic principles of citizens' rights; students learned to write reports but not to write petitions.[4]

The social stratification of education was ensured by the manner in which the United States established funding for its public schools. From the beginning the principle of local funding was laid down. Poor communities had less money to run their schools than rich communities; richer northern states had more money to run their schools than poorer southern states. Schools for the lower classes were overcrowded, there was no money for field trips, and advanced science classes were not offered. Schools for the upper classes taught ballet and advanced physics, there were frequent field trips, and classes were smaller and individual attention was given.

Actual comparisons of school districts (see Table 11.1) highlight the inequalities. Jonathan Kozol provides some examples of the contrast between spending for city schools and spending in the wealthier suburbs.

Table 11.1 Comparison of Spending Per Child Between Poorer and Richer School Systems[5]

Chicago area (1989)	Chicago $5,265	Niles Township $9,371
New Jersey (1989)	Camden district $3,538	Princeton district $7,725
New York metropolitan area (1987)	New York City $5,585	Manhasset $11,325 Jerico $11,325 Great Neck $11,265

Local property taxes as a way to raise money for schools are discriminatory because rich school districts can spend more money than poor ones on each student, and at a lower taxing rate. In Texas, for example, the residents of Edgewood Independent School District—a poor and mostly Hispanic area—has property taxes of almost $1 per $100 of assessed valuation and spends $3,596 per student. Another Texas school district, Santa Gertrude—which is rich in oil—has property taxes of 8 cents per $100 assessed valuation, yet spends $12,000 per student.[6]

When a single school serves students from several class levels, a system of tracking is often used. Students who come from homes where parents have more education, where books and magazines are read, and where private lessons and tutoring can be afforded are automatically tracked into the higher levels. "Achievement" tests basically measure a student's home environment and parents' educational level. The racial segregation of American schools is only a clearer and more obvious example of the social class segregation that has also occurred. Lois Weis's excellent ethnographic study of Freeway High School concludes: "This emphasis on form [rather than substance] fuels the contradictory attitudes toward education and knowledge in evidence among working-class youth. The school also encourages separatist race and gender spheres, emphasizing white-male dominance."[7]

Ideological control in the public schools has been based on persuading students that if they played by the rules and learned what they were supposed to know, they could succeed. The son of a poor Polish refugee might have seen success as being able to get a union job making cars at the Dodge Main plant in Detroit; the daughter of an African American share cropper in Alabama might have seen success as being able to attend the local state teacher's college and becoming a schoolteacher; the son of a Korean immigrant might have seen success as starting up his own small grocery; the son of an Iowa farmer might have seen success as earning a scholarship to an engineering school and becoming an engineer. In all these cases success was relative—it meant doing better than your parents. Education was the key to that achievement.

During the last century, an expanding economy continually needed more and better- trained workers and the education system expanded to meet those needs. With the exception of the depression period, the economy of the United States has been able to deliver on those dreams—until recently. Ideological social control had been accompanied by a *reason* for believing. The "greatest country in the world" was the country that allowed those who worked and played by the rules to achieve what they saw as success.

Following World War II, there was a significant shift in technology. The United States and other industrializing nations began moving from a mechanical base to an electronics base. Making that move required doing things differently. The skills required for computer programmers and electronic technicians were different from the skills required for assembly- line workers. The massive school bureaucracies that had emerged since the early 1900s resisted the changes. They were bureaucracies and acted in many of the ways already discussed in Chapter 9. The United States was not changing fast enough and those perceived as competitors—Japan, the Soviet Union, West Germany—were ahead of us in certain areas.[8]

Just as the social movement for public education in the beginning of the century had coincided with industrialization, so the social movement for civil rights coincided with Cold War competition and the introduction of robotronics into industry. The Cold War included an ideological component. Socialism promised a better life to the "masses"and its ideology blamed the capitalists for society's ills. America could not meet that ideological challenge without attempting to ameliorate the glaring racism, sexism, and economic inequalities of our society.

A school system that refused to recognize a bright African American as a physicist, a creative woman as a mathematician, or stressed memorization instead of critical thinking was actually hurting the national interest. When the Soviet Union put Sputnik into the sky in 1957, the elite became convinced that the schools had to change.

It was at this point that the federal government moved into the arena of public education. Massive funds and new programs were introduced to improve the courses and skills that would meet the needs created by the new technologies. These government initiatives were based on research and initiatives being put forward by "think tanks" such as the Ford Foundation, Rockefeller Foundation and Carnegie Foundation, representing the interests of the large multinational corporations. At the same time, the civil rights movement was making its own demands.

Curriculum reform, affirmative action in hiring, and remedial and special education were all changes that opened the existing bureaucratic structures of education. The result was a reshaping of American education in the 1960s. A debate was begun that included the competing ideologies of equality and democracy. As resources to improve the quality of education were poured into the schools, creative teachers and students took advantage of the opportunities.

Students who were introduced to black history courses were more likely to march or lobby for equal rights; students who were introduced to the philosophy of science in an Honors program were more likely to critically evaluate the control over medicine by white, wealthy males; students who were introduced to gender in a psychology course were more likely to challenge sexist remarks and demand more female instructors.

The challenges is this period were not guns in the schools, drugs in the playground, and drive-by shootings in the neighborhood. Instead, the challenges were students sitting in, and taking over, their schools; women demanding to play sports equally with men; minority students lobbying for legislation to mandate multicultural curriculum. There was a chance for young people to connect to the massive social movements of that time, and their goals were aimed at creating a more equal society.

When the social movements of the 1960s died down, the young lost the leaders who articulated the visions of expanded democracy and equality. Instead of role models like Martin Luther King and John Kennedy, young people today are offered athletes who promote hamburgers and rock stars who sing naked on stage. This does not mean that student activism has ended. But the resistance of today's young has no larger social movement that can express their anger and frustration in terms of social change for justice and equality.[9] Instead, the society offers them drugs as a means of both rebellion and escape.

Despite the movements for integration and women's rights, the current research indicates that schools continue to track minorities, women, and the poor, and that opportunities in the school system close down far more quickly for these groups.[10] Poor and minority children continue to have far higher drop out rates than Euro-American middle class children. Wealthier families can still afford to send their children to "Magnet schools" or private schools and insure their access to opportunity.

Two hundred students at Suitland Senior High School, in Suitland, Md., recently completed a new class: "How to behave when getting arrested." A group of police officers from Prince George's County Police Department taught the two-hour course in the school auditorium. They told the students to speak when spoken to and not to strain against handcuffs.

The students were selected by school administrators who felt that, due to their past behavior, they stood the greatest chance of having a confrontation with police. "We wanted to try to get young men (and women) who have either had some difficulty with police or have been in some situations here at school," says Sterling Marshall, Suitland's principal. Suitland's student body of 2,500 is 87 percent black.

When women do go on for higher education, they are still being tracked into "female" (and lower-paying) occupations.[11] In the fields of sciences, for example, women continue to be placed on the lower rungs of the educational ladder. Women make up only 1 percent of working environmental scientists,

2 percent of mechanical engineers, 3 percent of electrical engineers, 4 percent of medical school department directors, 5 percent of physics Ph.D.s, 6 of close to 300 tenured professors in the country's top 10 mathematics departments, and so on.[12]

By the early 1980s the technology of the electronic revolution had begun to bear fruit. Good-paying jobs were disappearing. (This is more fully discussed in Chapter 13.) The parents of the current generation of students were losing their jobs and being forced to accept lower-paying jobs, and/or having to accept welfare. The promise of success could no longer be realistically offered.[13] Students were told "you'll be lucky if you get a job making half of what your dad used to make."

The new generation was looking at employment defined by part-time work, minimum or subminimum wage, and no benefits. The chances of making enough money to get married, buy a house, and raise kids were rapidly diminishing. *The ideological control maintained by the schools was also breaking down because it could not deliver—the reward for obeying the rules and believing the ideology was no longer there.* [14]

As the need for large numbers of unskilled and semiskilled workers has decreased, corporate America has led a campaign to decrease funding for public education. Instead of adequate funds for all schools, corporate think tanks are now arguing that only a few elite schools should focus on "excellence." Powerful lobbyists and local businessmen have campaigned to reduce corporate taxes and cut back educational spending.

Today most public school systems are cutting programs like music, art, and foreign language and laying off counselors, social workers, and special education teachers. Despite the rhetoric about the need for computers in every classroom and video technologies, poorer schools are years behind in teaching these skills. Over and over again, one hears public pronouncements about new "approaches" to the problems of education. But very rarely does one hear a politician or big businessman call for additional spending on education; instead, the funds are being continuously cut.

School administrators, politicians, and police chiefs talk of installing metal detectors in the schools, putting up electric fences around the junior high, and doing search and seizure of school lockers. Direct social control—force, coercion, and intimidation—is rapidly replacing ideological social control as the failure of the system becomes more and more apparent. An inner-city Chicago high school begins to resemble a concentration camp or a plantation—where the overseers spend more time protecting themselves than teaching and where nobody in the building really wants to be there.[15]

Today the elite are arguing for a "two-tier" system of education. The economy still needs some highly educated workers. Why not set up elite schools where the promise of success will still hold true? Education can continue to occur in those schools because the students will have been preselected for the privileged slots in society and will obey the rules in order to win the prize.

The other schools can take the children of the homeless, of the unemployed, of the struggling single-parent families and keep them off the streets. The education provided in these schools will prepare students to work at a McDonald's or WalMart.[16] The ones who reject that future will be kicked out and can make their own way on the street.

The traditional assumption is that young people drop out because of personal failures. Schools rarely look at the ways in which the educational system fails the youth. Studies of the perceptions of dropouts themselves provide evidence that the characteristics of the school contribute to the dropout problem. Minority youth who have dropped out of urban schools are highly critical of their educations.[17] Stevenson's study found white dropouts from a working-class school strongly critical of irrelevant curricula, teachers, counselors, and administrators for their lack of caring and negative attitudes and of school policies for their insensitivity to students' emerging adult status.[18]

If one analyzes all the educational proposals made by both major political parties for "reform" in American education there is one thing conspicuously missing. Where are the promises and dreams for those who do not "qualify" for the elite programs and schools?

THE MEDIA

Media in our society are often called "mass" media because of their ability to reach and affect millions of people. A war or a sports event can be so projected that the normal everyday activities of the nation are suspended. Kennedy's assassination and its subsequent events glued the entire country to their television sets and radios for several days.[19] The Super Bowl becomes a major social event, where evening church is canceled and a family gathering is reorganized so "the game" can be watched. O.J. Simpson's trial occupied the nation for months.

Students may have no idea what is happening in sub-Saharan Africa or no understanding of the recent decisions of the Federal Reserve, but they do know Shaq O'Neal's scoring percentage and that Princess Diana and Prince Charles have divorced. Most young people do not know what the national debt is or the cost of the savings and loan collapse, but they know the words to the latest MTV video and how many CDs it has sold.

The media shape our consciousness in two important ways—they decide what we *should* know and they decide what we *should not* know. This is not a criticism in itself. This book you are reading right now was written by a person who has decided what she thinks you should know and is shaping that knowledge through her own distortions, emphases, and omissions. In other words, all media—books, movies, television, radio, art, and music—will do that. *The point for our analysis is that you, the reader, have so few sources from which to choose.*

If you could flip the channels between CBS, NBC, ABC, PBS and CNN and get different stories, different emphases, and different information you would have a far greater ability to decide for yourself what it is that you want to know and what version you should accept. But if you watch the evening news, you know that all the major stations run the same lead stories and pretty much say exactly the same thing.[20]

You can also observe that they all agree on who the "bad" guy is. Before Saddam Hussein invaded Iraq, the Iranians were the bad guys. Even though Saddam Hussein had used poison gas to wipe out entire Kurdish villages, he was a good guy who deserved getting massive amounts of military, technological, and social aid from the United States and Europe. Almost no major news coverage was given to Hussein and the genocide of the Kurds at the time he was receiving this aid.

But when the elite decided that American troops should be deployed to protect the interests of the emir of Kuwait (who is a dictator, but was never called that), *then* Saddam Hussein became evil, a new Hitler. None of the major media challenged the government's reversal of Hussein's status—overnight the American people had an evil image of Hussein drummed into their heads. In *The Persian Gulf TV War* Douglas Kellner shows how the media were used to sell the Gulf War. His study is an excellent example of both media manipulation and the networking relationships between so-called independent journalism and the Pentagon.[21]

The media used the ideology of democracy as a cover-up. Saddam had "invaded" another country. Since most of the informed media knew very well that Kuwait was a dictatorship, they did not actually use the word "democracy," but instead relied on the concept of "independence" as a way to win the sympathy of the American people. Since most Americans equate our independence with our democracy, it served the purpose. And because few Americans know real history, little was said about the fact that the land "invaded" had originally belonged to Iraq, but was given to Kuwait by the British colonizers!

But when the United Nations also condemned Indonesia's invasion of East Timor or South Africa's occupation of Namibia the media never rallied the public in defense of *those* nations' independence. It is not so much a question of what it is we are being told; it is also a question of what we are *not* being told.[22]

In the winter and spring of 1990 the media were full of stories about "gangs." These stories portrayed inner-city youth as minority gangsters, carrying out random violence and dealing drugs. In the same time period, a national movement was organized to put pressure on HUD (the federal housing agency) to provide homes for the homeless. On 1 May in Detroit, Minneapolis, Philadelphia, Oakland, and New York, a coalition of the Union of the Homeless, Up and Out of Poverty Now, and the Welfare Rights Organization seized empty HUD properties to dramatize the condition of the homeless in America. These people were not carrying guns, selling drugs or preaching hate. They were following in the footsteps of Abolitionists, suffragettes, civil rights marchers in Selma, Alabama, and union activists. It is a time-honored American tradition to challenge dominant group norms through civil disobedience— breaking a law that is seen as immoral.

These protestors were talking about dignity and the inalienable right of Americans to shelter and health care. They were led by homeless veterans, homeless autoworkers, and homeless schoolteachers. The dramatic story of those takeovers did not become a major news story. Dan Rather did not send investigative reporters to seek out the corruption in HUD or the landlords who own the sleazy "welfare hotels" that charge the New York City a monthly rent of $1900 for a family of four.

Jonathan Kozol points out that rental costs alone over the course of three years would be equal to the purchase price of a nice home.[23] If the government spent that money building homes for the homeless, thousands of people would be employed in that construction. Instead, that money goes into the pockets of handful of slum landlords. In either case, middle-class taxpayers pick up the tab. The question is: who benefits? But the average American watching television only knew that people in the inner city were organizing gangs.

There are many more examples of important political and social events that are left out. Newspapers continually define "society" events as the events of the upper class. Expensive charity balls and cocktail parties held at elegant country clubs are reported on the society pages, but the State Conference of the black Baptist church gets a two-line "announcement," even though the latter will include creative Gospel music, a delicious banquet, and the networking of people from across a large geographical area. A corporate chief executive officer who makes an announcement of a merger to the chamber of commerce will be reported on the front page, but the announcement that a working-class community group lowered the crime rate by starting a youth recreation program will be a short news story on the back page. In this way the media project what is important, what is acceptable, and what is known about other sectors of society.

The vast majority of Americans have nowhere else to go for an alternative point of view. Who controls the media? Most journalists would argue that they are not controlled. That is true and not true.

Principles of fair reporting, freedom of the press, and balanced coverage are important ideals accepted by the vast majority of those who work in these bureaucracies. At the same time, those who work in the media learn quickly what is acceptable in order to keep their jobs and get promoted. Careers depend on being accepted by the networks within the bureaucracy, that is, being "socially acceptable" for the cocktail parties and golf games. Those who control the travel funds decide who gets sent where to investigate what story. Powerful editors decide what should get printed, what page it will be on, and whether changes should be made.

On 19 February 1990 some 500 people marched to the entrance of the *New York Post* building. They were protesting landlords who "warehouse"—holding vacant apartments off the market to take advantage of tax breaks, rent hikes, or who tear down old low-income housing to put up expensive luxury apartment buildings. They were chanting "Warehousing is a crime; Kalikow should be doing time." The next day the *New York Post* ran a story about homelessness but never mentioned the march or the issue of warehousing, in a city with 75,000 warehoused apartments. But the *Post* is owned by Peter Kalikow, who along with his brother is one of the city's largest warehousers and has greatly profited from New York's housing crisis.[24]

Ultimately, the advertisers pull their weight. Will women's magazines that make money advertising *Eve* cigarettes run major stories exposing tobacco's links to cancer? Will the *Reader's Digest*, full of automaker's advertising, attack the subsidies of government to Chrysler in the same way they attack welfare as a government subsidies to the poor?

Even "scientific" findings are manipulated by the press according to Cynthia Crossen, a *Wall Street Journal* editor. In her study *Tainted Truth: The Manipulation of Fact in America* she exposed how research is reported and distorted by special-interest groups using the press.[25] According to Crossen, the media uncritically report the results of studies that have been designed to prove whatever the sponsor wants proved. Since 1954, the tobacco industry's research group paid more than $165 million to 800 scientists who have overwhelmingly tended to reassure smokers. A "study" also found that eating white bread won't make you gain weight. The sponsor of the study was Wonder Bread. After environmentalists warned of the long-range danger of disposable diapers clogging up landfills, Procter & Gamble (makers of Pampers and Luvs) and the American Paper Institute sponsored studies that showed there was no big problem.

"Freedom of the press" requires the ability to access, use, and buy the press. If poor people, minorities, or groups pressing for change cannot get the sympathetic ear of a reporter, they have no way to get their story told to any larger audience. Even if a reporter shows up, the editor or editorial board makes the decision on how much emphasis a story receives, if it is reported at all. Well-to-do editors often argue that people pay to read about crime and accidents because it is "exciting." Yet they often report the dull and boring news that relates to *their* status group in society—the proceedings of the Junior League, the symphony's new director, or elections by the chamber of commerce.

Despite the social movements of the past three decades, the media (especially television) continue to report in a way that projects whiteness, wealth, maleness, and environmental domination as that which is most desirable. In the same way, stories that focus on women, the poor, minorities and environmentalists continue to use a "victim" approach, focus on activities by the few that relate to violence, and perpetuate stereotypes of inner-city violence, environmental "extremists," and radical feminists.[26]

Kellner, in his study of television, concludes:

> It is an historical irony that the 1980s marked the defeat of democracy by capitalism in the United States and the triumph of democracy over state communism in the Soviet bloc countries. At present, the "free" television media in the United States are probably no more adversarial and no less propagandistic than Pravda or the television stations in the Eastern European countries. Hence the very future of democracy is at stake—and development of a democratic communications system is necessary if democracy is to be revitalized. If radical transformation of the system of communications and broadcasting is not undertaken, segments of the society will be condemned to perpetual information poverty; they will lack access to communications and social power. Indeed, the empowerment of individuals to participate in a democratic society must be an important part of a democratic communications system.[27]

RELIGION

Religion is an important part of any culture. The language we use (what words are "cuss words"?), our sacred symbols (a Cross, Star of David, or a Buddha), our rites of passage (weddings, funerals, baptisms), and our personal habits (diets, clothing, choice of sexual partners) are all influenced by the codes of our religion. To the extent that any one religion is dominant it can then degrade and oppress those who practice other rules for living which are different than those of the dominant religion.

Thomas Jefferson fought hard for the separation of church and state because he saw a new nation composed of thousands of different religions and sects, many of whom had fled the Old World to escape religious persecution. Jefferson attributed his own atheism to the way religion had been used to justify the brutal and bloody wars of Europe in the sixteenth and seventeenth centuries.

Despite the promise of the founding fathers to separate church and state, ideological control over a large and diverse population required a dominant religion. Just as English became the dominant language, and the history of England became the history of "civilization," so the religion of Christianity became the American religion. Judaism, Islam, Hinduism, Native American religion, and Buddhism were all defined as "outside" the definitions of Americanism. Real Americans were not only white but Christian.

The idea that the "moral basis" of America has to be God (and a Christian God, at that) assumed this cultural domination. What does it mean to a Hindu, Muslim, or Native American child to be told that "in God we trust" is required for his or her country to be "moral?" The message is clear—living under the codes of the deities of Hinduism, Allah, or the divine natural forces of Native American religion is not moral!

The Christian religion taught by most of the European churches in the sixteenth, seventeenth, and eighteenth centuries provided a divine basis for the ideologies of social stratification. God had made Africans a "lower order" creature so they could be slaves and Native Americans were not even real humans; God had meant for wives to serve their husbands and suffer in childbirth; God rewarded those who invested their money; and God meant for man to have "dominion over the earth."

The early New England churches blessed the land that was drenched in the blood of the Native Americans and burned women at the stake who questioned male authority. The Southern churches sanctified slavery and quoted the Apostle Paul as to the "proper" place of the slave. As national leaders used the U.S. Calvary to clear the American West, it was declared a Manifest Destiny ordained by God. The calvary massacre of 250 Arapaho and Cheyene—mostly women and children—was led by John Chivington, a Methodist minister.[28] White wealthy Americans could console themselves that the atrocities committed in the name of God and the flag were necessary to "civilize" the savages and bring "real" religion to the heathen.

Religion in eighteenth and nineteenth-century United States was a powerful ideological force. The vast majority of citizens could not read or write, did not understand basic principles of natural or social science, and did not have an historical background by which they could judge and appreciate other cultures. But they did have the Bible and the church interpreted that Bible for them to rationalize and justify what those in power wanted and needed to do.

Although we are focusing in this chapter on the ways in which religion has reenforced social stratification and inequality, it is important to understand that those same religions can also be used as powerful ideologies in support of equality and democracy. The story of Jesus driving the money changers out of the temple has been used to show that the greed of capitalism is a sin. Jesus' intervention in the stoning of the prostitute has been used to expose the hypocrisy of Christian male supremacy. The story of Moses leading the enslaved Hebrews out of Egypt was used by abolitionists to argue that God did *not* condone slavery. Nat Turner, leader of one of the largest slave rebellions, was called "The Prophet" for his religious vision of freedom. John Brown was a deeply religious man.

Martin Luther King argued he was a "fundamentalist" who preached the most fundamental teaching of Christianity—the brotherhood and sisterhood of all people. Yet King's ministry and social activism directly contradicted the racist and restrictive "fundamentalism" of right wing racist Christianity. Similarly, Mahatma Gandhi came from a religious culture that had created castes and untouchables, but Gandhi reinterpreted that religion into a powerful force for freedom and individual dignity in India.[29]

Social stratification is not the theological and ethical core of religion. What we are talking about here is the *use* of religion to justify and rationalize ideologies of power. Any group or individual can interpret religious doctrine to fit its own interests or select only those parts of religion that justifies its own ends. When religion becomes a mechanism for achieving or changing social power, it becomes part of the political ideology of a social movement; when religion is used to justify and legitimate existing power structures, it becomes part of the political ideology exercising social control.

As pointed out above, there is a long history of individuals within those bureaucracies resisting the use of their religion as a justification for dominant group ideologies. But these resisters are constrained by the rules and structures of bureaucracy. It is not surprising that the most powerful challenges to dominant group religion has come from individuals who express their religion through social movements—Anne Hutchinson, John Brown, Martin Luther King, and Malcolm X.

We are analyzing contemporary religion and its churches as bureaucracies of social control. To be acceptable to the dominant culture, religion in America had to accommodate itself to the materialism and consumerism of the society. The ideologies that allowed a small class of people to exploit, degrade and oppress were the ideologies of the society and could not be questioned without questioning Americanism.

But values that defined individual behaviors relating to lifestyle could be challenged without threatening the social structure. Thus, as social problems in this society deepen, it is not surprising to find that the religious bureaucracies are increasing their emphasis on individual sin. It is far safer to blame problems of society on the moral breakdown of the victims than to blame the powerful elite for their greed and indifference. The churches and the preachers who focus on the hereafter are no threat to those who are benefiting for the here and now.

Emphasis on individual differences—how people pray, how they dress, how they have sex, what they eat and drink—divides those who are on the lower rungs of the ladder among themselves. Instead of being united against the system's oppression, exploitation, and degradation, individuals are pitted against each other based on their individual tastes and cultural differences. While some churches wage concerted campaigns against homosexuality there are no parallel campaigns against interest rates that rip off the poor, banking practices that discriminate against loans to minorities, and tax policies that give breaks to the wealthy. The mainline denominations are funded by, and supported by, the very social class to which these criticisms would have to be aimed.

POLITICAL RELIGION: THE EXAMPLE OF ABORTION

Abortion is an example of an issue defined by the political use of religion. The United States is the only major industrial nation without a national policy on children. We have no mandated maternity leave; no national policy for day care; and no guarantee that all children will have health care. In other words, profits from shopping malls are more protected than our children. In some states a low income mother who is pregnant with a third or fourth child she cannot afford is being told her welfare benefits will not be increased; she may have to quit her job or college because there is no affordable day care; and she got pregnant in the first place because she could not afford the doctor's visit required for a birth control prescription.

To address the factors that lead many women to consider an abortion would require higher taxes on someone, better social services, and an acknowledgment that *all* children are equally valued. Instead, the issue is defined morally—that if a woman chooses an abortion she is sinning by committing murder. This definition advanced by religion, but reinforced by the media, avoids all the issues regarding the powerlessness of many women in our society.[30] In addition, the Bible tells women to serve men, which means submitting to the sexual demands of husbands and allowing the husband to decide whether birth control should be used or not.

True choice would mean that the society protects the rights of women to keep and raise healthy, happy children as much as it means protecting the right of women to choose not to have a child. Some middle- and upper-class women who argue for the right to abortions are only trying to protect their individual options and class privilege. An upper-class woman may want the right to abortion, but would not support public programs that would provide day care, health care, or other supportive services to allow a poorer pregnant women to choose to keep the child.

When religion enters the political arena and defines the issue of children as one of individual morality, religion is legitimating the current power relations in our society—*a social structure that has created a society in which one-fourth to one-third of all our children will be born into poverty.*

All the research collected on population control in the developing countries indicate that whether it be birth control or abortion, women are freed from the burden of unwanted children *only* as their educational level increases. In other words, if our schools were indeed seeking to empower women—to give them the knowledge to control their own bodies and to give them the education to hold rewarding jobs many of the problems related to abortion would disappear.

RELIGION AND SOCIAL CRISES

As the quality of life for millions of Americans declines, more people begin to raise questions about the dominant ideologies. Is it really a good thing that we pollute our air in pursuit of more profits? Is it really a good thing to deregulate the banks and leave the taxpayer with the bill for their failures? Is it really a good thing to cut taxes for the wealthy while millions of Americans are homeless? Is it really a good thing to give large government subsidies to businesses that install robots to replace workers' jobs? Why are we forced to compete with each other for jobs? Why is there so much hate?

These may appear to be questions of economics or politics but they are also questions about values—the values that place wealth and power for the few over meeting the needs of the many for health care, housing, and jobs. These are questions that look at the way our social structure distributes the rewards and benefits of the society. Is this distribution moral? *Those who control ideology in our society do not want the questions asked in this way.*

For those who have wealth and privilege, the ideology that explains crime, unemployment, and pollution is the ideology that sees individuals or families as being at fault. Homelessness is not the result of real estate corruption and profit-seeking but the result of mental illness, alcoholism, or laziness. Unemployment is the result of people not looking hard enough for work. Juvenile delinquency is the result of a breakdown of family morals and not a result of lack of jobs and poor education. The air, water, and earth are polluted because individuals smoke and litter, not because factories spew pollution into the environment.

Thus the question of blame becomes an ideological question of morality. As the economy has worsened in the last two decades, there has been a major effort to blame the immorality of individual lifestyles for the socio-political crisis. Millions of dollars have been spent by the Religious Right to convince Americans that if mothers stayed home, abortions were outlawed, homosexuality were criminalized, prison sentences were lengthened, more prisons built, and prayer put back into schools, all would be right with America again.

The dominant ideologies in America have always stressed individualism over community. They say ambition and incentive are what has made America great. Failure is the individual's fault. Religion that stresses individual salvation, and an individual's relationship to God can easily be manipulated into a religion that ignores the individual's responsibility to other human beings. Even charity becomes an act by which an individual can help assure his or her way into heaven. If you give to the poor, you are deemed more worthy. Of course, you are not supposed to question the existence of so many poor, or how their existence is connected to your wealth. *When religion fails to make the sins of exploitation, degradation, and oppression central then it becomes the religion of the oppressor.*

Again, it is important to note that what we are discussing here is the political use of religion. An analysis of the political use of Islamic fundamentalism suggests that the anti-democratic leadership of many Islamic countries is interpreting Islam in many of the same ways that the Religious Right is interpreting Christianity in the United States. Religion is playing a much different role in Latin America. Unlike the individualistic fundamentalism described above, many Christians in Latin America are embracing a liberation theology that calls on the poor to confront their oppressors and change the social structure.

The right-wing death squads in many Latin American dictatorships have been forced to assassinate priests and even bishops. The most famous assassination was that of Bishop Oscar Romero in El Salvador in 1980. For decades, the U.S. government has been providing military aid to these right-wing governments. Both sides claim to represent "Christianity" so it is clear that the question is the political interpretation of the religion!

Religion is a powerful ideological force, and the question of who controls our religious ideas, our religious teachings, and our religious bureaucracies is as serious a question as that of control over schools and the media. A religion that questions the morality of stratification is dangerous for those who benefit from the current system. Those in power would prefer to teach that alternative social structures are "utopian" and we have to wait until we get to heaven to have enough to eat (milk and honey) and find justice.

This textbook has a moral basis that can be interpreted in a religious sense. I see the sins of society as lying in the exploitation, oppression, and degradation of other human beings. Our existence as humans is fuller and more meaningful if we are live in a society in which all life is treated with respect, dignity, and given equal opportunities to develop to the fullest of its potential. From my own religious perspective, I see the love of neighbor that Christianity teaches as being the willingness to create a world that reflects this potential. As a social scientist, I would also argue that as our weapons of destruction spread, as unrest and disease increase, and as the hole in the ozone layer widens, we must seek the alternatives for *more* than moral reasons—we must seek them if we are to survive.

This chapter has stressed the negative uses of the bureaucracies of ideological social control. I, myself, am part of such a bureaucracy—the higher education system of West Virginia. Thus it should be apparent that there are many of us within these bureaucracies who question the dominant group ideologies and seek to resist in those ways we can. For example, the publisher of this book is a small independent company that has resisted being taken over by the large bureaucracies that dominate American publishing.

But individual efforts at resistance are limited. Only when large groups of people unite in a common understanding that they must make change is it possible to change society. We examine the growing potential for that type of change in Chapter 15. At this point we need to examine one more important way in which ideology controls us—science.

SUMMARY

This chapter examines three bureaucracies that are responsible for ideological control in our society. Education, religion, and media are three important means for teaching and maintaining our ideas and beliefs about stratification. In the United States, the content of such ideological control is deeply influenced by our ideas about the accumulation of material goods. We are taught that it is good to consume and good to evaluate others based on what they own and consume. This is not something innate but the result of socialization.

Public education in America was originally just for the children of the elite. As our society industrialized, it became necessary for workers to have more formal education. At the same time, it became necessary to provide immigrants with the socialization that would teach them American culture. Schools in the early twentieth century reflected the needs of an industrial factory society. They also reflected the patterns of social stratification—where girls, children of color, and poor children accessed fewer educational opportunities.

Following World War II, the educational system underwent major changes. Some were the result of the major social movements and clash of world political systems. Others were the result of the changing technologies. There was less demand for certain kinds of labor and less opportunity for social mobility. Ideological control based on positive rewards has been increasingly replaced by direct social control within the schools as students become more cynical and more rebellious.

Mass media are another major source of ideological social control. They decide what we know about the world and what we do not know. Very few persons have alternative sources of information. The media are able to shape our perception of world events and choose what is important or unimportant in our reality. These perceptions largely reflect the existing stratification system providing continuing justifications for the way things are.

Many people are deeply influenced by religious teachings. Religion can be used to justify many of our norms—both dominant and egalitarian as well as many of our arbitrary norms. When any one religion is used to define what is "right" and "wrong," individuals with different religious beliefs are oppressed and often discriminated against.

Religion can also be a powerful ideological force for social change. There are many individuals in our history who questioned dominant group norms by appealing to more egalitarian religious norms. Usually these individuals had to act outside the powerful religious bureaucracies, which were resistant to social change.

Today religion is being used in many political debates. Groups currently in power do not want to answer questions about fundamental inequalities—why the rich are getting richer while homelessness increases, children go hungry and our environment is poisoned. They would rather the debate be focused on religious issues related to personal lifestyle.

Discussion Questions

1. Do you have friends or relatives who dropped out of school? Can you analyze the factors related to social stratification that may have contributed to their dropping out? If you were a dropout and came back for your GED, can your analyze your own experience—sociologically?

2. Achievement tests primarily measure one's home environment. But one's home environment is an ascribed and not achieved status. So why do we call them achievement tests?

3. In the 1960s, the "student movement" was one of the major social movements in this society. Why is there no student movement today? What has changed? Why? Do you think it is possible that there will be one in the near future? What demands for change would it make if it happened?

4. Within your class, what knowledge do you have of "current events?" Can you explain the sources of the trade deficit or the historical causes of the current international crises? Why or why not? What *can* you explain?

5. For those of you who received a religious socialization, can you identify the religious norms you were taught as either dominant group, egalitarian, or arbitrary norms? Why is it so hard for us to admit that persons of other religions may hold differing norms that are equally "right" for them?

6. All societies must have basic rules to ,ensure ordered and predictable behavior. At the same time in a democracy, we try to allow different religions to follow their own rules as much as possible without interference from the government. Debate the "line" that separates these two points regarding: (a) prayer in schools; (b) abortion; (c) physician assisted suicide; (d) organ transplants; (e) laws preventing discrimination against homosexuals.

Resources

Videos: *Stand and Deliver*

This film tells the story of one teacher's attempt to overcome the problems he encounters in an inner-city school. Based on a true story, his methods were controversial within the educational community. The movie is good for a discussion—do you agree or disagree with the way he did it? Can you identify problems in that method that the movie does not address? Stars Edward James Olmos and Lou Diamond Phillips. Rated PG.

Broadcast News

This movie asks the question—what are the qualifications that make a "great" anchor on the evening news? The answer is the plot of the movie as two individuals (William Hurt and Albert Brooks) compete for the anchor spot and the girl (Holly Hunter). It's a fascinating "inside" look at television and the way our news is made. Rated R.

Book: Douglas Kellner, *The Persian Gulf TV War.*

Kellner looks carefully at the way in which information regarding the Persian Gulf War was presented to the American public. He then presents information that either contradicts or disputes what the media was saying. He also analyzes how this war was turned into a "media event" through the network of politicians, journalists, and the Pentagon. It is a fascinating book, but after you read it you may never trust the news again!

NOTES

Complete citations are provided in the Bibliography.

1. *Rethinking Schools* 1991.

2. The single-best history of the multicultural basis on which America's economic development was based is Takaki 1993.

3. Eitzen and Zinn 1993, 339–40.

4. Apple and Weis (1983) provide a collection of articles critical of an educational system that functions only to meet labor markets. Stern (1992) provides an analysis that argues for, and justifies, schooling for that purpose.

5. Kozol 1991, 236–37.

6. Tifft 1989, 48.

7. Weis 1990, 115.

8. Note the use of the word "perceived." Although the general public is led to believe that there is national competition, the reality is that American capital has always been invested in these other countries and that a section of the American ruling class was benefitting from the advantages that the more advanced technologies provided to our so-called competitors.

9. Weis and Fine (1993) have collected essays that document the ongoing struggles in public education.

10. Two important studies in the mid-1970s pointed out the failure of educational reform in relationship to social stratification. See Bowles and Gintis (1976) and Persell (1977). By the end of the 1980s, the inequalities among schools had grown so deep that education writer Jonathan Kozol titled his (1991) study *Savage Inequalities*.

11. American Association of University Women 1993.

12. Holloway 1993, 94–103.

13. Ray and Mickelson 1993.

14. Weis 1990; also see Weis and Fine 1993.

15. Kozol 1991.

16. Michael Apple 1983.

17. Kozol 1991; Fine and Rosenberg 1983; Rist 1973.

18. Stevenson 1993; also Weis 1990.

19. Barbie Zeilzer, a reporter, in 1992 analyzed the way in which the media shaped the "collective memory" of Americans regarding the Kennedy assassination.

20. Bagdikian 1993; also see Tuchman 1978.

21. Kellner 1992.

22. The best overall analysis of the mass media has been done by Parenti 1986, 1992.

23. Kozol 1988, 18.

24. Barak 1991, 71.

25. Crossen 1994.

26. Cantor 1987, 190–214. The magazine *Extra!* published by the organization FAIR (Fairness & Accuracy in Reporting) regularly analyzes these stereotypes as they appear in the dominant media.

27. Kellner 1990, 219.

28. *Interpreter* 1996.

29. Gandhi's philosophies deeply influenced the leaders of both the South African freedom movements and the leaders of America's civil rights movements.

30. Briggs 1987, 408–41.

12

FACT OR FANTASY? SCIENCE AND THE CONTROL OF IDEAS

"If the misery of our poor be caused not by the laws of nature, but by our institutions, great is our sin."

—Darwin, *Voyage of the Beagle*

Today we are in a "scientific age." Science has created its own ideology. Scientists no longer work in dark and damp cellars or small garages, creating new discoveries. Science today is as bureaucratized as the other areas of society. Huge university research complexes, government research agencies, and corporate research and development departments concentrate the work and power over science, in the hands of a very few. We turn now to a discussion of the way in which that has happened—the growth and development of science.

SCIENCE AS A WAY OF KNOWING

The laws and patterns of the natural world exist regardless of our own knowledge or understanding. **Science** is a system of ideas subjected to testing, critical evaluation, and retesting in the light of observable results. This contrasts with other ideologies, which are belief systems held to be true only because we have been taught by our society that they are true or our experience suggests they are true.

Giordano Bruno, an astronomer who challenged the medieval church's ideas of the solar system, was burned at the stake. Galileo was placed under house arrest. Yet their persecution by a powerful bureaucracy did not alter the way the solar system was organized. The world was round; what people thought about it in their heads didn't change the *fact* of a round world. Today we laugh at the people who thought the world was flat.

What happens when science cannot explain something? Up until the time of Bruno and Galileo, Europeans did not have a scientific understanding of the heavens. (Note that we say Europeans, because other cultures of that time—including the Mayans in Central America—had developed a more sophisticated understanding of astronomy.) The Church provided answers not based on scientific inquiry but based on religious ideology.

The medieval Christian church socially blocked scientific development by declaring any finding or fact outside of a Biblical interpretation to be heresy. In contrast, the Islamic religion was more tolerant of critical inquiry. The contributions of Egypt, Greece, and Rome were preserved and kept alive during Europe's Dark Ages in African universities, especially the great Islamic University of Timbuktu in Africa.[1]

Without understanding modern biology, European religion explained differences in skin color as God's punishment of the children of Ham by making them darker. People explained disease as the result of evil spirits or God's punishment. These explanations sound far-fetched to us; we now know that skin color is an adaptive mechanism to sunlight based on the amount of melanin in the skin and that disease is spread by germs and viruses.

People still believe homosexuality is a personal choice, and therefore a sin, instead of understanding it as a result of the natural continuum of sexual potentials that all humans possess. A century from now people may laugh at our antiquated ideas about homosexuality just as we laugh at those who saw dark skin color as a result of God's punishment.

The previous chapters have argued that those who control ideology can have power over others. Whether it is because God said so, because it is natural, or because it is the American Way, the elite use various ideologies to present their power and control as right and good. When scientists like Galileo and Bruno provide evidence that challenges the power of the ruling classes, they will attack that evidence as well as the scientists.

SCIENCE AS "PROGRESS"

The rise of industrialization demanded new ideologies to justify the accumulation of property and wealth and define social status for an emerging class of capitalists. At the same time, industrialization would not have been possible without breakthroughs in science. Galileo's discoveries made modern navigation possible. Isaac Newton laid the basis for modern physics, which in turn made possible mechanics and the production of machinery. Linnaeus and

Darwin established the groundwork for biology. Science was encouraged as necessary, and it soon became a "good thing."

A new social ideology was created, that of "progress." This ideology directly linked science and technology to the interests of the emerging elite of industrialists and bankers. By knowing and understanding atoms, gravity, proteins and metabolism it was possible for the ruling classes to harness and use nature for their own ends. Ordinary people were "sold" on this new ideology because the elite promised that "progress" would also improve their lives.

Chapter 6 pointed out that we have been taught to see all norms as necessary and not distinguish between dominant group norms and egalitarian norms. In a similar way, we have been taught to see all progress as good for everybody. The very word "progress" implies something positive. We have *not* been taught to distinguish between science and technology that is beneficial to the earth, and science and technology that allows an elite to enrich themselves and better manipulate and exploit us.

Anthropologist Richard Robbins argues that the ideology of progress has prevented us from seeing the costs of our technology and the benefits of simpler lifestyles:

> Those who claim that modern food-producing techniques are far more efficient than any other point out that in American society, only one calorie of human energy is needed to produce 210 calories for human consumption, while hunter-gatherers produce less than ten calories of food for every calorie they use collecting the food. Others argue...at the same time we vastly decreased the amount of human labor required to produce food . . . we vastly increased the amount of nonhuman energy required for food production. From that perspective, we expend one calorie of nonhuman energy in the form of nonrenewable fossil fuels (e.g. oil and coal) for every eight calories we produce.

He goes on to compare potato production in a small New Guinea community with American potato production:

> in addition to the human energy that goes into American farming, vast amounts of nonhuman energy are expended. For example, in the state of Washington in the 1960s, 60 percent of potato acreage was airplane-sprayed five to nine times each season to control insects; another 40 percent was treated for weeds. American potato farmers need specialized machines to cut, seed, harvest, dig, and plant, In 1969, 36,000 tons of fertilizer was applied to

> 62,500 acres—over 1,000 pounds per acre. Thus while the Washington system produced more potatoes, the actual energy costs per calorie were far higher than in New Guinea. Moreover, all kinds of hidden costs, as social erosion and pollution were incurred.[2]

One can add to Robbins's observations the point that millions of young Americans are unemployed or underemployed while our idea of "progress" tells us that machines that replace labor are a good thing.

Several generations have been told that televisions, interstate highways, and advanced health care are the result of the progress brought about by science. But have the benefits truly outweighed the negative impact of much of the technology? Our televisions also glorify violence, sexism, and consumerism in order to create artificial markets.[3] Instead of mass transit systems, interstate highways were built and made consumers hostage to powerful oil companies and made the concrete industry rich. Health care that is too expensive for the poor has provided profits to corporations that are double or triple the rate of profit in other sectors of the economy.

The progress that appeared to benefit some also often came at the expense of the many, sometimes in other parts of the world. According to Bruce Rich, an Environmental Defense Fund attorney and an expert on international development policy, there has been an international program of ecological destruction fostered by the World Bank. In the name of progress, the World Bank has plundered natural resources and impoverished millions.[4]

THE IDEOLOGICAL USE OF SCIENCE

As "scientific progress" replaced other ideologies in the modern world, it became necessary for the ruling elites to use science to justify their higher status. Science was now expected to reenforce the ideology of male supremacy. It is not surprising that the emerging medical profession did studies that found women to be childlike, dependent, hysterical, and not as intellectually competent as men.

In the late 1800s medical men actually came close to defining femaleness itself as an illness, as proof citing Darwin (incorrectly) and his theory of evolution. Evolution, they claimed, had played a dirty trick on women of the middle and upper classes: through excessively high development, their uteruses had become diseased. While these male "thinkers" found it unfortunate that so many uteruses were in so much trouble, they also found beauty in the thought of their women as overbred evolutionary anachronisms. For it was evolution, too, they claimed, which had done away with ladies' sexual appetites. Only "low" women, the story went, suffered from the indignity of sexual desire.[5]

The slaveowners also looked to science to justify their exploitation of people of color. Using Darwin, a whole generation of "scientists" claimed Africans were a subspecies and not capable of the level of civilization that the white man had achieved. Today we know that such scientific explanations distorted and manipulated reality. Just as belief in a flat world didn't make the world flat, neither does belief in the inferiority of people of color or women make them inferior. The only difference is that instead of citing God, the ruling elites tried to use science.

If the scientific method attempts to discover actual laws and patterns, how is it possible for so-called scientists to discover patterns and laws that are false, as in the examples above? One answer is that science is always the process of trial and error and that early theories must first be tested and proven false if science is to continue to grow and develop. But that answer assumes that science, and scientists, is separate from society and are neutral. Instead, scientists are part of the social structures of their society, and are socialized by the same processes that socialize other members. Scientists pass through the bureaucracies of "higher education," which reflect the dominant ideologies, and the well-paid full professors are overwhelmingly white and male.

Harvard professor Ruth Hubbard, introduces her study *The Politics of Women's Biology* with this statement: "Nature is part of history and culture, not the other way around. Sociologists and historians of science tend to know that. Most scientists do not."[6] In her more recent study of the political use of genetic research she goes on to explain:

> Scientific Education initiates students into a cultural enterprise, with its own history and system of beliefs. One of those beliefs is that the march of science is immune from political and societal pressures, that scientists can function in an ideological vacuum. This belief has been proved wrong time and again. Scientists, as a group, tend to provide results that support the basic values of their society. This is not surprising, since scientists live in that society and make their observations with that society's eyes. This is particularly true when scientists are studying people.[7]

Research funds come largely from the government and big corporations, and rewards are controlled through publishing and media exposure. Scientists, like journalists, may perceive themselves as impartial seekers of the truth, but they, too, are products of their own socialization. They cannot ignore the networks and bureaucracies that allow them to advance.[8]

These processes are clearly illustrated by the history of biological determinism. Two biological characteristics (race and gender) are used in our society to rationalize stratification. The ruling elites have attempted over and over again to find some explanation in physiology or genetics that justifies racial and gender differences.

In the 1800s and early 1900s, it was not at all unusual for a scientist to begin a research project with the underlying premise of biological inferiority: "People of African descent are obviously less intelligent, since so few are doctors, or scientists, or writers. What is it that makes them less intelligent?" (One could substitute any oppressed ethnic group, or women, into that statement.) The research carried out, then, *began* with the assumption of inferiority and then searched for causes or explana tions. Lewontin, Rose, and Kamin explain:

> [Biological] Determinists are committed to the view that individuals are ontologically prior to society and that the characteristics of individuals are a consequence of their biology. The open question for determinists, to the extent that there has been one, is the degree of determination of various traits, and how these traits might be manipulated by means of or in spite of their biology."[9]

Compare the statement above with this statement: "People of African descent have all the biological potentials that any other group have. What is it then that prevents them from succeeding in medicine, science or banking?" The research design for this second statement begins with the assumption of equality and would therefore have to look for the answer in the social structure—the institutionalized racism that creates a degrading atmosphere in school, the discrimination in employment, wages, and civil rights, and the social controls that punish people of color who challenge the system.

Today we associate outright racism with groups like the Ku Klux Klan. But through our history, respected and influential institutions of research have promoted and given credence to these racist beliefs. Louis Agassiz was a famous naturalist and geologist who helped establish the Museum of Comparative Zoology at Harvard University in 1860 and became its first director. In 1863 he aided in founding the prestigious National Academy of Sciences. His research and writings were read and respected throughout the world. Agassiz was a racist, and agitated against ever letting people of color attain social equality with whites.

Louis Agassiz was a great scientist who is credited with discovering the evidence for the ice age. How is it possible that a man of such intellect could scientifically argue such a racist position? His memoirs, however, reveal that he was a man who had been socialized as a racist and professed a total repungence for people of color. In other words, he was a product of his times. And the system rewarded scientists who held such views.

In 1975 Harvard University published a book by an entomologist (insect specialist) who rephrased Agassiz's arguments in a different, but similar vein. According to E.O. Wilson, race, gender, and nationality genetically influence behavior in the same way that animal behaviors are based in instinct.[10] Wilson argues there is a genetic basis for male jealousy, competitiveness, and warfare. Those who seek gender equality, cooperation, and peace are then obviously going "against nature." E.O. Wilson's book was quickly discredited and dismissed by a broad spectrum of social scientists. Stephen Gould points out the flaw in E.O. Wilson's reasoning:

> I believe that human sociobiologists have made a fundamental mistake in categories. They are seeking the genetic basis of human behavior at the wrong level. They are searching among the specific products of generating rules—Joe's homosexuality, Martha's fear of strangers—while the rules themselves are the deep structures of human behavior.
>
> For example, E.O. Wilson writes:' "Are human beings innately aggressive? The answer is yes." As evidence, Wilson cites the prevalence of warfare in history and then discounts any current disinclination to fight: "The most peaceable tribes of today were often the ravagers of yesteryear and will probably again produce soldiers and murderers in the future." But if some peoples are peaceable now, then aggression itself cannot be coded in our genes, only the potential for it. If innate only means possible, or even likely in certain environments, then everything we do is innate and the word has no meaning. Aggression is one expression of a generating rule that anticipates peacefulness in other common environments. The range of specific behaviors engendered by the rule is impressive and a fine testimony to flexibility as the hallmark of human behavior.[11]

We might ask why Harvard University would print a book containing arguments that had essentially been dismissed fifty, even one hundred years ago? We could also ask why even today in the 1990s these theories continue to emerge? The search for a biological basis of human behavior has not gone away.

A current popular version of biological determinism is that of James Q. Wilson and Richard Hernstein, a political scientist and psychologist. Their 1985 *Crime and Human Nature* reduced "criminal activity" to a series of equations that focused upon what they called "constitutional factors." According to Wilson and Hernstein, these factors are "usually present at or soon after birth, whose behavioral consequences appear gradually during the child's development. Constitutional factors are not necessarily genetic, although there may be some traits that are to a degree heritable, such as intelligence and temperament, affect to some extent the likelihood that individuals will engage in criminal activities."[12]

More recently there was yet another attempt to base stratification in genes. Although dismissed by serious academics, *The Bell Curve: Intelligence and Class Structure in American Life* was receiving widespread media publicity.[13] This study claimed to have found that blacks, poor people, and people who were accident prone were all less intelligent due to "genetic traits"! The ruling classes continue to need an explanation for poverty, crime, and illness that directs attention away from the system.

SOCIAL SCIENCE AND THE JUSTIFICATION FOR SOCIAL STRATIFICATION

In medieval Europe, social stratification had been based on the divine right of kings." Individuals were born into their statuses, according to God's plan. With industrialization, the social structure of Europe was radically altered. New classes—entrepreneurs, bookkeepers, factory workers, and bankers—replaced serfs, craftsmen and nobility. How were these new classes to be explained and justified? In part, a new religious ideology emerged to explain the economic success of the few at the expense of the many—Protestantism and predestination. The **Protestant Ethic** said God looked favorably upon those who worked hard, saved, and invested. Worldly success in terms of material wealth was a sign that one was favored by God.

Social scientists and historians have long argued over whether the Protestant Reformation created the ideological basis for the Industrial Revolution or the Industrial Revolution required the new ideology of Protestantism. Neither simple "cause and effect" theory is true. As technology advanced and social institutions began to change, there was pressure on the church to change. As the church changed, it made possible transformations in the economic institutions. There is a close interdependency between both of these phenomena, with each changing in reaction to one another.

Religious ideology was not the only explanation that emerged, however. Just as science had been used to justify racism and sexism, new attempts were made to explain the origin of modern classes using science. There were three main, and conflicting, ideologies that emerged in the nineteenth century—Social Darwinism, Freudian and other psychological theories, and Radical Socialism.

The first, **Social Darwinism**, based itself upon Darwin's ideas of a hierarchy for the natural world and applied them to human hierarchies. Charles Darwin never claimed that his theory applied to humans. But because it was such a useful explanation for why some were winners and others losers, it was quickly picked up and distorted to fit the needs of stratified society. Herbert Spencer, a philosopher who deeply influenced early American sociology, was the first to use the term "survival of the fittest," several years before Darwin. His perspective is an example of Social Darwinism.[14]

Like biological determinism, Social Darwinism ignored qualities that separated humans from other species. It asserted that humans and animals were all subject to the same laws. According to this argument, the uppers classes were a result of some people's "superior adaptation" and fitness to survive, while the lower classes were poor because they were maladapted and less able to survive in the competitive jungle. Some theorists went so far as to say that the poor who died of hunger, disease, or overwork deserved their fate, and that society would be better off for having eliminated them from the breeding gene pool of the society!

Sigmund Freud's theories sought explanations for human behavior inside the "psyche," which he described as id, ego, and superego. According to this theory, we were all born with "animal" instincts that society had to channel and control. Particularly important to Freud were the instincts having to do with sex drives and desires and the differences between men and women. Women, he argued, had "penis envy" because they could not be men!

Freud was a brilliant man who did make some significant contributions, particularly in his methods of psychoanalysis. Like Louis Agassiz, however, Freud was a product of his times. His initial research revealed that the hysteria of his female patients was caused by experiences of sexual abuse and sexual assault at an early age. Freud wrote a paper detailing his findings. Had he pursued this line of inquiry, he would have raised, one hundred years ago, the psychological costs of domestic violence and abuse that we now understand.

But Freud was warned that such research might prevent his advance in the profession, and he was persuaded to change his theory, attributing women's hysteria to repressed fantasies and other alleged aspects of their gender. Freud's sell-out of science in the interests of his career became known when his private papers were opened in the mid-1980s.[15] Yet few textbooks reveal this aspect of his career and many social science texts continue to treat Freud's sexist ideas as having a basis in science.

Although Freud is the most famous, other psychologists also sought the reasons for differences in gender and racial status inside individuals. One theory was that of "collective" or "tribal" consciousness. According to this idea, our attitudes and behavioral patterns are somehow passed on through birth, deeply embedded in our brains. Thus, statistics that show some ethnic groups have higher rates of violent crime can be attributed to their inheriting the violent characteristics exhibited by their ancestors of long ago![16]

Such arguments made sense to the wealthy, who were justifying their mansions and jewels while their workers died of tuberculosis exacerbated by the overcrowded and polluted conditions in the factories. Those workers, however, were far more inclined to believe the arguments of the socialists who saw their conditions as the result of an economic system that oppressed many while allowing a few unlimited wealth.

In general, **Socialism** sought to find remedies for social problems by changing society instead of blaming individuals. Within socialism, there were many different perspectives. Some were anarchists, who believed that governments set the conditions for the exploitation and oppression of the working classes. Anarchists argued society could not be free and prosperous until governments were disbanded and there were no restrictions whatsoever on individual freedom and liberties. Others were syndicalists, who focused on factory owners' oppression and exploitation of workers. They contended that the key to power was in the formation of powerful unions that could take over the factories and run them for the benefit of the workers. Utopian Socialists were those who prophesied that advances in technology could create enough material well-being for all to share and have a good life. But the most influential theory of this the last half of the nineteenth century was that of Karl Marx.

Marxist socialism saw the problem as the conflict between two major classes: the workers and the capitalists. The social relationship between these two classes was a contradiction. On the one hand, each class needed the other. Indeed, Marx argued that capitalist accumulation had been necessary for the development of industrialization. On the other hand, the inevitable conflict between these two classes would eventually destabilize society, according to Marx, and lead to class warfare. As wages were forced down and workers began to starve, they would have to overthrow the class that held them in bondage. This would lay the basis for a reorganization of society in which the productivity of new technologies could be designed to serve human needs and provide material well-being for all.

Marx called his scientific approach **dialectical historical materialism**. He saw events as arising out of a past, with a present and a future. He believed that nothing could be understood without understanding its context and its opposite. And he argued that underneath all the arguments about ideology, the bottom line was always material. Did you have enough to eat? shelter? protection for your children?

Marx believed that if ordinary working people could understand their own social conditions, they could and would change those conditions. Marx also argued that modern class relations cut across national boundaries and that workers around the world all shared a common oppressor and exploiter. For Marx there was no "other" outside the social boundary; there was no invisible class. His philosophy was internationalist. His theory required individuals to sense their own historical importance and actively participate in making history. In other words, Marx was an activist as well as a philosopher. He joined workers' organizations and pushed people to "do something!"[17]

Marxism, as Marx's theory came to be called, was an enormous challenge to the ideologies of the ruling classes of that time. Marxism and the other socialist theories swept Europe, leading to mass working class uprisings, the formation of unions, and other radical movements. Marx, himself, did not claim to be a "Marxist." As a scientist he was continually updating and revising his theories. As happened to Darwin's theories, others have turned Marx's writings and theories into dogma—that is, "the truth."

Large and important political parties were founded on Marxist, or other socialist, principles. Even today, Marxism continues to be a respected and important intellectual study in European Universities. Despite the great inequalities present in American society, Marxism failed to become an ideology for the majority of the American working class in the nineteenth and early twentieth centuries. This was partly the result of the unique conditions under which American culture developed and partly the influence of American social sciences as an alternative theory to explain social stratification.

AMERICAN SOCIOLOGY AND SOCIAL STRATIFICATION THEORIES

American social science in the late nineteenth and twentieth century divided into three main schools of thought regarding class stratification: a revised form of social Darwinism, social reformism, and structural functionalism.

The first school was another adaptation of Social Darwinism. These were social scientists who attempted to find the explanation for one's status in society within the natural laws of evolution—survival of the fittest and competition.

There were those who sought to explain criminal behavior by measuring skull size and shape. They argued that the higher crime rate of southern European immigrants could be explained by skull size instead of poverty and unemployment. Cesare Lombroso is the most famous name associated with this school. An entire field of "criminal anthropology" was based on his theory, and individuals were actually convicted of crimes because they had a head of a certain shape or some other physical characteristic![18] Paul Broca did research attempting to explain women's behavioral traits in the particular characteristics of their brains.

More insidious were those who attempted to prove that intelligence was an inherited trait. American social scientists seized on the findings of the British social scientist Cyril Burt who had "proven" that intelligence was inherited. Burt's research tracked identical twins (with the same genes) who had been separated at birth and raised in different environments. Burt claimed that these twins were measured at similar intelligence levels, proving that intelligence was genetic and not the result of social factors.

In the late 1970s Cyril Burt was exposed as having fraudulently manipulated his data. The two "research assistants" who collected the original information never existed at all. Reanalysis of his studies showed sloppy mathematical work and unfounded conclusions. But since Burt had been saying what the elites wanted to hear, for several decades his research had gone unchallenged. Had such poor research been done by someone who threatened the elites it would have been *immediately* exposed.

If intelligence were genetic, that is, a physiological trait, it could be tested and measured like other traits. Thus the American testing industry was born. Millions of children (and adults) have been processed through this testing system, with the "failures" separated out and tracked into courses that are less demanding and less rewarding.[19] The fact that scores on these tests are more highly correlated with family background (parent's education and income level), that children of color perform at lower levels, and that girls begin to decline in scores when they reach a certain age have all been used to buttress the argument that intelligence is somehow inherited.

One of the early and most important of these tests was that developed by Alfred Binet, a French psychologist. His original purpose was to identify children whose lack of success in normal classrooms suggested the need for some form of special education. In developing his scale, Binet insisted on three things:

1. The scores are a practical device; they do not buttress any theory of intellect.
2. The scale is a rough, empirical guide for identifying mildly retarded and learning disabled children who need special help. It is not a device for ranking normal children.
3. Whatever the cause of difficulty in children identified for help, emphasis shall be placed upon improvement through special training. Low scores shall not be used to mark children as innately incapable.

Psychologists at Stanford University seized upon the Binet scale and created the most famous of all IQ tests—the Stanford-Binet. Those who were seeking to rank children on the trait of intelligence overturned all of Binet's intentions and translated his scale into written form as a routine device for testing all children.[20]

These cases of fraud, subjectivity and data manipulation point out a very important fact: *so far, the only way to provide scientific proof of a biological basis for social ranking on the basis of class, gender or race is to make it up!*

SOCIOLOGY, SOCIAL REFORM, AND FUNCTIONALISM

The second sociological approach did look at the social structure. Sociology as a discipline in America grew out of work by sociologists who had been church ministers, social workers and ethical philosophers. These early sociologists could see that the cause for crime, low test scores, and poverty for the lower classes lay in the social conditions of the society. They deplored the conditions under which so many Americans lived and wanted to better the lives of the unfortunate. Their attempt to scientifically determine why poverty and crime existed led to the founding of sociology departments in several major universities.

Marx's premise had been that the working class would become more and more impoverished and the capitalists would become more and more oppressive. Those premises did not seem to hold true for nineteenth-century America. Indeed, what looked like a more valid proposition was that capitalism could be *reformed*. Living standards for the workers could improve even if the capitalists maintained their class position. Unions could be organized and win better wages and working conditions and companies would still be profitable. In other words, reform was possible within the given system of class relations.

Early studies in sociology were designed to provide insight into reforms that could be made in the existing system. The United States was an expanding economy, and it seemed reasonable that in a land where wealth appeared to be unlimited, the benefits could be more equitably shared. In other words, the hierarchies of power themselves were not questioned; the idea was to pressure those with power to be more fair and equitable in their administration of that power.

It is important to note that none of these sociologists understood the larger connections being made in this book. They did not see a relationship between white middle class prosperity, the brutality of slavery, the genocide of Native Americans, the oppression of women, the rape of the land and exploitation of natural resources, and the expansion of American economic interests into Central and South America. The "invisible classes" discussed in Chapter 4 were as invisible to these early sociologists as they were to the rest of the population.

The Great Depression of the 1930s radically changed the country, and sociology. Although most economists use the stock market crash of 1929 as the starting point of the depression, it is more accurate to see its start in the early 1920s. In that decade, the small farmers of America were driven off their land by a combination of falling prices and drought. Angry and frustrated, they were easily persuaded by groups like the Ku Klux Klan to blame Jews, Negroes, and communists for their problems. As a result, Klan membership reached into the millions and the number of lynchings grew rapidly. The country was already in social crisis when the stock market crashed.

The continued control over the educational and media bureaucracies by the elite has meant that the struggles of each generation are soon rewritten, or written out, of the history books. At the same time, every generation has produced scholars, writers, and artists who have put on record "the other side of the story." During the upheaval of the 1920s and 1930s, the historian and sociologist W.E.B. Du Bois was able to challenge the racist premises of Reconstruction history.[21]

During the depression, it appeared that the predictions of Marx and other radicals might hold true for America. Marxism became fashionable in some intellectual circles in the United States. (Du Bois was a Marxist.) An entire generation of young sociologists were exposed to Marxist arguments and sought to apply his theories to America. But within a decade the world was at war and economic prosperity had returned. Marx faded from fashion, and as wages went up and the United States became the dominant world power, an attack on writers, scholars, and teachers who had been influenced by Marxism was launched—McCarthyism.[22]

The prosperity of this period still did not extend down into the poorer two-fifths of the population, although there was an *illusion* of general prosperity. That illusion was not openly challenged until Michael Harrington's book *The Other America* exposed the existing poverty of the country to astonished Americans.[23]

A new approach was needed—a theory that could explain social stratification and power in the prosperous consuming society that was postwar America. The new ideology of America was framed by anticommunism. This theory would have to explain how inequality could exist in a country that was supposed to be characterized by freedom and equality and the pursuit of happiness for all.

In contrast, the "totalitarian" systems of the communist countries claimed to have done away with economic inequality. It was embarrassing that the enemy's systems provided health care for all and free university education whereas the greatest democracy in the world did not. How was such a discrepancy to be explained? Was there a scientific theory that could offer an answer? American sociology offered structural functionalism.

Following World War II, a new Department of Social Relations was created at Harvard that brought together historians, social psychologists, political scientists, sociologists, and anthropologists. In the next ten years this group of leading scholars developed a theory that would explain, justify, and rationalize the continued existence of the most highly developed class system in the modern world. In sociology this theory was called structural functionalism and its major theorist at Harvard was Talcott Parsons.

Unlike Marx, who took sides, Parsons claimed to be purely objective and scientific. To a country weary of war and eager to buy vacuum cleaners, cars, and a house in the suburbs, a theory that was "apolitical" was comforting.[24] Parsons argued that his new theory was "value free." Parsons drew heavily for his theory on the writing of the German sociologist Max Weber, who saw class as a function of status, prestige, and power.

Like other intellectuals, Max Weber was a product of his own socialization. His writings on stratification, bureaucrac,y and technology were useful, but he never made the connections between an industrializing Germany and the brutal repression of Germany's African colonies. Tanganyika (now Tanzania) was one of Germany's East African colonies. In the early nineteenth century German troops mercilessly repressed a revolt (the Maji Maji rebellion) in which tens of thousands of Africans were slaughtered, crops were destroyed, and diseases and famine killed thousands more.

Nor was Weber capable of seeing the oppression of women or the degradation of environment that was present. Weber felt that bureaucratization of society was inevitable and nothing could be done to change it. The elites preferred Weber's theories to Marx because they explained social hierarchy without raising the moral issues of who benefited.

Sociology has failed to understand the connections between the theoretical perspectives of well-to-do European men who thought that models of "society" could be explained by Europe alone and the internationalization of the world which was occurring at that time. Walter Rodney's analysis of the relationship between the Europe of this time, and Africa, is helpful in understanding the connections.[25]

Parsons professed no political leanings, other than his desire to discover social reality. But Charles O'Connell, a doctoral student in the history of sociology, found documents that revealed Parsons's clear political leanings—he was vehemently anti-communist. Indeed, his political sympathies led him to use his personal power and influence to bring ex-Nazis to Harvard despite State Department regulations banning their immigration.[26]

According to Parsons and other functionalists, stratification is an unconsciously evolved device by which societies insure that the most important responsibilities are discharged conscientiously by the most qualified persons. A hierarchical ordering of individuals helps to maintain the stability of the society. A system of differential rewards is the inescapable by-product of the division of labor in society, and existing differences in status and income reflect and encourage both conscientious performance and stability.[27] In other words, those who were rewarded by the system "contributed" more and deserved their higher status. Competition functioned to assure that the most capable and intelligent would "rise to the top."

This "system" theory was much like Freud's box of id, ego, and super-ego. Somehow, internally within the system, there was a sense of what was needed for balance.[28] Social relationships which preserved that balance were "functional"; social relationships which upset that balance were "dysfunctional."[29] The fact that the American social system had created the richest and most powerful nation in the world was proof enough that it was functional.

According to the structural functionalists, American families were happy because women knew their function was at home. The American economy was prosperous because workers knew their function was to labor, and owners knew their function was to invest. People received the rewards that society had to offer by following the rules and working hard. This meant that those who did not succeed must not have followed the rules or must not have worked as hard. They had been deviant in some way and deserved their misfortune. Indeed, structural functionalists argued that without social hierarchy there would be no motivation to achieve.[30]

The structural functionalists did not go unchallenged. C. Wright Mills was one of the first postwar sociologists to argue that positions at the top of the hierarchy in America were factually not based on individual merit and achievement. Nor did such hierarchies necessarily function for the good of all. In *The Power Elite*, Mills painstakingly documents the power that certain elite sectors had over American society in the 1950s. Mills's scholarship inspired a new generation of critical sociologists who broke new ground in researching actual power relationships of class in modern America. William Domhoff followed Mills in the mid-1960s with his study *Who Rules America?*[31]

Because history provides the data for sociological analysis, it is probably even more important that a new generation of historians also arose, led by the work of William Appleman Williams. Others included David Horowitz, Gabriel Kolko, James Weinstein, and Howard Zinn.[32] These scholars began to restudy the conventional truth and show it to us in new ways. George Rawick, a sociologist, went back to the oral histories of formal slaves collected during the depression, and wrote *From Sundown to Sunup*.[33] In this book he showed that African-Americans on the slave plantations had created a vibrant culture of survival and resistance, when the Master wasn't around.

His work, and others like him, destroyed the myth that the slaves were passive and accepting.

In his introduction to *The Power Elite and the State: How Policy is Made in America*, G. William Domhoff observes:

> For all its seeming relevance, however, few social scientists want to talk about how power operates in the United States, let alone try to study it. Whatever the reasons for avoiding the study of the power structure in America, it has no disciplinary home in the social sciences. Research on power therefore crops up at the edges of disciplines, or in the interstices between disciplines, especially between political science and sociology. The pariah status of power in the social sciences can be seen most glaringly in economics. There, in the most celebrated of the social sciences, is virtually no concern with power.[34]

The focus of Marxist theory had been on social class, economic exploitation, and class struggle. Social Darwinism focused on the biological determination of human behavior. The focus of structural functionalism was on social stability, the positive functions of class and the interdependency of all sectors of society. None of these approaches, as they were interpreted in mid-twentieth century America, fully accounted for or analyzed the inequality of women, people of color, or the degradation of the earth.

The debate was framed in the more narrow terms of social class and even critics such as Mills and Domhoff confined themselves to the issues of economic power and control. Sociology as a discipline did not even begin to seriously address the relationships between class, race, gender and speciesism until the powerful social movements of the 1960s spread from the South, the ghettos and barrios, and the kitchens of America into the insulated and isolated halls of ivy.[35]

Mainstream sociology is an academic discipline within a powerful educational bureaucracy.[36] As such it has actually contributed little to our understanding of social stratification and power. There are powerful networks that control the discipline and determine who receives the prestige and rewards. Irving Louis Horowitz compared the social stratification of sociology in 1968 to a feudal empire: an association of 7,500 "believers," 350 or so bishops and archbishops (the theorists); the College of Cardinals (the presidents of the American Sociological Association); and 850 or so elite secularists who have access to the money of the great foundations. "sociology thus has two principal estates: the priests and the princes. The third estate are the 7,000 nuclear members".[37]

There is a rich history in sociology of resistance to the power of these elite networks.[38] Alternative organizations, such as the Society for the Study of Social Problems and the Association of Humanist Sociology, both spearheaded by Al and Betty Lee, have been attempts to provide alternative perspectives within the discipline. The journals *Critical Sociology* and *Humanity and Society* have provided an alternative publishing outlet.

The rules in sociology, however, ensure the status quo. Those who hold positions at the elite universities are given more research funds and lighter teaching loads and are thus more able to publish and gain prominence. To network, one must have the money to go to professional meetings that are held in expensive hotels. In order to be promoted, one must publish. In order to publish, one's research must be based in the existing literature (and if your perceptions are new or challenge the dominant theories, to whom to you turn?) Your findings are seen as more legitimate if you use mathematics, quantify all variables, and carry out confusing and often uninterpretable statistics.

The most famous and prominent sociologists are those who develop theories that explain society without criticism. These sociologists help legitimate stratification. For example, the "Wisconsin School" of status-attainment developed theories to explain social mobility in America.[39] These theories were based on the assumption that a modern industrializing society needed social mobility and that the middle class would continue to expand. This is what people wanted to hear. But these theories have not been able to explain why today the middle class is shrinking and the lower- and upper-class levels are becoming more polarized.

The "rules" also go against the research of politically sensitive topics. Many sociologists believe the decision by Washington University in St. Louis (a private school controlled by the elite Pew family) to close down the sociology department was because it had generated research and teaching that offended decisionmakers in St. Louis.

Nor does the discipline want to tackle controversial topics. For example, in the late 1970s I wrote an article analyzing the participation of the Ku Klux Klan in the textbook protest of West Virginia. I argued that the textbook protest and the Klan's participation were part of a right wing social movement against multicultural education, and against unions. I could not use the "social movement" literature for my framework of analysis because it was largely irrelevant. I had been able to interview both Klan members and those opposing the Klan for my research, but could only cite historians (and not sociologists) for my academic references.

My article was turned down by several leading sociology journals because I did not cite the "correct" literature or quantify variables. Between 1950 and the time I submitted my article only *one* article had been published in a major sociological journal dealing with the Ku Klux Klan—although the KKK had been a major force in the country for a century. But there had been numerous studies of the "student" movement. Such studies were "safe" and easily done, using a researcher's own campus and network for informants. Ironically, my research *was* used by the West Virginia Education Association and then the National Education Association and I was asked to be a consultant in their study of right wing opposition to multicultural education and public employee collective bargaining.

But a sociologist who offers a "new" version that can be used *to justify* social stratification may be quickly rewarded. The meteoric rise of William Julius Wilson and his "underclass" theory is an example of a sociologist who is suddenly taken *very* seriously by *Time* magazine, the *New York Times*, and major government funding agencies.[40] Wilson's research has been used to reinforce the stereotype of poverty as black and urban. Wilson, who is an African American professor of sociology at the prestigious University of Chicago, has become nationally famous by explaining poverty as the result of breakdowns in roles and the isolation of the black subculture. Like E.O. Wilson, who provided a new dressing for genetic theories of behavior, William J. Wilson's work has been used to provide a new dressing for the old arguments that blame the victims.

His analysis has been thoroughly criticized by those in sociology who understand the bankruptcy of his model, including the leadership of the Association of Black Sociologists.[41] Because his model is one of structural functionalism, Wilson ignores major historical and political events that shaped the inner city. For example in *The Truly Disadvantaged* he does no analysis of the impact of the civil rights movement on the inner city, the repression of the Chicago police on civil rights activists, or the flood of illegal drugs into that community at the very time of his observation of "disorganization."[42] Nor does he explore areas of the country in which such "social disorganization" is found among predominantly white populations.[43]

Historian Jacqueline Jones concludes her study of poverty in America with a critique of Wilson's concept of underclass:

> Scholars tended to focus on racially segregated, 'hyperghettoized areas' and to suggest that the "concentrated poor" were by definition "isolated" from mainstream society. In fact, even the poorest urban census tracts consisted of some people who were blue-collar workers and others whose wages were insufficient to raise them above the poverty line. These residents took pains to distance themselves from the youth culture that surrounded them and too often invaded their own homes.

> The definition of the underclass in terms of "antisocial behavior" was especially misleading. The entrepreneurial impulse that led some youths into selling newspapers and other into selling stolen goods *was less inherently "destructive" than the context in which it was carried out* (emphasis added). Among the poor, household strategies for survival assumed a number of different forms, but usually the goal was a predictable, ordinary one—to care for children and maintain ties among the generations. Thus the charge that the underclass had priorities quite different from the middle class confused means with ends.
>
> Like the sharecroppers forced to scrounge for wage work to supplement their inadequate furnishings, inner-city folk faced the undeniable fact that one minimum-wage job was insufficient to feed, clothe, and house a mother and her children. Hence individuals and groups of neighbors and networks of kin devised diverse ways to survive. They rearranged their households, pooled their resources and parceled out tasks on the basis of age and sex. Income came from "working off the books," negotiating around, or manipulating the welfare bureaucracy: part-time jobs; and soliciting aid from friends, parents and former boyfriends. The adults who work in fly-by-night sweatshops with false Social Security cards did so not because they were criminally inclined but because they knew that, if they reported extra income, their welfare payments would be docked in proportion to their own initiative in supporting themselves.[44]

The important task of understanding actual and real power relations in this society—the mechanisms of oppression, degradation, and exploitation—have been left largely to independent journalists, to activists within the movements of equality and environment, and to the grassroots organizers who have, of necessity, been forced to study and understand the power relationships they must change in order to survive. A forceful example of how such an organizer learned the principles of social power in America can be found in Septima Clark's biography, *Ready from Within.*[45] Her teachers were not prominent sociologists; they were her own friends and neighbors and activists at the Highlander School in Tennessee. Using that knowledge, Clark organized the literacy campaigns in the South that laid the basis for the civil rights movement.

CONCLUSION

Scholars who hope to challenge inequality in America cannot rely on the very bureaucracies whose task it is to control and delegitimate those challenges.

Social science that seeks to further the cause of democracy and equality must link with the emerging social movements that are challenging social stratification in America. At the same time, the emerging social movements must be informed by scientific scholarship that helps them understand the real world which they are confronting.

The difficulty of accurately understanding the changing real world is clear when we consider the amazing and rapid changes in modern technology. Technology is applied science, and as such can be used to further dominant group ideologies or egalitarian ideologies. The next part of this book looks more closely at the new technologies and their implications for American society.

SUMMARY

Science, like religion and politics, has an ideological base. People "believe" in science and to a certain extent, our society socializes us to accept basic scientific principles. But, like religion or politics, science can also be used to justify and rationalize the ladder of stratification. Scientists who discover facts that challenge the power of the elite are subject to negative sanctions just as political or religious leaders who challenge dominant group norms.

One of the most important ways in which science has become an ideology is through the idea of "progress." Americans have been taught that science and technology create progress—which is a good thing. But progress has both positive and negative aspects. Often progress for one group creates great social pain for another group. In other words, some progress is defined by dominant group norms.

Over time, science has come to replace religion as the major way of defending and justifying social stratification. A study of the history of science shows that "great" scientists found proof of the inferiority of women, people of color, and of the poor. Many scientists continue to argue that humans should continue to dominate other forms of life.

Sociology has been defined as a "social science" and as such is part of the contradictions of science. The Protestant ethic was a reworking of religious ideology that made a more scientific outlook on life possible. But it was also used to rationalize the difference between those who were "the elect" and those who were damned. Another social science ideology popular in the last century was Social Darwinism, which distorted Darwin's findings about the natural world to argue that humans were subject to the laws of "natural selection."

These conceptions of science were challenged by movements for greater equality and democracy that wanted to apply more egalitarian norms to science. In the nineteenth and early twentieth centuries these views were expressed by various socialist thinkers. The best known was Karl Marx, who developed a scientific method called dialectical historical materialism to try to understand the fundamental laws of human society.

American sociology has reflected all of these different interpretations of science as applied to our culture. IQ tests and other "genetic" arguments for human differences have been used, and continue to be used, to explain why some groups are higher on the ladder than others. After World War II another theory, structural functionalism, was developed at Harvard. This view argued that our places on the ladder were not genetic but were given by the "needs" of the system.

There have been sociologists and other social scientists who have continued to challenge the schools of thought that justify stratification. But because academic sociology is a bureaucracy like all others, most of these challenges have had to come from outside the legitimate structures. Social scientists who are critical of the existing system find greater support among leaders and participants of social movements for change than from within their own institutional arena.

Vocabulary

Science. A system of ideas subjected to testing, critical evaluation, and retesting in the light of observable results.

The Protestant Ethic. A reinterpretation of religious ideology that was more suitable for an emerging industrial age; beliefs that God looks favorably upon those who work hard and will save those who "do well"—therefore failure in society is a sign of failure in God's eyes.

Social Darwinism. Trying to apply (incorrectly) Darwin's conclusions regarding the natural world to the study of society; argues that human hierarchies are the results of "laws of nature."

Socialism. A political approach to social problems seeking to find solutions by changing unequal social structures into forms that would give more economic equality.

Dialectical Historical Materialism. An approach that sees society arising out of the past in the context of contradictions within society; argues that stratification is an undesirable effect of the scarcity of resources and that advances in technology will make greater equality possible; identified with the writing and work of Karl Marx.

Structural Functionalism. An approach that sees society as guided by system imperatives that place individuals into necessary roles; argues that stratification is an unconsciously evolved device by which societies insure that the most important responsibilities are discharged by the most qualified persons.

Discussion Questions

1. What is your definition of "progress?" How were you taught that progress was part of science? Can you see things in your life where "progress" has not helped but hurt you or your family?

2. What are the differences between the ideology of religion and the ideology of science? Do you believe that science will eventually answer all questions and replace the need for religion? Why or why not? Discuss the ways in which both religion and science are used by the ruling elites to justify stratification.

3. The argument about whether our behaviors are based in our genes or in our socialization is often called the "nature-nurture" debate. In your view how do humans, who have intelligence and the capacity to evaluate consequences, differ from other animals? Can you identify traits about yourself that are connected to your genetic makeup? How do these traits interact with your socialization and your current social environment?

4. What were you taught regarding IQ testing? How has your academic career been affected by the way you performed on certain tests? Discuss the ways in which an IQ score could create a self-fulfilling prophecy for a young person who performed poorly on a certain test.

Resources

Books: Randy Shilts, *And the Band Played On*

The movie based on this book was recommend as a resource in Chapter 10 for analysis of bureaucracy. The book is more detailed, and gives an amazing inside view of the way science is manipulated and used in the struggle to find the cause of AIDS. It is also a detailed study of the interaction of those who tried to define the disease religiously (it is God's punishment for the sin of homosexuality) and those who tried to define the disease scientifically. Shilts was a newspaper journalist and he writes the book like a detective story, so that although it is long, it is hard to put down!

Septima Clark, *Ready from Within.*

Although this book could have been used for either of the chapters about social movements, it is also a study of how science and knowledge is used. Mrs. Clark was an African-American school teacher in the South after World War II who laid the groundwork for the successful voting rights campaigns there. She did not learn to do that in her formal education, but was trained by her own experiences and at the Highlander School, an alternative educational institution in Tennessee that advocates social change. Her story is told in her own words—simple and powerful. She also has some fascinating insights into the leadership role of Martin Luther King.

NOTES

Complete citations are provided in the Bibliography.

1. Bennett 1982, 13–22.
2. Robbins 1993, 34–35.
3. Cannon 1993, 16–21.
4. Rich 1994.
5. Hymowitz and Weissman 1978,72
6. Hubbard 1990, 1
7. Ibid. 1993, 7.
8. Littrell (1993, 207–31) explores the consequences of such social position for sociologists.
9. Lewontin, Rose and Kamin 1984, 35.
10. Wilson 1975.
11. Gould 1981, 330
12. Wilson and Hernstein 1985, 69.
13. Hernstein and Murray 1994; for both an academic and political criticism of this book, see Newby 1995.
14. Ritzer 1992, 35.
15. Masson 1984.
16. Carl Jung is the most famous psychologist identified with the theory of the collective unconscious. This same theme runs through the recent bestseller, *Women Who Run with the Wolves* (1992).
17. Marx and Engles's call to action in *The Communist Manifesto* remains a classic example of the combination of social analysis and the need for people to respond with action.
18. Gould 1981, 122–45.
19. Hilliard 1990, 135–42.
20. Gould 1981, 146–58.
21. DuBois 1992.
22. This attack was named McCarthyism after Senator Joseph McCarthy, who led a campaign against anyone and everyone who might have any sort of "leftist" leanings by calling them communists. In the process McCarthy ruined the careers and lives of scores of intelligent and sensitive people whose only "crime" had been to question some aspect of the system. See Goldman 1960, 202–36.
23. Harrington 1963.
24. Ehrenreich 1989, 17–56.
25. Rodney 1982.
26. O'Connell 1988; also *The Nation*, 6 March 1989.
27. Susan Boyle (1989, 34–36) summarizes the major concepts of the functional approach to stratification, while also pointing out that it has never been possible to accurately measure the claims made by the theory.
28. In graduate school at the University of Wisconsin we used to joke about the fact that nobody had ever really read the entire book—it was too abstract, confusing, and obtuse. I rose to the challenge and read the entire book. What people said was true. Had anyone written such a book with the purpose of critiquing the power elite, it would have immediately been attacked as

abstract, confusing, and obtuse. But Parsons was at Harvard, had influential friends, and his theory provided social science justifications needed by the elite.

29. Parsons 1951.

30. The early debate between Kingsley Davis, Wilbert E. Moore, and Melvin Tumin on functionalism and stratification may be found in Bendix and Lipset 1966, 47–95.

31. Mills 1956; Domhoff 1967.

32. See the bibliography for some of their more influential studies from this period.

33. Rawick 1972.

34. Domhoff 1990, xiii. Susan Boyle (1989, 4) argues that sociology's failure lies in its refusal to incorporate an historical perspective as well.

35. During my five years of graduate study at the prestigious University of Wisconsin , I was *never* required to read a book by a woman social scientist or an African-American social scientist. I was never exposed to the analytical writings of the great nineteenth century feminists nor was I ever introduced to the historical and sociological genius of W.E.B. DuBois. Of course at the time I was there (1965–70) the large sociology department faculty was entirely Euro-American and entirely male.

36. Sjoberg and Vaughan 1993, 54–113.

37. Horowitz 1968, 130.

38. Oppenheimer, Murrar,y and Levine 1991. Also see Vaughan, Sjoberg, and Reynolds 1993.

39. Knottnerus 1993, 252–68.

40. Wilson's most famous book was his 1987 *The Truly Disadvantaged: The Inner City, the Underclass, and Public Policy.*

41. A leading member of the Association of Black Sociologists thoroughly criticized Wilson's analysis in a paper at the American Sociological Association meetings (Newby 1988). Also see the critical review by Duster in *Contemporary Sociology* (1988) and his subsequent criticisms in *The Black Scholar* (1988). Also see Reed's critical review in *The Nation* (1988).

42. William J. Wilson 1987.

43. Ewen 1989.

44. Jones 1992, 275–76.

45. Clark 1991.

PART IV

FORCES OF SOCIAL CHANGE

We have already discussed how social stratification in America was changed in the past by powerful movements demanding greater democracy and equality. These movements reflected peoples' beliefs that change was possible; that there was a better way to organize society. Usually, then, these movements have occurred when possibilities for change are seen as attainable.

Today everyone acknowledges that technology is changing our society. This part of the book looks at the relationship between this technological change and the possibilities it opens for changes in our social stratification system.

- **Chapter 13** discusses the relationship between technology and social change. This is not the first time in human history that people have been frustrated, angered, and frightened of new technologies. And in every historical case, the new technologies have meant social changes. The chapter looks at the social consequences of technological change in terms of the middle and working classes, corporations, and the government. Ultimately, the question is one of "who benefits?" Will computers and robots (robotronics) be used to create greater unemployment, more pollution, more poverty and hunger or do the new technologies have positive possibilities as well?

- **Chapter 14** examines in greater depth some of the negative consequences that robotronics is having on our society. Many groups are being pushed farther down on the ladder and their social pain is increasing. This chapter looks at ways in which people are coping, or not coping, with their loss of social status. Some of the ways of coping—crime and drugs—are clearly not healthy for our society. At the same time, it is possible to begin to see how robotronics could also be used to make our society, and our earth, a better place.

- Changes in the system of social stratification require social movements. **Chapter 15** looks at emerging social movements. Some of these movements are based on the ideologies of democracy and equality. They want to continue expanding opportunities for individuals and groups to participate in society. But there are movements that is reacting to change by wanting to go backwards, to an earlier time when the ideologies of racism, classism, sexism, and speciesism clearly defined everyone's place. They long for "the good old days." At the present time, these movements are largely defined by conservative religion, which equates the values of the past with religious ideals.

- **Chapter 16** argues that indeed we must have social change. Our society, as we know it, will not survive the extreme inequalities of social stratification that have been unleashed by the new technologies. There must be a reorganization. What kind of reorganization it will be is a question of who has the ability to project a vision of change. If the solutions to our social problems are resolved within a democratic context, we will be able to move forward, as a society and a world. Thus, the main struggle in this next period will be to reaffirm and redefine our democratic ideology in a way that can overcome the social structures of inequality and hierarchy.

13

TECHNOLOGY AND STRATIFICATION: ON WHICH RUNG DO THE ROBOTS GO?

WHAT'S WRONG?

When Communism collapsed and free markets blossomed around the world, the peace dividend and capitalism together were supposed to spur rapid economic growth. Ultimately, they may. But so far the world economy has faltered. Higher unemployment, slow growth, and severe wage and price competition are rampant in the industrialized nations. Welcome to the new economic order nobody expected.

—*Business Week*, 2 August 1993.

Throughout human history there have been stages of development. We usually link a new social stage with the discovery of new technologies. The discovery of how to use and control fire moved humans to a different stage. The Industrial Revolution that occurred in Europe approximately five hundred years ago was a more recent stage in human technology. Up to that point, humans had to rely on sources of power that existed naturally in the environment. Fire, water power, animal power, and human energy were the sources that societies used to move objects, heat homes, and smelt metals.

When the societies of northern Europe discovered how to use steam power to drive machinery, and then discovered how to control and use electricity, they attained a technological edge on the rest of the world. White supremacists have used this fact to "prove" the superiority of European cultures. But the European Industrial Revolution would not have been possible without the discoveries that had been made previously by more advanced societies in Asia and Africa. Metalworking is believed to have originated in Africa. When the Arabs discovered the decimal numbering system, science advanced. And during Europe's "Dark Ages," the knowledge of the great civilizations of Egypt, Greece and Rome was kept alive in the African University at Timbuktu.[1]

With the new technology, huge machines could be driven by external energy sources that were portable. Mills and factories could now be built away from streams and water wheels. Each new development in energy allowed new developments in machinery and the production process.

But no matter how powerful the machine, it required a human being to turn it on, tell it where to run, how long or how fast to run, and when to turn it off. In other words, power-driven machinery may have replaced the water wheel, the mule, and the human being as a source of energy, but it did not replace the need to have humans control the production process.

The breakdown of feudalism created an unprecedented period of social turmoil and suffering. Society seemed to disintegrate. People increasingly turned to superstition and magic. The church became a totalitarian institution and the Inquisition persecuted and tortured dissidents. Groups of armed bandits roamed the countryside. Massacres of Jews and Gypsies were frequent. Fathers had to leave their families to seek work, and the family structure broke down. Roving armies destroyed crops and community structures broke down. Disease was rampant, and the Black Plague descended. Writers at that time were convinced the world was coming to an end and that the prophecies of Revelation from the Bible were at hand.[2]

The "glue" that had held the feudal society together was no longer working. The power of the church and the lords was being undermined by a new power—the emerging classes of capitalism. Eventually order was restored, organized around the new technologies and new social structures. At the time it was almost impossible to see or understand what was happening, for the transition from feudalism to industrial nationstates took between three and four hundred years.

If the description of the breakdown of feudalism sounds disturbingly like today, there is a good reason for the similarity. Senseless violence and urban unrest characterize our cities, the traditional family appears to be breaking down, and hunger and homelessness have created millions of displaced and hopeless people. Government is no longer trusted or respected and preachers, astrologers, and television personalities all claim to have the answer to what is happening.

There is one important difference. Today the higher level of education and the tools of social science allow us to see and understand the processes that are going on around us. We know that radically new breakthroughs in technology will create social disruption and force changes in the social order.

We, as informed and educated citizens, can struggle to understand and help shape the emerging new order.

THE CHANGING NATURE OF TECHNOLOGY

What is this radical new breakthrough in technology? Just as the new sources of power replaced the water wheel, the mule and the human as sources of power, today the computers, intelligent robots, laser beams and fiber optics are replacing the need for human guidance of production. We have reached an era of intelligent machinery. We will use the term **robotronics** to describe this new stage in the development of technology.[3]

This new stage is characterized by three main features: (1) it has introduced machine intelligence into production, (2) it has made possible the collection and analysis of quantities of information never before possible and (3) these changes have occurred at a faster rate than any other technological revolution in history.

When I was a graduate student at the University of Wisconsin, the computer on campus took up a three-story building and required constant air conditioning all around it. We punched our data onto cards and had to wait in line to have our programs run. Today's tiny hand-held computer of 640K has more memory and computing power than that huge computer![4] The first microprocessor invented by Intel in 1971 used 2,300 transistors to run a calculator. Intel's 1995 chip uses 6 million transistors![5]

There has been an interaction between the new technologies themselves and new scientific knowledge. Scientists use the new machines to gather even more information that leads to better machines for gathering information that in turn leads new information that can be used for even better machines, etc. This process is especially evident in biology, where lasers, fiber optics, and new powerful microscopes have allowed scientists to see the structure of cells, microbes and genes. In turn, science has provided industry with ways to alter plants and develop new bioorganic medicines.

In communications, satellites have made it possible for messages from radio, television, cellular phones, and laser beams to be rebeamed anywhere in the world almost instantaneously. What is called the "Information Superhighway," or Web, is transforming communications around the world.

Most of us are aware of some of the more obvious technological innovations—we have our home computers and CD-ROMs and microwave ovens that can be intelligently programmed. AT&T promises us that soon we will be able to have video communication with those we "talk" to on the World Wide Web. Few of us are aware of the *full* scope of the new technology, for unless it touches our lives directly we tend not to see it. Many experts predict that we have only activated the tip of the iceberg; the *real* technological revolution has barely begun!

This chapter is not a catalog of the immense scope of technological change unfolding in our society and in our world. The chapter, instead, looks at how this technology is altering the economic relationships of our society with which social stratification is so tightly interwoven.

TECHNOLOGY AND SOCIAL STRATIFICATION

Capitalism reorganized social hierarchies to fit its needs. Industrial machinery was expensive. A group of people who could save the money to buy and put that technology to use was needed. These were the capitalists. A group of people who came to work every day to run the machines was needed. They were the blue-collar workers.[6] As capitalism developed, other groups became necessary. Office workers, bankers, stockbrokers, insurance salespersons, and health-care workers all reflected the increasing division of labor that capitalism was creating.

But no matter how complex the social structure, it operated on a relatively simple premise. I would go to work and produce a product or carry out a service. I would get paid. I would take my pay and go out and buy products and services. When I did that, two things happened: I had to go back to work to earn more pay, and I had consumed things that now had to be reproduced by workers like myself.

This process was a "flow," or an exchange, you probably remember studying in economics classes. Even the bankers and stockbrokers were necessary. They were the people who gathered up extra money and pooled it into large enough amounts to finance the expansion of more factories, more jobs, and more products. Advertisers informed us of what products there were and encouraged us to buy so that we would spend our wages, go back to work, and create more jobs for ourselves and others.

To the extent that the flow worked, or balanced out, we would have a "healthy" economy. As the earlier chapters have pointed out, a healthy economy required certain groups to remain at the very bottom, as the most exploited, oppressed, and degraded. The perception of "health," then, was that of the upper and middle classes. We also know that there were times in American history when the economy became unbalanced, when there were not enough jobs and too many products. The most famous of these times was the Great Depression of the 1930s, but there were other serious periods of unemployment, high inflation, and fiscal imbalance.

In the late 1970s, it became apparent that our economy was beginning to be seriously unbalanced. Many economists and politicians argued that our troubles were like the earlier times and could be solved if we would pass some new regulations, find some new investments, and increase productivity. It is now apparent that the economic problems our society is facing are deeper and of a different character than other dislocations in American history. Why?

PREVIOUS ECONOMIC DISLOCATIONS

Our society has undergone several major economic dislocations that changed our power structures. The United States began as a society based on small farms, craft production, and slave plantations. Of these three, the production from the slave plantations was the most profitable. Power in early American society lay with the plantation owners, and it was this power that prevented the emancipation of slaves after the American Revolution. As industries in the North developed and farmers in the West prospered, economic growth and power shifted from the South to the North.[7]

The Civil War was the breaking point in the power of the plantation South and opened a new stage of economic development. Railroads and the industries that grew up around the railroads provided employment and profits to a large sector of society. Once the railroads were built there was another shift, this time to industrial production of consumer goods. Henry Ford and the assembly line became the symbol of this period. Automobiles, refrigerators and other consumer goods were mass produced, making affordable goods available to the working classes. Automobiles spawned the industries that built the highways and operated the gas stations.

When World War II ended and the United States emerged as a world power, a new industry opened up: international finance. American banks led the world in investing in the new nations emerging from colonialism, and the lucrative profits from these loans could be reinvested again and again.

This brief review of economic history is important because certain patterns emerged each time there was a major shift. The first effect of a major industrial shift was always a major dislocation of the workforce. The freed slave who did not want to remain on his or her former master's plantation was not prepared to move West suddenly and work on the railroad. A worker who drove railroad spikes and was now unemployed did not automatically become an autoworker.

Economic shifts require learning new skills and physically locating to new areas. Because these changes were unplanned and largely not understood, they were accompanied by human suffering and social disorder. The farmers who lost their farms in the dust bowls of the 1920s did not understand economic forces and became easy prey for groups like the Ku Klux Klan, who blamed the nation's woes on Jews and black people.

A second effect of a major economic shift is reorganization within the political structures of our society. Existing political parties are always controlled by the interests of the status quo. With each economic shift, new leaders and interest groups had to enter the political arena, challenging the former leadership. At some points this meant that new parties were formed, as in the case of the Republican Party prior to the Civil War; at other times this meant a "takeover" of an existing party, as happened to the Democratic Party under Roosevelt and the New Deal. [8]

The third effect of each economic shift is a transition from competition to concentration. Each new industrial stage begins with many entrepreneurs rushing to meet a new market possibility, attracting investment funds from areas of slow growth. The new technologies become possible because market competition keeps prices close to cost. But over time a few market leaders emerge: companies that have easier access to capital; those that have better political connections; those that make the best decisions regarding product development. Eventually a situation of monopoly and oligopoly develops where a tiny number of companies dominate production and prices no longer reflect real costs.

This pattern of concentration occurred with the railroads, automobiles, steel, banking, airlines, food products, and is happening now in health care. The only major area of production that is still competitive (and in which prices are falling instead of rising) is computers and electronics—the newest industry. One could safely predict that within several years that area will also become concentrated.

The elite who control these companies and financial institutions can make decisions that affect millions of workers and millions of consumers. In contrast to a hundred years ago, when the economy of this country was characterized by small businesses and independent farmers, our economy today is characterized by giant institutions that control markets, supply, and create demand by spending billions on advertising. The implications of this kind of concentration have already been discussed in terms of the social power wielded by bureaucracies in general. The new technologies have only accelerated this concentration in both private corporations and public bureaucracies.

The discussion above focuses on the control over, and use of, technologies. It would be easy to assume that the problem is just simply "who controls?" But this perspective ignores the fact that the new technologies themselves create directions and imperatives for human society. In other words, technology itself is not neutral. There is a complex interaction between the development of new technologies, the possibilities that development engenders, and the decisions about the direction future development should take.[9]

Jerry Mander compares two competing technologies in terms of their social impact:

> A prime example is nuclear energy, which cannot possibly move society in a democratic direction, but *will* move society in an autocratic direction. Because it is so expensive and so dangerous, nuclear energy must be under the direct control of centralized financial, governmental, and military institutions. A nuclear power plant is not something that a few neighbors can get together and build. Even control by city or state governments is proving impossible, as is now obvious to those locales attempting to block the movement and disposal of radioactive wastes within their borders.
>
> The existence of nuclear energy, and nuclear weaponry, in turn requires the existence of what Ralph Nader has called a new "priesthood"—a technical and military elite capable of guarding nuclear waste products for the approximately 250,000 years they remain dangerous. So if some future society, tiring of the present path, should determine to move away from a centralized technological society and toward, say, an agrarian society, it would be impossible. The technical elite would need to remain, if only to deal with the various wastes left behind. So it is fair to say that nuclear technology *inherently* steers society toward greater political and financial centralization, and greater militarization.
>
> Solar energy, on the other hand, is intrinsically biased *toward* democratic use. It is buildable and operable by small groups, even by families. It does not require centralized control. It is most cost effective at a small scale of operation, a reason why big power companies oppose it. And solar energy requires no thousand-year commitment from society.
>
> So where nuclear energy requires centralized control, solar energy functions best in a decentralized form. These attributes are inherent to the technologies and reflect the ideological bias of each.
>
> What is true for energy systems is equally true for other technologies. Each new technology invariably steers society in *some* social and political direction, by its very nature. Each new technology is compatible with certain political outcomes, and most technology is invented by people who have some specific outcome in mind.[10]

We are often presented with a view that the social changes due to robotronics are mandated by the technology; we have no choice but to go along if we want to reap the benefits. The argument that humans cannot control the march of technology has been called "technological determinism." This view is a smokescreen to cover up the fact that the new technology is indeed controlled—by those who will benefit from it.

Science writer Rudi Volter makes this point clear:

> Every society has its distinctive characteristics, and a particular technology will not necessarily produce identical social consequences for all that employ it. The actual consequences of a particular technology depend on why people have developed or adopted it in the first place. Having invented gunpowder, the Chinese employed it primarily for fireworks, while in late medieval Europe, gunpowder was immediately used for weaponry. The uses to which a technology is put depends on history, existing social arrangements, and the particular needs of the populace. Technological changes produce social changes, but at the same time technological change is a product of the society in which it takes place. Technologies exert a profound influence on human affairs, but they do not do so in a narrowly deterministic manner.[11]

Volti argues for democratic control of technology.[12] But this assumes the schools, universities and media provide an open forum for critical and dissenting views. As pointed out in Chapter 12, this is unlikely. Scientists whose research threatens the profits of General Electric, DuPont, or Union Carbide, will rarely find funding for their research. Authors who write books critical of technologies favored by the ruling class will not receive prominent reviews in the *New York Times Book Review*.[13] Without the knowledge of technological consequences, Americans have little choice or control over how those technologies may affect their lives.

The ideology of speciesism assumes that humans can always control nature. There is an arrogance in the belief that no matter what problems are created by new inventions, science can solve them. We debate only our own human interests; our viewpoint does not ask what are the interests of the atmosphere, the oceans, the global balance of life? What are the interests of the unborn generations?

Every new technological stage has created social consequences, but since the rate of change in the past was relatively slow, there was more time for social reaction, debate, and discussion. In every case, however, the stages were within the general system of labor. Workers created goods that other workers consumed. *The stage of robotronic technology is not the same kind of technological and economic change*.[14]

Between August 1990 and February 1992 Sears. Roebuck & Co. eliminated 40,500 jobs. The most recent layoffs involved 600 salaried positions in regional management structure. The company also cut pay for salespeople in its U.S. stores.

The elimination of workers at Sears and other similar companies is possible because of the increased use of robotronics in the service sector. For example, new automated cash registers and customer service kiosks in the stores were responsible for 7,000 of the lost positions. According to Sears, this new system would cost $60 million but would save the company $50 million a year. The system includes 28,000 terminals and 6,000 customer service kiosks installed in 868 retail stores in the United States and Puerto Rico.

Although such systems are expensive ($60 million), it should be noted the cost would be recouped by Sears within fourteen months!

THE CURRENT ECONOMIC TRANSFORMATION

When computers and electronics began to develop as an industry, it was viewed as just another stage, like the ones above. People believed that displaced autoworkers' sons would get jobs programming or building computers and everything would eventually work out, just like it had in the past. This held true for the first and second generations of computers, for the technology was still not very advanced and production still required large numbers of workers.

Fifteen years ago the robots used in industry were likened to a worker who was wearing a blindfold, had one hand behind him or her, and was wearing a baseball mitt on the hand that was free. Obviously this type of robot could do only very minimal and simple kinds of jobs. It took workers to build the robot, so it was just a matter of relocation, wasn't it?

Now we have robots that can see with laser eyes and have robotronic fingers that are sensitive enough to pick up and pack the finest crystal. These robots are being built by other robots and computers, not by workers. We now have factories covering acres of space and running assembly lines twenty-four hours a day that use only three or four workers in the entire production.

This does not mean that all workers are replaced. If the cost of labor is less than the cost of robotronics, then workers will still be used. In this way, robotronics intensifies the competition between workers. This is increasingly a competition that crosses international boundaries, as we discuss in the next chapter. But as more robots, computers and other electronic devices are mass produced, their cost relative to labor continues to fall.

The dilemma that ensues can be summarized as follows: *if robots and computers build the cars, and robots and computers don't drive the cars, and the laid-off autoworkers can't afford the cars—who buys the cars?* In other words, there has been a major change in the cycle described earlier—the production of goods and services is now being increasingly done by intelligent machines and the workers who have been replaced cannot purchase the goods and services that robotronics are placing on the market.[15]

SOCIAL CONSEQUENCES OF ROBOTRONICS

This transformation of the economy has not happened overnight. Although this revolution will not take the two or three hundred years that the Industrial Revolution took, it will take several decades for the full implications to be felt. Initially there have been ways for governments, companies and workers to adjust. All these adjustments are designed to preserve the system of social stratification that currently exists.

Those who sit on the top of the ladder will use robotronics to increase their privilege and power—not in ways that would increase the power and resources of those on the lower rungs. Thus, ordinary people often view the new technologies negatively because robotronics has meant greater hardship and a deterioration in the quality of life for them. We have not had the opportunity as a society to consider the ways of implementing new technologies that would make life better and the planet healthier.[16]

In the past twenty years we have seen several of these adjustments. Although these adjustments are interrelated and interdependent, we list them in terms of the sector impacted. The working (middle) class and their families have made five major temporary adjustments:

- Wide-scale application of robotronics was done first in the manufacturing sector and it was the industrial working class who felt the first effects. It was argued that the service industries would remain "labor intensive" and that laid off autoworkers, coal miners, and steelworkers would find employment selling insurance, repairing automobiles, and flipping hamburgers. Those jobs, however, paid on the average only *one-half* the average industrial wage.
- The loss of good-paying industrial jobs by predominantly male workers was partially compensated for by the entrance into the workforce of the women in the household. In many cases this was not based on the woman's desire to have a career, but a "bitter choice" between staying home with children and living in poverty or going to work for low wages but helping the family stay off welfare.[17] Among

married couples with children, the average wife was employed 32.3 percent more hours in 1989 than in 1979, the equivalent of nearly seven weeks of full-time work.[18] With two incomes, the family was able to temporarily maintain a similar standard of living. The entrance of women created a demand for services that gave a temporary boost to the service industries in fast foods and personal services.

- Workers met the growing competition of robots by agreeing to take cuts in wages and benefits. As long as the new technology was expensive, companies could be convinced to maintain the workforce if these concessions were made. Cuts in benefits were not immediately felt — the loss of a pension or a health care plan did not *immediately* affect a family.
- Consumers maintained their standard of living by going into debt. For approximately a decade the ratio of consumer debt to savings increased and reached record heights in the early 1990s. This meant that families are now in debt for their homes, their cars, their refrigerators, and the clothes on their backs. More and more of a family's income is consumed by debt payments instead of the purchase of

It is easy to picture robotronics in assembly line production. But the impact of the new technology in agriculture has been just as profound, if not more so. In the past two decades, there has been a dramatic decline in the number of small and medium sized farms. The individual farm owner cannot amass the capital necessary to compete with the amount that corporations are able to invest.

For example, cotton yields are rising across the United States even though there are fewer farmers to grow the crop. One driver, at the wheel of a $135,000 mechanical picker, *can do the work of 500 people* (emphasis added). Cotton farmers in the United States spend $500 million on pesticides, only to find that they must spray more often or use stronger chemicals. Meanwhile, many beneficial insects that would have helped control harmful bugs have been destroyed, leaving crops vulnerable to a whole new series of pests. (The deadly gas that escaped from Union Carbide's plant in Bhopal India in 1984, killing more than 3,000 people, came from a pesticide often sprayed on cotton crops.) (Thompson, 1994.)

A *National Geographic* describes a new operation in Ahmadabad, India:

"In a nearby building a machine opened bales of cotton, gobbled it up with mechanical fingers, and sucked it into more machines to be cleaned, combed, and spun. Here the white floors and walls were spotless. I saw a delivery boy who took the spun yarn to the mill, but there were few other signs of life, and I envisioned a time when the manager would sit alone in his air-conditioned glass booth watching over a crew of robots.

Factories like this one could take away thousands of jobs from desperately poor people if they replaced India's small mills and traditional hand-weavers." (Thompson, 1994.)

goods. Banks are pushing credit cards and extending debt limits to take advantage of the profits that can be earned from a debtor's economy.

- In the past decade more people have turned to the "underground economy." Yard sales, roadside stands, and informal hiring have cut costs for millions of families as they are able to buy cheap second-hand goods and find marginal employment on which they pay no taxes. Although second-hand goods sold in flea markets are a means of survival for low income persons, the government collects no sales taxes or employment taxes, further eroding the economic base of the country.

Corporations have made adjustments as well:

- New technology that increased productivity while lowering the costs would make a corporation more competitive. Companies that installed computers and efficient robots first were able to make higher profits. But as other companies then installed the same technology the first company would no longer have the edge unless it installed even newer technology. The rapidly changing pace of robotronics meant that companies had to invest large amounts in updating plants and equipment. They began to organize politically to pressure the government to give them tax breaks or subsidies to carry this out.
- Corporations had to take long hard looks at the "padding" of their corporate expense accounts and their workforce. Companies began to restructure and downsize to become leaner and more efficient. This meant that increasing numbers of middle level managers lost their jobs as well.
- Increasing competition and greater productivity meant that divisions and plants that had previously been marginally productive were completely closed down or disbanded. In Flint, Michigan, for example, within *one* year General Motors closed plants idling over 30,000 workers. Companies also shifted production to reflect the changing consumer markets. If lower-income Americans could no longer afford to buy cars, the low-priced dependable Chevette would be discontinued and emphasis would be placed on higher-priced models. Fewer cars might be sold, but the higher prices and profit per car would help make up the difference. At the same time, dealers were encouraged to extend credit and draw out installment payment periods. Increasing competition also meant that bankruptcies reached record numbers, causing even more unemployment.
- Since the costs of adding workers to a payroll is high, companies began to extend the practice of overtime. While more and more

workers were losing jobs, those who still had jobs were working record amounts of overtime in order to cut costs and increase profits. If new workers were needed, companies turned to temporary help that could be hired part-time and would not require benefits to be paid. In the early 1990s, the temporary-help industry, which comprised less than 2 percent of total employment, accounted for 27.7 percent of the new jobs.[19]

- Corporate America began a publicity campaign to blame the problems of un employment on the Japanese and immigrants. American workers were told they would have to work as hard and accept the same living standards as workers in other countries if we were to remain competitive and keep their jobs.
- Corporations sought deals with other companies leading to a decade of "megamergers" and LBOs (leveraged buyouts) that fueled stock speculation and allowed a small handful of stock brokers and money managers to become rich overnight. This economic activity had very little productive value—in other words, no new goods were manufactured or jobs created. Yet the government continued to count stock market prices and trading as part of its indicator of the health of the economy.

The government has also made major adjustments. Because most of these adjustments occurred under President Reagan, they have been called Reaganomics. But no individual president is to blame for what are clearly problems of the social system. These adjustments did the following:

- The government increased its spending beyond what it could raise in taxes in order to pump money into the economy. Much of this spending was in defense, which provides jobs without flooding the consumer market with goods, and supports the profits of the politically powerful defense industries.
- The government agreed to provide American corporations with large subsidies and tax breaks in the name of keeping America competitive. This further increased deficit spending.
- The government rescinded regulations that were costly to industry but that had protected the consumer and average citizen. Funding for meat and poultry inspectors, for example, was cut drastically. The result is that eggs are today contaminated with salmonella and we cannot use raw egg whites or eat "runny" fried eggs. We are told to cook all beef and poultry thoroughly because of bacterial contamination. Enforcement of environmental laws was inadequately funded and pollution increased.

- The restrictions placed on the stock market after the big crash of 1929 were largely removed and speculation and trading practices formerly illegal were made legal. The result was that insiders and "big players" were able to make large gains, while small investors lost.[20] The culmination of deregulation was the collapse of the savings and loan Industry. The taxpayer was left with the bill, which now exceeds $500 billion.
- The government attempted to pay for some of its deficit spending by cutting human services, education and welfare programs. Student grants and loans were reduced. Housing subsidies for the poor and child immunizations were cut back. Because government spending in social services creates twice as many jobs, dollar for dollar, as does defense spending, the effect was to increase unemployment as well as increase social problems.
- The government raised the "acceptable" rate for unemployment. In the 1950s a national unemployment rate of 3 percent was considered scandalous. Today, government economists boast if the unemployment rate is as low as 7 percent.
- The government increasingly raised taxes on the shrinking middle class, further eroding their ability to purchase goods and services.
- Lucrative sources of profits in gunrunning, gambling, drugs, and other illegal activities became more attractive as it became more difficult to make high profits in legitimate business. The deregulation of banks during Reagan's presidency made it easier for large sums of illicit money to pass through normal channels. The election of a president (Reagan), whose administration saw communism as a greater threat than drugs and the repression of human rights, made it easier for government officials and agencies to be corrupted by illegal interests.[21]

We are arguing that these have all been temporary adjustments because none of them have addressed the fundamental problems underlying the emerging economic crisis—the fact that under the current system, human beings are increasingly superfluous to the production process! In the next chapter we will examine how robotronics have affected the broader arenas society—in employment, our communities and our personal lives.

SUMMARY

Major changes in technology are always accompanied by major social changes. In the past, advances in technology still required human control—

In his Presidential address to the American Society of Criminology, William Chambliss made the following observations regarding changing laws and gun and drug trafficking: "the contradictions that are the force behind state-organized crime today are the same as those that were the impetus for piracy in 16th century Europe. The accumulation of capital determines a nation's power, wealth, and survival today, as it did 300 years ago. The state must provide a climate and a set of international relations that facilitate this accumulation if it is to succeed. Laws prohibiting assassination and arms smuggling enable a government to control such acts when they are inimical to their interests. When such acts serve the interests of the state, however, then there are pressures that lead some officials to behave criminally. Speaking of the relationship among the NSC, the CIA, and drug trafficking, Senator John Kerry, chairman of the Senate Foreign Relations Subcommittee on Terrorism, Narcotics and International Operations, pinpointed the dilemma when he said 'stopping drug trafficking to the United States has been a secondary U.S. foreign policy objective. It has been sacrificed repeatedly for other political goals' (Senate Hearings 1986)."

Despite the demise of socialist states, corporate competition remains a major force behind the U.S. government's contradictory policies and actions regarding drugs and weapons traffic.

someone to "run" it. Robotronics is the first technology in human history that creates intelligent machines.

During other times of technological change, there has been social disruption while humans have had to learn the new skills and ways of relating to the changes. But after a while, displaced workers have been absorbed and it appears that the circle of production and consumption is once again working.

Robotronics poses new problems. In the early stages of the "robotronics" revolution it was believed that the new technologies would also absorb workers. Increasingly, machines build the machines, run the machines, repair the machines and control the machines, while more and more workers become superfluous for production. Those workers who are still employed in production find that they are competing with machines, which are becoming cheaper. The result is an increased competition among those workers who still have jobs.

Like other changes in industrial technology, the production of robotronics initially was very competitive. But over time, these new industries are also becoming concentrated, and a few companies are beginning to dominate the field.

When new technologies create social problems people always ask "whose fault is it?" One can blame the machines themselves for creating the problems, or one can blame the people who have made the decisions in regard to the use of the machines. Like the question of "progress" discussed earlier, the real question is "who is benefiting from the way technology is now being used?" That is the question of social stratification.

We can see major adjustments that American society has begun to make to accommodate the new technology. The working or middle class has adjusted by accepting lower wage jobs, by women entering the workforce, by agreeing to pay cuts and cuts in benefits, by going more deeply into debt, and by engaging in the underground economy.

Corporations have adjusted by meeting competition with increased use of the new technology, by restructuring and downsizing, by closing production that is marginally profitable, by extending the practice of overtime and hiring temporary help, by blaming foreign workers, and by carrying out mergers.

Government has adjusted by increasing deficit spending, providing large subsidies to business and cutting back social programs, removing government restrictions financial industry, raising the acceptable rate of unemployment, and making it easier for profits to be made in activities such as gambling and drugs.

Vocabulary

Robotronics. A stage of technology characterized by intelligent machinery; it has three main features: (1) machine intelligence is introduced into production; (2) information can be collected and processed faster and better than ever before; (3) the rate of technological change is rapidly accelerating with each advance in the technology.

Discussion Questions

1. A generation ago, a college degree almost guaranteed someone a good-paying job. Is that still true? How do you feel about your employment opportunities, in comparison to those that were available twenty-five years ago? If you feel they are not very good, who are you likely to blame? Is the relationship between your life chances and the new technology obvious to you? Why or why not?

2. Does the book accurately describe the adjustments that your family has made to the current economy? In what ways is your family different? Why?

3. Many people blame President Reagan (or Reaganomics) for the serious problems in the economy. Do you think having another president at

the time would have made a big difference? How is this an example of seeing a situation as both microsociologically and macrosociologically?

Resources

Video: *Roger and Me*

This documentary is both a serious and funny look at what happened to one city (Flint, Michigan) when General Motors laid off 30,000 of its workers. The moviemaker (Michael Moore) grew up in Flint. He focuses on how the layoffs impacted the lives of people and the city itself. There is little discussion of the cause of the layoffs except to suggest that foreign workers may be to blame. Still, it is a valuable look at the social pain caused by decision makers (in this case "Roger," chairman of the board of General Motors).

NOTES

Complete citations are provided in the Bibliography.

1. Bennett 1982.
2. Tuchman 1987.
3. Other names that have been given to this new complex of technology includes "The Information Age," "Digital Technologies," and "The Computer Revolution." I prefer the use of "Robotronics" because it combines electronics, which underlies information technology and computer application, with the idea of intelligent machines—robots.
4. Also see Jones 1982.
5. "Can This Chip Make the Next Quantum Leap?" *Business Week*, 21 November 1994, 96–100.
6. For a detailed analysis of how the new technology is restructuring the labor force see Jones 1982, 46–79. He argues that we must completely rethink our ideas of "employment" and "productivity" in light of the massive changes occurring due to the new technology.
7. John Keller (1983) analyzes this relationship between economic stages and political shifts in American history.
8. Ibid., 1983, 51–89.
9. Jones (1982, 210–38) points out that the emphasis upon humans as "tool-using" animals ignores the fact that humans are also animals who create language, myth, religion, music, ritual, and art.
10. Mander 1992, 35–36.
11. Volti 1992, 236–37.
12. Ibid., 1992, 269–72.
13. This is not to imply that critical books do not get written or distributed; it is only to compare the extent to which critical books are "pushed" by the dominant media. It is interesting to note that Jerry Mander's book was published independently of the major media; it was published by the environmental organization Sierra Club.
14. Jones (1982, 254–56) makes a similar argument from the perspective of an economist. The historian Barbara Tuchman (1987) also argues that the twentieth century is analogous to the fourteenth, when feudalism began to collapse but industrialization had not yet emerged.

15. Aronowitz and DiFazio 1994.

16. Moore (1996) attempts to address what programs might be necessary to reverse the trends of worker displacement. Sheak and Dabelko (1993) argue that if there was the political commitment, full employment could become a viable goal.

17. For an excellent study of how women in one community coped with the changing economic conditions see Rosen 1987.

18. Mishel and Bernstein 1993.

19. Ibid.

20. Zey (1993) documents the fraud-facilitated leveraged buyouts engineered by Michael Miliken and the firm of Drexel Burnham Lambert. She traces the direction of the power relationships between corporations and investment bankers and between investment bankers and the congressmen relevant to banking interests. Her study is an excellent example of how corporate, banking and social networks are used by the upper classes in American society, with little concern for the consequences to the middle classes, whose savings and investments were often wiped out.

21. The common term, "money-laundering" applies to such illegal profits that are entered into the economy and the legally reinvested. Ehrenfeld (1992) discusses this process as regards to illegal drugs. The corruption at the highest levels of government that such activities generate has been openly discussed. See for example McCoy (1991) and "Guns for Drugs" in *Newsweek*, 23 May 1988. A far more detailed discussion is provided in *The Guns 'n' Drugs Reader* (1991).

14

THE BRAVE NEW WORLD—A SCARY PLACE

"We also predestine and condition. We decant our babies as socialized human beings, as Alphas or Epsilons, as future sewage workers or future..." He was going to say "future World controllers," but correcting himself, said "future Directors of Hatcheries," instead.

. . . there is always soma, delicious soma, half a gramme for a half-holiday, a gramme for a week-end, two grammes for a trip to the gorgeous East, three for a dark eternity on the moon; returning whence they find themselves on the other side of the crevice, safe on the solid ground of daily labour and distraction, scampering from feely to feely, from girl to pneumatic girl, from Electromagnetic Golf course to. . .

—*Brave New World*[1]

Bedridden patients in nursing homes will now be able to use voice commands to tilt their beds, dim room lights, turn on the television and answer the telephone. The electronic system uses voice-recognition technology based on digital signal-processing chips and special software that translates speech into computer commands. According to *Business Week*, this technology is now "economically feasible."[2]

Nursing home chains are replacing nurses' aides and other workers with these and other similar devices. Patients now have many of their needs met, except one—the need to have a friendly, caring human being share their emotional space. To cut costs and temporarily make greater profits, nursing home owners install these robotics and lay off nursing home workers. The patients' mental health deteriorates. An alternative would be for the nursing home operator to take the money saved with the robotic devices and hire human beings to read, play games, and do crafts and physical therapy with patients.

> Luxury is the hottest concept in nursing homes: Oriental rungs in the lobby, a la carte dining, and the right to choose the carpeting and curtains in the room. The betting is that retirees will be willing to spend their own money—and lots of it—for these comforts. Beverly has 78 luxury facilities, out of 911 nursing homes, and expects to get 20 percent of its profits from them this year (1985). Manor Care Inc., which earned $23 million on revenues of $364 million in 1984, runs only first-class homes, Even nonmedical companies are getting in on the action. Owens-Illinois, the glassmaker, has acquired an upper-class nursing home chain based in Ohio. And Marriott Corp. is developing condominiums that offer medical services to residents (Fisher 1985, 142).

The second alternative may sound more logical and rational to us because it might be *our* grandparent who has been isolated in a room surrounded by robotronic devices. We would argue the first priority should be the emotional and mental health of the patient. If we happened to be very wealthy, we could place our relative in a nursing home that did provide quality human contact like the luxury homes described in the box. But a middle-class person cannot afford the most expensive nursing home. The nursing home that cuts costs by using robots may be the only one we can afford. This is the dilemma facing our society—how can we use this new technology for the genuine benefit of human beings?

The problems arising from these changes have been examined in great detail by social scientists and journalists. But rarely do these examinations link the social problems to the larger picture of sweeping technological change and structural transformation. Our interest here lies in understanding how specific problems reinforce exploitation, oppression and degradation or, conversely, how specific problems hold opportunities for equality and democracy.

We analyze these problems by examining the relationship between technological change and social change in six areas:

1. The changing nature of employment
2. The redistribution of wealth
3. The accessibility to information
4. The acceleration of ecological damage
5. The destruction of traditional community
6. The social psychological stress on individuals of unexplained change and failure

THE CHANGING NATURE OF EMPLOYMENT

Technology has radically altered the nature of employment in our society in three ways: it has increased the numbers who have no jobs at all, it has increased the numbers who have marginal employment (part-time work and/or work that pays so poorly one cannot live on the wages), and it has increased the burden of overtime for workers who do work. These changes have in turn affected family and community relations.

The preceding chapter pointed out that industries using large numbers of manual laborers were the first to profitably install robotronics. By the early 1980s, coal mining towns and cities with steel, auto, and rubber factories were devastated by layoffs.[3] Old factories using labor-intensive machines were replaced by new factories that could produce twice as much with one-half or one-third the workforce.

Companies cut costs further by building the new factories in the South and Southwest (where it is more difficult to form unions and wage scales are lower) or in countries like Mexico or Brazil. It was assumed that the hundreds of thousands of Americans would find new jobs, just as in other painful economic shifts. Those who did not find new jobs were often not counted as unemployed because of the way that information is collected.

Government statistics grossly underestimate the real extent of unemployment. Even though the statistics are debatable, one can use government figures to track the trends. In 1980 the unemployment rate had reached 7.1 percent. Public anger at this rate was one of the major reasons for Jimmy Carter's defeat and Ronald Reagan's election. Under Reagan (see Chapter 13) adjustments were made and the unemployment rate appeared to be heading down, reaching a low in 1989 of 5.3 percent. But by 1991 the rate was up to 6.7 percent and was greater than 7 percent again in 1993. Most sociologists agree that actual unemployment is between two and three times greater than that shown by government figures.[4]

One must be "actively seeking employment" to be counted as unemployed. The government does not count middle-aged workers who were laid off several years ago and have given up looking for work. If such a laid-off worker does get a temporary job in a store at Christmastime and works for one week, he or she will be counted as "employed" for that month. Students who are going to college because there was no job for them after high school are not counted as unemployed, nor are the workers forced into early retirement. A mother who stays at home with her children but would work if she had a chance is not counted as unemployed, nor are most of the homeless.

There are a surprising number of homeless persons who work minimum-wage jobs but have to live in homeless shelters because they cannot afford to pay big city rents. A front-page *Wall Street Journal* article described a family in which both the parents work ten-hour shifts for minimum wage at a local poultry plant in Springfield, Missouri but must live with their two children in a homeless shelter because they can't afford their own place.[5]

Jobs in unionized industries such as rubber, auto, steel, electrical, and coal were expensive to employers. These jobs included good health coverage and pension plans, union protection of seniority rights and health and safety, grievance procedures, and high wages. In contrast, robots are an employer's dream come true. They work twentyfour hours a day, never come in with hangovers, report themselves if they make a mistake, don't go on strike, and never ask for a raise. Robots don't develop expensive medical problems from heavy lifting or breathing fine oil particles in the air. Robots don't complain about wearing bulky protective wraps and heavy goggles when they work in front of a hot furnace. They do precisely what they are programmed to do—in the same way every time. Japanese-built cars were so popular in the late 1970s and early 1980s because the Japanese installed robotronics in their factories before U.S. factories did. A robot makes the same weld late Friday afternoon as it did on Monday morning. The joke in Detroit used to be that one should never buy a car built on Friday!

It is wrong to see only robots as responsible for unemployment in industry. The new technology reaches further than robotic assembly line production. Computer Aided Design (CAD) enables computer programs to turn out—in minutes—what used to take skilled draftsmen and design engineers weeks to produce. Computerized inventory has replaced thousands of bookkeepers and warehouse workers. Computer-managed quality control has replaced thousands of inspectors.[6] These changes did not occur overnight and many companies initially absorbed the employment losses through early retirement plans, retraining, and other workforce shifts. Older workers were the most likely to be protected in this way.

Young adults have been the most affected—either because they bore the brunt of the layoffs or because the job opportunities that used to be there for high school graduates have now disappeared. Minorities and women have always faced the problem of being "last hired, first fired," but in the 1980s the layoffs began to include more white males. By the late 1980s working class white males were facing the many of the risks that had been traditionally faced only by women and minorities (see Table 14.1).

Workers who had earned annual incomes of $50,000 or $60,000 a year had large house payments, furniture payments, car payments, and credit card debts. Once unemployment compensation ceased and savings dried up these workers could not economically survive. A minimum wage job could not maintain the payments and many of these workers became homeless. Today, the unemployed homeless on the street corners of America include both

African American and EuroAmerican school teachers and steelworkers as well as African American farmworkers and Chicano garment workers.

The use of robotronics in the service sector did take longer, and the demand for services created by the entrance of wives and mothers into the workforce initially did generate employment opportunities. But now the service sector is rapidly developing the new technology. Across the country sweeping changes in retailing, food services, business services, communications, and health care have made some workers more productive, but have also cost other workers their jobs.

According to *Business Week* in the first three months of 1994 employers announced an average of *3,106 cutbacks per day*.[7] The 25 largest announced staff reductions since early 1991 were listed in the same article.

Table 14.1 Job Death: 25 Large Downsizings

Company	Staff Cutbacks	Company	Staff Cutbacks
IBM	85000	Proctor & Gamble	13000
AT&T	83500	Phar Mor	13000
General Motors	74000	Bank of America	12000
U.S. Postal Service	55000	AETNA	11800
Sears	50000	GE Aircraft Engines	10250
Boeing	30000	McDonnell Douglas	10200
NYNEX	22000	BellSouth	10200
Hughes Aircraft	21000	Ford Motor	10000
GTE	17000	Xerox	10000
Martin-Marietta	15000	Pacific Telesis	10000
DuPont	14800	Honeywell	9000
Eastman Kodak	14000	U S West	9000
Philip Morris	14000		

Other sources have cited similar reductions. These layoffs include not only industrial positions, but positions in the service industry (Marriott hotels) and layoffs of white-collar managerial staff (See Table 14.2)[8].

Layoffs have not been limited to the private sector. In 1991 the U.S. Postal Service announced plans for automation that would culminate in loss of 47,000 jobs by 1995.[9] In May 1994 New York Mayor Giuliani cut 15,000 city jobs and in October cut an additional 7,600 jobs.[10]

Today we have become accustomed to pumping our own gas out of automated electronic pumps that measure the amount and calculate what we owe. The computer in the pump enters that information into central computers of

Table 14.2

Additional Lay-offs cited in other sources:	
TRW (1991)	10000
Marriott (1991)	2500
Trinova (1991)	3713
Sara Lee (1994)	8500
Northrop Grumman (1994)	9000
Higher Paying White Collar Lay-offs	
Morgan Stanley Group	45
Amdahl Corp	400
Bank of New England	800
McGraw Hill	1000
PWA Corp	1900
Shearson Lehman	800
Wang Laboratories	2000

the gas chain, which track when more gas will be needed. We pay by sticking a credit card into a slot on the pump . Gas stations used to be a major source of employment for unskilled young men. Those jobs are gone.

If we want our windshields cleaned, we have to do it ourselves. Much of the new technology demands that work that cannot be completely automated now be done by the consumer! We pick up our food at the counter rather than having it served, we wheel our own grocery carts around rather than have a grocery clerk fetch us the goods, and we bag our own groceries in the discount stores. Feminists have noted that much of this work is done by the female consumer who may have labor-saving devices in the household, but who has to work harder at shopping.[11]

Many unemployed have found alternative work, but at much lower wages. The robotronic revolution has deskilled a large number of jobs which once required some basic training and skill.[12] The example of the fast food industry is instructive. This service industry has combined the new technology with management techniques that allow it to use unskilled labor that is nearly interchangeable.

Rather than hire one responsible worker for a five-day eight- hour shift, the fast-food chains hire workers at minimum wage for three, four, and five-hour shifts or for full shifts less than five days a week. They do not have to pay pensions or health benefits and other supplemental costs of full-time workers. If a worker is sick, another worker is called, and the sick worker has no way to make up the lost pay. Someone who is sick too often is simply fired.

A twentytwo-year old with a high school education may work fifteen hours a week at a minimum-wage rate flipping burgers, but the government will count him or her as employed. She or he may be able to find two such jobs and end up working thirty hours a week. She or he may have to pay for uniforms and transportation to and from work. If she or he is a single parent childcare expenses may be incurred. Such situations are becoming more and more common for many young people in America.

The working poor may be able to afford car payments, but not house payments. They can survive if they live at home with parents or relatives and if they do not have to pay utilities. They will fall in love and have children, but they cannot afford to set up their own households, an economic prerequisite in our society for marriage. Increasingly, these marginal workers are forced into the ranks of the homeless.

Elliot Liebow, in his study of homeless women, makes a critical point:

> Don't look at me," says the employer. "I'm paying them what they are worth. If you force me to pay my employees more than they are worth, I will have to go out of business." In the long run, he is probably right. From that perspective, it is as if the market system requires human sacrifice for its good health.
>
> One result of these system failures (unemployment, underemployment, and substandard wages) is a growing number of working poor yet homeless men, women and families, and a lot of discouraged workers. Then, through welfare programs, through shelters and soup kitchens and vouchers and a wide variety of purchased goods and services, our whole society goes about the business of subsidizing those employers who are unable to pay their employees enough to live on. As if by magic, however, the onus of welfare and dependency is lifted from the system of work and the employers and placed on the workers and the unemployed right in front of our very eyes, and no one is any the wiser.[13]

The simplification of manual skills is not the only way in which labor has been deskilled by technology. Computer programs that calculate and evaluate have also deskilled a number of white-collar professions. For example, life insurance agents once had to learn complicated formulas for figuring maturities and interest rates. To be a successful agent required mathematical and problem-solving skills. Today the average agent fills in a questionnaire, enters the data into the computer, and all possible plans and options are immediately printed out.

Deskilling has also occurred in the area of accounting. Office workers using accounting software can obtain results that once were calculated by highly trained accountants. Typesetting in the publishing industry was once a well-paid unionized skill. Today anyone who types and has a elementary understanding of word processing can do basic desktop publishing.

In many areas of the service sector humans have been almost eliminated. Computers carry out "interactive learning" with elementary school children and teacher's aides are laid off. Satellite courses and remote phone hookups replace professors. Automated teller machines (ATMs) replace bank tellers. Voice Mail and menus replace human operators and receptionists. ("Please push * 1 * followed by your account number if you wish to find out how much you currently own on your credit card.") This process is continuing, as the example of the nursing home at the beginning of the chapter made clear.

Many believed that the electronics/computer industry would provide enough jobs to make up the losses due to robotronics. Another belief was that hi-tech jobs would be more interesting and healthier than the traditional industrial job.

The emerging computer industry did initially provide some employment. Although its *rate* of growth has been high, the real number of workers employed has never been great, in comparison to those industries in which the layoffs occurred. Ttable 14.3 compares the rate of growth of certain job categories with the actual increase in number of jobs. The projected growth rate is based on the U.S. Bureau of Labor Statistics projection for "moderate" growth.

Table 14.3 Rate of Growth versus Real Job Growth (1992–2005): A Comparison of Job Categories

	Rate of Increase %	Projected Number of Jobs by 2005
Home health aides	138	827000
Human service workers	136	445000
Personal and home care aides	130	293000
Computer engineers and scientists	112	447000
Systems analysts	110	956000
Salespersons, retail	22	4446000
Cashiers	25	3417000
General office clerks	24	3342000
Waiters and waitresses	36	2394000
Janitors, cleaners, maids, and housekeepers	19	3410000

As can be seen from Table 14.3, the actual number of jobs in the "high-tech" fields are very small in comparison to the number of low-paying jobs (maids, waitresses, home-care aides) that will be created. It is likely that even the predicated rate of growth in high-tech will be less than projected. There are two reasons: (1) the market is beginning to be saturated and demand is falling, and (2) increasingly computers are writing their own new programs and robots are building their own superior replacements.

This does not mean no human labor is involved but that there may only be one or two highly skilled electronics engineers involved in a complex process that previously might have involved hundreds of workers. Recently a number of the major firms in the computer and electronics industry have announced major layoffs and plant shutdowns. The cycle is beginning there as well.

Some have argued that the workers who were laid off were paid less than the engineers and technicians who are now required at the workplace. This argument ignores the fact that a middle-aged skilled draftsman in the unionized auto industry could make $65,000 a year with excellent benefits. Today it is possible to hire an electrical engineer for that amount—or less!

Likewise, the projection that electronics work would be more interesting and provide a qualitatively better work environment has not been borne out. Dennis Hayes studied the workers in Silicon Valley, home to many of the nation's most important electronics industries. He found that their workers experience some of the nation's highest divorce rates and most stressful work and that 60 percent or more were in therapy.[14] The San Jose Police Department told the McNeil-Lehrer Report that 60–80 percent of Silicon Valley employees from assembly line to top management, use drugs.[15]

But companies have no choice. They must implement the newest technology or lose the competitive edge to their competition—whether it be another American company or a foreign company. Under the current economic structure unemployment and marginal employment will continue to grow. Fewer people will have the resources to purchase goods and demand will continue to fall, increasing competition. It is truly a vicious cycle.

CONSEQUENCES OF THE REDISTRIBUTION OF WEALTH

Chapter 3 discussed the changes in wealth and income that have been occurring in American society. The data show that the rich are getting richer and the middle class is getting smaller. What are the consequences to society when fewer people earn more and more people earn less?

The vast majority of us use up our incomes when we have bought food and paid our bills. Statistics show that the poor spend 42.6 percent of their actual income on food whereas those in the wealthiest fifth spend only 9.2 percent of their incomes on food. These statistics are computed from the U.S. government's Consumer Expenditure Survey for 1990 based on quintiles. The wealthiest are the top 20 percent and the poorest are the lowest 20 percent. The percentages given above are based on the ratio of food expenditure to income. If the same ratios are calculated for actual expenditure the poor spend 18.6 percent of their actual expenditures on food and the wealthy spend 12.9 percent. Thus, the difference is reduced, although it is still substantial. These differences reflect the fact that the "income" of many poor families is in the form of subsidies (food stamps, welfare, etc.).

Statistics also show that the poor actually spend more than they have, the middle classes spend what they have, and the wealthy have money left over, which they reinvest. These reinvestments have been largely going into more productive machinery (robotronics), replacing or deskilling jobs and creating more unemployment and marginal employment. B*ut if the purchasing power of the poorer classes is decreased, who buys the goods produced by the investments of the rich?*

The new technology has made it possible for companies to use the entire world as their production and market base. There are no unionized semiconductors plants in the United States but the industry still finds that the low wage rates of other countries are more profitable than minimum wage in the United States. In February 1983 Atari (the home computer giant) moved its Silicon Valley production to Hong Kong and Taiwan (where, at the time, workers earned $1.20 and $.90 an hour in wages and benefits). Atari already had assembly plants in Singapore, Puerto Rico and Ireland. The vast majority of the workers in these factories are women.[16]

> In the spring of 1993 a fire in a factory in Thailand that makes toys killed 240 workers and injured 500 others. Like the factory in North Carolina, the doors were also locked. Many broke limbs when they tried to leap to safety from upper floors. Many of those who didn't jump died of smoke inhalation. Dozens of other bodies were found on collapsed staircases or piled up at exits.
>
> The factory buildings had no fire escapes, no sprinkler systems, not even a fire alarm. Yet executives of the company said they complied with government regulations. The company (Kader Holding Co., Ltd.) supplies toys to companies such as Fisher Price, Tyco and Hasbro and to stores like Toys R Us and Wal-Mart. Most of the workers were women and their average pay (in American dollars) was about $140 for a six day workweek (Swartz 1993, 20).

All the major tennis shoes and sneaker firms that sell shoes in America use lower-paid foreign labor. The NIKE and Reebok ads that fill up NBA time-outs certainly do not advertise this fact! Ryka, Inc. sells athletic shoes specifically designed for women. The company's founder, Sheri Poe, was a rape victim and has promised to devote a percentage of the profits to aid women victims of violent crimes. This effort has been hailed by the women's movement as "progressive" marketing. But Ryka, too, uses cheap Asian labor, many of them women, to produce these shoes.[17]

In the very poor countries an American company that makes shoes and pays wages of $4 an hour is seen as providing "economic development." That firm is now paying a foreign worker $4 instead of paying an American worker $10.34 in wages and benefits.[18] In 1991 the average wages *and* benefits per hour of industrial workers in Mexico were $2.17; in Hong Kong they were $3.58; in Korea they were $4.32.[19] *As workers in every country become competitive with workers in other countries the worldwide standard of living is driven down.*

And ultimately all workers have to compete with robotronics. A news story describes the impact of robotronics in a Mexican factory:

> CHALCO, Mexico (AP) Panasonic's TV factory in this working class neighborhood has an unexpected message for the free trade era: Sales are rising and output is up a third, but it is being done with 50 fewer workers than a year ago. After NAFTA took effect, the number of Mexican workers producing goods like TVS and tractors decline 7 percent through August. Meantime, production of such goods rose 9 percent, according to the National Statistics Institute. The Mexican garment industry has laid off 1 of every 10 workers since January. Te immediate response of businesses big and small has been to replace man with machine. 'Maybe in the Far East wages are low enough to assemble by hand, but here it's still cheaper to bring in machines,' said Edgardo Leyva, personnel manager for Panasonic's Chalco factory. Machines don't need costly job training, don't quit and don't get paid vacations, he said. Only a handful of female workers, wearing white lab coats and goggles, inspect row upon row of TV circuit boards being assembled by new whirring robot arms under blue lights. A year ago many of those arms were human.[20]

The foreign worker who makes $4 an hour can now buy meat to go with his or her rice or beans but will still not be able to afford the shoes. It is also very probable that when the American company built the new factory in the low wage country, they installed the latest robotronics and are using fewer workers than they did when the company operated in the United States. So there are fewer workers, in total, who can buy the shoes.

In order to be "competitive" the American worker would have to be willing to work for $4 an hour with no benefits as well. Thus, the "development" that is occurring in Asia, and countries like Chile and Mexico, is only a temporary development that in the long run lowers the purchasing power of workers globally. In other words, who will be left to spend $125 on a pair of sneakers?

In a special cover story "Detroit South: Mexico's Auto Boom: Who Wins, Who Loses?" *Business Week* compared an "average" Mexican autoworker with an "average" Detroit-area autoworker:[21]

Dario Sanchez Delgado	*Michael Schultz*
Age 26. Married. Two Children.	Age 36. Married. One Child.
Welder at Chrysler plant in Toluca, Mexico	Welder at Chrysler's Sterling Heights (Mich.) plant
Seniority: 5 years	Seniority: 17 years
Pay: $1.75 an hour	Pay: $16.00 an hour
Benefits: Mandated profit-sharing, extra vacation pay, one month's bonus at Christmas, a one-cent lunch	Benefits: Paid vacation full health care income protection for layoffs
Education: Jr. High	Education: High school, working on an associate degree

The deterioration of wages and working conditions around the world has not occurred without resistance from workers. Strikes, slowdowns and political unrest are frequent in those areas where such working conditions are typical. A wave of strikes by women factory workers in Indonesia has been so brutally repressed that even the U.S. government had to cite human rights "abuses."[22] Such labor unrest is rarely reported in the media. The governments of these countries, in an attempt to maintain a friendly atmosphere for investment, usually move quickly against independent union organization.[23]

If workers are unemployed or receiving low wages, consumer markets shrink and investors must adjust. The purpose of investment is to make more money. In today's shrinking consumer market, the most profitable businesses are those that are either essential to life (heat, electricity, health care, etc.) or those that do not cater to the normal consumer market—stock speculation and illegal addictive drugs.

There are limits to the extent to which stock speculation can continue without causing even more serious problems for the economy. But there appears to be almost no limits to the amount of money that can be made in drugs. Thus there are powerful economic forces, with devastating social consequences, supporting and driving the trade in cocaine, crack, heroin, and other drugs. These consequences are examined in more detail in our discussion of the changes in our communities and in our personal lives.

The "fit" of drug dealing, youth unemployment, and capitalism is eloquently explained by Terry Williams in his ethnographic study of eight youthful cocaine dealers:

> These studies took me to areas of high unemployment and diminishing resources, especially for young people. But while quality entry-level jobs were disappearing, illegal opportunities were emerging with considerable force because of the growth of a powerful and profitable multi-national drug industry.
>
> Every teen aspires to make good. In the cocaine hustle, that means to "get behind the scale"—to deal in significant quantities; it is like landing a top sales job in a major corporation, or being named a partner, after a long apprenticeship, in a brokerage firm with a seat on the Stock Exchange. The kids who get that far have some control over prices and selling techniques, direct the work of subordinates, and, above all else, make large amount of money. Their work has been essential to the growth of a major industry.
>
> these kids and others like them simply want respect; they are willing to risk their lives to attain those prized adult rewards of power, prestige and wealth.[24]

THE CONSEQUENCES OF INFORMATION ACCESSIBILITY

Government, credit card companies, and police agencies can keep track of what we spend, who we talk to, and where we go.[25] Control over these vast amounts of information is a source of power. Huge personal data base files can be used for credit checks, job references, and insurance claim investigations with little knowledge or agreement on the part of the parties involved. Marketing firms can target us for an advertising campaign based on their knowledge of our consumer habits without our ever knowing we are marked. Police departments can access information on both drug dealers and political protestors.[26]

Computers can talk to other computers and pass on information without any humans even being involved. At the current time, the government is seeking the legal right to "eavesdrop" on computer conversations. In the end someone will use the information for a purpose. If we do not know the information is being used, nor understand how it is being used, how do we protect ourselves from potential misuse?

The new technology bombards us with information. We can download databanks using the Web. We are subjected to information telling us what to wear and what to eat as we ride the subway. We can tune into twentyfour hour television news and watch death and destruction as it happens. In order to win our attention the talk-show hosts on radio and TV beguile us with weirder and more sensational people and events.

The lies, deceit, and hypocrisy that have always existed but were formerly unreported have become the gist of a talk show, an evening news show, or a tabloid front page. A low income person with Parkinson's disease can hear on TV that an expensive new treatment is available and know that she or he cannot afford it. A teenager in the inner city who is selling illegal drugs watches a news report about defense contractors who have bribed government officials and knows those in the government themselves put personal gain over the law.

This kind of information breaks down belief in the system but rarely provides alternatives to the beliefs it is destroying. If government is corrupt, what are the means by which government by the people, for the people, and of the people, can actually be attained? If quality medical care is not available to the working poor, what is the plan that will guarantee lower costs and availability for all and not just change the bureaucracy of the existing system? If our city streets are flooded with drugs, who are those responsible for getting them there and why aren't they prosecuted?

Bruce Wright, an African American who served on the New York Supreme Court, made a similar observation:

> Punishment without pity, urged President Nixon as he pressed for wholesale revision of criminal law codes. And yet, was it not pity that resulted in his pardon? Or was it simply the rule of the inner circle and clubbiness? Clearly there was no punishment without pity for those sent off to the genteel and comfortable prisons. It is possible to regard such sojourns as no punishment at all. And now, all are successfully "rehabilitated." Nixon is much honored and shamelessly received his presidential pension, his free office space in a federal office building, a staff and secret service protection
>
> Poor minority prisoners and white ones as well are aware of such goings-on. They saw Vice President Agnew plead no contest

> to charges that he plotted some of his offenses in his White House office. He arrived at court in a chauffeur-driven limousine, he took his rap on the wrist and departed as he had arrived—in style. He is now a success in business and an author as well. He never served time in prison.[27]

In this Age of Information many Americans know less than their grandparents. Early colonists of America, who could not read, gathered around as someone read to them the debates later called *The Federalist Papers*. Then these unschooled farmers and tradesmen argued for hours over the politics of federalism versus confederacy. Abraham Lincoln and Stephen Douglass campaigned for the presidency in 1858 giving complex speeches several hours long to midwestern farmers and city factory workers.

Union members and ladies' club members of the early 1900s flocked to hear speakers discuss philosophy, drama, and theology by traveling guest lecturers. Young African Americans who marched into the segregated restaurants of America in the 1960s carried their school books with them and while they waited for the police to arrest them, they studied.

Just as technology has created new jobs that deskill labor, so the age of information is really a deskilling of knowledge. The "Information Age" has lowered our thinking and analytical skills. Depriving ordinary citizens of thinking skills is a form of degradation. The image of the superstitious "brutish" peasant of the Middle Ages is an image of an uneducated person, who could not think and analyze for himself or herself.

Research indicates that today's children know less math, less geography and have fewer writing skills than a generation ago. History lessons are not remembered, and science is to be avoided. Americans can reel off the National Basketball Association rankings or tell you the latest gossip about Princess Diana's death, but cannot intelligently discuss the real reasons for the federal deficit, the moral implications of gene-splicing, or the historical reasons for the Arab-Israeli conflict. We can tell you the favorite food of presidential candidates and whether they have had any marital affairs, but do not know their position on the GATT agreement.

American youth now *listen* to music more than *playing* or *composing* their own music; they *observe* baseball, basketball, and hockey more than *playing* their own games; they *watch* drama on TV or videocassetes more than *acting* in our own productions; they *listen* to a political debate on C-SPAN more than *debating* politics. Just as robotronics produces more goods but there are fewer who can buy them, so the new technology produces more information about life but fewer who have knowledge or life experience.

A premise of democracy is that all citizens are capable of understanding and evaluating their social reality. It assumes we are able to debate and evaluate historical precedents and future consequences. To work, democracy requires that all parties with different views are heard and understood.[28] The current debate over who will control and access the new "information superhighway" is really about power in America. Poor children do not have home computers or the skills to access the knowledge that will allow them to fully participate in society. Information technology has become another way in which the social stratification of our society is maintained.

As a society, we have become less able to do those things that democracy requires. As citizens become less knowledgeable those who *do* have knowledge and the understanding that knowledge provides become more powerful. They can justify their power by saying that the masses are ignorant—all the people care about is their beer, baseball, and latest royal romance. But it is not the American people who are to blame for our society's political impoverishment nor is it our computers, modems, CD-ROMS and TV sets. It is the use and control over that technology that we must criticize.

THE ACCELERATION OF ECOLOGICAL DAMAGE

Although early factories polluted the air and streams and lumbering and mining stripped the mountains, the impact was limited. Industrialization was occurring in only a small portion of the globe, and the global ecosystem could absorb it, to some extent. Prior to the chemical revolution, most pollutants were "natural"—elements already existing in nature and capable of being dumped into the air by a volcano or prairie fire as well as a factory. The modern age has changed this.

Today the entire world is industrialized and the entire global ecosystem is threatened. Mining operations in Zambia that supply copper to U.S. industries are dumping waste into the water and air of interior Africa; timbering for teak in Nepal is leading to massive floods in Bangladesh; the toxic chemicals produced in Louisiana are dumped by rain into the most northern Canadian lakes; the nuclear accident in Chernobyl poisoned the farms of northern Europe.

Gribbin, writing about the hole in the ozone layer, pointed out:

> The story of the hole in the sky, and its implications for humankind, is far from over. Joe Farman, who discovered the hole, wrote in his article in *New Scientist* on November 12, 1987, that "no one predicted these depletions. The lesson is plain: existing policies on the production of CFCs are based on a false premise—that we understand the processes controlling the ozone layer. The past few years have shown that we do not." And Sherry Rowland,

> in his talk at Chapel Hill on March 11, 1987, pointed out that "any agreement which affects only North America, Western Europe, and Japan will soon be overwhelmed by the increased usage outside these regions. If the goal is to prevent the organochlorine concentration of the atmosphere from growing much beyond that which has already produced the Antarctic ozone hole, then a phase-out of about 95 percent of existing uses will be required without *any* exceptions."
>
> Even if by some miracle direct released stopped immediately, Rowland concludes, ozone depletion would continue to increase for another two decades, because of the long lifetime of CFCs in the atmosphere. Ninety percent of the CFC molecules already in the air in 1987 will still be there in 2000 A.D.; 39 percent will still be there in 2100 A.D.; and 7 percent even in 2300 A.D. The damage we have *already done* to the ozone layer will be with us, and our children and grandchildren, throughout the twenty-first and twenty-second centuries.[29]

It is not just that the damage is global and therefore more extensive. The damage is also more dangerous. Science has created new chemicals and chemical combinations and they are used in ways that nature does not. One of the first lessons was DDT—a chemical pesticide. After years of use it was discovered that DDT not only killed insects but that it killed birds, fish, and small animals and was entering the food chains of humans.

Once a "chain," or balance, is interrupted in this way, the long-range damage is far greater than the initial damage that the insects were causing. Some farmers had better crops for several years and the companies that made DDT had better profits for several years. But the *social and environmental costs* were thousands of times greater than any of these limited benefits.

Today there are thousands of new chemicals invented every year and only a few hundred are tested by the federal government. In other words, we really have very little idea of the long-term effects of many of the products that are used daily in industry and everyday living. We do know that the cancer rate in our country continues to climb. We do know that mental disorders, particularly stress disorders, are accelerating. We also know that birds are disappearing, with two-thirds of all species on the decline and 1,000 threatened with extinction. Destructive insects are developing resistance to more and more poisons, with a least seventeen species now unaffected by any insecticide on the market.[30]

But like the scientists of the early twentieth century who were products of their socialization, the scientists of this century have been socialized to see any application of technology as "progress." Twenty years ago few asked what we would do with millions of pounds of disposable baby diapers that were not biodegradable, or run off into the water supply from fields fertilized with toxic chemicals, or radioactive waste that would take hundreds of thousand of years before it was safe.

The new technology has not only chemically polluted the earth but has allowed a few to manipulate biology.[31] Unfortunately, the main interest of those who provide most of the funds for such research is the profit margin. Scientists today are altering the basic genetic structures of plants and animals with little knowledge of the long-range consequences.

We do know that the creation of "domesticated" varieties of seeds—corn, wheat, rice—produced higher yields in many areas of the world initially. However, these varieties could not withstand the droughts or diseases that the natural strains could survive, and had to be discarded. Now in many cases the original natural strain has died out or been completely destroyed. This is one of the major sources of hunger from drought in the Third World today—an effect of the destructive power of technological "progress." And now the problem is "coming home." According to a *Business Week* article on worldwide food shortages, such genetic manipulation is now a potential catastrophe in the United States:

> The world's harvests face a greater threat from pests and diseases than ever before. Why? Because the new crop varieties are striking in their genetic uniformity. Millions of acres of the Midwest are planted every summer with endless snaking rows of corn plants that are nearly as alike as identical twins. If one of those plants is vulnerable to a new strain of disease, they all are.
>
> Last summer that threat nearly became reality. Pioneer 3394 and many of its relatives were highly sensitive to a disease called gray leaf spot. The conditions were right for gray leaf spot to become an epidemic. And that's precisely what happened. The disease marched across cornfields in Missouri, Iowa, Illinois, and Indiana. Such epidemics will recur, and the next one could be worse.[32]

Already the biosphere project is researching how we can build domed cities that protect us from the lethal sunlight and provide us with a balanced and healthy environment. It is a frightening scenario, for such "safe" places would be available only to the few. Will the future create a new stratification system—between those who must live on an overheated world bombarded with lethal sunlight and breathing poisoned air and those who are tucked away into artificially safe environments?

The 1994 Worldwatch Institute Report argues that we must view the crisis of our environment as a global crisis:

> In an environmentally interdependent world, no country can separate its fate from that of the world as a whole. Failure to deal effectively with such issues as climate change, the loss of plant and animal species, stratospheric ozone depletion, and population growth means that all countries will suffer.
>
> Eliminating these threats to our future requires a fundamental restructuring of many elements of society—a shift from fossil fuels to efficient, solar-based energy systems, new transportation networks and city designs that lessen automobile use, redistribution of land and wealth, equality between the sexes in all cultures, and a rapid transition to smaller families. It demands reduced consumption of resources by the rich to make room for higher living standards for the poor. And with current notions of economic growth at the root of so much of the earth's ecological deterioration, it calls for a rethinking of our basic values and vision of progress.
>
> Faced with this degree of change, we are tempted to deny the severity of environmental threats and assume we can get by with minor adjustments to business-as-usual. Action depends on overcoming denial, among the most paralyzing of human reponses. Denial often runs particularly deep among those with heavy stakes in the status quo, including the political and business leaders with the power to shape the global agenda.[33]

Today there are a minority of scientists who are raising these, and other, questions. They are arguing that we have reached the point of irreparable harm to the globe's ecology—that we have unbalanced the essential relationships between water, air, energy, and earth. The new technologies that give the promise of curing arthritis and diabetes are the same technologies that created the hole in the ozone layer and may have created, or contributed to, the disease AIDS. In other words when we create something technologically new, who uses it, who controls it, and who benefits from it—a select few or the earth?

THE DESTRUCTION OF COMMUNITY

The large social structure—society—is made up of substructures that sociologists call **community**. As individuals we cannot possible connect to, and relate to, our 250 million fellow citizens. But we can relate to and feel a part of our own communities. Within community, there is a sense of belonging and a sense of obligation toward one another.

This is not to say that communities are ideal places. In the slave South, a community included the plantation owner's family, the slave overseers, the slaves, and the poor whites. In rural America a community included wealthy bankers, prosperous merchants, small farm families, and poor hired hands. The stratification within these communities mirrored the general patterns of our society—they were divided by class, gender, and race and often exploited the earth.

As the chapter on networking pointed out, communities are an important way in which the lower classes and oppressed groups can fall back upon social obligations and reciprocity. Communities extend the networks provided by families so that the high school football team, the local garden club, and the bands at the Moose Club can all be part of community pride, sharing and enjoyment. A strong and rich community life shows children the practical results of caring about your neighbor. Carol Stack's study of a poor African American community in a midwestern city in 1970 documented the many social mechanisms by which people could survive through networking and sharing, even if they were considered "urban poor."[34]

Sociologists have documented the strains created in our society when small-town communities began to be replaced by large urban centers in the early 1900s. Yet over time the functions of community were re-created in those urban centers. The neighborhood around the factory consisted of plant workers, the foremen, their families, the neighborhood merchants, the local school, and the local churches. Residents shared participation in the union, in the schools, and in local activities centered in bars, churches, and interest clubs.

The initial impetus for urbanization was the need to bring together the resources for major industry or services (e.g., Detroit was the car city, New York and Los Angeles were financial centers, Chicago was the stockyard city, and Billings was the copper mine city.) Suppliers to these factories, and support services, created another source of employment.

Within a city such communities were often ethnically based. In Detroit, the white autoworkers at Ford's giant Dearborn complex lived in the town of Dearborn; the black autoworkers at the Ford complex lived in the town of Inkster. In New York, San Francisco and Los Angeles, ethnic communities of Chinese, Puerto Ricans, and Koreans developed their own networks and resources.[35] They read their own newspapers, ate in restaurants owned by their neighbors, and shopped in local stores run by local merchants.

Children growing up in these communities saw opportunities for a good life and upward social mobility. The undertaker, grocery store owner, and minister lived just up the street. If you worked hard, maybe you too could

I moved into a small working-class community in 1975 in West Virginia. The local grocery store was "Harry Ford's Key Market." Everyone knew Harry and Harry knew everyone. If a kid in the community was in trouble, Harry would give him or her a job dusting cans or stocking. There were always four or five teenagers working in Harry's store. Harry supported all the youth athletic teams and contributed to the fire department and the PTA. A big new Kroger's opened up the road and Harry had to work longer hours to compete. He had a heart attack and retired.

Today Ford's Key Market is gone and we have a Seven-Eleven, owned by Southland Corporation. The prices of groceries are exorbitantly high. Clerks are paid minimum wage, and two or three workers are expected to do all the work of the store. Seven-Eleven supports the Special Olympics, a charity controlled by corporate sponsors but the company rarely contributes anything to local efforts. The store's profits go to stockholders who live in suburbs far away and their corporate policy has nothing to do with the health or destruction of our community.

Recently the corporation announced that they would have to hire extra security guards at the store because the rate of shoplifting was so high. Harry Ford rarely had a problem with shoplifting.

become a professional or community leader. But even if you just finished high school, you could get a decent job in a nearby factory and support a family.

The community was the source of The American Dream. The civil rights movement of the 1960s was fueled in large part by minorities who wanted a greater part of this dream. They saw that their communities were being denied the better jobs, the better schools, the bank loans for improvements, and adequate city services. Their anger and frustration turned to violence, and our society experienced a rash of urban rebellions as sections of Los Angeles, Detroit, Newark, Atlanta, Cleveland, and other cities burned. These rebellions were more than just a part of the demand for civil rights; they were also a demand for the right to participate in community.

The urban rebellions of the 1960s occurred at the time when America's industries were still hiring and using industrial labor. By the mid-1970s the layoffs began, and with the disintegration of the employment structure came the disintegration of the community.[36] Young people were no longer needed in the plants—where were they to go? Instead of marrying the girl of your dreams and having a baby, young men stood on street corners, had the babies, and depended on welfare to feed them.

Along with the closing of the factories came urban renewal. Many leaders in low income communities called these programs "urban removal."

Interstates highways, massive impersonal housing projects, and shopping malls destroyed the local churches, grocery stores, and neighborhood parks. Not only has it been a physical destruction—it has also been a social destruction. The local grocery store owner cannot compete with the national grocery store chain; the local restaurant cannot compete with McDonald's and Wendy's. The service sector is now dominated by huge chains that charge higher prices and pay lower wages and whose owners no longer live in, or care about, the communities they serve. This is an important aspect of "the disappearing middle class."

Urban problems receive most of the attention of the media. These same social forces, however, have also had devastating effects on rural community life. As small farmers have been forced into bankruptcy, those who have not migrated to the cities remain as part of the isolated, and often forgotten, rural poor.[37]

Unemployed and marginally employed youth have now become a new market and the market is drugs. Like slavery or the genocide of Native Americans, we can stand above the problem and it looks like a giant plan or "conspiracy." But we have argued throughout this book that individuals, groups, bureaucracies and the government respond to social forces. After the urban rebellions, it was clear that unemployed youth were a destabilizing element in our society. Radical groups could organize the anger and challenge the system. But young people addicted to heroin, speeding on crack, or mellowed out on weed were far less dangerous.

Thus there were social benefits (from the perspective of social stability) to providing an outlet for the potential anger and aggression that was arising out of society's inequalities. The growing economic crisis that created a pool of permanently unemployed, or marginally employed youth, also provided a fertile ground for drug sales in poorer communities.

Cyril Robinson, in detailing the evolution of black gangs as drug sales organizations, points out that once the work option for maturing gang members disappeared, stable families became problematic, and the gang became the substitute family and the survival technique for many youths. These youths had the organization to merchandise drugs either through the use of their social networks or through the organized gangs, and the big drug cartels were quick to see the possibilities of the market.[38]

Youths and the unemployed are the most widely publicized users of drugs and alcohol. But drugs have penetrated all levels of society where individuals feel alienated and cut off from community. Michael Malone asserts that the Drug Enforcement Agency of the U.S. government has called Silicon Valley one of the biggest cocaine users in the United States.[39] This area of the country is home to the electronics industry, where well-educated and well-paid workers live.

The exorbitantly high profits of the drug trade are a powerful incentive to a society that rewards "smart" investments. One could make returns of 100 percent to 1,000 percent investing in drugs whereas an investment in a company that produced refrigerators might return as much a 11 percent or 12 percent. Our society has never found drug addiction to be contradictory to the morals of capitalism—the liquor and cigarette industries prove that. Nicotine, the addictive substance in tobacco, is as addictive as heroin and probably more physically destructive. Cigarettes have been sold for decades as fashionable, and the U.S. government provides taxpayers' dollars to subsidize the profits of the tobacco industry.

Beginning with the sale of illegal liquor during Prohibition, major "legitimate" interests in the ruling class have allied themselves with organized crime to take advantage of the high profits from drugs.[40] Illegal drugs create a social basis by which control and power within communities is vested in individuals and groups outside the limits of legitimate structures. Just as control over retailing in communities is now held by powerful corporate interests, so the income and jobs of the drug-controlled community is held by modern warlords—those who have the guns and who "own" enough politicians and government officials.

Drug addiction breaks down the traditional relationships of network reciprocity. Youths who need a fix will steal from their neighbors. Young mothers hopelessly addicted to cocaine will abandon their addicted babies. Honest law enforcement officials are prevented from arresting and/or convicting the powerful businessmen behind the scenes because those businessmen are networked into the highest levels of power.[41]

Drugs have become the most pronounced form of exploitation, oppression and degradation in our society. The high rate of AIDS among drug addicts, the birth of deformed and ill babies, the murders and injuries, and the fear that this trade brings rivals the brutality of slavery or the slaughter of the Native Americans. Activists within drug-controlled African American communities have accused the government of genocide.

Harlon Dalton, writing about AIDS in the African-American Community, points out:

> Less strongly, the term genocide reflects a widespread belief that the federal government willingly let AIDS spread as long as it was confined to populations that straight white America would rather do without. The grist for this view is provided by the government's own spokepersons, among others. In its weakest form, genocide signifies a reckless indifference to, or deliberate disregard of, the black community's vital interests, or at a minimum the subordination of those interests to the distinct concerns of the larger society.[42]

The effects of the drug trade are most obvious in communities that are the most economically vulnerable. These communities are usually minority communities. But as the economic situation worsens, these same effects are increasingly visible in poor and working-class white communities as well. We cannot just blame poverty; there is too much historical evidence to prove that even the poorest of communities in America have managed to construct stabilizing community structures.[43] Nor are middle-class youth immune from the disillusionment of our society—although they are more able to afford the drugs and avoid the public prosecution and discussion of their problems.

In Chapter 4 we pointed out that the starving Guatemalan who picks our bananas is invisible to us. Likewise, the starving Peruvian or Colombian peasant who grows the cacao leaf is also invisible to us. His hunger and poverty create the conditions for his exploitation by international drug dealers, just as unemployment and poverty create the conditions for the exploitation of American teenage street dealers. But in both cases, those who are benefiting—the banks who make the investments, the politicians and officials who accept the bribes, and the big businessmen who organize the major deals—have the power.

Drugs have not *caused* the breakdown of community in America; drugs are a *consequence* of the destruction of community structures that have been the social units of "normal" society. In this stage of the social crisis, the powerful forces driving forward the new technology are leaving in their wake a trail of twisted minds, broken bodies and evaporated dreams.[44]

INDIVIDUAL STRESS AND ADAPTATION

Communities are the basic social unit of our society and the individual is the basic unit of the community. Families and communities socialize individuals to survive in the society. In Chapter 7 we discussed the ways in which we are socialized to accept our places on the ladder of stratification. The ideology of individualism teaches us that if we fail to succeed or fit in it is our own fault. Our culture does not teach us to seek answers in structural changes and the social forces acting on us; it teaches us to see the answer in terms of individual motives.

When a man who has supported his family all his life is laid off, he is likely to define his unemployment as his fault. Even if an unemployed man is able to find a low-paying job, if he cannot "support" the family he may still feel this way.

Research shows the initial reaction to joblessness is for the man to blame himself. If he had not lost so many sick days; if he had been willing to accept a pay cut; if he had not argued with a foreperson—then he might still have his job. If he doesn't blame himself, he seeks other individuals to blame—women and blacks who took the job through affirmative action, or the Japanese. The anger at those who "caused" the problem may be expressed as domestic violence, violence against a foreman or some other official, or violence against minorities.

Many unemployed go through a second stage of feeling worthless. Life is not worth living and they have failed all of those who depend on them. These feelings can lead to withdrawal (sitting in front of the TV all day), alcoholism or drug dependency (prescriptions for depression or illegal drugs) or suicide. Domestic violence increases. Stress-related illnesses emerge, creating medical bills that generate more stress.[45] Normal family life is disrupted and divorces are far more likely to occur.[46]

All these problems are translated into social psychological stress on children. These stresses are then acted out in school, on the street or in the forms of illness.[47] At the same time, the economic contraction has led to severe cutbacks in government funding for social service counseling, mental health services, and preventive medical care.

What is being described *is* the breakdown of the family. Traditional roles define the man as the breadwinner and if he cannot play that role, his authority in the household is undermined. In cases where the wife has to find a job (usually at substantially lower wages), the self-concept of the male is further eroded by the idea that his wife is supporting him.

In contrast, wives who are laid off are much less likely to suffer lowered feelings of self-esteem. Rosen found that women in blue-collar jobs experienced ambivalent feelings about lay-offs: on the one hand, they worried about the loss of income to their families, but on the other hand, they felt relief that they could spend more time with children at in the home.[48]

A lay-off for a single female parent was perceived differently. In this case, Rosen found, women had accepted the responsibility of being the "breadwinner" and worried far more about their failure to support the family. For them, the only recourse is the welfare system.[49] To "go on welfare" is a degrading and humiliating experience. It is another way in which "good" people get to punish those who don't "deserve" the good life, by causing social pain.

In earlier times, unemployed individuals were usually supported through family and community networks. Odd jobs were found, neighbors and churches pitched in to help pay medical bills, and the school teachers in the community helped out with the children. This process, however, assumes two things: that communities are still viable, and that there are enough employed workers to provide the resources of the unemployed. In a housing project that holds 2,000 households, people who hardly know each other, who will take care of the guy who loses his job? When a plant shuts down and suddenly 38 percent of all the workers in the community are jobless, it is impossible for those who are still working to provide the support necessary.

Today, large numbers of younger unemployed or marginally employed workers and their families are being supported by parents or relatives who still do have good jobs, benefits, or pensions. But as that older generation passes on, that support network will also disappear.

Because layoffs and unemployment are proportionately greater for minorities, the social consequences of an economic crisis are more severely felt in the communities and families of African Americans, Latin Americans, and other oppressed minorities.[50]

The media are constantly talking about crime, the breakdown of the family, and the need to restore traditional values. Our analysis is not denying that families are breaking up and that individuals are turning to crime. What we are arguing is that blaming the victim will not solve these problems.

Why do those in power not realize that the creation of job programs, adequate housing, better health care, and better education are the answers we need? It actually costs more to send a young person to maximum security prison for a year than to send him or her to Harvard University. As Chapter 8 pointed out, the estimate of the social costs of crime in our society were placed at $425 billion a year by *Business Week*.

Yet our society is investing millions of dollars in new prisons and cutting back support for higher education. Schools boards are hiring security guards to patrol the halls of the high schools and laying off the social workers who can counsel parents and teenagers. This appears to be irrational. Why send youths to prison instead of college?

Remember that social order requires one of two things—either belief that the system will work in your benefit or coercion to make you obey a system you no longer believe in. The "choice" to coerce is because the system is increasingly not working for those on the bottom rungs. Millions of people—old and young—are increasingly facing a bleak future. They cannot find jobs; they cannot pay medical bills; they cannot read; they cannot walk the streets safely.

The system is not working for millions of young people. If they had good college educations that had taught them history, and critical thinking skills, they would become a powerful threat to the existing order. In the existing system, education is reserved basically for those who are still necessary for the economy and who will still receive some of its rewards.

This loss of belief in the system is an ambiguous factor, but it is real. If you were to interview a young man busted for drugs and a seventeen-year-old unmarried woman who has just had her second baby, they would not talk to you about social psychological stress, social forces, or ideological controls. Just as most of us can't name the viruses that make us sick or name the organs that are infected, most people cannot name or identify the social forces that are making them sick. But we can see sickness whether we know its name or not.

The most valuable resource of our society—our people—are being disabled from participation in life. The creativity, talent and intelligence that each person brings to society in a unique way is being denied. Instead of being given the potential to develop and blossom, people are being stunted and beaten to the ground. The new technology is not benefiting them.

ROBOTRONICS IN A KINDER AND GENTLER WORLD

Are the new technologies capable of being used in a different way—a way that extends equality and democracy and raises the quality of life for the entire planet? The answer to that question is yes, theoretically. But the *historical* answer lies in the emergence of social movements that challenge the existing power structures and make demands for social change.

Currently, the new technologies are being researched, developed, and applied by massive bureaucracies—the government, research foundations, and corporations. These bureaucracies are described in Part III. They are social structures and reflect the ideologies and norms of our general society.

The scientists, administrators, and public officials who work in these bureaucracies perform their work without critically looking at the underlying assumptions of much of what they do. Is their research a further manipulation of the balance of nature? Will the profits earned from the technology further enrich only a few? Are the benefits of the medical research available only to the affluent who can afford it? These bureaucracies are incapable of asking these questions between the hierarchies of power within them reinforce the existing structures of power.

Barry Jones, an economist, has analyzed the implications of robotronics for the job market.[51] The greatest hope for future employment opportunities in a post-service era lies in work that is:

1. labor/time-absorbing (and consequently low in productivity);
2. not subject to direct competition from technology;
3. not subject to foreign competition (or needing tariff protection or quotas to survive)
4. not based on large-scale capital-intensive enterprise;
5. not based on a new invention or technological form;
6. low resource-using (not entropic);

7. aimed at the satisfaction of individual needs (e.g. providing a million different garments rather than the same garment a million times);
8. based on fulfilling human needs on a continuing basis (e.g. restaurants, entertainment, sex-related employment), not once and for all;
9. in itself an output of production (i.e. activity for activity's sake, such as professional sport, research, gardening, music and craft, welfare industries).

The most likely areas for future work expansion, not all of them desirable, are in:

1. education, including recurrent education and training for the semi-skilled and unskilled;
2. home-based employment, including domestic work, maintenance and gardening on a contract basis, home security;
3. leisure, tourism, sport and gambling;
4. dinging out;
5. provision of drink, drugs and commercial sex (and treating their adverse affects);
6. craftwork, the arts and entertainment generally;
7. individualized social, welfare, and counseling services (especially geriatric or psychiatric);
8. individualized transport systems, e.g. taxis, personal drivers, fixed-route minibuses (such as *perseros* of Mexico), courier services, point-to-point delivery;
9. public-sector employment, armaments, armed forces, police;
10. hobby-related work, including DIY (do-it-yourself) work in the informal economy, antiques and collecting;
11. small-unit energy generation (solar, wind and growing crops for 'biomass') and subsistence farming;
12. manufacture of leisure and solar-energy equipment (boats, games, solar heaters and collectors);
13. materials recycling;
14. recognizing that some existing forms of work are essentially 'welfare industries' where the main output is *employment*;
15. nature-related work, including gardening in the widest sense; the care and preservation of wildernesses, forests, deserts and natural parks, coastlines, the development and care of footpath networks;
16. care of animals, including selling, breeding and grooming pets.

Jones's analysis does *not* take into account the issues we are raising here of exploitation, oppression, and degradation. His options (sex for sale or gambling, for example) illustrate our argument that the issues are political and social as well as economic. So the question remains: *for whose benefit* will the new technologies be used?

It is not inevitable that social movements will make demands that reflect the ideologies of democracy and equality. The economic crisis after World War I in Germany gave rise to conflicting social movements. One was a radical left-wing movement, and the other was the Nazi movement, led by Hitler. The Nazis won, and a vicious system of slave labor, genocide, and militarism was put into place in one of the most "civilized" nations of the world.

This text has argued that to understand social stratification and power in America we had to study history—to know how and why the structures of power emerged as they did. We are also going to argue that to understand social stratification and power in America we have to ask questions of the future. What current dimensions of power suggest the patterns for the next decade? the next century? What social forces will be involved in setting those patterns. Is democracy no longer really necessary for a "healthy" economy, as a 7 June 1993 *Business Week* article suggests?[52] Or can the new technology lay the basis for a society in which all citizens more freely participate and live in harmony with their neighbors and the earth? It is to these questions that we turn in Chapters 15 and 16.

SUMMARY

The new technology is having major consequences for stratification in six major areas: employment, distribution of wealth, control over information, acceleration of ecological damage, destruction of community, and social psychological stress on individuals.

Beginning in the later 1970s and early 1980s, large-scale industry "retooled" by building new factories with more robotronics. These newer factories were often built in states with weaker union laws or in countries with cheaper labor and fewer pollution controls. Urban areas in the United States that had been dependent on these industries faced soaring unemployment rates. Shortly thereafter, layoffs began in white-collar industries. The service sector was soon feeling the effect of robotronics. The unemployed able to find new jobs usually received less pay and fewer benefits. The industry that was producing the computers and other equipment for robotronics utilized relatively few workers—it was increasingly using robotronics to create robotronics.

Not all suffered. Those who did have jobs in the new sectors of the economy often did well. Corporate heads and bankers were actively ensuring that the upper classes were reaping the financial benefits of the changes. As laws were changed, it became easier for companies and financial institutions to enter the world market and take advantage of cheaper labor and resources in other countries. The gap between rich and poor has increased.

Robotronics has also meant new technologies for the media. People now are given news and information instantaneously—over satellite dishes, the Web and Internet, and cellular phones. But more information has not led to a better informed citizenry. The educational level of the population appears to be decreasing. Greater access to information has given those in power greater control over individuals.

Damage to the earth has been accelerating as new chemicals and even life forms have been discovered and put to use without adequate consideration of their long term-effects. The destruction is now happening so rapidly and spreading so quickly that some ecologists fear that within a decade the damage may be irreparable.

All these consequences have had an impact on communities. The networks that have sustained communities in the past are shredded by the control that organized crime brings into a neighborhood. Drugs, gambling, and other such activities continue to drain the communities of human and material resources.

Individuals who are on the lower rungs of the ladder have experienced more social pain. This takes the form of greater stress, more resistance, and increased sickness. Some turn to alcohol or other drugs to escape. Some act out their frustrations within the family. Others become severely depressed and give up hope. The impact on the family, and especially children, is devastating.

One can ask whether robotronics can be applied in more positive ways. First the question of social power—who controls the new technology for whose benefit?—must be answered.

Discussion Questions

1. Can you identify the consequences for you and/or your family in the six areas discussed in this chapter? On this personal level (the microsociological) have these consequences been positive or negative? How are these consequences related to your position on the social ladder?

2. As this book is being written Congress is debating legislation that would cut Social Security, Medicaid, welfare, grants to college students, and aid to education. Individual states will be given more control over what federal monies are distributed for social programs. What do you think the consequences of these political changes will be in the six arenas discussed above?

3. The discussion in this chapter is pretty "gloomy." How is this gloom related to the fact that the book is titled "the view from below?" If I were writing from the perspective of the upper classes, how would this alter my analysis?

Resources

Video: *Poletown*

This is a documentary and would have to be rented from a library or academic source. Still, it is worth the trouble. It is the story of a community in Detroit that resisted General Motors in its plan to buy up a large portion of the community to construct a new and more modern plant. The city government cooperated because GM promised jobs. Included in the demolition was an old and beloved Catholic church. The parishioners camp out in its basement, hoping to save it and the police come and drag them bodily away. My students react by saying that thought these things happened only in places like Russia!

Looking back, ten years later we can see the long-range consequences. The plant did not create new jobs, GM got richer, and a community was destroyed.

Book: Aldous Huxley, *Brave New World.*

This novel was required reading for senior high school and freshman college students in my generation. Huxley paints a vivid and scary picture of what can happen to individuality and freedom in a technological society controlled by the few. In his vision of the future he hypothesizes that social control will be accomplished through drugs. I wonder why it is no longer being required?

NOTES

Complete citations are provided in the Bibliography.

1. Huxley 1932, 1946, 14, 67.
2. "Flipping Off the Lights from your Sickbed," *Business Week* 22 March 1993, 88A.
3. One of the earliest studies to explore the implications of the current economic shift was Bluestone and Harrison 1982; they updated their arguments in 1988.
4. Even *Business Week* argues that official unemployment rates are depressed. The cover story for the week of 7 November 1994 is highly critical of several official government statistics.
5. Horowitz 1994.
6. James Bozeman (1989) was one of the earliest scholars to lay out the full implications of this technology in his paper.
7. *Business Week* 9 May 1994, 61.

8. These are upper level managerial lay-offs that occurred in 1990 and 1991 (*Wall Street Journal*, 12 December 1991; 15 January 1990).

9. *Wall Street Journal*, 27 September 1991.

10. *Business Week*, 7 November 1994.

11. Cowan 1983.

12. See Attewell's (1992) review of the debate regarding skill upgrading and deskilling of the manufacturing labor force.

13. Liebow 1993, 225–26.

14. Hayes 1989, 135–59.

15. McNeil-Lehrer Report, 19 April 1984.

16. Griede 1994; Also see Fuentes and Ehrenreich (1983, 56)

17. *Business Week*, 14 June 1993, 82–84.

18. Mishel and Bernstein 1993, 134.

19. *Business Week*, 19 April 1993, 84.

20. "Mexican workers still waiting for new jobs from NAFTA," AP report, 18 December 1994.

21. *Business Week,* 16 March 1992, 100.

22. Grieder 1994. Fuentes and Ehrenreich (1983) document ten major strikes in Mexico, Taiwan, Thailand, South Korea and the Philippines involving thousands of workers, many of them women.

23. Amnesty International (1993) documents known cases in which such labor repression result in human rights violations.

24. Williams 1989, ix–x.

25. For a discussion of the political misuse of such power by government, see Davis 1992.

26. FBI director J. Edgar Hoover used the technologies of wiretapping to collect information that vastly increased his personal power. His example illustrates the potential misuse of technologies by law enforcement authorities. See Theoharis 1993; Kelley and Davis 1987; Powers 1986; Welch and Marston 1984.

27. Wright 1987, 205–6.

28. Douglas Kellner (1990, 179–222) concludes his critique of today's television with several proposal for democratization of the broadcasting system.

29. Gribbin 1987, 180–81. Gribbin updated his analysis with further scientific information in 1990.

30. Worldwatch Institute 1994; also see Brown 1992.

31. Harvard biologist Ruth Hubbard and coauthor Elijah Wald (1993) argue that the interests of profit and careers are driving genetic research, with potentially disastrous consequences.

32. "The Catastrophe Lurking in America's Farmlands" *Business Week,* 20 May 1996, 84.

33. Brown 1994.

34. Stack 1975. The full effects of the economic crisis and the consequent rise of the drug trade had not yet been fully felt in "The Flats," the community studied by Stack.

35. For a discussion of how this occurred over the last century, see Takaki 1993. An excellent description of how this process is continuing in American society is found in Lamphere 1992.

36. A well-researched study of this is to be found in Perrucci et al 1988.

37. See Conger and Elder 1994.

38. Robinson 1993, 310–14.

39. Malone 1985, 398.

40. Pearce 1993, 169–93.

41. Freemantal 1986; Potts, Kochanb, and Whittington 1992.

42. Dalton 1989, 137–38.

43. For an excellent example of how a poor African American community used networking and sharing to survive, see Stack 1975. Stack's study was done in 1970, before the full effects of the economic crisis and the consequent drug trade had been felt.

44. The angry language in this section and the section following is the result of the way in which my own life has been touched by the disintegration of community and the individual destruction of those I have known and loved. A social scientist who can write "objectively" about human suffering is not better informed—indeed she or he is only revealing either not understanding such suffering or not caring.

45. In 1957, 13 percent of Americans had seen some kind of psychological counselor. By 1985, the number was nearly 30 percent—or 80 million people (Meredith 1987). Fourteen percent of all workers' compensation claims filed in 1987 were stress-related, up from 5 percent in 1980 (Miller 1988).

46. Voyandoff and Donnelly 1988, 97–116.

47. Rayman 1988, 119–34.

48. Rosen 1987, 120–27.

49. Rosen 1987, 127–29. Also see Gordus and Yamakawa 1988,38–54; and Perrucci and Targe 1988, 55–72.

50. Bowman 1988.

51. Barry Jones 1990, 239–40.

52. "Is Democracy Bad for Growth?" *Business Week*, 7 June 1993, 84–88.

15

SOCIAL CHANGE IN THE TWENTYFIRST CENTURY

What's it going to take? That's the question.
We know we need some big changes,
but how are we going to get them?
I think it's going to take the courage of people
who refuse to stand silently by.

—Pete Seeger

The previous chapter examined reactions to the growing social crisis. It does not take a genius to predict that movements for change will arise as life becomes more difficult. Not all people would agree that something is terribly wrong. The extent of agreement will probably vary inversely your social status—the higher you sit on the ladder of social stratification the less likely you are to have personally experienced the growing social pain. You are more likely to believe the system is working, even if it needs some fixing. At what point do enough people lose faith in the system to organize serious challenges to the power structure?

THE CHANGING CHARACTER OF TWENTIETH CENTURY SOCIAL MOVEMENTS

The social movements of the 1960s demanded equal access to the promises of democracy and the prosperity of capitalism. Women and minorities believed that they should be paid equally and treated the same in the workplace; that they should be given equal opportunities to learn and study any career or profession; and that their cultures and ways of behaving should be equally accepted as valid.

Today's social movements are different. They are beginning to challenge the premises of the system itself. That challenge has taken two directions. One is the struggle to expand democracy and improve the quality of life for all on our planet. The other asserts we should go backward, to an earlier time when people accepted and believed in the social hierarchies as "good." Obviously, this book believes that it is best to move forward with the expansion of democracy. Today, this view is called the "liberal," or "left" view. The belief that we should go backward in time to a more stratified society is a "conservative" view from the "right." We first look at the movements that are fighting to expand democracy. We shall then discuss the conservative reactions.

The movement for expanded democracy and equality has several dimensions. There are those within the environmental movement who argue that we must change our priorities on consumption, profit, and materialism or we will inevitably destroy the earth. The movement for accessible, quality health care asserts that enriching insurance companies, drug companies, hospital corporations, and a tiny minority of health professionals is incompatible with providing health care for millions of Americans. The movement to reform politics contends that a "democracy" based on million-dollar television campaigns, financed by powerful interest groups, and leaving millions out of the political process is not a democracy at all.

THE ENVIRONMENTAL MOVEMENT

The political squabbles between nations was based on the assumption that humans should decide who controlled the earth. Who controlled whose resources? Where was the border drawn? Who got to invest where? The answers to these questions justified the creation of immense nuclear arsenals. Since World War II, massive amounts of nuclear material has been released in the air, ground and water supply during nuclear testing. For example, in southern Utah, communities downwind from the Nevada test site suffer from rates of thyroid and bone cancers eight to ten twelve times higher than the national average, and women in the South Pacific islands (site of numerous nuclear tests) have been giving birth to deformed and critically ill children. Other women cannot conceive at all.[1]

Research and development have promoted automobiles rather than mass transit and nuclear energy rather than solar or water power in order to protect the interests of energy corporations. The power industries that use oil, gas, coal, and nuclear argue that solar and water power have not proven "feasible." But the research into these technologies is only a tiny fraction of what has been spent on developing other power sources. Had government grants and subsidies been equally allocated to water and solar power it is probable that they would be feasible. One can joke that the companies could not put a meter on sunlight or wind!

This was not an evil conspiracy. Individuals responsible for such decisions were functioning in bureaucracies where they were rewarded for making decisions that reinforced existing interests and were punished for questioning those decisions.[2]

The challenge for change had to come from outside those power structures. That challenge was the environmental movement. Until recently the environmental movement has been based on middle-and upper-middle class whites who had above-average educations. Their concerns were primarily wilderness and wildlife preservation, wise resource management, pollution abatement, and population control.[3]

As the environmental crisis has deepened, the movement has broadened. There are those who are asking about the connections between the application of ecologically destructive technology and our changing social class structure. How is it that women are more degraded by speciesism than men?[4] Why is it that communities most often targeted for toxic waste dumps are the communities of the poor and people of color? As those relationships become clearer, the defense of the whale, spotted owl, and songbirds can also be seen as a challenge to the more general social processes of exploitation, oppression and degradation.

Robert Bullard raises the issue of the relationship between speciesism and racism:

> Racism plays a key factor in environmental planning and decision making. Indeed, environmental racism is reinforced by government, legal, economic, political, and military institutions. It is a fact of life in the United States that the mainstream environmental movement is only beginning to wake up. Whether by conscious design or institutional neglect, communities of color in urban ghettos, in rural "poverty pockets," or on economically impoverished Native-American reservations face some of the worst environmental devastation in the nation. It has thus been an up-hill battle convincing white judges, juries, governmental officials, and policymakers that racism exists in environmental protection, enforcement, and polity formulation.[5]

The environmental movement has had some success in raising public consciousness and creating public pressure. But it faces a formidable force—the drive to maximize profits in a contracting economy. This force not only affects corporations, it affects individuals. The Native American in Brazil who has been forced off his ancestral land by a giant lumbering company may seize the opportunity to slash and burn a plot of tropical forest for the promise of two or three seasons of harvest. The American small farmer, facing bankruptcy, may see toxic pesticides as his/her only way of staying in business next year.

Environmentalists not only confront the structures that create these problems, but they must educate and involve those who will be the immediate victims of change. In an economy where jobs are scarce, the threat to the worker from the environmental activist may appear more serious than the long-range threat of planetary destruction. Perhaps the most outstanding example are the industrial workers whose jobs are threatened by environmental protection. The fight to end strip mining was seen as a threat to miners' jobs; the fight to control air pollution was seen as a threat to chemical and steel workers' jobs.

These contradictions are being resolved, however, as conditions worsen. Decades of environmental degradation are now being felt on a personal, as well as occupational, level. When a worker realizes that his or her daughter may have leukemia as a result of the plant pollution or that his or her house will have no resale value because of the toxic waste dump three blocks away, the question of environment becomes an individual concern. Because populations that are poor or marginalized by racism are more likely to face the worst environmental problems they have been among the first to connect ecological destruction to the broader issues of the economy and political power.

In West Virginia (one of the poorest states in the country,) government leaders are proposing that counties depressed by coal mine layoffs pursue "economic development" by allowing out-of-state waste corporations to use mountain hollows as enormous waste dumps. In some of these communities, laid-off coal miners are leading the resistance to these dumps. They no longer have jobs to protect, and their mountains and communities are the only thing they have left. Poor African Americans in Greene County, Alabama, discovered their status made them prime targets for one of the country's largest toxic waste facilities.[6] Native American peoples have organized to fight the environmental degradation and devastating health consequences of the uranium industry.[7]

The problems are not confined to the poor or minorities. Middle-class families, such as those in Buffalo's Love Canal area, discovered their homes had been built over what had been a toxic waste dump. And all Americans are threatened by an increasing cancer rate that is highly correlated with the carcinogens being dumped into the air, water, and food. In 1994 consumers (including toddlers and small children) ate over 110 million boxes of contaminated cereals (Cheerios, Lucky Charms, Trix, Kix, and others) before the FDA detected the unapproved pesticide Dursban that had been sprayed on the oats used. The 1993 National Academy of Sciences report on pesticides and children concluded that some children already receive ten times the "safe" level of cholinesterase-inhibiting organophosphate pesticides just from eating fresh fruits and vegetables.[8]

As citizens have become more aware, and more angry, about the exploitation of the environment and their bodies, there has been an attempt to coopt and redirect the demands. Businesses have used the growing awareness of waste disposal as an investment opportunity. Today, several huge corporations are announcing record earnings, taking lucrative contracts from federal, state and local governments to haul and dispose of waste. But the priority of these companies is profit, not concern for the environment. Industrial interests have not always been able to coopt the movement, and there has been a growing backlash against environmental protection. Intense lobbying in Congress has already resulted in the weakening or elimination of many environmental regulations.[9]

Over and over again, local watchdog groups have shown that these companies charge high rates and do minimal work, often simply transferring the poison from one vicinity to another. Across the country local communities are organizing to fight back. As they link their struggles and understand the common roots of their problem, they will grow as a powerful force.[10] At the same time, every effort will be made by those in power to divert and undermine the emerging strength of such grassroots resistance.

The environmental crisis is evident even to the ruling class. Their approach, however, is to "manage" the problem without addressing the fundamental assumptions of speciesism. Those who want to manage only the *effects* of speciesism see the question very differently from those who raise the issue of speciesism and the larger inequalities of stratification. These two sides were clearly shown in the arguments about the environmental impact of the North American Free Trade Agreement (NAFTA).[11]

Environmentalists with the critical perspective charged some conservation groups of compromising to get NAFTA passed. They called these groups the "Shameful Seven." and pointed out the corporate connections:

- World Wildlife received a $2.5 million donation from Eastman Kodak, whose chief executive officer is co-founder of a corporate lobby for the treaty;
- The National Wildlife Federation, according to its 1992 annual report, gets support from such NAFTA boosters as Dow Chemical, DuPont, Monsanto, 3M, Shell, Duke Power, Pennzoil and Waste Management Co.
- Audubon gets contributions from General Electric, Procter & Gamble, and Waste Management Co.

- The Nature Conservancy received more than $2 million from Coca-Cola, and other large sums in the $250,000-$500,000 range from Canon USA and Tenneco, all NAFTA supporters.[12]

The issue was whether the treaty would ensure that Mexico would enforce the same environmental controls as the United States. If part of the reason that companies want to relocate in Mexico is to avoid the controls found in the United States, then they would certainly not want the treaty to include clauses that toughen environment protection.

As the older generation passes on, the personal costs of speciesism will be more sharply felt. A younger generation that drinks Coke for breakfast, eats potato chips for lunch, and has a Big Mac for supper is coming of age. They have grown up breathing polluted air, drinking questionable water, and consuming food filled with chemicals of undetermined effect. Just as unemployment is related to the falling academic achievements of the younger generation, so is food and health. No corporate research department is studying how sugar-coated chemically colored breakfast cereals and fake fruit juice is affecting the learning of the young.

Our external environment is closely linked to our internal environments—our bodies. The long-range effect of environmental degradation on our health is just now becoming apparent to many. Yet it comes at the very time our health-care system is increasingly unable to provide quality services to a large proportion of Americans.

THE HEALTH CARE MOVEMENT

The socialist countries and industrial capitalist nations of Europe made health care a social right, like education. The United States was the only industrialized Western nation that developed almost all health care as a marketplace commodity. As long as the economy was healthy, Americans could purchase health care, just as they purchased housing and food. Government medical programs for the poor and elderly provided a basic "safety net" for disadvantaged Americans. But the contraction of the economy has created a large group of working Americans who cannot afford the health care they need. At the time of writing this book 38 million Americans, many of them the "working poor," had no health insurance whatsoever.

At the same time, the new technologies in health care have provided a bonanza for large corporations that sell hospital equipment and services. While the price of computers and robots is rapidly falling, the subsidized health care technologies remain astronomically expensive. What would a CT-SCAN machine really cost if it had been subject to the same market pressures as the new generation of laptops and fax machines? Marketplace concerns also affect how research and development decisions are made.

In June 1993 the Food and Drug Administration announced that it would require drug researchers to disclose whether they have financial stakes in the drugs they are testing. "Can a financial stakeholder approach scientific inquiry without introducing some bias?" asked Dr. David Kessler, the FDA commissioner. "I think probably not." This means that up until this point such disclosures have *not* been a requirement. The fact that it is now being asked reflects the pressure of public opinion and the growing anger over high drug company profits.[13] As long as profitability concerns rule, more emphasis will be placed on curing cancer than preventing it.[14]

A recent National Public Radio program interviewed a French government official regarding the generous medical plan automatically provided to all French citizens. He was asked whether it would be possible to develop such a system in the United States. The French official answered that the French plan was put in place at a time when modern medicine was just emerging. In France, medical services developed under the assumption that citizens had a *right* to basic health care and that health was not a marketplace commodity sold only to those who could pay. He observed that the system in the United States is too firmly entrenched—powerful insurance companies, drug and medical equipment companies, hospital corporations, and medical associations all function on the premise that any health-care system must protect their profitability.

This official's observation reflects the argument of this text. Medicine in the United States reflects social stratification. Research tests and development are based largely on samples of white males, usually middle class. If the research is hoped to be beneficial (lower heart attack rates, for example) the generalization that white males are the test group holds true. Large charities raise money for the health problems that affect the wealthy, such as arthritis, diabetes, and heart disease. Research into illnesses like gum disease, sickle cell anemia, or asbestosis that affect primarily the poor, minorities, or workers is given lower priority.

If the medical tests are risky, the sample group will be different. An example is the infamous experiment at Tuskegee Institute in which the government purposefully exposed black men to syphilis to study the natural course of the disease. Although an effective treatment was developed mid-experiment, the men were never told about it and were never treated, lest the research be compromised.[15] Today drug companies are doing such risky research on Third World poverty populations, where people will eagerly participate for a small fee.

Epidemiology is the scientific study of how diseases are transmitted and spread. The reaction by the government to the outbreak of AIDS in the United

States was a patriarchal reaction, not a reaction based on the principles of epidemiology. AIDS first emerged in the United States as a disease among homosexuals, who are labeled as undesirable by our society. Patriarchal ideology saw the disease as justified punishment for sinners rather than a fatal virus capable of spreading throughout the population. Even after the blood test was developed, the Red Cross delayed using it because it was too "expensive." As a result, tens of thousands of hemophiliacs developed AIDS unnecessarily.[16]

The need for quality accessible health care brings together groups in our society who have formerly been divided by their own particular group issues. Poor men and middle-class women, heterosexual and homosexual, Hispanic and Native American—are all facing similar problems. Any catastrophic disease such as cancer, Alzheimer's, or AIDS will bankrupt the average family.

Community networks have attempted to meet this need but can hardly make a dent in the bills. One sees bake sales raising money for leukemia treatments or jars at a local store requesting change to help pay for dialysis. Families on welfare are afraid to take jobs to get off welfare and lose medical coverage for their children. Small businesses complain they cannot afford health coverage for their employees, and big corporations are instituting larger deductibles and more restricted coverage.

More sick and injured people are dying in the street after medical care is denied or terminated. While some doctors break regulations to keep patients who need continued care in the hospital past the HMO "guidelines," other doctors impose unnecessary and expensive tests and operations in order to pad their bills and milk the government and insur-ance companies.[17] Hospital corporations with links to insurance companies process inflated bills that are paid without question. At a time in history when technology should be laying the basis for the best-quality care humans have ever known, the health care delivery system in the United States is breaking down.

One hundred years ago the local doctor arrived at the home of a heart attack victim and did what he could. Often the patient died and no one vilified the doctor. Today it is different. Technology exists to save many heart attack victims. If an ambulance arrives quickly with a trained paramedic crew, the patient will be kept alive. If the hospital room is staffed with well-trained personnel and the victim is cared for correctly, she or he may make a full recovery. But if ambulance crews have been cut back because the city can no longer afford to run them; if the emergency room personnel are overworked, underpaid and poorly trained; and if the victim has no medical coverage—she or he may not survive. The victim's death is now due to social causes, not medical causes. Those who die as a result of inadequate health care have been murdered by the system. The more the general public understands the *systemic* causes of these "murders," the greater will be the demand for change.

Unequal access to quality medical care is not the only consequence of how the health system in America is currently run. According to Laurie Garrett's study *The Coming Plague: Newly Emerging Diseases in a World Out of Balance*, the government's neglect of public health surveillance and prevention may lay the basis for major epidemics in the United States.[18] Diseases are not separate from society but are often a consequence of social problems. For example, a new and drug-resistant tuberculosis strain is now a major threat, due in large part to the growing homeless population in America. In 1983, when the federal government was subsidizing immunization for children, fewer than 1,500 children contracted measles. After the cutbacks in immunization funds the 1990 total was 27,000 cases of measles reported and 100 children died. Basic standards of public health are norms that are cultural imperatives; if they are widely violated, they can threaten the very existence of the society itself.

President Clinton tried to carry out some reform, but only in the context of the networks that helped elect him. The bureaucratic structures that protect the interests of a powerful few (insurance companies, hospital corporations, highly paid health professionals) will not reform themselves in a way that undermines their profits and privileges. Why would the American Medical Association, who represents members with an average annual salary of $177,000, work for legislation that makes medical care more affordable?

The challenge to the health-care system in the United States must come from outside. Could lawmakers have extended voting rights in 1964 had there been no massive civil rights movement? Real change in the health-care system will not come until there is a similar social movement making that demand. How many people will have to be denied medical care and die on the street before millions march to Washington?

"Life, liberty and the pursuit of happiness" are the self-evident truths of living in a democracy. If the elderly are stacked away in poorly regulated nursing homes, if children go without immunization and preventive checkups, as the incidence of cancer continues to grow and AIDS spreads—people are being denied their lives and their pursuit of happiness. The failure of government in the face of the threats to our environment and health have led to increased questioning of government itself. Do we really have "liberty" when we cannot safely breathe the air and when we cannot afford a doctor? Why does government fail to respond to these issues in a meaningful way? Increasingly, those concerned about the future are organizing around the issues of how our government works.

THE SOCIAL MOVEMENT FOR DEMOCRACY

The history of this country is the history of the proud struggle to extend democracy to more and more people. Our pride in being American is not that traders stole people from Africa to work as slaves but that we fought a bloody war to end slavery; is not that we created a nation that was an industrial power but that the workers who did this were guaranteed decent wages, health plans and basic rights to express grievances and have their own organizations.

In Chapter 5 we argued that past social movements were specific groups objecting to the exploitation, oppression, and degradation that they, as a group, faced. This could be called "group politics." Their challenge rarely extended to the general exploitation, oppression, and degradation underlying *all* social stratification. Trade unions politically educated their members to vote for labor candidates; women's organizations politically educated their members to vote for prosuffrage candidates; the NAACP politically educated their members to vote for candidates supporting desegregation.

Today a candidate with the support of the National Organization of Women could win an election but may vote against the unions; a candidate with strong labor backing could win an election but may vote against women and minorities. Groups who were relatively small in number, such as Native Americans, or groups who had no resources, such as the homeless, were left out of this kind of democracy.

Disenfranchised groups have always had advocates—usually well-meaning middle-and upper-class individuals who feel morally compelled to "speak for" the powerless. The problem with advocacy politics is that those who do the advocating can afford to compromise. They often end up acting as restraints on their constituencies, whose anger is then never fully expressed. The result is a system of professional lobbyists for the poor and other disenfranchised groups, who roam the corridors of power and, in fact, protect the politicians from ever having to confront those who are actually doing the suffering.

Today women, minorities, and unions all face an erosion of rights won in the 1960s. Media exposure of scandals, the breakdown of basic government services, and the failure of candidates to address clearly real issues have disillusioned millions of Americans. This disillusionment is giving rise to two kinds of social movements. The first is the attempt to continue the progress by recapturing democracy and returning it to the people. The second movement arising out of the failure of "group politics" to win genuine and lasting change is the conservative reaction, which is discussed later.

The movement to recapture democracy is now expressing itself in three ways: (1) a demand for reform of the political process, (2) a demand for respect of multicultural and personal diversity, and (3) a demand for economic equity.[19]

The Demand for Political Reform

Today's political system has been endlessly analyzed by television commentators, journalists, and social scientists. Everyone seems to agree the media are too powerful and that campaigns are too expensive; everyone seems to agree there is a "gridlock" in politics that stifles reform; everyone seems to agree that too many Americans don't vote and don't believe the system represents them. There is less agreement on what it is that has caused these problems. People are beginning to wonder if a system in which the rich get richer and the poor get poorer can reform itself.

The public is beginning to confront the hypocrisy of today's "democracy."[20] The first demand is to take campaigning out of the hands of expensive advertising consultants and slick media commercials. To the extent that candidates for major offices need to raise *millions* of dollars to campaign they become hostage to the interest groups that fund their campaigns. Limiting campaign spending and providing funds from the public sector is one mechanism by which such hostage taking could be prevented.

Once in office, politicians become subject to intense pressures from well-trained and highly paid lobbyists. The politician is offered trips, gifts, offers of jobs after retirement and high fees for speeches. Stricter rules regarding lobbying and more disclosure of lobbying activities are now being demanded.

On state and local levels, districts could be organized to make candidates more responsive to the ordinary citizen and less controlled by political machines. This point is often not understood. If a county is allowed four state legislators and all four are elected countywide, then candidates must campaign in the entire county. On the other hand, if the county is divided into four sub-districts and candidates campaign only in their own district, they could be better known, personally, and could rely less on paid advertisement and the machines that supply poll workers and political bribes. The smaller the territory in which one has to campaign, the easier it is for a candidate to be independent of wealthy interest groups.

What appear to be logical and even innocuous reforms are strongly opposed by many currently in power. The demand for such reforms is so strong that politicians are being forced to give lip service to them. But the new laws currently being considered are full of so many compromises and loopholes that they change very little. A federal candidate must accept caps on donations—$1,000 from individuals, $5,000 from political action committees (PACs). But parties can bag limitless money if it goes to things such as voter registration (called "soft money") and not directly to candidates. The Republicans are winning the money race: In 1995 its national committees got $34 million in soft money vs. $25 million for the Democrats. Table 15.1 shows the top donors to the two national party committees.

Table 15.1 Top Donors to Party Committees[21]

To Democrats		To Republicans	
Dirk Ziff	$380,000	Philip Morris	$992,149
AT&T	313,684	RJR Nabisco	696,450
Seagram's	285,000	AT&T	370,000
MCI	279,750	American Financial	330,000
Miramax Films	276,000	ARCO	322,175

If many of those who do *not* vote are minorities and the poor, what would happen if large numbers of poor people suddenly showed up to vote for candidates that truly represented *them*? Such a situation developed when the Reverend Jesse Jackson ran for the nomination of the Democratic party in the 1980s. The power structure within the Democratic Party itself, as well as the mass media, functioned to discredit his candidacy and block him as a serious candidate, revealing the basic mechanisms by which those in power maintain their control. The reality is that the networks who run the political machines do not want large numbers of angry people to get involved in the political process; they want them to stay home and be swayed by slick television advertisements.

In *Land of Idols: Political Mythology in America* , Michael Parenti argues that the American people must first get over the political myths that have been used to mislead and confuse them.[22] His analysis of those myths runs closely parallel to the analysis of this text.

The current system insures that the highest levels of our government are overwhelmingly composed of white, upper-class men. But in a society of many different ethnic and nationality groups, democracy means an individual is not judged based on his or her group membership. In a society of many different religions and differing moral and ethical standards, democracy means an individual with a different lifestyle and beliefs is accorded respect and access to opportunity. Recapturing democracy requires the demand for cultural and personal diversity.

The Movement for Diversity

Whether it be the "Bloomer" girls who first dared to wear pants, the beatnik of the 1950s, the hippie or yuppie, or the lesbian or gay—democratic ideology declares you should be who you are as long as your lifestyle does not infringe on others' rights. The social movement for diversity exposes the way in which dominant group norms and their ideologies undermine democracy in American society. Dominant group norms are *not* necessary for the survival of the society; dominant group norms *are* necessary for the survival of stratification within society. Dominant group norms allow the groups at the top to retain privileges that lower groups do not have. That very fact is antithetical to democracy.

We have already discussed how our socialization teaches us labels and stereotypes. Many people believe that Hindus would rather starve to death before eating meat and that the Native Americans smoke peyote and get high. We do *not* know why these customs are important to these groups and the historical reasons for them.[23] In other words, we are not taught to *respect* Arabic or Native American culture.

Democratic ideology is more than simply respect for differences. It also holds that culture is improved and strengthened when people of different backgrounds and ideas inform one another and share their perspectives. Do we not all have something to teach each other? But as respect for diversity enters into the socialization of our young, serious questions willbe raised. The answers that justify inequality ("they aren't as smart as we are" or "they were less civilized" or "they are born weird") will no longer be correct. Respect for Native Americans, Hispanics, and Africans; respect for different religions and lifestyles; and respect for unique personal qualities that make people different challenge the social mechanisms of inequality.

For some people, their "pursuit of happiness" has required exploiting, degrading, and oppressing others. When the tobacco industry claims it has the right to addict teenagers to cigarettes, it is really defending its right to exploit and oppress them. Nicotine, which is as addictive as heroin, is a legal drug. Once hooked, the tobacco industry can be guaranteed a lifetime of profits, while the smoker or chewer is risking cancer.

The white supremacists who argue they have the right to distribute hate literature against Jews and Blacks are really defending their right to maintain white privilege. In other words, all "rights" are not equally valid *in a democracy*. The right to take the land of the Native Americans could be justified on the basis of economic interests or the racism of the politicians—*but it could not be, and still cannot be, justified by any standard considered democratic.*

The dream of equality and democracy has been one of the most powerful glues holding our society together. Groups who have been oppressed, exploited and degraded by social stratification in our culture have clung to this dream, believing that sometime, equality and democracy would triumph over racism, sexism, classism, and speciesism.

If the struggle to recapture democracy is not successful, our society *will* fracture across all our lines of differences. The only way a society such as ours can prevent fragmentation is to deepen our respect for differences and diversity. This is the opposite viewpoint to those who argue that multicultural education and respect for non-Christian religious perspectives will create fragmentation. I argue that it is the contracting economy that is laying the basis for possible fragmentation—but those in power do not want to acknowledge *that* perspective.

As the economy contracts, it becomes easier to blame someone who is different. When basic needs are not met, human beings may fight only for survival. A functioning democracy requires a system that provides for the basic needs of individuals and their families. How must democracy be redefined in an era of robotronic revolution that is creating unemployment, hunger, and homelessness?

The Demand for Economic Equity

Unequal access to opportunity in America has been mitigated by another reality—upward social mobility. Parents at the bottom of the ladder dreamed their children would be able to move up a rung, and often they did. As long as the economy was expanding it was possible for society to provide better standards of living for succeeding generations. This process kept alive the hope.

Successful capitalism and access to opportunity were synonymous in many people's minds. To a whole generation of American citizens, defense of democracy meant the defense of your refrigerator, recreational vehicle, a college education for your children, and a house fully paid for. As the economy has contracted, this definition of democracy is being questioned. Keeping your job meant working harder than the other guy, but how can you beat a robot? Who pays the taxes when you aren't working and the robots don't pay taxes? Where's the hope for the future when your college-educated children have to continue living at home after graduation because their jobs don't pay enough to support them?

The movement for economic equity is demanding that the material benefits of the new technology be used to better the quality of life for all, rather than continue to enrich the few. Instead of a few workers working long overtime hours, why aren't more workers employed in shorter work weeks? If robots can make cars and refrigerators, why can't human beings be freed to help the disabled, the elderly, and the youth? If high tech requires more education, why can't displaced workers be used as teachers' aides and why can't everyone go to college? Underlying these rather simple questions are some very challenging premises. Our society bases much of its ideology on the idea of individualism and private property. The stockholder of a robotronics firm will argue he "owns" the profits earned from a factory producing machines that puts workers out of work.

But one could look at it in a different way. The factory that builds those robots is also a social product. Thousands of workers' labor was involved in making the steel and building the original machines that made the machines now making machines. Countless mothers raised children to participate in that process. Hundreds of teachers taught those workers and generations of scientists added their knowledge. As long as the private ownership of that factory, and those before it, provided livelihoods for those workers, mothers, teachers, scientists, and other members of society, few questioned that such private ownership was in conflict with democracy.

Now technology is no longer seen as providing jobs; it is seen as depriving people of work. Technology is no longer providing a better quality of life; it is providing weapons of destruction and more pollution, sickness, and homelessness. How do we create meaningful work for people in a society ruled by robotronics? What kind of democracy do we need for the people to be able to answer that question? Citizens have a democratic right to question an economy where technology is being used against the majority.

It is in the poor minority communities of America that the full effects of gross economic inequity can be seen. In some areas of the inner city, real unemployment for young adult males is as high as 40 to 50 percent. Caol Stack, in her ethnography of a poor African American section of a Mid-western city notes that the emptiness and hopelessness of the job experience for black men and women, the control over meager (AFDC) resources by women, and the security of the kin network, militate against successful marriage or long-term relationships in The Flats. Stack concludes:

> Distinctively negative features attributed to poor families, that they are fatherless, matrifocal, unstable, and disorganized, are not general characteristics of black families living substantially below economic subsistence in urban America. The black urban family, embedded in cooperative domestic exchange, proves to be an organized tenacious, active, lifelong network.[24]

Instead of analyzing how unemployment and drugs force communities into alternative social arrangements, American society is much more likely to focus on some sort of "moral breakdown" by young blacks as being the problem. This way of looking at the economic crisis—in moral terms—is the basis of the conservative response, or the "Backlash."

THE BACKLASH

All the questions raised by the social movements discussed above challenge a power structure based on racism, sexism, classism, and speciesism. If the elite cannot argue with the *facts* of un employment, ecological destruction, and deteriorating health, they must find explanations that do *not* threaten their control. We cannot discuss social movements for democracy and equality without also discussing movements that arise to defend the existing system and its ideologies. What is the character of these backward movements?

Dr. Martin Luther King was accused of creating a backlash to the civil rights movement. He responded by saying that the forces of the backlash had always existed. But as long as racism was the norm and accepted, the racists did not have to go to the streets to protect their ideology and behavior. Only when racism was challenged in a major way did the racists have to *overtly* defend what they had defended for years.

The movements of the 1960s—against the war in Vietnam, against nuclear arms, and for expanding rights to women, people of color, and other excluded groups—were characterized as coming from the Left.[25] This political label connected the demands of these movements—for peace, civil rights, and greater equality—to socialism and communism. In contrast, movements organized to preserve the privileges of the elite and give greater power to the rich, whites, Protestants, and males were characterized as coming from the "right." This political label connected the agenda of these movements to fascism, racism, and patriarchy.

In Chapter 7 we pointed out that labels and stereotypes are often too simple and are used merely to "call names." Thus, in the political debates of the 1960s, the terms "leftist" and "rightwinger" were more often used to try to discredit the opponent than explore the political differences between the positions of the debaters.

During the period of the Cold War, the labels of "socialist" and "communist" were used to discredit movements that expanded democracy and equality. Well-financed organizations such as the World Anti-Communist League, the John Birch Society, and the Heritage Foundation supported political candidates who were willing to oppose civil rights and peace, and who would protect the privileges of the elite.[26] These same organizations used their money and influential networks within the media to convince Americans that communism was a greater threat than poverty, unemployment, domestic violence or racism. This perspective, acted out in foreign policy, has now created what *The New York Times Magazine* writer Tim Weiner called "blowback".[27] The U.S. government was willing to support any dictator or drug-dealing ruler as long as they were "anticommunist."

They have now been proven historically wrong. The socialist governments have collapsed, not by violent revolution or by attacks from without. Yet the United States still faces severe internal problems, and they can no longer be blamed on the communists! Those who want to preserve the status quo, or even return to a time when the elite had greater power, have had to find a new way to attack and discredit the emerging social movements.

THE CONTEMPORARY BACKLASH

According to many politicians, television preachers, and journalists everything was fine before today's "moral breakdown in values." These conservatives blame changing values for crime, unemployment, and homelessness.[28] Conservatives want to return to what they believe was a better value system of an earlier time. These values, of course, were those that justified the systems of stratification.

According to this conservative view, when women knew their places, divorce and juvenile delinquency were not problems. According to them the women's movement is responsible for the breakdown of the family. Television programming in the 1950s and 1960s helped establish the myth of a "happy family" that used to exist—back in the days of *Little House on the Prairie*, *The Waltons*, *The Partridge Family,* and the Beavers.[29]

Unemployment is blamed on pushy groups of minorities and women who took jobs away from the good workers. According to the conservatives, our schools gave better educations back when children could pray the Lord's Prayer at the beginning of the day. Teenage pregnancies were not a problem until girls learned about birth control and watched love scenes on television. Americans had pride in our country when we could cheer John Wayne as he slaughtered Native Americans. Men could be men back when manhood was not threatened by aggressive women and gay and lesbian rights activists. Everything was fine in the Good Old Days of social stability and "normality."

Our socialization usually did not teach us the facts about those "Good Old Days." We did not learn the real history of the American West and the slaughter of Native Americans. We did not learn the real history of how women were legally beaten by their husbands, denied access to birth control and died by the hundreds of thousands from self-induced abortions. We were not told of the ecological damage caused by the timbering of our mountains and the pollution of our air.

In the nineteenth century, the age of sexual consent in some states was nine or ten, and alcoholism and drug abuse were more rampant than today. Teenage childbearing peaked in the family-oriented 1950s. Marriages in pioneer days lasted a shorter time than they do now. Stephanie Coontz's study of the myths about American families argues that American families have always been in flux and often unstable. She concludes that we must see family pains as part of a larger social predicament and not react with guilt and blame.[30]

We are rarely taught how our actions and our choices are conditioned by powerful social forces. Only when social structure begins to break down does it become apparent how much our lives are dependent on outside forces. During the Great Depression of the 1930s, for example, millions did begin to question the social structure, as did the youth of the 1960s when they were forced to fight a war with which many did not agree.

The appeal to a better past—a more secure time when Mom stayed home, Dad had a job, everybody went to church, and you could walk the streets safely at night—is really an appeal to a time that described, at the most, ten percent of the population at any given time in our history. But these arguments touch a nerve with many Americans. First, this perspective reinforces our belief that individuals are totally responsible for their own problems. Second it speaks to the growing sense of powerlessness that is a result of the loss of community.

Conservatives resist extending democracy and equality past traditional boundaries. They see jobs, civil rights, and good education as the prerogative of whites, heterosexuals, and middle- and upper-class Christian people. For them, everything was fine until Hispanics, homosexuals, atheists, and the poor trash start wanting the same rights. The clearest popular expression of this position has been that of radio commentator Rush Limbaugh. The fact that he has been given wide publicity and access to the media indicates the extent to which those in power agree with or tolerate his views. There is no equivalent of Limbaugh from the opposite political perspective present in the national media.

In the conservative mind, our forefathers were able to defend their privileges against the demands of these outsiders. If we could only put such threatening groups back into their places, everything would be fine. In its most popular expression, this conservative ideology is linked with religion, but it would be a mistake to see it only in its religious form. Chapter 9 has already discussed how the very powerful Trilateral Commission was making essentially the same argument in 1976. At the same time, the conservative movement has readily used religion as a way to justify its ideology.

RELIGION AND CONSERVATISM

Religion meets two primary needs. It provides individuals with answers about the purpose of life and the meaning of death and it provides ethical and moral standards for social interaction. The religious ideological base ofconservatism is often identified as "fundamentalism." Many analysts refer to conservative religion as fundamentalism. But there are serious problems with that conceptualization. The real question is which religious beliefs one holds to be the most fundamental. Dr. Martin Luther King argued that he was a fundamentalist Christian but his social activism was based on the fundamental truths spoken by Christ—to love God and our neighbor.

Conservative fundamentalism urges individuals to see salvation as the main point of life, and not to worry about the rest of society. God's love for them is a reward because they have adopted a certain lifestyle, which includes giving money to the church and carrying out certain individual behaviors like prayer and church attendance. They may also improve their chances of getting to heaven if they don't drink, if women don't wear makeup or they shave their heads. In other words, individual life style behaviors are more important than how one treats other people.

They then claim to be the elect who are chosen because they are better people, and God prefers their lifestyles and beliefs to all others This kind of religion can even go so far as to assert that only white people will get to heaven or that only members of the Disciples of the Christian Church of the Little Valley will go through the Pearly Gates.[31]

Conservative fundamentalism provides participants with a sense of belonging and personal power that the larger society denies them. It promises to return the Good Old Days by restoring local control over school boards, local governments, and the media. But this local control is based on the demand to hold back multicultural education and return to education that reinforced patriarchy, class privilege, white supremacy, and speciesism. Pride in America can be restored by once again telling the glorious story of how the West was won and the savage heathens were driven from the land given to Euro-Americans by God.

In local elections where conservative fundamentalists have conducted campaigns, they have usually done so with what has been called a "hidden agenda." In other words, they have not openly told the voters what they real goals are. Like the politicians discussed earlier, who vote to cut taxes for the rich and oil companies but would never talk about that while campaigning, the conservative fundamentalists cannot reveal their agenda because it does go against the egalitarian norms of democracy and equality that so many Americans hold dear. Instead, the candidates with conservative fundamentalist views concentrate on attacking the lifestyles and values of their opponents. This effectively prevents public discussion of issues and programs—the very things that should be discussed in a campaign.

Martin Marty and Scott Appleby's study of contemporary conservative fundamentalism from a cross-cultural perspective suggests that rapid social change is affecting religion throughout the world. The United States is not the only culture experiencing a rise of religious conservatism. In searching for common themes that unite conservative fundamentalist movements in Christianity, Islam, Judaism, Hinduism and Confucianism they suggest the following definition:

1. They are *fighting back*. They are reactive, and see themselves as militants. Funda mentalists begin as traditionalists who perceive some challenge or threat to their core identity, both social and personal.
2. They are *fighting for* something. They are fighting for a worldview that they perceive as threatened. When the threat grows sufficiently intense, they will enter the secular realm to fight politically.
3. They are *fighting with* resources that they think of as weapons. They have selected those things in their ideology that they believe to be fundamental. They choose those features that will best reinforce their identity, keep their movement together, maintain boundaries and keep others at a distance.
4. They are *fighting against* others. Their enemy may be generalized or specific, but they are the agents of social change against all that is held dear.
5. They are *fighting under* God, or under some other transcendent power. This lifts their cause beyond rational debate, compromise, and toleration—for they alone have the truth.[32]

Conservative fundamentalism in the United States is intensely nationalistic. Fundamentalists have linked American military and economic might to the guarantee of their right to evangelize the world. The United States is the "city on a hill" ordained by God as the light to the nations.[33] A global world community in which all humans live in harmony with their cultural dif ferences and in balance with the environment is in polar opposition to the fundamentalist idea that the world must be reshaped in the form of their beliefs and reflective of their social position. Likewise, within American society, fundamentalists can assert their moral superiority by targeting and blaming certain groups who, because they are different, are the cause of society's evil and sins. An example of this perspective is the current backlash to the gay rights movement.

THE GAY RIGHTS MOVEMENT AND THE CONSERVATIVE RELIGIOUS BACKLASH

Many people find homosexuality to be a troubling idea. Our socialization in a patriarchal society includes not only the idea that men should play the leading role in sex but that sex ought always to be between a man and a woman. These beliefs are reinforced by religion ("anything else is a sin") by biological ideas ("it is not natural") and by popular culture ("it is disgusting").

It is useful to remember, however, that one hundred years ago a white person might have made exactly the same remarks in reaction to a textbook asserting African Americans were equal to European Americans and that the two races should "mix." When we discussed the Civil War it was pointed out that granting slaves their freedom did not automatically erase racism from America—many of the myths and beliefs still linger after one hundred years. So it is not surprising that heterosexual people have difficulty with the acceptance of homosexuality.

Many heterosexuals find it hard to believe two human beings of the same sex can truly love each other in the way that two heterosexuals can love. The stigma of the labels and stereotypes directed at gays and lesbians is so powerful that it is now estimated somewhere between one-third and one-half of all teenage suicides are committed by homosexual teenagers so fearful of the social sanctions that they take their lives.

The earlier discussion pointed out that democracy requires respect for lifestyle differences. What two human beings do in their private homes together does not impinge on the rights of others. Democracy guarantees minimal government regulation and control of one's private affairs. This allows those from different cultures and backgrounds to eat their own foods, pray in their own way, raise their children as they see fit, and keep a boa constrictor as a pet. Advocates of cultural and personal diversity ask that society not discriminate against a person because of choice of partner any more than society would discriminate against persons who feed their children cold sandwiches of pickled fish for breakfast or keep a snake named Snooky.

Most Americans, even those who do not approve of homosexuality, do not condone beating up people or firebombing their house because they are gay or lesbian. But once the conservative movement begins to blame social problems on gays and lesbians, those individuals who have reached the breaking point of stress have an "approved" target on which to vent their hostility. The young man who cannot get a good job and fulfill society's expectation of his role as a provider can go out and "gay bash" to prove he's still a man. The principal of the school that is underfunded and understaffed can redirect parents' anger by attacking a lesbian teacher. Parents who are afraid their daughters will get pregnant and their sons start using drugs can direct their fears on the homosexuals who have "undermined American values."

If one considers the enormity of the social crisis facing our society—between 4 and 6 million people homeless, thousands of babies born with AIDS, and an atmosphere so polluted that we can get cancer from the sun—the issue of whom one chooses for a partner seems trivial. But because the conservative religious movement has no real analysis or solutions for the larger problems, and because the issue of homosexuality can be defined as a breakdown of morality, they have made it a point of attack.[34] It acts to divide us further instead of bringing us together to seek constructive solutions to serious problems. And it serves to protect the privileged position of the elite.

THE ATTACK ON IMMIGRANTS

Just as gays and lesbians have been easy targets for blame, so have recent immigrants. The contraction of the economy, the lowering of wages, and the cutback in social services have heightened the competition between workers. Instead of seeing a system that fails to provide *all* workers with decent jobs, the conservatives focus on those who they say have taken "our" jobs. The idea that America "belongs" to Euro-Americans was easier to support at a time when most of the population was white. But as Figure 5.1 shows, that situation has changed dramatically.[35] America now belongs to many different ethnicities.

These feelings of hostility are fanned by the media and right-wing political commentators. Because on the face of it the charges appear to be true, Euro-American workers, and even some Chicano and African American workers, deeply resent the immigrants who have come to America to find a better life. Violence against persons of other national origins, particularly immigrants, has been on the rise as a result.

Immigrants from poverty-stricken countries are willing to accept wages and working conditions that many Americans would refuse, such as stoop labor in the fields. But even they are being affected by the robotronic revolution. In California, agribusiness has been mechanized, eliminating thousands of jobs for farm laborers. Large firms like Green Giant and Birds Eye have begun shifting to Mexico the growing of crops as well as the packing of vegetables. The operations manager of Birds Eye calculated that Mexican-grown broccoli cost his company about 25 percent less than identical California broccoli.[36]

Americans do not understand that these immigrants have been part of our social structure all along as "the invisible class"—sewing our shirts, picking our bananas, and making our athletic shoes. To the Conservative, "Americanism" translates into white, Christian, and English-speaking. Thus the backlash movement uses the color and cultural differences of the immigrants to reinforce racism.

Rarely does one see attacks on immigrants from Great Britain who have come to find a better life! Figure 5.1 shows that indeed the Lady of Liberty has increasingly raised her torch for non-European immigrants. In the first decade of this century, 93 percent of immigrants were European; in 1992 only

15 percent were European. Did the poem under the Statue of Liberty really mean "huddled *white* masses, yearning to be free?"

Figure 5.1

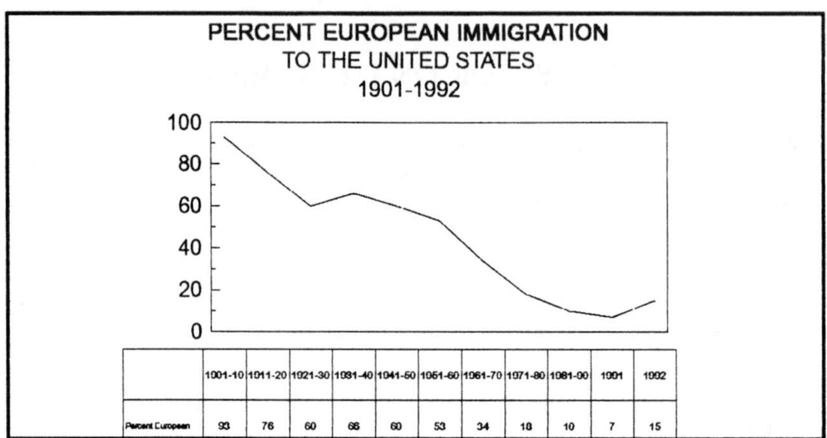

	1901-10	1911-20	1921-30	1931-40	1941-50	1951-60	1961-70	1971-80	1981-90	1991	1992
Percent European	93	76	60	66	60	53	34	18	10	7	15

Ellen Rosen, in her study of blue-collar women in a New England industrial town, found women born in America, with youth and education and previously held high-wage jobs, had the worst time becoming reemployed after a layoff. These are the women who had benefited most from the wage gains blue-collar women had made in the postwar period. Ironically, this wage advantage becomes a disadvantage when they lose their jobs and face the prospect of taking some of the worst wage cuts. Their perception of lost wages led many to refuse jobs they could have had. In contrast, the immigrant women in this community (in this case Portuguese) perceived the low-wage jobs as better than what they had worked for in the old country, and were more likely to accept the employment.[37] Instead of seeing the problem as an industry forcing down wages in order to maintain profit, many workers see the situation as "the Portuguese [or some other immigrant group] taking Americans' jobs."

The conservative backlash also accuses immigrants of "costing" America more in terms of social services. Although economists debate this issue, there is an argument to be made for the fact that as workers and consumers, the immigrants put more into the economy than they "take out."

The attack on immigrants plays on the anger of Americans who already resent the taxes they pay. This also directs their anger at those *below* them on the ladder, thereby deflecting the anger away from those *above* them on the ladder (who pay less and less in taxes).[38] Thus, the backlash again serves the purpose of confusing the issues and setting people against one another rather than solving the problems created by the system.

THE BACKLASH: LEADERS VERSUS FOLLOWERS

Many participants in the conservative movements do not see or understand the antidemocratic ideology of their leadership. For example, good people, truly concerned about our society's neglect of children and disregard for human life, can easily be organized around an antiabortion platform. Many do not see that the right of a woman to decide when to have children as key for women in modern society. In order to pursue education and careers, women must have the right to choose when to have their children.

The leaders of the antiabortion crusades are fundamentally opposed to women playing any role but that of wife and mother. They want to turn the clock back to the time when women were "barefoot and pregnant." If questioned, one finds that many of those leaders are also opposed to birth control of any kind, except "natural rhythm." The politicians elected by these movements have voted *against* government funding for day-care centers and expanded health care for poor children. In other words, the simple principle that "killing a fetus is murder" really overlays a more fundamental principle that uncontrolled pregnancy and childrearing keep women "in their place."

Mimi Abramovitz argues that the Conservative attempt to restore "family values" is really an attempt to regulate women:

> The family ethic derives from patriarchal social thought that sees gender roles as biologically determined rather than socially assigned and from standard legal doctrine that defines women as the property of men. The idea of natural differences between the sexes causes individuals to see their femininity and masculinity solely as part of human nature rather than as the product of socialization.
>
> The implication that biology is destiny also obscures the historical impact of differential socialization and unequal opportunities on the choices made by individuals of different sexes, races, and ages, By making these choices seem natural and rational, the family ethic helps to justify discrepancies between societal promises and realities, to rationalize prejudice, discrimination, and inequalities, and to promote the acquiescence of the oppressed in their oppression. Finally, the direct appeal to nature as the source of gender differences minimizes the cultural determination of women's sexuality, the significance of changes in

> women's position over time, and the importance of women's private domestic labor to both capitalist production and patriarchal arrangements. Like most ideologies, the ideology of women's roles represent dominant interests and explain reality in ways that create social cohesion and maintain the status quo.[39]

Conservative religious leaders want to define the problems facing today's children as moral issues arising out of sins. According to them, abortion and homosexual child molesters are the most important issues. This focus keeps the attention of the public away from the real attack on our children and families—cutbacks in educational opportunities for young women, lack of accessible birth control, and too few day care centers.

In contrast, those who represent the movement for democracy argue we should address the fact that nearly 20 percent of this nation's children go hungry.[40] But ending abortion rights will not cost the elite any money while programs to feed the hungry might put pressure on the wealthy to pay more taxes!

The conservative movement not only supports elitist ideologies, but is elitist in its own structures. The leaders of such movements have some "truth," and their followers must acquiesce to their superior knowledge. If democratic ideology is premised on the idea that all should participate in decisions that affect them, the conservative movement is based on providing answers to those below. Whether it be television evangelists, politicians, or militia leaders, the fears and frustration of the "masses" can be manipulated by those who know the "truth."[41]

The belief that ordinary human beings are capable of intelligent and moral decisions is the very cornerstone of a democratic society. What will happen as these two strong currents— the movement to increase democracy and equality and the movement to conserve stratification—meet head-on in the twenty-first century?

SUMMARY

Previous social movements in American history have focused on improving the life chances of particular groups—slaves, women, workers. In the 1960s there was a new wave of social movements to include groups on the bottom rungs within the general prosperity of the country. These movements were known as civil rights movements and included minorities, the aged, women, gays and lesbians, the disabled, and other groups that have faced oppression and exploitation.

Today's social movements are facing issues that cut across group boundaries because they affect the quality of life for all—health care, the environment, and the existence of democracy. There are two different directions arising. One direction is that of expanding equality and democracy and egalitarian norms. A second direction is to return to earlier dominant group norms and the protection of privilege.

Dominant group norms of speciesism violate cultural imperatives and actually threaten the survival of the planet. As toxic wastes and other dangers increase, groups at the bottom of the ladder are the most susceptible to exposures—a form of environmental racism and sexism. Some companies have used public awareness of pollution as the basis for profits without genuine concern for the long-range impact of policy. Other companies have attempted to avoid environmental policies in the United States by operating in countries with less restrictive standards.

As the cost of health care has skyrocketed, the proportion of Americans without health insurance has risen dramatically. Meanwhile, cutbacks in public health programs have opened the door to threats of new epidemics. Increased pollution of air, water, and food has increased the rate of cancer and other diseases. Public awareness of these factors and the enormous profits of the health industries have led to a growing social movement to provide policies that would ensure quality affordable health care to all.

The corruption of public officials and the growing control over politics exercised by lobbyists representing wealthy interests has raised awareness of the need to evaluate how democracy functions. This has led to demands in the area of electoral reform, legislation to protect and enhance diversity, and policies to provide economic equity.

Rapid social changes and the increase of social pain have led many Americans to view the past as a time when everyone was happy. This view distorts the fact that large groups of Americans were enslaved, oppressed, and exploited for the benefit of the happy few. The "backlash" desires to return to a time of Good Old Days when social boundaries were clear (men were men and blacks knew their place). This longing is most often expressed in terms of religious ideology—the demand to return to "old-fashioned" values.

The political movement to restore dominant group norms is currently taking the form of conservative fundamentalism. This movement links the insecurity felt by millions of Americans to the return to traditional religious values. This movement sees alternative lifestyles as a major threat and thus fails to address issues of social stratification and power.

Discussion Questions

1. Sociologists and anthropologists have studied how societies react to change. In general, people find social change difficult to accept. Once we

learn what to believe and how to do something, we like to continue to do it that way. At the same time, we all like the possible benefits that new technologies may bring. Discuss the ways in which your parents and/or grandparents have resisted certain technological changes that you have accepted. Why is it easier for the young to accept change?

2. This chapter raises the issue, what *kinds* of social change? What is the appeal of the social movements that argue we must react in terms of "values?" What values would be the most important to you in reacting to social change? How is it possible that your "values" may make it difficult for someone who is different than you to enjoy the same democratic rights and equality that you may experience?

3. Which direction of social movements do you think the super rich find the most threatening? Why?

Resources

Book: Stephanie Coontz, *The Way We Never Were: American Families and the Nostalgia Trap*

Novels, television and the movies have given us our view of the past. In this book Coontz argues that this view has been highly distorted. We are operating on false premises and that is dangerous. Some of these data are shocking, and sometimes amusing. But if you want a "reality check," you might want to read this book.

NOTES

Complete citations are provided in the Bibliography.

1. Alston and Brown 1993,182–84.
2. Snell 1991.
3. Bullard 1993, 22.
4. The relationship between the oppression of women and the ideology of speciesism is analyzed by Warren and Cheny 1995. Also see Warren and Wells-Howe 1994.
5. Bullard 1993, 17.
6. Bailey et al 1993,107–12.
7. Churchill and LaDuke 1992, 241–66; Alston and Brown 1993, 182–83.
8. *Organic Gardening* 42,1, January 1995, 22.
9. Ladd 1993.
10. Bullard's (1993) collection of essays on such struggles documents the growth of what he calls the "environmental justice" movement.
11. An excellent example of that debate can be found in the two opposing articles on this issue in the November 1993 *Scientific American*: Bhagwati's "The Case for Free Trade" and Daly's "The Perils of Free Trade."

12. *The Nation*, 28 June 1993, 895.

13. *Charleston Gazette*, 16 June 1993.

14. An early, but cogent critique of the failures of the American health system was made by the Health Policy Advisory Center 1970.

15. J. Jones 1981.

16. Shilts 1987. Brandt (1988) explains the difficulties of dealing with an epidemic such as AIDS and why political and value-laden programs won't work.

17. DRGs are Diagnostic Related Groups and set limits on what Medicare and Medicaid will pay for certain problems. These kinds of regulations were the subject of the movie *Article 99* about doctors forced to break the law to deliver health care to patients in a Veterans Ad ministration hospital. Today DRGs are being replaced by similar restrictions from HMOs.

18. Garrett 1994.

19. I am grateful to feminist philosopher Sandra Harding for her analysis that we must "recapture democracy," which I heard at the Eastern Sociology Society meetings in 1992. Her ideas are developed in *The Racial Economy of Science: Toward a Democratic Future* (1993).

20. Grieder's (1992) analysis of the federal government is typical of these current critiques. A parallel critique from a Conservative perspective is that of Kevin Phillips 1994.

21. *Business Week*, 18 March 1996, 4.

22. Parenti 1994.

23. Harris 1989.

24 Stack 1974, 109, 124.

25. The terms "left" and "right" originated in France after their Revolution. The represen tatives of the royalty and aristocracy sat on the right and the representatives of the common people sat on the left in the parliamentary chamber.

26. See Bellant 1991a and 1991b.

27. Weiner 1994.

28. A powerful rebuttal to their position that the "breakdown" of the family is a result of changing values is made by the readings in Voydanoff and Majka 1988.

29. Spigel 1992.

30. Coontz 1992.

31. I made up the name of this church. But such churches, and beliefs, do exist.

32. Marty and Appleby 1991, ix–x.

33. Ammerman 1991, 40; Finch 1983.

34. See "The Coors Family and Gay Rights" in Bellant 1991b, 62–66.

35. Data adapted from Kivisto 1995, 86 and *Statistical Abstract of the United States 1994*.

36. Takaki 1990, 308.

37. Rosen 1987 139–41.

38. Bartlett and Steele 1993.

39. Abramovitz 1988, 36–37.

40. Center on Hunger, Poverty and Nutrition Policy, Tufts University, June 1993.

41. Bellant 1991b.

16

A VISION FOR THE FUTURE

From the cowardice that dares not face new truth,
from the laziness that is contented with half-truth,
from the arrogance that thinks it knows all truth,
Good Lord, deliver me.

—Kenyan Prayer

AIDS is rapidly becoming the number-one killer of young men in our society, but the richest nation on earth is unable to allocate enough funds to prevent its spread or research its treatment fully. According to the *Journal of the American Medical Association* federal researchers analyzing 1990 mortality data found that AIDS and illnesses related to HIV were the number-one killer of young men in five states and sixtyfour cities nationwide. Among young women, AIDS and AIDS-related illnesses were the leading killer in nine cities.[1]

The U. N. World Health Organization report for 1996 warns that the global spread of untreatable forms of malaria and tuberculosis and the emergence of killers like AIDS and Ebola threaten to undermine recent advances in health care. The organization in the United States that must lead the fight against infectious disease, the Centers for Disease Control (CDC) had a fiscal budget last year of $7.2 million, of which $1.8 million alone was spent on stopping the Ebola epidemic. Compare these dollar amounts with what was spent make a *movie* about Ebola—*Outbreak*. The production budget for the movie was $54 million and the star of the movie (Dustin Hoffman) received a salary of $54 million![2]

We face a crisis of clean water in the next century, but we continue to pour toxic chemicals into our precious groundwater. Our inner cities are deteriorating into war zones, and we continue to build prisons and cut back education. Life in America as we know it will not continue into the twenty-first century. No matter what cultural, egalitarian, and dominant group norms characterize a society, that society cannot violate basic cultural imperatives.

This textbook has not only attempted to *describe* stratification and power in America, but has explored the *consequences* of this stratification and power. Although most of us can observe some of these consequences in our everyday lives, we have no way of knowing or understanding the full range of problems until we study a text such as this. As you have read the preceding chapters, you may have reacted, as my students did—all right, what can we *do* about this? What is the answer? If I, the author, am the "expert" (and I must be if I wrote this book) then surely I have some solution to propose that will tell you what we need to do to restore our society to health.

But I have no such solutions, nor do I believe that any easy solution exist. If I, as a sociologist, tried to impose "my" answers on society, no matter how well meaning my answers might be, I would be an elitist. My ideas and arguments can only become part of the people's search for their own answers. But I do believe certain conclusions emerge from this textbook that can guide us in the search for those answers.

THE SEARCH FOR POTENTIALITY

Stratification has often been viewed as a necessary evil. If someone had to do stoop labor in the fields, scrub the floors, and mine the coal, who was to get the dirty jobs? If someone was needed to administer and make decisions, who was to get the clean and safe jobs? In other words, almost all social hierarchies believe that lower classes were inevitably necessary and there was nothing that could be done to change that. God, fate, or luck determined who ended up on top or bottom. This necessity meant the full creative and intellectual potentials of the majority of human beings could never be developed.

Human beings exhausted and mentally drained by hours on the assembly line or in front of a hamburger counter cannot go home and write poetry or solve math problems. Women exhausted by childbirth and running around after small children cannot paint pictures and design space technologies after the children are put to bed. People of color who must daily confront hostility and prejudice and suffer the stresses of hate cannot concentrate on their studies and become great doctors. The talents and energies locked up inside every human being must be given a *supportive* environment in order to grow and develop.

For the first time in human history the possibilities of robotronics allow us to contemplate the entire potential of the world's population. The new technologies can produce the necessities of life with a minimum of human labor. With intelligent machines to do work that is routine, boring, dangerous, and tiring, we can free humans to do those things the machines cannot. The implications of this for democracy are astounding.

People freed from demeaning and exhausting labor and supplied with the necessary supportive environment can become truly informed and educated about the world around them. Ordinary people will be able to participate in debates about issues that affect them—the global economy, medical discoveries, environmental issues. Individuals will have access to the material necessities that make their lives good—food, health care, recreation, and the arts. They will have time to develop their own skills and hobbies—art, photography, computers, literature, architectural design. And individuals will be freed to participate in community life—working with children, the elderly, and environmental improvement.

This vision is the alternative to the ugly realities described in this text. The existing structures of power are using the new technologies against human beings and against nature. Paul Kennedy's *Preparing for the 21st Century* describes a new century in which the poor get poorer, the rich richer and the environment increasingly the victim of grave, irreversible damage.[3] He forecasts increasing social unrest, both at home and globally, and mass migrations from the poor countries to the rich. His depressing analysis does not include an understanding of human resistance to exploitation, oppression or degradation, nor does he see the important role of social movements acting in history.

But the new technologies hold a potential for being used in the different manner—to free our human capabilities and to restore our ecological balance. We cannot search for those potentials unless we first believe they are there.

I started writing this book on a 386 computer using WordPerfect 5.1, changed to a 486SX and WordPerfect 5.2 for Windows, and have finished the book on a Pentium computer using WP 7. In comparison to my previous two books, written on a typewriter, this book has been immeasurably easier and more fun. With computers, anyone can draw, design, do desktop publishing and analyze data. What were once skills of the elite can now be used by anyone with the interest and time. These skills can produce community newsletters, make videos for the schools, publish stories written by sixth graders, and keep track of the finances of the local recreation center.

The new communication technologies now make true global understanding possible. Citizens around the world can watch each other's television programs and communicate via satellite using phones, modems, or videos. If robotronics were organized to produce food and medical services based on need instead of selling the highest priced goods to the richest people, the world's population could be fed and clothed.

A recent article in the *National Geographic* poses the existing contradiction between the old, dangerous and unhealthy machinery and the new, safe, and clean robotronics, that puts people out of work. The author of the article describes two factories:

"In Ahmadabad (India), where Mahatma Gandhi held his first fast—in support of textile workers striking for higher wages—I walked through a mill owned by Arvind Mills Ltd. An enormous weaving shed was packed with more than 400 looms. Shipped from England to India, some of these machines are nearly a hundred years old.

Inside the mill the industrial revolution was a reality. To drive the looms, huge wheels along the ceiling clattered and clanked, now run by electricity but powered by steam engines in the 19th century. Cotton dust had accumulated on the windows and on every pipe and loom and wire.

Overhead the pipes sprayed mist into the air to moisten the cotton fiber. The workers, all men, wore only cotton loincloths, or dhotis, because of the unbearable heat and humidity. I stopped to talk with one of them, but he couldn't hear me. Then I realized he was deaf. Although some of the workers were speaking, no sound came from their mouths. They were lip-reading—some of them permanently deafened by the unrelenting noise. How could this mill, with its antiquated machines and intolerable conditions, be the world's second largest maker of denim, as I'd been told?"

The author then enters the plant's new operation, based on robotronics. (His description of this new part of the factory was used in Chapter 13.) He concludes: "(New) Factories like this one could take away thousands of jobs from desperately poor people if they replaced India's small mills and traditional handweavers. Recognizing that danger, the Indian government restricted the growth of modern mills and is attempting to expand the market for handicrafts" (Thompson, 1994).

Here is the dilemma—should people be kept in low- wage jobs that create deafness and trap them forever in poverty or should modern factories be built and those people be left with no job at all? The *National Geographic* author does not offer the third option. The son or daughter of the deaf and poverty-stricken mill worker could be given an education and given an opportunity for creative and useful work—while the machines do the dangerous, dirty, and boring work.

There is a widely held belief that starvation in today's world is due to overpopulation. Although population must ultimately be controlled, today's famines are *not* caused by a shortage of food but the misallocation of agricultural resources. Meeting the needs of the world's hungry requires more than birth control; it requires a response to global stratification and global ecological damage.

Food is not grown to meet the needs of hungry people; food is grown to meet the need of the world's markets to get the highest price. Thus, fields that once grew corn and rice now grow artichokes and celery. At the same time, the long-term consequences of using pesticides and chemical fertilizers are increasing the threat of eventual starvation due to the poisoning of the environment. Identifying and choosing technologies based on protection of the earth and real human need could reverse the destruction of the environment.

Most people do not understand the wonderful potentials of the new technology because they see its application only under the current system. It is easy to blame the technology for our problems and more difficult to see the problems as a result of the social structure. *Yet that is the first step toward a solution—correctly identifying both the positive potentials of the robotronics revolutions and identifying the forces that are holding back that potential.*

CREATING THE CHANGE

You may agree with this analysis so far, but still ask how we get to the point of realizing such potential? How do we make these changes in the social structure?

The answer to the question lies in the process of recapturing and redefining what we mean by democracy in this new age. If we wait for some leader who has all the answers, we are merely reinforcing elitism. In a large and diverse society, there can be no one "right" answer that any single individual thinks up.

I know what I think, and that is based on my socialization, my religion, my experiences,and my interests. These may be very different from yours. It is the *debate* and *dialogue* between many people with many different ideas about how we make the change that the answers emerge. Democratic ideology provides the parameters of that debate—*your ideas are valid if they promote opportunities for all; if they are based on respect of differences; if they acknowledge the contributions that everyone can make. Your ideas are not valid if they continue to advocate exploitation, oppression and degradation of some for the benefit of others.*

Our country was originally founded upon such a debate—the debate over our Constitution. But that debate violated the parameters above, for it was framed by the necessity to keep African Americans in bondage, to build a military force capable of taking Native American lands, to maintain women in a subordinate status, and to exploit the earth. If today's debate is framed by the necessity to keep using the cheap labor of foreign workers and exploiting the natural resources of less powerful countries it will also be invalid. The understanding of democracy must be expanded to include all peoples. The poor peasant of Mexico, the slum dweller of Rio de Janeiro, the factory worker of Taiwan, and the copper miner in Zambia all have an equal right to share the good life with the middle-class college student in Iowa.

NATIONALISM VERSUS GLOBAL DEMOCRACY

One of the most powerful ideologies of social stratification is nationalism. White supremacy in our history has been closely connected to patriotism and nationalism. Just as conservative religious ideology argues that only certain people deserve heaven, so nationalism argues that one's nation is more deserving than other nations. According to them, we Americans have a greater right to the good life.

The conservative movement discussed in the previous chapter defends nationalism because it fears a "World Government" that will destroy "Americanism." They are right. A world government run by the elites of the world will not only destroy our national identities, but create a global stratification system where the many will continue to be poor while a few grow richer and richer. The "New World Order" advocated by former President George Bush is *not* a vision of global democracy; it is a vision of global elitism.

But what the conservatives want is a return to the Old World Order, where a majority of the American people maintained high standards of living off the exploitation, oppression, and degradation of minorities within their own countries and peoples of the less developed nations. There is another alternative. That alternative is a vision that sees people of the world organized as equal partners in an effort to create peace, provide a good life for all, and protect and safeguard our planet.

Does the slum dweller in Chicago receive any benefit from maintaining poverty in the slums of Rio de Janeiro? In the summer of 1993, wire services shocked American readers with reports that a "hit squad" had killed seven homeless children in Rio de Janeiro, Brazil. The country has an estimated 7 million street children and over the past year alone 320 abandoned minors have been killed. Amnesty International charged that store owners were hiring the death squads to eliminate street children suspected of stealing. The squads were said to be composed of drug traffickers, off-duty police, and freelance gunmen. Are such killings really much different than the drive-by shootings that are killing so many American youths?

The Latino fruit picker in Florida and the Tanzanian fruit picker in Arusha will both get sick from the same chemicals used to increase fruit production. The deformed child born in Vietnam suffers from Agent Orange just as the Vietnam vet exposed to Agent Orange suffers in the United States. In other words, the destructive effects of the robotronics revolution are shared across the globe.

A WORLD WITHOUT THE IDEOLOGIES OF STRATIFICATION

The ideology of equality rejects patriarchy and strikes at the heart of stratification. If our children are raised in homes that are governed by egalitarian norms, and in which exploitation, oppression, and degradation based on gender is absent, are they not more like to recreate such egalitarian relationships in the larger society?

If every woman across the globe asserts her right to raise her child to his or her fullest potential, what will be the basis for continuing social stratification? Under patriarchy, men run governments and fight wars while women are charged with the responsibility for ensuring the survival and happiness of the next generation. Increasingly women are saying that they cannot raise their children in this kind of world unless fundamental changes are made.

The international women's movement is beginning to articulate some of these principles.[4] In refugee camps in Asia and Latin America, women are stepping forward to maintain life when the patriarchal social structure breaks down. In the Middle East, Jewish, Christian, and Muslim women have tried to come together to seek their common ground.

An article in the *Dar es Salaam News* described the role of women in the ethnic wars of Africa:

> [In the refugee camps] Traditional, male dominated society structures often breakdown in the upheaval of flight and resettlement. Men cannot claim any longer to be the main providers for the household and women may have to assume this role. The psychological consequences of becoming a refugee can be worse for men because they have lost their previous position of power and status. They are unemployed, often idle and confined. On the other hand, many women who have always been on the lower ranks of society, have less to lose. Women keep on doing the basic and crucial tasks, they have always done: domestic and productive work, childcare, fetching fuel and water.[5]

Environmentalists are making the same arguments. All people of the world share the oceans and the atmosphere. The nuclear emissions of one nation contaminate all nations. When a plant species that could be used to cure cancer is eliminated by deforestation, cancer victims in every country are affected. An ideology that would put the long-range protection of our planet ahead of monetary advantage would strike deep at the heart of elitism.

The terrible civil war in Bosnia, the ethnic slaughters in Somalia, Rwanda, and India, and the gang wars of our inner cities all speak to the terror that befalls when individual groups continue to put their power and control ahead of the community good. Behind all these wars lays the powerful interests of the arms manufacturers of the world, who make billions of dollars in blood money from promoting and encouraging armed conflict. *The world can no longer afford nationalism and racism—they will destroy us all.*

DEFENDING DEMOCRACY

Our forefathers used the ideas of democracy to found a nation in which only white educated men who owned property could vote. The ideas of democracy have been continually expanded, not through the leadership of the elite but by powerful social movements from below. These demands used the ideology of democracy as a basis for explaining and legitimating their cause.

The early chapters pointed out that there were different definitions, depending on where you sat on history's ladder. The elite didn't even actually use the term democracy—they wanted a republic where "freedom" meant the right to own slaves, take land from the Native Americans, and to exploit immigrant labor. To the majority of Americans, however, freedom meant the right to a decent life, land, and opportunities for your children.

Today we are again facing the question of "what do we mean by democracy?" What if the robotronics revolution requires that the old ideals of democracy be abandoned as "unworkable"? The elite want us to believe that to stop crime we must give up the constitutional right to bear arms, the protection against search and seizure, and other civil liberties. Just as Huxley predicted in *The Brave New World*, stability and order in a highly stratified world means redefining democracy.

You might reply, "But that is ridiculous! No one in this country would suggest we shouldn't have democracy." You are wrong. We have already pointed out that the Trilateral Commission publicly argued for the "moderation" of democracy in 1976. *Business Week*, a popular and widely read magazine of business, makes an argument in a major article in 1993 that under certain conditions, dictatorship is preferable to democracy for economic growth and development.[6]

As social conditions for the majority continue to deteriorate, direct social control will become more and more an "answer." We have already discussed the use of prisons, drugs and gang warfare as ways to control populations that can no longer be promised the good life. Direct social control, however, implies that ideological control is no longer there. That means the consensus of the ruled has disappeared. This consensus has been the underpinning of American democracy.

As funds for education are cut back and more prisons, longer prison sentences, and expansion of the death penalty is mandated, we can see the choices the politicians are making.[7] *The ideological struggle in the next decades will be between the arguments to protect the elite at the expense of democracy, and the arguments to expand democracy at the expense of the privileged elites.*

Few of us believe we have much power. Yet we do, but not as individuals. History tells us that our power comes from joining in social movements. These movements do not have to spring to life as massive national movements. They can begin as small movements, in our own communities, on our own campuses, and in our own workplaces.

We will not get drugs out of our communities until community organizations take back the streets. The police, judges, and courts are all part of the bureaucracies that are gridlocked and bribed. Our schools will not be able to truly teach our children until ordinary parents, grandparents, and concerned citizens wrest them away from the massive bureaucracies that are paralyzing learning. Our air, water, and wildlife will not be cleaned or safe until we demand that the earth comes before profits for the few. The political parties who run candidates and control local offices on behalf of the elite must be thrown out by organizations whose power is based on the ordinary people.

While we are struggling to reorganize the structure of our society, we must also struggle to change ourselves and our children. This book discussed how our socialization has planted ideas in our head that continually reinforce inequality. Only when we begin to see ourselves in harmony with each other and the earth; only when we can respect each other and value our differences—will we be able to achieve the democratic dream.

The American people believe in democracy. But they are also frightened. They are frightened by economic insecurity, crime, and the threat of illnesses they cannot afford. They are worried about their children and grandchildren. They are confused by the new technologies.

Some leaders will try to do what Hitler did—provide a scapegoat to blame. **Scapegoats** are those who with less power who can be blamed for social problems. The social movements of the right-wing will target the "others"—people on the rungs below us rather than those who sit at the top. Whether it be "niggers," "japs," "fags," "treehuggers," or "feminazis," there will be a temptation to let stereotypes and hate explain inequality. It is much more difficult for people to see the problem as systemic, and to realize they have to fully participate in the solution. It is easier to sit home, watch television, and send your money in to some demagogue who has found the people you can blame.

But at the same time, Americans are deeply committed to the ideologies of democracy and equality. They accept the fundamental idea that all human beings are created equal and they want peace and prosperity and a healthy planet for their children and grandchildren to inherit. We have to believe that our society can be reorganized around *these* ideologies. Who will be the leaders to provide *this* vision? Who will be the thinkers and activists that organize around these principles?

The answer to that question lies with you, the reader.

SUMMARY

How do we find the solutions for the serious social problems generated by inequality? How do we use new technologies to create new potentialities for all human beings? There are no easy answers. Any one person who tries to "give" answers is only providing his or her own viewpoint.

The answers for a better society must be generated out of a process of debate and dialogue. That process must be governed by egalitarian norms—the answers must provide equal opportunities for all and an end to the degradation, oppression, and exploitation of any groups.

This extension of democracy will have to be global. The world government so feared by many today is a world government of elites, that would force all people down to a level of extreme exploitation. The alternative view must be of a world where all peoples can equitably share the benefits of knowledge and technology.

Finding these answers requires that all people participate. Relying on a few leaders with a "quick fix" that blames some one else will not provide the solutions. It will be up to ordinary people like us to create our future.

Vocabulary

Scapegoats. Groups with less power who can be blamed for social problems; the most famous example were Germany's Jews, whom Hitler blamed for the economic depression following World War I.

Discussion Questions

1. A popular saying is "Think globally, act locally." In the light of the discussion in this chapter, what does that mean to you?

2. When you hear that there is war in a place like Bosnia or Liberia, how are you supposed to respond? Do you know the history, politics, and geography of that region? How can you know what is best for equality and democracy? Discuss the difficulties of being "informed citizen." Why is your own education such an important part of this?

3. Do you believe that the problems described in this book will be solved through the existing political channels open to us? Or will we need another era of social movements? In your answer discuss the ways in which you think *you* will end up responding.

4. If you were drafting legislation to address the question of who benefits from the new technology, what kinds of policies would you suggest? Why?

NOTES

Complete citations are provided in the Bibliography.

1. *Journal of the American Medical Association,* June 1993.
2. *Business Week*, 21 August 1995.
3. Kennedy 1994.
4. *Ms.* magazine carries a section in every issue entitled "Sisterhood Is Global: International News."
5. "Refugee Women Hold Families Together" by a Correspondent writing for World Food Programme. Special Feature, *Dar Es Salaam News*, 8 March 1991.
6. *Business Week.*
7. Chapter 11 discussed the problems of the schools—cutbacks in funding, elimination of programs, and diminishing career prospects. Yet more and more states are now trying to "solve" the problem of student alienation, and poor attendance, by *jailing parents* if their children don't attend class!

BIBLIOGRAPHY

Abramovitz, Mimi. *Regulating the Lives of Women: Social Welfare Policy from Colonial Times to the Present.* Boston: South End Press 1988.

Adler, Paul S. *Technology and the Future of Work.* New York: Oxford University Press 1992.

Allen, Gary. *None Dare Call It Conspiracy.* California: Bucaneer Books 1990.

Alston, Dana, and Nicole Brown. "Global Threats to People of Color," in Bullard 1993, 179–94.

American Association of University Women. *How Schools Shortchange Girls.* Wellesley, MA: Wellesley College Center for Research on Women 1993.

Ammerman, Nancy T. "North American Protestant Fundamentalism." in Marty and Appleby 1991. 1–65.

Amnesty International. *The 1993 Report on Human Rights Around the World.* Alameda, CA: Hunter House 1993.

Amott. Teresa L. and Julie A. Matthaei. *Race, Gender and Work: A Multicultural History of Women in the United States.* Boston: South End Press 1991.

Anand, Valerie. *The Ruthless Yoemen.* New York: St. Martin's Press, 1991.

Anderson, Margaret and Patricia Hill Collins, eds. *Race, Class and Gender.* Belmont, CA: Wadsworth 1992.

Apple, Michael. "Curricular Form and the Logic of Technical Control." in Apple and Weis 1983, 143–65.

Apple, Michael and Lois Weis. *Ideology and Practice in Schooling*. Philadelphia: Temple University Press, 1983.

Applebome, Peter, "Scandals Aside, TV Preachers Thrive." *New York Times*, 8 October 1989, 12.

Aronowitz, Stanley and W. DiFazio. *The Jobless Future*. Minneapolis: University of Minnesota Press, 1994.

Aronson, Steven M.L. "Luce Talk." *Town and Country, 147 no. 5155* (April 1993): 74–79, 127–31.

Attewell, Paul. "Skill and Occupational Changes in U.S. Manufacturing." Adler: 1992, 46–88.

Aulette, Judy Root, and Raymond Michalowski. "Fire in Hamlet: A Case Study of a State-Corporate Crime." in Kenneth Tunnell, ed. *Political Crime in America: A Critical Approach.* New York: Garland 1993, 171–206.

Bagdikian, Ben. *The Media Monopoly*. Boston: Beacon Press, 1993.

Bailey, Conner, et al. "Environmental Politics in Alabama's Blackbelt." in Bullard 1993, 107–22.

Barak, Gregg. *Gimme Shelter: A Social History of Homelessness in Contemporary America.* New York: Praeger, 1991.

Barlett, Donald L., and James B. Steele. *America: Who Pays the Taxes?* Kansas City, KS: Andrews & McMeel 1993.

——. *America: What Went Wrong?* Kansas City, KS: Andrews & McMeel 1992.

Barnett, Harold C. *Toxic Debts and the Superfund Dilemma.* Chapel Hill: University of North Carolina Press, 1995.

Barrera, Mario. *Race and Class in the Southwest: A Theory of Racial Inequality*. Notre Dame, IN: University of Notre Dame Press, 1979.

Barrera, Mario, et al. *Work, Family, Sex Roles and Language: Selected Papers of the National Association for Chicano Studies.* Berkeley, CA: Tonatiuh-Quinto Sol International, 1980.

Bassuk, Ellen L., et al.. *Supplementary Statement on Health Care for Homeless People*. National Academy of Sciences, Washington, DC, 1988. In McKenzie 1990, 409–13.

Bellant, Russ. *The Coors Connection: How Coors Family Philanthropy Undermines Democratic Pluralism.* Boston: South End Press, 1991a.

——. *Old Nazis, the New Right, and the Republican Party.* Boston: South End Press, 1991b.

Bendix, Reinhard, and Seymour Martin Lipset. *Class, Status, and Power: Social Stratification in Comparative Perspective. 2nd ed.* New York: Free Press, 1966.

Bennet, Lerone. *Before the Mayflower: A History of Black America.* New York: Penquin Books, 1982.

Berk, Sarah Febstermaker. *The Gender Factory: The Apportionment of Work in American Households.* New York: Plenum Press, 1985.

Bhagwati, Jagdish. "The Case for Free Trade." *Scientific American 269, no. 5 (*November 1993).

Blea, Irene Isabel. "Bruheria: A Sociological Analysis of Mexican American Witches." In Barrera, et al. 1980, 177–93.

Bluestone, Barry and Bennett Harrison. *The Great U-Turn: Corporate Restructuring and the Polarization of America.* New York: Basic Books, 1988.

——. The *Deindustrialization of America: Plant Closings, Community Abandonment, and the Dismantling of Basic Industry*. New York: Basic Books, 1982.

Bonacich, Edna. "Inequality in America: The Failure of the American System for People of Color." Andersen and Collins, eds., 1992.

Booth, Alan, ed. *Contemporary Families: Looking Forward, Looking Back.* Minneapolis, MN: National Council on Family Relations 1991, 341–60.

Bowles, Samuel, and Herbert Gintis. *Schooling in Capitalist America: Educational Reform and the Contradictions of Economic Life*. New York: Basic Books, 1976.

Bowman, Phillip J. "Postindustrial Displacement and Family Role Strains: Challenges to the Black Family." In Voydanoff and Majka 1988, 75–96.

Boyce, Joseph. "L.A. Riots and the 'Black Tax'." *Wall Street Journal*, 12 May 1992.

Boyer, Richard O., and Herbert M. Morais. *Labor's Untold Story*. New York: United Electrical, Radio & Machines Workers of America, 1955.

Boykin, A. Wade, and Forrest D. Toms. "Black Child Socialization: A Conceptual Framework." In McAdoo 1985, 33–52.

Boyle, Susan C. *Social Mobility in the United States: Historiography and Methods*. New York: Garland 1989.

Bozeman, James. "Genesis and Technical Anatomy of the Scientific and Technical Revolution." Paper presented at the annual meeting of the Association of Humanist Sociology, Howard University, 1989.

Brandt, Allan M. "AIDS in Historical Perspective: Four Lessons from the History of Sexually Transmitted Diseases," *American Journal of Public Health*, 78, no. 4 (April 1988): 367–71.

Brewton, Pete. *The Mafia, CIA & George Bush: The Untold Story of America's Greatest Financial Debacle.* New York: S.P.I. Books, 1992.

Briggs, Sheila. "Women and Religion." In Hess and Ferree 1987, 408–41.

Briscoe, David. "As Chaos Threatened, Marcos Pleaded with Washington." Associated Press, 18 February 1996.

Brown, Dee. *Bury My Heart at Wounded Knee*: *An Indian History of the American West.* New York: Henry Holt 1991, 1970.

Brown, Lester. et al. *State of the World: 1992 A Worldwatch Institute Report on Progress Toward a Sustainable Society*. New York: Norton 1992.

Brownmiller, Susan. *Against Our Will: Men, Women, and Rape*. New York: Simon and Schuster 1975.

Bullard, Robert D., ed. *Confronting Environmental Racism: Voices from the Grassroots.* Boston: South End Press, 1993.

——. "Anatomy of Environmental Racism and the Environmental Justice Movement." In Bullard, ed. 1993, 15–39.

Burton, Clarence M., William Stocking, and Gordon Miller, eds. *The City of Detroit, Michigan, 1701–1922.* Deteroit-Chicago: SD.J. Clarke 1922.

Business Week. "The Catastrophe Lurking in America's Farmlands." 20 May 1996, 84.

——. "Gross Compensation?" 18 March 1996,:32–33.

——. "The List: Political Angels." 18 March 1996, 4.

——. "Is America Becoming More of a Class Society?" 26 February 1996, 86–91.

——. "The Point Man in Germ Warfare." 21 August 1995, 72–73.

——. "Washington to the Rescue. Now, About the Price..." 30 January 1995, 47.

——. "Can this Chip Make the Next Quantum Leap?" 21 November 1994.

——. "Who's Hurt by Rate Hikes? Hint: It's Not the Rich." 21 November 1994, 71–72.

——. "What Made Giuliani Jump Ship," 7 November 1994.

——. "The Pain of Downsizing." 9 May 1994, 61.

——. "The Economics of Crime: The Toll is Frightening. Can Anything Be Done?" 13 December 1993, 72–80.

——. "Is Democracy Bad for Growth?" 7 June 1993, 84–88.

——. "Flipping Off the Lights from your Sickbed." 22 March 1993, 88A.

——. "Detroit South: Mexico's Auto Boom: Who Wins, Who Loses?." 16 March 1992, 100.

Cannon, Carl M. "Honey, I Warped the Kids." *Mother Jones*, July/August 1993, 16–21.

Cantor, Muriel G. "Popular Culture and the Portrayal of Women." In Hess and Ferree 1987, 190–214.

Chaiklin, Harris. "Soup Kitchens and Shelters: The Private Sector as Safety Valve for Public Sector Irresponsibility." Paper presented at annual meeting, Society for the Study of Social Problems, Washington, DC, 1985.

Chambliss, William. "State-Organized Crime." In *The Guns 'n Drugs Reader* 1991, 145–57.

Chesler, Phyllis. *Women and Madness*. New York: Avon. 1972.

Children's Defense Fund, *The State of America's Children: 1992*. Washington, DC, 1992.

Churchill, Ward, and Winona LaDuke. "Native North America: The Political Economy of Radioactive Colonialism" In Jaimes 1992, 241–66.

Clancy, Tom. *Clear and Present Danger*. New York: Berkeley Books, 1990.

Clark, Septima. *Ready from Within*. Trenton, NJ: Africa World Press, 1991.

Cohen, Jody. "Constructing Race at an Urban High School: In Their Minds, Their Mouths, Their Hearts." In Weis and Fine 1993, 289–308.

Colby, Gerard. *DuPont Dynasty: Behind the Nylon Curtain*. New York: Lyle Stuart, 1985.

Collier, Peter and David Horowitz. *The Rockefellers*. New York: Holt, Rinehart and Winston, 1976.

Collins, Patricia Hill. *Black Feminist Thought: Knowledge, Consciousness, and the Politics of Empowerment*. New York: Routledge. 1990.

Conger, Rad D., and Glen H. Elder. *Families in Troubled Times: Adapting to Change in Rural America*. Hawthorne, New York: Aldine de Gruyter, 1994.

Cook, James. "The American Indian through five Centuries." *Forbes* 9 November 1981.

Cookson, Peter W. Jr. and Caroline Hodges Persell. *Preparing for Power: America's Elite Boarding Schools*. New York: Basic Books, 1985.

Coontz, Stephanie. *The Way We Never Were: American Families and the Nostalgia Trap*. New York: Basic Books, 1992.

Cowan, Ruth Schwartz. *More Work for Mother*. New York: Basic Books, 1983.

Crossen, Cynthia. *Tainted Truth: The Manipulation of Fact in America*. New York: Simon and Schuster, 1994.

Crozier, Michael J., Samuel P. Huntington, and Joji Watanuki. *The Crisis of Democracy: Report on the Governability of Democracies to the Trilateral Commission*. New York: New York University Press, 1975.

Dahl, Robert. *Who Governs?* New Haven: Yale University Press, 1961.

Dalton, Harlon L. "AIDS in Blackface," *Living with AIDS*, Pt. 2, *Daedalus, Journal of the American Academy of Arts and Sciences*, Summer 1989. In McKenzie 1991, 122–143.

Daly, Herman E. "The Perils of Free Trade." In *Scientific American. 269 No.5* (November, 1993).

Davis, James Kirkpatrick. *Spying on America: The FBI's Domestic Counterintelligence Program*. New York: Praeger, 1992.

Davis, Marilyn. *Mexican Voices, American Dreams: An Oral History of Mexican Immigration to the United States*. New York: Henry Holt 1990.

Delumeau, Jean. *Sin and Fear: The Emergence of a Western Guilt Culture 13th–18th Centuries*. New York: St. Martin's Press, 1990.

Denzin, N. ed. *Studies in Symbolic Interaction. 6*. Greenwich, CN: JAI 1985.

Divine, Robert A. *The Johnson Years, s.1 and 2*. Lawrence: University of Kansas Press 1987.

Domhoff, G. William. *Who Rules America?* Englewood Cliffs, NJ: Prentice-Hall, 1967.

——. *Who Rules America Now?* New York: Simon and Schuster, 1983.

——. *The Power Elite and the State: How Policy Is Made in America*. New York: Aldine de Gruyter, 1990.

DuBois, Ellen Carol, and Vicki L. Ruiz. *Unequal Sisters: A Multicultural Reader in U.S. Women's History*. New York: Routledge, 1990.

DuBois, W.E.B. *Black Reconstruction in America: An Essay toward a History of the Part Which Black Folk Played in the Attempt to Reconstruct Democracy in America, 1860–1880*. 2nd ed. New York: Macmillan 1992.

Duster, Troy. "Book Review." *Contemporary Sociology 17* (1988): 287.

——. "Social Implications of the 'New' Black Urban Underclass." *Black Scholar*, May/June, 1988, 2–8.

Eckert, Allan W. *A Sorrow in Our Heart*: *The Life of Tecumseh*. New York: Bantam, 1992.

Edelman, Marian Wright. "The Sea Is So Wide and My Boat Is So Small: Problems Facing Black Children Today" In McAdoo, 1985: 72–84.

Ehrenfeld, R. *Evil Money: Encounters Along the Money Trail*. New York: Harper Business 1992.

Ehrenreich, Barbara. *Fear of Falling: The Inner Life of the Middle Class*. New York: Harper Perennial 1989.

Eitzen, D. Stanley, and Maxine Baca Zinn. *In Conflict and Order: Understanding Society, 6th ed.* Boston: Allyn and Bacon 1993.

Eschholz, Paul and Alfred Rosa. *Subject and Strategy*. New York: St. Martin's Press, 1990.

Estes, Clarissa Pinkola. *Women Who Run with the Wolves: Myths and Stories of the Wild Woman Archetype*. New York: Ballantine, 1992.

Ewen, Lynda Ann. *Corporate Power and Urban Crisis in Detroit*. Princeton: Princeton University Press, 1978.

——. "All God's Children Ain't Got Shoes: A Comparison of West Virginia and the Urban 'Underclass'," In *Humanity & Society. 13, no. 2*, (1989): 145–64.

Fainstein,Susan and Norman Fainstein. "The Political Economy of American Bureaucracy" In C. Weiss and A. Barton, eds.1980.

Faludi, Susan. *Backlash: The Undeclared War Against American Women*. New York: Crown 1991.

Fisher, Anne B. "The New Game in Health Care: Who Will Profit?" *Fortune*, 4 March 1985, 142.

Franks, David. "Role-taking, Social Power and Imperceptiveness: The Analysis of Rape." In N. Denzin 1985.

Franks, David, and D. McCarthy, eds. *The Sociology of Emotions*. Greenwich, CN: JAI 1989.

Frazier, Thomas R. *The Underside of American History*. New York: Rutgers University Press 1990.

Freemantle, Brian. *The Fix: Inside the World Drug Trade*. New York: TOR 1986.

Finch, Phillip. *God, Guts, and Guns*. New York: Seaview, 1983.

Friend, Richard. "Choices, Not Closets: Heterosexism and Homophobia" In Weis and Fine 1993, 209–36.

——. "Power and Role-Taking" In Franks and McCarthy 1989.

Fuentes, Annette, and Barbara Ehrenreich. *Women in the Global Factory*. Boston: South End Press, 1983.

Garrett, Laurie. *The Coming Plague: Newly Emerging Diseases in a World Out of Balance*. New York: Farrar, Straus & Giroux, 1994.

Garrison, Jim. *On the Trail of the Assassins*. New York: Warner Books, 1991.

Genovese, Eugene D. *The Slaveholders' Dilemma.* Columbia: University of South Carolina Press, 1992.

——. *The World The Slaveholders' Made*. Middletown, CN: Wesleyan University Press, 1988.

Geschwender, James A. *Racial Stratification in America.* Dubuque, IA: Wm. C. Brown 1978.

Goldberg, Gertrude S. "The United States: Feminization of Poverty Amidst Plenty" In Goldberg and Kremen. 1990, 17–58.

Goldberg, Gertrude S., and Eleanor Kremen. *The Feminization of Poverty: Only in America?* New York: Praeger. 1990.

Goldman, Eric F. *The Crucial Decade—And After: America, 1945–1960.* New York: Vintage, 1960.

Gordus, Jeanne Prial, and Karen Yamakawa. "Incomparable Losses: Economic and Labor Market Outcomes for Unemployed Female Versus Male Autoworkers" In Voydanoff and Majka, 1988, 38–54.

Gould, Stephen Jay. *The Mismeasure of Man*. New York: Norton 1981.

Gove, Walter R., Carolyn B. Style, and Michael Hughes. "The Effect of Marriage on the Well-Being of Adults." *Journal of Family Issues* 11 (March 1990): 4–35.

Green, Jim. "The Brotherhood." *Southern Exposure*, 4, nos. 1–2 (1976): 21–29.

Green, Rayna. "The Pocahontas Perplex: The Image of Indian Women in American Culture." In DuBois and Ruiz 1990, 15–21.

Greenberg, David F. *The Construction of Homosexuality*. Chicago: University of Chicago Press, 1988.

——. ed. *Crime and Capitalism: Readings in Marxist Criminology*. Philadelphia: Temple University Press, 1993.

Grieder, William. "The Global Sweatshop." *Rolling Stone*, 30 June 1994, 43–45.

——. *Who Will Tell the People? The Betrayal of American Democracy.* New York: Simon amd Schuster 1992.

——. *Secrets of the Temple: How the Federal Reserve Runs the Country*. New York: Simon and Schuster 1987.

Gribbin, John. *Hothouse Earth: The Greenhouse Effect and Gaia.* New York: Grove Weidenfeld 1990.

——. *The Hole in the Sky.* New York: Bantam 1988.

Grinde, Donald A. *The Iroquois and the Founding of the American Nation.* San Francisco: Indian Historical Press 1977.

Guns 'n' Drugs Reader. Berkeley, CA: Prevailing Winds Research 1991

Gurganus, Allan. *Oldest Living Confederate Widow Tells All*. New York: Ballantine Books 1984, 1989.

Hacker, Andrew. *Two Nations: Black and White, Separate, Hostile, Unequal.* New York: Ballantine Books 1992.

HaHall, Jacquelyn Dowd. "The Mind That Burns in Each Body: Women, Rape and Racial Violence," In Anderson and Collins, eds. 1992, 397–412.

Halle, David. *America's Working Man: Work, Home, and Politics Among Blue-Collar Property Owners.* Chicago: University of Chicago Press 1984.

Harding, Sandra. *The Racial Economy of Science: Toward a Democratic Future.* Bloomington: Indiana University Press 1993.

——. *Whose Science? Whose Knowledge? Thinking from Women's Lives.* Ithaca, NY: Cornell University Press 1991.

Harrington, Michael. *The Other America: Poverty in the United States.* Baltimore: Penguin 1963.

Harris, Marvin. *Cows, Pigs, Wars and Witches: The Riddles of Culture.* New York: Random House 1989.

Harrison, Algea O. "The Black Family's Socializing Environment: Self-Esteem and Ethnic Attitude Among Black Children." In McAdoo 1985, 174–93.

Hayes, Dennie. *Behind the Silicon Curtain: The Seductions of Work in a Lonely Era.* Boston: South End Press 1989.

Hernstein, Richard and Charles Murray. *The Bell Curve: Intelligence and Class Structure in American Life.* New York: Free Press 1994.

Hess, Beth B. and Myra Marx Ferree. *Analyzing Gender: A Handbook of Social Science Research.* Newbury Park, CA: Sage 1987.

Hewlett, Sylvia Ann. *When the Bough Breaks: The Cost of Neglecting Our Children.* New York: Harper Collins 1992.

Hilliard, Asa G. III. "Limitations of Current Academic Achievement Measures." In Lomotey, ed. 1990, 135–142.

Hills, Stuart. *Corporate Violence: Injury and Death for Profit.* New York: Rowman and Littlefield 1987.

Hine, Darlene Clark. "Rape and the Inner Lives of Black Women in the Middle West: Preliminary Thoughts on the Culture of Dissemblance." In DuBois and Ruiz 1990, 292–97.

Holloway, Marguerite. "A Lab of Her Own." *Scientific American 269, no. 5* (November 1993): 94–103.

Holm, Tom. "Patriots and Pawns: State Use of American Indians in the Military and the Process of Nativization in the United States." In Jaimes 1992, 345–70.

Horowitz, David. *The Free World Colossus: A Critique of American Foreign Policy in the Cold War.* New York: Hill and Wang 1965.

Horowitz, Irving Louis. *Professing Sociology*. Chicago: Aldine 1968.

Horwitz, Tony. "Getting Nowhere: Boomtowns Lure Poor with Plenty Of Work—But Not Much Else." *Wall Street Journal*, 16 June 1994.

Hubbard, Ruth and Elijah Wald. *Exploding the Gene Myth: How Genetic Information Is Produced and Manipulated by Scientists, Physicians, Employers, Insurance Companies, Educators, and Law Enforcers.* Boston: Beacon Press 1993.

——. *The Politics of Women's Biology*. Boston: Beacon Press 1990.

Huggins, N. *Black Odyssey: The Afro-American Ordeal in Slavery*. New York: Random House 1990, 978.

Hughes, Langston. "October 16," In *Selected Poems of Langston Hughes.* New York: Vintage 1959, 10.

Hurt, Henry. *Reasonable Doubt: An Investigation into the Assasination of John F. Kennedy*. New York: Henry Holt 1985.

Huxley, Aldous. *Brave New World*. New York: Harper and Brothers 1932, 1946.

Hymowitz, Carol and Michaele Weissman. *A History of Women in America.* New York: Bantam Books 1978.

Hynes, Charles J., and Bob Drury. *Incident at Howard Beach.* New York: Putnam 1990.

Interpreter. July–August 1996, 26.

Jaimes, M. Annette, ed. *The State of Native America: Genocide, Colonization and Resistance*. Boston: South End Press 1992

Jaimes, M. Annette and Theresa Halsey. "American Indian Women." In Jaimes 1992, 311–44.

Jensen, Joan M. "Native American Women and Agriculture: A Seneca Case Study" In Du Bois and Ruiz 1990, 51–65.

Jernegan, Marcus W. "Laboring and Dependent Classes in America, 1607–1783." In Frazier 1971.

Jones, J. *Bad Blood: The Tuskegee Syphilis Experiment*. New York: Free Press 1981.

Jones, Barry. *Sleepers, Wake! Technology and the Future of Work*. New York: Oxford University Press 1982 (1990 ed.).

Jones, Jacqueline. *The Dispossessed: America's Underclasses from the Civil War to the Present.* New York:Basic Books 1992.

——. *Labor of Love, Labor of Sorrow*. New York: Vintage Press 1986.

Josephson, Matthew. *The Robber Barons: The Great American Capitalists 1861–1901.* New York: Harcourt Brace Jovanovich 1934, 1962.

Josephy, Alvin M., ed. *America in 1492*. New York: Vintage 1993.

Juzang,, Ivan. *Reaching the Hip Hop Generation.* Princeton, NJ: Robert Wood Johnson Foundation 1993.

Kaplan, Robert D., *The Arabists: The Romance of an American Elite.* New York: The Free Press 1993.

Karnow, Stanley. *In Our Image: America's Empire in the Philippines.* New York: Ballantine Books 1990.

Katz, William Loren. *Black Indians: A Hidden Heritage.* New York: Atheneum 1986.

Keller, John F. *Power in America: The Southern Question and the Control of Labor.* Chicago: Vanguard Press 1983.

Kelley, Clarence M., and James Kirkpatrick Davis. *Kelley: The Story of an FBI Director.* Kansas City, MO: Andrews, McMeel and Parker 1987.

Kellner, Douglas. *The Persian Gulf TV War.* Boulder, CO: Westview Press 1992.

——. *Television and the Crisis of Democracy.* Boulder, CO: Westview Press 1990.

Kennedy, Paul. *Preparing for the 21st Century.* New York: Random House 1994.

Kivisto, Peter. *Americans All: Race and Ethnic Relations in Historical, Structural, and Comparative Perspectives.* Belmont, CA: Wadsworth 1995.

Klanwatch Project of the Southern Poverty Law Center. *Terror in Our Neighborhoods: A Klanwatch Report on Housing Violence in America.* Atlanta: Southern Poverty Law Center.

Knottnerus, J. David. "The Rise of the Wisconsin School of Status Attainment Research." In Vaughan, Sjoberg and Reynolds 1993, 252–68.

Kolko, Gabriel. *The Triumph of Conservatism: A Reinterpretation of American History 1900–1916.* Chicago: Quadrangle Books 1963.

Komarovksy, Mirra. *Blue–Collar Marriage.* New Haven: Yale University Press 1987.

Kozol, Jonathan. *Rachael and Her Children: Homeless Families in America.* New York: Crown 1988.

——. *Savage Inequalities: Children in America's Schools.* New York: Crown 1991.

Ladd, Anthony E. "From Cold War to a Warming Planet: Redefining International Security as Environmental Sustainability," Speech delivered at Loyal University, New Orleans. 19 April 1994.

——. "The Environmental Backlash and the Retreat of the State." *Blueprint for Social Justice, no. 5* (January 1993).

La Dou, Joseph. "Deadly Migration: Hazardous Industries' Flight to the Third World." *Technology Review*, July 1991, 46–53.

Lamont, Michele and Marcel Fournier. *Cultivating Differences: Symbolic Boundaries and the Making of Inequality.* Chicago: University of Chicago Press 1992.

Lamphere, Louise. ed. *Structuring Diversity: Ethnographic Perspectives on the New Im migration.* Chicago: University of Chicago Press 1992.

Lane, Mark. *Plausible Denial: Was the CIA Involved in the Assassination of JFK?* New York: Thunder's Mouth Press 1992.

——. *Rush to Judgement.* New York: Thunder's Mouth Press 1992.

Lee, Howard B. *Bloodletting In Appalachia.* Parson, WV: McClain Books 1969.

Lekachman, Robert. "The Specter of Full Employment" In Skolnik and Currie 1991, 66–71.

Liebow, Elliot. *Tell Them Who I Am: The Lives of Homeless Women.* New York: The Free Press 1993.

Limerick, Patricia Nelson. *The Legacy of Conquest: The Unbroken Past of the American West.* New York: Norton 1987.

Littrell, Boyd. "Bureaucratic Secrets and Adversarial Methods of Social Research," In Vaughan, Sjoberg, and Reynolds 1993, 207–231.

Litwack, Eugene, and Peter Messeri. "Organizational Theory, Social Supports, and Mortality Rates," *American Sociological Review* 54 (1989): 49–66.

Lomotey, Kofi, ed. *Going to School: The African American Experience.* Albany, NY: State University Press of New York 1990.

Lundberg, Ferdinand. *America's Sixty Families.* New York: Vanguard 1937.

Lusane, Clarence. *Pipe Dream Blues: Racism and the War on Drugs.* Boston: South End Press 1991.

Lyman, S. and M. Scott. "Accounts." *American Sociological Review* 33 (December): 46–62

Malone, Michael. *The Big Score.* New York: Doubleday 1985.

Mander, Jerry. *In the Absence of the Sacred: The Failure of Technology and the Survival of the Indian Nations.* San Francisco: Sierra Club Books 1991.

Manis J., and B. Meltzer, eds. *Symbolic Interaction.* Boston: Allyn and Bacon 1972.

Marsden, George M. *Fundamentalism and American Culture.* Oxford: Oxford University Press 1980.

Masson, Jeffrey M. *The Assault on Truth: Freud's Suppression of the Seduction Theory.* New York: Farrar, Straus, and Giroux 1984.

Marty, Martin E., and R. Scott Appleby. *Fundamentalisms Observed.* Chicago: University of Chicago Press 1991.

Marx, Karl and Friedrich Engles. "The Communist Manifesto" In Robert C. Tucker, ed. 1978, 469–500.

Matsumoto, Valerie. "Japanese American Women During World War II." In DuBois and Ruiz 1990: 373–86.

McAdoo, Harriette Pipes and John Lewis McAdoo. *Black Children: Social, Educational and Parental Environments.* Beverly Hills, CA: Sage 1985.

McCartney, Laton. *Friends in High Places: The Bechtel Story—The Most Secret Corporation and How It Engineered the World.* New York: Simon and Schuster 1988.

McClain, Leanita. "The Middle-Class Black's Burden." In Andersen and Collins 1992, 120–22.

McCoy, Alfred W. *The Politics of Heroin: CIA Complicity in the Global Drug Trade*. Brooklyn, NY: Lawrence Hill Books 1991.

McIntosh, Peggy. "White Privilege and Male Privilege: A Personal Account of Coming to See Correspondences Through Work in Women's Studies." In Anderson and Collins, eds. 1992, 70–81.

McKenzie, Nancy F., ed. *The AIDS Reader: Social, Political and Ethical Issues.* New York: Meridian 1991.

——. *The Crisis in Health Care: Ethical Issues.* New York: Meridian 1990.

McPherson, James M. *The Battle Cry of Freedom.* New York: Oxford University Press 1988.

——. *The Negro's Civil War.* Urbana: University of Illinois Press 1982.

Meier, Linda K. and Brian K. Zoeller, "Taking Abusers to Court: Civil Remedies for Domestic Violence Victims." *Trial no. 6* (June 1995): 60–65.

Melendez, Edwin and Edgardo Melendez, eds. *Colonial Dilemma: Critical Perspectives on Contemporary Puerto Rico*. Boston: South End Press 1993.

Meredith, Nikki. "Psychotherapy: Everybody's Doin' It, But Does It Work?" *Utne Reader*, March/April 1987.

"Mexican Workers Still waiting for New Jobs from NAFTA." AP report, 18 December 1994.

Miller, Annetta. "Stress on the Job." *Newsweek,* 25 April 1988.

Millman, Marcia. *Warm Hearts and Cold Cash: The Intimate Dynamics of Families and Money.* New York: Free Press 1991.

Mills, C. Wright. "Situated Actions and Vocabularies of Motive." In Manis and Meltzer, eds. 1972.

——. *The Power Elite*. New York: Oxford University Press 1956.

Mirande, Alfredo. *Gringo Justice*. Notre Dame, IN: University of Notre Dame Press 1987.

Mishel, Lawrence and Jared Bernstein. "The Joyless Recovery: Deteriorating Wages and Job Quality in the 1990s." Washington, DC: Economic Policy Institute 1993.

——. *The State of Working America*. Armonk, New York: Economic Policy Institute 1993, 1994.

Moore, Robert B. "Racist Stereotyping in the English Language," In Anderson and Collins, eds. 1992, 317–29.

Moore, Thomas. *The Disposable Work Force: Worker Displacement and Employment Instability in America*. Hawthorne, New York: Aldine de Gruyter 1996.

Morrison, Toni. *Playing in the Dark: Whiteness in the Literary Imagination.* Cambridge, MA: Harvard University Press 1992.

——. *Beloved*. New York: Knopf 1987.

Ms. magazine, "Sisterhood is Global: International News." Section in every issue.

Muñiz, Humberto Garcia . "U.S. Military Installations in Puerto Rico: Controlling the Caribbean." In Melendez 1993, 53–65.

Musto, David. *The American Disease: Origins of Narcotics Control.* New York: Oxford University Press 1988.

The Nation. "Bringing Nazi Sympathizers to the U.S.: Talcott Parsons' Role." 6 March 1989, 303, 306–309.

National Academy of Science. "Homelessness, Health and Human Need."In McKenzie,1991, 377–408.

New York Times Service. "Old Boy Network Gets a Facelift." *The Charleston Gazette-Mail* (WV), 8 November 1992.

Newby, Robert, ed. "The Bell Curve: Laying Bare the Resurgence of Scientific Racism." *American Behavioral Scientist, 39, no.1* (Sept./Oct. 1995).

——. "Critique of William Wilson's *The Truly Disadvantaged*." Paper delivered at the 1988 annual meetings of the American Sociological Association, Atlanta, August 1988.

Newsweek, "Guns for Drugs?" 23 May, 1988.

O'Connell, Charles T. "Talcott Parons and the German Summer of 1948: Science and Politics in Early Soviet Studies at Harvard University." Unpublished paper, August 1988.

Oppenheimer, Martin, Martin J. Murray and Rhonda F. Levine. *Radical Sociologists and the Movement: Experiences, Lessons and Legacies.* Philadelphia: Temple University Press, 1991.

Organic Gardening, 42, no. 1 (January 1995): 22.

Parenti, Michael. *Land of Idols: Political Mythology in America.* New York: St. Martin's Press 1994.

——. *Make Believe Media*. New York: St. Martin's Press 1992.

——. *Democracy for the Few*. New York: St. Martin's Press 1988.

Parsons, Talcott. *The Social System*. New York: Free Press 1951.

Pearce, Frank. "Organized Crime and Class Politics" In Greenberg 1993, 169–93.

Perrow, Charles. *Complex Organizations: a Critical Essay*. 2nd ed. Glenview, IL: Scott Foresman 1979.

Persell, Caroline Hodges. *Education and Inequality: The Roots and Results of Stratification in America's Schools*. New York: Free Press, 1977.

Perruci, Carolyn C., Robert Perrucci, Dena B. Targ, and Harry R. Targ. *Plant Closings: International Context and Social Costs.* New York: Aldine de Gruyter 1989.

Perrucci, Carolyn C. and Dena B. Targ. "Effects of a Plant Closing on Marriage and Family Life." In Voydanoff and Majka, 1988, 55–72.

Perrucci, Robert, and Harry R. Potter. *Networks of Power: Organizational Actors at the National, Corporate and Community Levels*. Hawthorne, New York: Aldine de Gruyter 1989.

Peshkin, Alan. *God's Choice: The Total World of a Fundamentalist Christian School.* Chicago: University of Chicago Press 1986.

Peters, Marie Feguson. "Racial Socialization of Young Black Children" In McAdoo 1985, 159–73.

Phillips, Kevin. *Arrogant Capital: Washington, Wall Street, and the Frustration of American Politics.* New York: Little, Brown 1994.

Potts, Mark, Nicholas Kochan, and Robert Whittington. *Dirty Money: The Inside Story of the World's Sleaziest Bank.* Washington, DC: National Press Books 1992.

Powers, Richard Gid. *Secrecy and Power, The Life of J. Edgar Hoover*. New York: Macmillan 1986.

Pulley, Brett. "Police Teach Getting Arrested Safely 101." *Wall Street Journal*, 16 June 1994.

Raichen, Steven, "Yes, We Have No Bananas." *Eating Well: The Magazine of Food and Health* 3, no. 15 (Jan./Feb.1993): 64–70.

Rawick, George. *From Sundown to Sunup: The Making of the Black Community.* Westport, CN: Greenwood 1972.

Ray, Carol Axtell and Roslyn Arlin Mickelson. "Restructuring Students for Restructured Work: The Economy, School Reform, and Non-college-bound Youths," *Sociology of Education* 66 (January 1993): 1–20.

Ray, Dixie Lee. *Environmental Overkill: Whatever Happened to Common Sense?* Washington, D.C.: Regenery Gateway 1993.

Rayman, Paula. "Unemployment and Family Life: The Meaning for Children." In Voydanoff and Majka 1988, 119–34.

Reed, Adolph Jr. "The Liberal Technocrat." In *The Nation*, 6 February 1988, 167–70.

"Refugee Women Hold Families Together" by a correspondent writing for World Food Programme. Special Feature, *Dar Es Salaam News*, 8 March 1991.

Reiman, Jeffrey. *The Rich Get Richer and the Poor Get Prison.* New York: Wiley 1979.

Rethinking Schools, "Scalping: A Practise Dating to Ancient Greece." September 1991, 22.

Rich, Bruce. *Mortgaging the Earth: The World Bank, Environmental Impoverishment, and the Crisis of Development.* Boston: Beacon Press 1994.

Rist, R. *The Urban School: A Factory for Failure*. Cambridge: MIT Press 1973.

Ritzer, George. *Sociological Theory.* 3rd ed. New York: McGraw Hill 1992.

Robbins, Richard H. *Cultural Anthropology: A Problem-Based Approach.* Itasca, IL: F.E. Peacock 1993.

Robinson, Cyril D. "The Production of Black Violence in Chicago." In Greenberg 1993, 279–333.

Rodney, Walter. *How Europe Underdeveloped Africa*. Washington, DC: Howard University Press 1982.

Rosen, Ellen Israel. *Bitter Choices: Blue-Collar Women in and out of Work*. Chicago: University of Chicago Press 1987.

Ross, Catherine E., John Mirowsky, and Karen Goldsteen. "The Impact of the Family on Health: The Decade in Review." In Booth, ed. 1991, 341–60.

Rossi, Peter, James Wright, G. Fisher, and G. Willis. "The Urban Homeless: Estimating Composition and Size." *Science* 235 no. 4794 (13 March 1987): 1336–41.

Rubenstien, Richard E. "The Los Angeles Riots: Causes and Cures." *National Civic Review* 81, no. 3 (Summer/Fall 1992): 319–24.

Rubin, Lillian B. *Worlds of Pain: Life in the Working-Class Family*. New York: Basic Books 1976.

Ryan, William. *Blaming the Victim*. Rev. ed. New York: Pantheon 1976.

Schwadel, Francine. "Sears to Slash 600 Salary Posts, Salespeople Pay. " *Wall Street Journa*l, 13 February 1992.

Schwartz, Barry. *George Washington: The Making of An American Symbol.* Ithaca, NY: Cornell University Press 1987.

Shawwith, J. Gary and, Larry R Harris. *Cover-Up: The Governmental Conspiracy to Conceal the Facts About the Public Execution of John Kennedy.* 2nd ed. New York: Thomas Publication 1992, 1970.

Sheak, Robert J. and David D. Dabelko. "'Full Employment' Proposals Reconsidered: The Limits of Incremental Reform." *Research and Social Stratification and Mobility,* 12 (1993): 329–59.

Sheffield, Carole J. "Sexual Terrorism: The Social Control of Women." In Hess and Ferree 1987, 171–189.

Shenkman, Richard. *Legends, Lies and Cherished Myths of American History*. New York: Morrow 1988.

Shilts, Randy. *And the Band Played On*. New York: St. Martin's Press 1987.

Sidel, Ruth. *Women and Children Last: The Plight of Poor Women in Affluent America.* New York: Viking 1986.

Sjoberg, Gideon, and Ted R. Vaughan. "The Bureaucratization of Sociology: Its Impact on Theory and Research." In Vaughan, Sjoberg, and Reynolds 1993, 54–113.

Skolnick, Jerome and Elliott Currie. *Crisis in American Institutions. 8th ed.,* New York: HarperCollins 1991.

Snell, Bradford Curie. "American Ground Transport. In Skolnick and Currie, 1991, 327–41.

Snipp, C. Mathew. *American Indians: The First of This Land.* New York: Russell Sage Foundation 1989.

Spigel, Lynn. *Make Room for TV: Television and the Family Ideal in Postwar America.* Chicago: University of Chicago Press 1992.

Stack, Carol. *All Our Kin: Strategies for Survival in a Black Community.* New York: Harper Torchbook 1975.

Steiner, Stan. *La Raza: The Mexican Americans.* New York: Harper Colophon 1970.

Stern, David. "Institutions and Incentives for Developing Work-Related Knowledge and Skil.l" In Adler 1992, 149–86.

Stevenson, Robert, and Jeanne Ellsworth. "Dropouts and the Silencing of Critical Voices." In Weis and Fine 1993, 259–71.

Stiffarm, Lenore A. and Phil Lane Jr. "The Demography of Native North America: A Question of American Indian Survival." In Jaimes 1992, 23–53.

Swartz, Sue. "A Remembering, a Memorial, and a Reminder, Dedicated to Those Who Sew for Us" *Sojourner: The Women's Forum.* 18, no. 11 (July 1993): 20.

Syfers, Judy. "Why I Want a Wife." In Eschholz and Rosa 1990, 387–89. (Published originally in *Ms. magazine*, 1971.)

Takaki, Ronald. *A Different Mirror: A History of Multicultural America.* Boston: Little, Brown 1993.

——. *Iron Cages: Race and Culture in 19th Century America.* New York: Oxford University Press 1990.

Theoharis, Athan. *From the Secret Files of J. Edgar Hoover.* Chicago: Ivan R. Dee 1993.

Thomas, David, D. Franks, and J. Calanico. "Role-taking and Power in Social Psychology." *American Sociological Review* 37 (October 1972): 605–15.

Thompson, Jon. "King of Fibers. *National Geographic*, 185, no. 6 (June 1994): 60–86.

Thornton, Russell. *American Indian Holocaust and Survival: A Population History Since 1492.* Norman: University of Oklahoma Press 1987.

Thurber, David. "Decade After Uprising, Philippines Faces New Doubt." Associated Press, 18 February 1996.

Tifft, Susan. "The Big Shift in School Finance." *Time.* 16 October 1989, 48.

Tuchman, Barbara. *A Distant Mirror: The Calamitous 14th Century.* New York: Ballantine 1987.

Tuchman, Gaye. *Making News.* New York: Free Press 1978.

Tucker, Robert C., *The Marx-Engels Reader.* New York: Norton 1978.

U.S. News and World Report. "The Living Legacy of Jim Bakker." 6 November 1989, 14.

Vaughan, Ted, Gideon Sjoberg, and Larry T. Reynolds, eds. *A Critique of Contemporary American Sociology.* New York: General Hall 1993.

Volti, Rudi. *Society and Technological Change.* New York: St. Martin's Press 1992.

Voydanoff, Patricia, and Brenda W. Donnelly. "Economic Distress, Family Coping and Quality of Family Life" In Voydanoff and Majka 1988, 97–116.

Voydanoff, Patricia, and Linda C. Majka, eds. *Families and Economic Distress: Coping Strategies and Social Policy.* Newbury Park, CA: Sage Publicaations 1988

Walker, Alice. *Possessing the Secret of Joy.* New York: Harcourt Brace Jovanovich 1992.

Wall Street Journal. "Where the Subsidies Go." January 1994.

——. "U.S. Postal Service Expects to Trim 47,000 Jobs by '95." 27 September 1991.

——. "Morgan Lays off 6% of It Bankers in Reorganization." 12 December 1991.

——. "White Collar Layoffs Open 1990, and May Close It, Too." 15 January 1990.

Warren, Karen, and Jim Cheny. *Ecological Feminism.* Boulder, CO: Westview 1995.

Warren, Karen, and Barbara Wells-Howe, eds. *Economical Feminism.* New York: Routledge 1994.

Weatherford, Jack. *Native Roots: How the Indians Enriched America.* New York: Crown Publishers 1991.

Weber, Max. *The Theory of Social and Economic Organization.* New York: Free Press 1947.

Weiner, Tim. "Blowback: From the Afghan Battlefield." *New York Times Magazine*, 13 March 1994, 52–55.

Weinstein, James. *The Corporate Ideal in the Liberal State: 1900–1918.* Boston: Beacon Press 1968.

Weis, Lois. *Working Class without Work: High School Students in a Deindustrializing Economy.* New York: Routledge 1990.

Weis, Lois, and Michelle Fine, eds. *Beyond Silenced Voices: Class, Race and Gender in United States Schools.* Albany: State University Press of New York 1993.

Weiss, Carol, and Allen Barton, eds. *Making Bureaucracies Work.* Beverly Hills, CA: Sage 1980.

Weitz, Shirley. "Sex Differences in Nonverbal Communication." Paper presented at the American Sociological ASsociation Annual Meeting, San Francisco, 1975.

Welch, Neil J. and David W. Marston. *Inside Hoover's FBI.* Garden City, New York: Doubleday 1984.

White, Deborah. "Female Slaves: Sex Roles and Status in the Antebellus Plantation South." In Du Bois and Ruiz 1990, 22–33.

Wigginton, Eliot. *Refuse to Stand Silently By: An Oral History of Grass Roots Social Activism in America, 1921–64.* New York: Anchor Books 1991.

Wildstrom, Stephen. "Books." *Business Week*, 18 January 1993, 19.

Williams, Janet E., Linda G. Caleca, and Suzanne McBride. "Statehouse Sellout." *Indianapolis Star*, 11 Feb. 1996 1A–13, 14A.

Williams, John Alexander. *West Virginia: A History.* New York: Norton 1976.

Williams, Terry. *The Cocaine Kids: The Inside Story of a Teenage Drug Ring.* Reading, MA: Addison Wesley 1989.

Williams, William Appleman. *The Tragedy of American Diplomacy: The Roots of the Modern American Empire.* New York: Dell 1972.

Wilson, James Q., and Richard J. Herrnstein. *Crime and Human Nature.* New York: Simon and Schuster 1985.

Wilson, William J. *The Truly Disadvantaged: The Inner City, the Underclass, and Public Policy.* Chicago: University of Chicago Press 1987.

Wolff, Leon. *Little Brown Brother: America's Forgotten Bid for Empire Which Cost 250,000 Lives.* New York: Kraus Reprint 1970.

Worldwatch Institute. "Vital Signs 1994." New York: Worldwatch Institute.

Wright, Bruce. *Black Robes, White Justice: Why Our Legal System Doesn't Work for Blacks.* New York: Lyle Stuart 1987.

Wright, James. *Address Unknown: The Homeless in America.* New York: Aldine de Gruyter 1989.

Yung, Judy. "The Social Awakening of Chinese American Women as Reported in *Chung Sai Yat Po*, 1900–1911." In Du Bois and Ruiz 1990, 195–207.

Zelizer, Barbie. *Covering the Body: The Kennedy Assasination, the Media, and the Shaping of Collective Memory.* Chicago: Chicago University Press 1992.

Zey, Mary. *Banking on Fraud: Drexel, Junk Bonds, and Buyouts.* New York: Aldine de Gruyter 1993.

Zinn, Howard. *A People's History of the United States.* New York: Harper and Row 1980.

INDEX